HISTORIANS IN SERVICE
OF A BETTER SOUTH

HISTORIANS IN SERVICE OF A BETTER SOUTH

Essays in Honor of Paul Gaston

~

Edited by Robert J. Norrell and Andrew H. Myers

Edward L. Ayers   Raymond Gavins
James H. Hershman   John T. Kneebone
Matthew D. Lassiter   Gregg L. Michel
Lynda J. Morgan   Andrew H. Myers
Robert J. Norrell   Stephen O'Neill
Robert A. Pratt   Steve Suitts
Randolph D. Werner

NewSouth Books
Montgomery

NewSouth Books
105 S. Court Street
Montgomery, AL 36104

Copyright © 2017
All rights reserved under International and Pan-American Copyright Conventions. Published in the United States by NewSouth Books, a division of NewSouth, Inc., Montgomery, Alabama.

Publisher's Cataloging-in-Publication data

Historians in service of a better South : essays in honor of Paul Gaston / Robert J. Norrell and Andrew H. Myers, editors.
p. cm.

ISBN 978-1-60306-446-0 (paperback)

1. Gaston, Paul M., 1928–. 2. United States—Southern States—History. I. Title.

2017937787

A hardcover edition has also been produced.

Printed in the United States of America

ACKNOWLEDGMENT

This book was designed and composed by Horace Randall Williams, a longtime friend and Southern Regional Council colleague of Paul Gaston. Williams is editor-in-chief of NewSouth Books, which published two of Paul's books: *Man and Mission: E. B. Gaston and the Origins of the Fairhope Single Tax Colony* and *Coming of Age in Utopia: The Odyssey of an Idea*. In addition, NewSouth brought back into print *The New South Creed: A Study in Southern Mythmaking* and *Women of Fair Hope*. Williams is an Alabama native, journalist, editor, and publisher. He has edited and/or published some seven hundred books, mostly on southern history and culture. For many years, he edited and designed the SRC's journals and special reports. He was an editor and investigator at the Southern Poverty Law Center for a decade and was the founding director of its Klanwatch Project.

To the memory of
Mary Gaston

Contents

	Introduction............ Robert J. Norrell	ix
1	The Black Church and Black Memory of Jim Crow.......... Raymond Gavins	3
2	From the Old to the New..... Randolph D. Werner	31
3	Virginia on the Cusp of Change............ James H. Hershman, Jr.	63
4	Publicity and Prejudice........ John T. Kneebone	90
5	Triangles of Change.......... Robert J. Norrell	110
6	Reparations and History......... Lynda J. Morgan	135
7	Bending Toward Injustice........ Robert A. Pratt	169
8	What We Remember, What We Forget............ Stephen O'Neill	204
9	Racial Buffer Zone.......... Andrew H. Myers	221
10	The Open Schools Revolt..... Matthew D. Lassiter	242
11	White Southern Students and University Reform in the 1960s..... Gregg L. Michel	272
12	Hugo Black and a Lost Alabama Political Tradition......... Steve Suitts	296
13	Southern Family Trees, Wrong and Right........... Edward L. Ayers	312
	Contributors.....................	324

Introduction

ROBERT J. NORRELL

Anyone who witnessed Paul Gaston's career at the University of Virginia from 1957 to 1997—or, more likely, who engaged him at some point during those four decades—knows of his remarkable impact on students. If Paul had a large influence on the students he mentored, including the Ph.D. students who contribute here, he enlightened hundreds who took his courses on the realities of the South. He changed the lives of many undergraduates who were struggling to cope with the racial and political unrest in the South and the nation. Indeed he extended great influence among students before he had even taught graduate students. In his autobiography, *Coming of Age in Utopia: The Odyssey of an Idea,* Paul describes with admiration the courage of a coterie of student activists in the 1960s, among them Howard Romaine, David Nolan, Tom Gardner, Roger Hickey, Bud Ogle, and Anne Cooke Romaine.

In the 1970s through to 1997, Paul continued to teach, advise, and inspire dozens of students every year. He was a model of courageous engagement with the social problems that pressed on Americans and southerners in particular. His dissent from conventional thought about race, class, and politics modeled a critical mind that inspired many students to question the world around them. His activism licensed students themselves to act.

This Festschrift honors Paul Gaston, in the tradition of this kind of book, by offering essays that are inspired by the teaching of the mentor. This book by no means includes all his students: Paul directed at least twenty-five dissertations, and this volume includes essays from only eleven of them. Others were invited and declined, and some of his earliest students are deceased. A few we could not locate. Still, the essays in this volume reflect the range of

Paul Gaston's interests as a historian and an activist. Indeed, a connection to Paul's own work is the unifying theme of this volume, rather than coherence of a single historical issue or perspective. They reflect Paul's expansive and evolving intellectual interests.

THE EARLIEST OF PAUL'S students among the contributors here is the late **RAYMOND GAVINS**, who in 1970 became the first African-American to receive the Ph.D. in history at the University of Virginia. Ray had been an activist during his graduate student days and an original collaborator with Paul in instituting a black studies curriculum at the University. Here Ray echoes some of Paul's interest in historical memory, now a fashionable enterprise but not so much when *The New South Creed* appeared in 1970. Ray explores the way that African Americans in North Carolina remembered the crucial role that black churches played in helping them endure the travails of white supremacy in the post–Civil War South. Reflecting Paul's original engagement as a scholar with the economic and political issues of the "New South," **RANDOLPH WERNER** charts the economic and social changes in the backcountry of the region surrounding Augusta, Georgia. Werner explains the growth of new, railroad-enabled towns and the changes it wrought in consumption, marketing, and even commonplace thinking. He notes the emphasis among postwar farmers in scientific farming and crop diversification. His observations about the newly emerging country editors provide an edifying contrast to Paul's about big-city newspapermen like Henry Grady, Richard Edmonds, and Henry Watterson.

Some of Paul's students contributing here continue his tradition of applying historical thought to contemporary struggles for justice. **ROBERT PRATT** gives a sober account of the many ways that partisan political action and court decisions have undermined the progress toward voting rights and democracy for African Americans and other minorities, even amid the triumphal election of America's first black president. **LYNDA MORGAN** analyzes the history of the movement for slavery reparations, relating the modern concern for justice about past wrongs to the failure of the nation to provide economic recompense to the freed people at the moment of emancipation. **STEPHEN O'NEILL** focuses on the efforts of white South

Carolinians to manipulate and misrepresent the memory of the civil rights struggle in order to preserve white privilege in recent times. "The past will always come out, will always come back," O'Neill warns about the moral obtuseness of many white southerners.

Many of Paul's later students undertook projects that suggested a southern past of people dissenting from the exploitation and prejudice that was all too often the norm in southern history. As **JOHN KNEEBONE** writes here, "Paul's larger teaching was that alternatives were possible." Kneebone's essay examines how a 1921 exposé of the reemerging Ku Klux Klan prompted activism against racial and religious bigotry. Kneebone's piece also resonates with Paul's analysis of southern and national propaganda in *The New South Creed* in which the South's reputation in the North shaped regional events.

Several contributors illuminate issues that pertain to the civil rights movement of the 1950s and 1960s, each of which connected to Paul's experience as an activist. **GREGG MICHEL** writes about students who formed the Southern Student Organizing Committee (SSOC), some of them Gaston protégées. A nearly all-white group, they were inspired to activism by the civil rights movement, but they eventually moved on to other issues, including the Vietnam War and university reform. In the late 1960s, SSOC chapters appeared on campuses across the South. **JAMES HERSHMAN** analyzes the course of Virginia politics during the turn away from "massive resistance" after 1959. In his early years in Virginia, Paul exerted continuous effort to thwart the forces of massive resistance in Virginia. Hershman concludes that the evolution of the Old Dominion's traditionally limited, rural-dominated "democracy" to a corporate-dominated, suburban-centered control brought a convergence of Virginia rule to American norms, albeit with little benefit to the state's poor and black citizens.

ANDREW MYERS uses modern mapping techniques to explain how and why African Americans stationed at Fort Jackson in Columbia, South Carolina, remained isolated from the evolving civil rights struggle in that city. Fort Jackson by contrast had few interruptions of its pattern of racial harmony, though neither did the many black soldiers stationed there engage in protest through most of the civil rights period. Myers explains this reality by following housing patterns and real estate developments in the section of Columbia around Fort Jackson. **ROBERT "JEFF" NORRELL** offers an overview interpretation of the Southern Regional Council (SRC), the interracial organization founded in 1944 as the successor to the Commission for Interracial Cooperation. Paul Gaston worked continuously on SRC projects from the late 1950s into the 1990s, including serving as an officer for several years. Norrell argues that SRC successfully "triangulated" among black organizations, the national media, scholars like Paul, and foundation philanthropy to advance the civil rights movement through its various stages of protest and change.

MATTHEW LASSITER offers an in-depth analysis of the "Open Schools" movement which grew out of the Southern Regional Council's leadership project to thwart segregationists' massive resistance to school desegregation. School desegregation was among Paul's main concerns in his work with the Council. Lassiter explains the work of the journalist Benjamin Muse, operating sometimes surreptitiously in the late 1950s and early 1960s, to encourage local leaders in southern towns and cities to comply with desegregation orders and to deflect pressure to close or abandon public schools. He shows the deft ways that SRC leadership used the pressure of the federal government to push local leaders toward moderation on the school issues, at the same time acknowledging the limitations of southern liberalism in countering white oppression.

Paul also had a great influence on his colleagues, both within the academy and without. Several of the contributors herein note the importance of Paul's role in bringing Armstead Robinson to the University of Virginia, and then supporting Armstead's work at the Carter G. Woodson Institute for African and African American Studies. Paul was instrumental in bringing the late Julian Bond to the Virginia history department in 1992, where the former Student Nonviolent Coordinating Committee (SNCC) activist engaged five thousand undergraduates with the civil rights movement over the next two decades. Julian and Paul were close colleagues throughout those years.

We have included historical essays from two colleagues, **ED AYERS** and **STEVE SUITTS**. When Ed came to Charlottesville in 1980, he saw that "Paul knew exactly who he was and what he was supposed to do and he did it with courage, grace, and success." Ed and Paul worked side-by-side mentoring many students, including several authors included in this volume. They could do that because each had an open mind about historical topics and historical methodologies. If Paul was more focused on historical thinking as the impetus for social change, Ed became a nationally influential agent for change in historical methodology. He is without peer as an innovator in digital history. In his contribution to this volume, Ed recounts the history of the practice of genealogy in America and shows the recent convergence between traditional academic history and the exciting work among genealogists during the past two generations.

Steve Suitts, the longtime executive director of the Southern Regional Council, builds on his biography of the Supreme Court Justice Hugo Black to discuss efforts to bring some measure of economic justice to the South during the Great Depression. Black, like Suitts and the Gaston family, were Alabamians focused on the profound injustices of the economic system created by entrenched elites. A Populist in origin, Black worked hard during his years in the United States Senate, from 1927 to 1937, to impose a measure of economic equality on a society and economy grossly stacked against the poor. He was not in fact very successful in his efforts, and historians have based his significance on his illustrious career on the Supreme Court. Suitts, however, under the influence of his long friendship with Paul Gaston, places emphasis on Black's Alabama Populist, oppositional background.

THESE ESSAYS ARE OFFERED in admiration of our friend and mentor Paul M. Gaston.

HISTORIANS IN SERVICE OF A BETTER SOUTH

1

The Black Church and Black Memory of Jim Crow

RAYMOND GAVINS

Raymond Gavins died on May 22, 2016. Besides contributing his writings, he supported the preparation of this Festschrift by helping to identify some of Paul Gaston's earlier students and by sharing his knowledge of publishing. His life came to an end before he could compose a preface or take part in the final editing. The essay that follows appears with the permission of his family, and it showcases his role as a pioneer in the field of oral history. As he said in an email to the editors: "Using mainly Behind the Veil: African American Life in the Jim Crow South Project oral histories, I'll explore roles of the black church and religion in empowering black southerners to endure and resist Jim Crow, sustaining a struggle for dignity and equal citizenship, long before 1954."[1]

∼

Since the emergence of social history in the 1970s, oral sources have been vital to studies of southern race relations noticeably during the decades of legal segregation and black struggle preceding the mid-twentieth century civil rights movement.[2] While facing the threats and realities of disfranchisement, lynching, illiteracy, and poverty in the segregated South, blacks relied on their own institutions—none more indispensable than the black church—for survival, affirmation, uplift, dignity, hope, and the will to resist. Many oral interviews in the "Behind the Veil" Collection at Duke University give voice to such ideals. My aim here is to discuss the role of the black church in the Jim Crow era, drawing from historiography, related literature, and a sample of "Behind the Veil" interviews.[3]

For its many adherents and observers alike, the black church was paramount. In 1903, W.E. B. Du Bois observed: "The Negro Church is the only social institution of the Negroes which started in the African forest and survived slavery; under the leadership of the priest or medicine man, afterward of the Christian pastor, the Church preserved in itself the remnants of African tribal life and became after emancipation the center of Negro social life." Thus "today the Negro population of the United States is virtually divided into church congregations which are the real units of race life." Central in their community, the church served as the crucible within which African Americans could forge a collective determination to survive and empower themselves. The question is how they would do that under iron-fisted segregation and violence. How might they pursue uplift in face of mass poverty? Citizenship in face of disfranchisement? Education in "the sight of the Veil . . . between us and Opportunity"?[4] Resistance in face of fear? Hope in face of despair? Churchmen and women's answers to such questions illuminate their world, "the meaning of its religion," and work by which the church inspired faith, racial solidarity, and steps toward equal citizenship.[5]

In the wake of emancipation, while they established or expanded their own churches and denominations, which competed for members, blacks cooperated to institute and preserve annual Emancipation Day and other sacred traditions.[6] These included the fifth Sunday union meeting; a weeklong "big meeting" or revival; family reunion and homecoming Sundays. Union meetings rotated among member churches. Attendees worshiped, raised funds, and ate lunch thanks to the host congregation. Revivals, reunions, and homecomings, ordinarily in late summer or early fall, not only called "sinners" home to Christ but celebrated ties that bound relatives and friends from near and far. Church would be crowded with kin who had migrated to the North or other regions. After the morning service and sermon by the revivalist of the week, kinfolk and others enjoyed a picnic dinner and went to evening service.[7]

Churches afforded parishioners a "range of ways to deepen their faiths and improve their lives," hereby undermining Jim Crow. Like the "invisible institution" of slaves, the post-slavery black church, Albert Raboteau maintains, was "an agency of social control, a source of economic cooperation, an arena for political activity, a sponsor of education, and a refuge in a hostile white world." Ministers and lay people formed and sustained religious, educational, fraternal, business, and civic organizations. Ex-slave pastor Alexander Bettis founded more than forty South Carolina Baptist churches before his death in 1895. During freed people's first crusade for schools (1860–1900), they opened and staffed Sabbath schools, modeled by the Sunday school, to furnish basic literacy instruction in evenings and on weekends. Before and beside the Freedmen's Bureau and missionary-sponsored schools, Sabbath schools sowed the seeds of universal schooling. "Public education for all at public expense was, in the South, a Negro idea," Du Bois affirmed. Fraternal orders, mutual aid societies, and clubs anchored churches' effort to promote morality, education, and freedom. Notable were the Prince Hall Masons, Oddfellows, Good Samaritans, Independent Order of St. Luke, and United Order of Tents. Lodge-church alliances, as in Richmond, Virginia, organized the first African American insurance companies and banks, infusing a group economy and ethos "within the Veil" that challenged white racism.[8] Churchgoers espoused equal rights in local and state civic groups, the Negro Convention Movement, National Association of Colored Women, and National Association for the Advancement of Colored People. Christian faith, race pride and unity informed their priorities and programs.

Consider these North Carolina strides. Even as the rank and file sang "I am bound for the promised land," the black clergy and press eyed public issues. Study "the great questions of the day," preached African Methodist Episcopal (AME) cleric E. George Biddle. His good shepherd would be educated, abreast of "politics and all economic subjects that relate to the health and wealth of his flock." Education would enable him to reference politics. The shepherd's leadership would reflect his preparation. "The pulpit is demanding prepared men for its occupancy. The pew demands talent that can lead and instruct it in the truths of the Gospel. Thought, well presented, must take the place of sound and noise, and senseless harangue and twaddle," announced the *AME Zion Church Quarterly*. "These will not do in this enlightened time." Church-founded Biddle and Shaw universities, St. Augustine and Livingstone colleges, and Scotia Seminary for women were providing theological and higher training. Scotia earned "an excellent reputation." "Over 1,800 women students of the Negro group [had] received instruction at the school" by 1884.[9]

Churches and voluntary associations grounded black Wilmington's middle class, which had leverage in the Republican Party and city government before the bloody Democratic coup of 1898. About fifty-one blacks died in it; hundreds were "exiled and scattered over the country from our pulpits and our people." The churches and lodges spearheaded blacks' recovery. Meanwhile, in Durham, a cadre of men from White Rock Baptist and St. Joseph's AME churches, and the Royal Knights of King David, chartered the North Carolina Mutual Life Insurance Company. Promoted as the "company with a 'Soul and a Service'," it grew to be the nation's largest black insurer and symbol of progress. It funded and patronized enterprises that, by 1925, made Durham the fabled "Capital of the Black Middle Class." Viewing the church as a bridge linking black enterprise and uplift, one pastor opined: "The influence of the pulpit in this regard can hardly be overestimated. It is a great . . . stimulant, affecting many, many lives that other influences fall short of."[10]

Never was its influence more needed than when voter disfranchisement and mob violence inscribed statewide Jim Crow in 1900. Led by Bishop James W. Hood of the AME Zion Church, black leaders met in Raleigh on Emancipation Day and issued "An Address to the White People of North Carolina" protesting proposed legislation to disfranchise blacks. "It is already urged by an influential portion of the . . . leading men that these amendments to the State Constitution are temporary expedients," they stated. "That the Thirteenth, Fourteenth and Fifteenth amendments to the Constitution of the United States must be repealed. Repeal them and slavery again becomes lawful." They added: "In view of these facts, it is natural that we should feel the greatest anxiety as to the outcome of efforts now being made not only to restrict our right to vote, but to deny that right altogether." Yet the Suffrage Amendment passed, instituting a grandfather clause, poll tax, literacy test, and property qualification. Statutes soon required absolute "separation of the races" and fueled extralegal white supremacy. Not counting black fatalities in the Wilmington riot, thirty-two blacks were lynched circa 1897–1918.[11] Rural blacks, fleeing oppression and seeking opportunity, migrated to Tar Heel cities and to the North by tens of thousands

Religion was central to blacks' ideology and strategy. In 1901, Principal Simon G. Atkins of Slater Normal School proclaimed that "now is the time for the Negro to show his faith in God and humanity," by believing "mob violence and uncontrolled outlawry" would end. "I do not believe that the white people of North Carolina have repudiated the spirit of Christ," he testified, urging patience. "I do not believe that race hate can thrive in any considerable part of the state's soil."[12] Braving their fears, the majority of blacks stayed in North Carolina. Many closed ranks to affirm and advance themselves.

Churchwomen in Wilmington (representing twelve churches in 1897 and twenty-two by 1920) illustrate blacks' evolving resistance to dependency and discrimination. Lodge and club women garnered "help for the poor, sick, and indigent." Love & Charity Lodge raised money for medical care and to rebuild its hall, which housed Alexander Manly's *Daily Record* newspaper operations and was burned down in 1898. Laywomen urgently supported a 1907 black "boycott of the city streetcars," a challenge to segregated seating. Their massive temperance rally in 1912 "drew more than 1,000 participants." They aided black migrants and families of servicemen in World War I, launched a library at St. Stephen's AME Church, opened a Youth Women's Christian Association (YWCA), and contributed funds to building a new Williston Industrial High School. From their ranks came nurses and the creators of an American Red Cross unit by 1917. They co-sponsored Emancipation Day exercises in 1919 at Shiloh Baptist Church, where the Congregational pastor gave the oration. "A parade was held with a drum and fife corps, and more than 100 black soldiers took part," reported the *Wilmington Dispatch*. Some Red Cross workers also marched as a unit in the parade." The same year, laywomen crusaded for women's suffrage and were pivotal founders of the Wilmington branch of the National Association for the Advancement of Colored People (NAACP). Between 1917 and 1920, blacks chartered ten NAACP branches, each church-affiliated.

As did Wilmington's branch, they vowed "to educate that men and women may know how to qualify and then exercise all the rights and privileges of citizenship." A church-NAACP partnership would last in the South and nation throughout the twentieth century.[13]

Individual memories enlarge the portrait not only of links between churches, families, and communities but also of thought and action relating to citizenship, education, empowerment, and equality. As Celestyne D. Porter, Ann E. Pointer, and Booker T. Federick point out, ethical and human values that they imbued coming of age enabled them to endure and reject segregation.

Celestyne Porter, retired educator and supervisor, inculcated precepts of tolerance, caring, and industry during childhood in Mathews County, Virginia. Located seventy miles north of Norfolk on the Chesapeake Bay, it had 7,784 residents (75 percent white) by 1930, a year after she entered Hampton Institute. Statewide, seventy blacks and sixteen whites had been lynched since 1880, though none in Mathews.[14] She portrays it as "an old plantation system county," a place of "fishing and small farming." Blacks, a number of them landowners, simply got along. Segregation was the rule, but blacks and whites lived in proximity and interaction. "There wasn't anything like that [violent conflict]," she vouches. "The white men and the colored men would go up to the courthouse and they'd drink their beer, their booze. . . . Then they would walk on home. You know, we'd laugh about it." Often, "if Miss Annie didn't have all the flour she needed, she'd send over home and get some. If Mama didn't have all that she needed, she'd borrow from Miss Annie. . . . We forgot about who was colored and who was white." If she was "Miss Annie" to us, "her children called my daddy and mama 'Uncle Wilbur' and 'Aunt Sue.' We used to have a joke [that] white folks would rather be kin to you than to call you Mr. and Mrs."[15]

Regardless, "you went to your own church." Her ex-slave maternal grandparents and their thirteen children; parents; and siblings (five brothers, four sisters) belonged to First Baptist Church, a haven for country folk. Both her grandfather and grandmother stood out, ever supporting and educating their children. To wit, Porter's mother developed a fine singing voice in the choir. She attended Hampton as a member of its noted Jubilee Singers and, until her babies were born, taught school. "The joke of it was, none of us had no voice. She didn't pass us down no voices." However, she pushed her own and the neighbors' children to learn. The "school didn't go any further than fifth grade," so she "started farming us out to everywhere else where we could get an education. And relatives helped each other. Where they had better facilities than you had." Porter thus moved to Norfolk with her oldest sister, who finished high school and was continuing at Presbyterian-run Norfolk Mission College. They joined a Presbyterian church. She went to Price Elementary and Washington High School, where her aunt "taught us all about the blacks. That was a part of her English course. You had to learn about that. And then Dr. [Carter G.] Woodson would come to speak each year to . . . black teachers and professionals called The Book Lovers in Norfolk." The famed scholar, founder of the Association for the Study of Negro Life and History, "was a friend of our family's, and he stayed at our house every time he came to speak." Woodson was keen to reach teachers as well as ordinary folk in promoting black history; his visits perhaps sowed seeds for Porter's career.[16]

Meanwhile, First Baptist hosted homecomings. "The older people, my grandparents and all had family reunions. They didn't call it family reunions." However, "everybody came home. If they went away to work, they came home in the summertime . . . back to Mathews County for homecoming." Together with preaching, singing, and fellowship "homecoming is always a very, very big thing. Everybody comes back, as near as possible, for that Sunday homecoming, all-day meeting and dinner on the ground." The event was a source of strength for the celebrants, writes William Wiggins, who "are certain to sing spirituals whose themes of freedom, justice, and hope still have a special relevance."[17]

The elders personified ideals of independence, moral character, and selflessness. Porter's grandparents were sharecroppers and domestics earlier, but when she was growing up the family owned "fifteen acres on the waterfront." The land "came to us through my maternal grandmother who was the illegitimate daughter of the plantation owner, and he willed her the place. It was to be her place and her heirs," she certifies. "My father was a farmer and a fisherman . . . he farmed the whole area, he and my brothers, as they grew up on the farm. And then his main occupation was fishing. He was a fisherman, a waterman they call them now." Also, "the girls didn't go in the field. We had to keep house and work for the [white] people in the neighborhood." Her papa was an upright, respected, and generous man. He sold produce, oysters, and crabs, and habitually gave away vegetables and fish to the less fortunate. Her "brothers took after him, and they were watermen until they left home."

It was her grandmother (107 years old when she died in 1938) who best practiced the ideal of giving. "About slavery. She could tell you the whole thing. She was a house servant, and she could tell you what's there." She taught Porter to cook and can, wait on tables, and clean. "I've got a picture of her. My grandmother was really and truly a very smart uneducated woman." For example, she prepared food and delivered it to people in need. "Every Sunday she would put my two brothers and my sister [and me]—we were the last of the children—put us in this surrey, an old surrey. You sat in the front, and she drove the mule," Porter assures. "And people would say . . . 'where you going?' 'I'm going to see the sick and afflicted, the poor and the needy, and the cast down on account of trouble.' We used to laugh about it and say 'What did Grandma . . . mean by the sick and afflicted?'"

In any case, Porter internalized the meaning of that mission: "We had good examples of transplanting of ideas." The church and family's teachings seemed to guide her. At Hampton "I took a double major in history and Bible and literature, and it was the best education that I really have had, my four years there." She participated in "the debating society and the Hampton Club and the Phillis Wheatley [Club]." Chapel service was mandatory. "If you had a little more than somebody else, you still had to do everything. You had to work, for one thing." Porter "worked at the president's house. . . . I could cook and I could set the table. You had to be able to set the table to get that job." Each summer "I was the housekeeper for a very wealthy lady" in Mathews. "I cooked and cleaned up and set the table for her" and she would pay "me Labor Day when I got ready to go back to college." Her most significant jobs, regardless, were teaching and cultivating black children. "My first job was at a one-room school just outside Williamsburg. I made $2.00 a day," she said. "But all my students were reading when I left there in May, and I had beginners, first grade [to] . . . eighth grade. My children were all reading." She received invaluable support from parents and donors. "The churches helped. They took care of large numbers of people who did not have anything. The churches took care of them, and you gave to the churches." As well, "in schools kids didn't mind wearing hand-me-downs. If the aunt had a nice dress and passed it to you, you didn't mind."

During her teaching in Norfolk, Porter mobilized lay and club women to play "every kind of role you could think of. We were fund-raisers for the first thing, and we attacked the needs of the community." They started a raffle to obtain "the first operating table" for the black hospital. "We'd go down after school in the evening and we'd go on Sundays to read to the children and to show them pictures and carry them bunnies and make things." Active in the Women's Interracial Council, YWCA, and Urban League, too, Porter exemplified church workers who fostered black self-determination and organization. She studied U.S. history at the University of Pennsylvania (summers 1938–43), becoming one of the first blacks to earn the M.A. there. "It was just the two of us on campus. We made the *Philadelphia Inquirer* on the front page," she verifies. "We were the first blacks that had been admitted to the College of Arts and Sciences," and still "I went to church on Sundays."

In the final analysis, Porter was proud of black churchwomen's activism. "During the age of separate and unequal, we developed, all of us developed, a society totally our own, and I don't think that we had any seriously bad attitudes about living together as black people," she declares. They "had to sit on back of the bus" but evinced great resilience. "You knew that you had your churches, your own school, your own—everything."[18] So, they aspired and struggled for a brighter tomorrow.

Ann Pointer came of age in fearful surroundings where the church was a mitigating force. A former Tuskegee, Alabama, hospital worker and sharecropper, she, four brothers, and a sister "were poor as church mice." Raised in rural Macon County, they knew a "world from the church to the community to the school." Paternal grandparents, both ex-slaves, were Christian paragons. "They lived, I would say a fourth of a mile away, on the same place where we were living. We all lived and rented from the same man that owned all the land in this area." Her grandmother "never knew her real mother because they sold her" and "my grandfather . . . could not read nor write but he was a Methodist minister." Carried away by Confederates in the Civil War, he was captured, "set free," and inducted into the Union army. "So my grandfather was compensated from the government. . . . They started giving him a check of one hundred dollars a month back then, which was good money back in that time." Suffering repeated injustices, "he was afraid of white people and he was until he died." For instance, "he had a son that was lynched in Tallapoosa County. When I say lynched, he was shot." He shot back at his attackers and escaped with a hip wound. Subsequently, he managed to see a white doctor who "put poison into his hip and killed him." Her grandfather got a warrant for the arrest of his killers, but death threats kept him going back to court. Moreover, when he bought "groceries and things," the grocer cheated him "out of that check."[19] It is not surprising that he feared whites.

Pointer notes that "those same fears were passed down to us, thus giving many of us . . . inferiority complexes." Even so, thanks to the ministry of their neighborhood church, they pulled together. "If you had sickness, it was everybody's sickness, and they could ring that church bell down here, it was a bell in that church." Neighbors lent a helping hand, even to "the hobos" who frequently passed through. "We had a woodpile and you know ain't nobody supposed to be out there chopping, everybody in the house. And papa would take a lantern and he'd go out" into the yard and find a hobo. "'Hey friend, nobody to hurt you, I'm just cutting up some wood if you all could give me a meal.'" Her mother fed him "and they'd fix him a pallet . . . And that happened all the time." Neighborhood elders also were examples of caring. "At church they would shout, shout, cry . . . and all that stuff." On Sunday evenings "they would sit down and talk about the old times and the work that they did and the hard time that they had." They admonished children to stay in church and attend school, to get an education and make good livelihoods, often giving them a nickel for encouragement.

Accordingly, Pointer and her siblings strove to learn, live by the Golden Rule, and prosper. School "went from October through April and the first of May the school was closed, where you get in the field." They "didn't have a well in the yard, we had to go to the spring for water," the house had "holes everywhere," and the owner "did not make it pleasant for his tenants." Pointer determined to protest. "My father [ruled] 'no,' and we would listen to him, 'easy way is the safest way home, just walk around it, don't get in their way.'" A semiliterate man who once was jailed ninety days for bootlegging, he accommodated to deflect trouble. "Mama wanted us to go to school, she wanted us to be good," and advance. She completed seventh grade, was highly independent, and made four dollars a week working in the white people's houses. "My mother was proud, we could not tell people that we didn't have anything." Thanks to her expectations and tutoring, they stayed "out front at school, at church, and everywhere else. . . . All six children had abilities other children couldn't touch." Her sister excelled in mathematics and her brothers "were great athletes . . . and smart in books as well." Teachers and church people applauded them for being outstanding and well behaved students. "God rest her soul. . . . God knows what to do for you," observes Pointer, who moved "from the cotton field to the white woman's kitchen" to Tuskegee Institute. "Now I started out teaching school" before retooling to be a practical nurse, restaurant cook, and hospital orderly. But it was a high school business course paid for by her mother that equipped Pointer to earn a decent living, which partially fulfilled her mother's dreams. In addition, she "taught us the morals of life." Pointer concludes that "the church and a good family, a loving close-knit family is what kept me going . . . in the right direction."[20]

Booker Federick, of Leflore County, Mississippi, came of age in a rural environment like Porter, Pointer, and probably 80 percent of black southerners prior to World War I and the Great Migration. His was a multigenerational sharecropping family. "I lived on plantations until I was about twenty-eight years old and then I moved into the little town here [Itta Bena]," he discloses. "I didn't get a chance to go to school that much . . . sometimes we may go around forty-five days out of a season." His parents "didn't have any education." Some croppers "had the learning, but they didn't have no rights. That's what throwed them to be just about in the same shape I was in myself."[21]

Oppression reigned. The owner "sold all of the cotton, but . . . if he got twenty-two cents a pound for cotton, he might would settle with you on thirteen or fourteen cents a pound." Federick "thought it was very unfair." Nonetheless, "we didn't know anything to do about it but try to make another crop with him or move to another plantation." Some blacks rented land and sold their own cotton, yet "still didn't get the fair price for it." Murder and whipping occurred. "I've heard them talk about how they would lynch people and how they hung them up in trees." Periodically, owners would "want you to do so much. If you didn't do it, they'd take you that night and strap you and things of that nature and make you do without food," he reminisces. "Every once in a while some black people defended themselves. . . . They would fight back and get by for a long time."

In the meantime, blacks fought back by means of the church. There they congregated and found solace, fostering confidence and self-help. "That's the one thing that I've been doing ever since I was fourteen years old, going to churches and visiting churches and trying to get whatever I could out of going, and then being among all kinds of people," Federick remembers. This was a legacy from his ex-slave grandparents and hardworking parents. "I avoided a lot of things in life that I could have got into by remembering what I was taught by some older person." He went to "the church over here and was a Sunday school teacher." Folks there "believed whatever they done in faith, the Lord would grant it to them in grace." He opines: "Nothing that I've done, not so much, I've been the kind of man the Lord would want, but it stayed in me to go to church and do all the service I can there," adding "during the time I come up, they didn't have pools in these churches to baptize. They would baptize us in the lakes and rivers, and sometime they'd have a little pond or something on the plantation."

To earn their "daily bread," blacks invented ways to cooperate. "If we would be fortunate enough to get through with what land we had traded with the man to work, we traded with him to work fifteen acres . . . and you wasn't through when we got through, we'd just take our hoe and go on over there without asking any questions," Federick indicates. "That's the way we'd help one another then. And go on over there and make sure, and if another person wasn't through, all of us" combined hands and pulled the "rows of corn that had some full ears on there" for a tenant family. "We would try to pull those ears, because the first load of corn" went to the owner's corn house. "Then we'd start putting some full ears on top" to deceive the owner. Sometimes, they would assist an abused tenant in slipping his "family away off a plantation" and remaining silent, particularly if "he left owing the man something." Usually, "he would stay around the place with his family already gone for two or three days, and then one night he would leave himself." Also, women assisted tenants with washing and cleaning. "There were some plantations, the ladies had little babies at the house. The older child stayed there with the baby." When a mother "got ready to nurse the baby, then that older child would carry it to the field."[22] Resistance evolved in such cooperative customs, deep-rooted in slave religion and serving as resources for Federick and his neighbors.

Others, especially those who grew up before 1940, speak to four themes: the significance of churchgoing; youth ministry; church-based networks of support; and the principle of faith. While "religion is essentially a subjective experience," their testimonies invoke a shared outlook on its value for life and coping among middle and working-class blacks.[23]

Churchgoing is a perennial and protean theme. Like schooling, it illuminates childhood worlds with grandparents, parents, siblings, kinfolk, neighbors, and employers. It provided a safe haven for fellowship—for praying, singing, learning, and sharing fundamental beliefs about God, humankind, and the world "beyond the Veil." Factory worker Tolbert Chism of Fargo, Arkansas, began a Methodist catechism at age five. "My people were always highly religious and Christian-like, so to speak," he recalls. "We went to church every Sunday. There wasn't no way out of that." Katherine Hinton, an Enfield, North Carolina domestic, "was brought up in the church. Along then the pastor didn't play with you long. You went to Sunday school and church." She went to regular church twice a month but to Sunday school every week. "If church didn't meet I stayed home . . . along then you won't running up and down the road like they do now." For educator Anthony Farmer of Danville, Virginia, being baptized in the river was a key incentive. "Always baptizing was big . . . at the church I grew up in, or started to grow up in, White Rock Baptist Church," he reminisces. Afterward, "they would have the service and give you what is called the right hand of fellowship which is communion. And everybody would come around and shake your hand and wish you well."[24]

Witnesses also disclose disciplinary aspects of churchgoing. "Oh well, you were going to join the church," attests Mary Dulin, a housewife from Drakesboro, Kentucky. "You were going to be a Christian in those days or else they were going to worry you to death with fear." New Iberia, Louisiana, laborer William Zepherin concedes: "Oh, yeah. Definitely. He [father] used to make us go to church barefooted sometime. Wash our feet, grease 'em and we go sit up in the front. . . . We just couldn't afford no shoes." Cotton Plant, Arkansas, farmer William Malone waited long Sundays on the pews. "They stayed at church longer then than they do now. The preacher would preach longer," he recollects. "And back there then looks like the people was more together than they are now." Educator Manuel Crockett went to church so often in Sunrise, Tennessee, that he avoided vespers as a student at Hampton Institute: "Everybody cut church if they possibly could." It "was just too long, and repetitious, too," confides Greenwood, Mississippi, health worker Daisy Livingston: "I remember Mama and them . . . use to stay at church all day long, and then they'd go back in the evening and stay till late at night."[25]

Many recollect churchgoing as voluntary and inspirational. Ernestine Clemmons, a New Bern, North Carolina, housewife, remarks that "the church used to be full. . . . And people used to take the children in; got an older person to go with you. You couldn't go in after dark without some older person taking you." She adds: "We used to have an old lady . . . all the children used to go to her for her to take us to church on Sunday nights if the parents didn't go." Wilhelmina Baldwin, a teacher from Tuskegee, Alabama, refers to "so much fun" in church. Her father was pastor of rural churches and the Blackburn Church at Boggs Academy, Keysville, Georgia. "We always had Sunday school and church on the campus every Sunday morning and we had prayer meeting on Wednesday nights, and some of the community people would come." Ex-sharecropper Willie Harrell of Memphis, Tennessee, went to church freely and joyfully. "My mama and grandpa and grandma used to load us up in the wagon. We used to go to church. Hook them mules up and go to church and man, you could hear them old church's bell a mile before you get there," he admits. "I loved church. I goes every Sunday now."[26]

Going to church was a communal ritual. "You'd walk and then it was an absent Sunday and it wasn't nothing but Sunday school. Now you walked that Sunday. But the Sunday what was real preaching . . . your mama and papa took and carried you . . . in the wagon," according to Josephine McCray, a nurse from Manning, South Carolina. A domestic, Ida Belle of Kentsvania, South Carolina, talks about the joy of attending church and its inclusiveness. "Church was much different. People were loving. Just what you had, if it's a gingham dress or homespun dress, you were good and clean. You would wash it and iron and starch it up and you'd go on to church. If your hair was braided you were respected, didn't matter who had their hair fixed," she recounts. "You went to church and love was there. And the church was full and we used to walk for three miles."[27] Church was a sanctuary for all the people, irrespective of class, where they could enjoy autonomy and nurture their hopes.

Loyalty to the church was chock full of meanings. "The people live for the church instead of the church existing for the people," wrote Monroe N. Work of Tuskegee Institute in his report for *The Negro Church*. Du Bois, in *The Souls of Black Folk*, said their "weekly sacrifice . . . at the altar of the 'old-time religion'" evoked a "common consciousness, sprung from common joy and grief, at burial, birth, or wedding; from a common hardship in poverty, poor land, and low wages." Business woman Cleaster Mitchell of Brinkley, Arkansas, agrees. "The lifeline of the community was the church, because they never had telephones, a lot of them couldn't write . . . but they would gather up on a Sunday. That's when they prayed together, they visit together, they talk, they caught up on everything that was going on, and I guess they shared recipes," she recites. "That was a glorious time when they got together on a Sunday."[28]

A second theme in the interviews concerns children and youths' religious training. Field researchers for *The Negro Church* emphasized that this commitment was essential to developing "intelligent congregations" and to retaining the church's "influence on young people." Training began with parents taking children to church. David Matthews, an Indianola,

Mississippi, pastor and teacher, tells of bonding on Sundays. "The father was there and the mother was there unless death or something. Rarity for a family to have a divorce situation in our community," he relates. "They would stick together and the family would be together . . . ate together and went to church together and programs, whatnot together. So there was more togetherness then."[29]

Parental and adult authority, the inspiration to hold ethical principles, youth programing, and the cultivation of friendly relationships permeate narrators' accounts. Since parents were at church, their children "couldn't get out of line." They either had to behave or bear chastisement. "But the father and mother were there. That made a lot of difference in the discipline," contends David Matthews. "The broad perspective was that the community observed the actions of the children and if they were out of line then any citizen in that community would be willing and ready to call you back in place. And of course if that didn't do they could even spank you and nothing would be done about it when you'd go home except you'd get a second one [laughter]." Discipline for New Bern laborer Leamon Dillahunt began with his father. "My speech, I think I had six words in it and I started saying it when I left my father's lap and before I [could] get up there and finish my speech I was back to my father sitting in his lap. I remember that the longest day I live," he says. Being guided and encouraged by his father "instilled something into me . . . and I can see now children when they're coming up . . . have to have role models. Well, we had good role models back then."[30]

Such were ex-slaves York D. Garrett II and Sarah R. Garrett of Tarboro, North Carolina, who reared seven children by the rules of church and school. York attended a freedmen's school and worked in a white grocery store. By 1895 he was its owner and operator. A voter and loyal Republican, he was twice elected as an Edgecombe County magistrate. Owner of an "eight room house" and a good provider for his wife, children, and ex-slave mother, he also did lay duties in Episcopal and Baptist churches, chiefly advocating for black schools, and became of one of the state's famous Masonic leaders. All his children graduated from college. The oldest, Beatrice G. Burnett, a teacher and civic activist, gives her account in *Hope and Dignity: Older Black Women of the South* (1983). A son, York D. Garrett, Jr., a Durham pharmacist and businessman, gives his in an interview.

Their accounts are revealing. Both recognize the mother's partnership in their guidance, stating "she'd let my father do the politicking. But she'd stick right behind him in anything he wanted to do" [Burnett] and "she was a member of those things too . . . Eastern Star, Household of Ruth and all that" [York, Jr.]. However, they attribute enduring ideals (race pride, the Golden Rule, or scholastic achievement) to their father's impact. Finishing Elizabeth City State Normal School in 1912, Burnett did graduate study at Hampton; taught seventh grade and physical education; and soon was a Sunday school, NAACP, and suffrage advocate. "My father often said, 'You're as good as anybody else. . . . And that's the philosophy we were brought up under. I'm telling you, and I have never taken low either,'" she asserts, applauding his self-confidence and courage. Just after World War I, "one of the deacons of my church and the superintendent of my Sunday school got a message to be out of town at such-and-such a time if he valued his life." He had objected to the policy of closing black schools "until the cotton was gotten out." York, Jr., called a meeting with white authorities at the Episcopal Church, but "the whites said, 'There is nothing we can do about it.'" Blacks announced: "'We will.' My father said, I don't even have a gun but I'm sending to get one." He led an armed patrol, protected the deacon, and the mob never came.

York, Jr., finished Elizabeth City Normal and Howard University academy in 1916 before joining the army during World War I. "I went in as a company clerk, which was the biggest job in the army then unless you were an officer," he insists. "It was segregated. I was in charge of the whole company, 250 blacks." He earned a Phar.D. at Howard and passed the North Carolina pharmacy examination in 1920. His father's model in education, fraternalism, and independence guided him. "So I've never known for my father to work for anybody because he was in business for himself when I was born [1894] and continued in business for himself until he died [1928],"[31] concludes York, Jr, who became a Durham pharmacist, drug store owner, and lay leader of White Rock Baptist Church from 1932 to 1977.

As portrayed with the Garretts, churches backed families in motivating children to learn and achieve. William Childs, a schoolteacher and

Wilmington truant officer, reveals the positive effects. He and five siblings grew up in a multigenerational household and St. Stephen's AME Church, each stressing honesty, education, and progress. His maternal grandparents (ex-slaves) got married at St. Stephen's in 1875. "I was twenty-two and my husband was twenty-two too not quite twenty-three. Not a year older than I was. He was a cooper. . . . My husband was good to me," Isabell Henderson, his grandmother, affirms in her Federal Writers' Project slave narrative. "We went in our own home and stayed there. . . . I have had five children. Three are livin.' Two are dead. I never worked until after he died." The young couple never forgot the city's bloodbath. "They did not really want to talk too much about the riot of 1898," Childs allows. "There was . . . a lot of information about it. But they did not like to talk about it." They were "positive people that looked forward rather than back," faithfully connected to St. Stephen's.[32]

Childs's parents, in particular his father, a railroad cook and preacher, reinforced church precepts. "My father was a stickler for good behavior and we addressed everybody as mister, white and black," Childs avows. Too, his father rarely mentioned segregation. "He did not approve of it but he didn't dwell on it. His thing was he wanted us to be in church and Sunday school and that kind of thing, you know. And in school. . . . And in the library." These were seeds for their future. "He was not that formally educated. I'm not sure how far he went in school but he didn't go that far," Childs discloses. "But he had this thing about reading . . . principally the Bible. He read the Bible all the time." From 1920 to 1941, every sibling finished high school, three finished college, and two earned M.A. degrees. Josephine McCray had demanding parents, too. "I'll tell you, you had to read something out of the Bible to my mother and father just like you read your school books. You couldn't go to bed if you didn't," she testifies. "Now I'm glad I accept it. I can read. . . . I'm eighty-four years old. My last baby I raised is in Korea, one of my daughter's sons. I don't have to ask nobody to write him. I can do it myself."[33]

Education and counsel molded youth ministries. Most enjoyable for Wilhemina Baldwin were the "family conferences," meeting in summers and coordinated by the Presbyterian Church. These gatherings connected adult and youth Bible study, worship, recreation, and "a talent night where we had to do some things as family," she thinks back. "We would try and race and beat other families there each year." Along with Mother's Day, Father's Day, Easter, and Christmas, "when I came along everybody would look forward to Children's Day, and great preparations were made for children to present programs," elaborates Durham health educator Mildred Page. "And sometimes the Children's Days were staggered so that you'd get to go to Children's Days at other churches."[34]

Children received invaluable training. "Well, they would get up and recite speeches and poems. Something to kind of motivate 'em to be something," Leamon Dillahunt reflects. "Have something to look forward to. And we really looked forward to that day." This was validated by what an investigator for *The Negro Church* discovered when he polled 1,339 children with "Are you a Christian?" Their responses were 494 yes and 845 no. "Nearly all go to church, however," he commented. They liked being in children's activities and seeing their friends. Training them were women such as New Bern schoolteacher Dorcas Carter. "I would give plays and I still do that. Sometimes programs. . . . That's what I liked doing and I got a lot of satisfaction and people would always say you're the talk of the town," she recognizes. "But my important role was as a teacher."[35]

Youth programs forged many enduring relationships. Leamon Dillahunt admits that the boys participated mainly "'cause the girls would be at the church." When Presbyterian families fellowshipped "we played with all the other family members," Wilhelmina Baldwin verifies, and she learned "how to get along with the boys." Cleaster Mitchell was in a youth band: "A lot of them would stay out under the shade trees there, and they would sit and talk and everything, and then we would go in later and have this Bible class, and we played with all the other children." Never a big churchgoer but a Methodist, Manuel Crockett confesses that he "became Baptist to marry [his wife] Myrtle." Elizabeth Pitts, a farmhand from Leflore County, Mississippi, confirms that people "would gather and socialize" during "baptism ceremonies at the local river. Yeah, they would go to church and meet people, you know." Engineer James Lewis, from Havelock, North Carolina, concurs. Baptists, Methodists, and others in his county came to "each other's church" regularly. He reckons that "people at Adam Creek were just friends. If they weren't friends, they were cousins or brothers."[36] Their exchanges, usually a result of the Baptist Training Union and Youth Days, generated lifelong friendships and marriages.

A third theme in the recollections uncovers churches as spaces for temporal and spiritual support. This mirrors Benjamin Mays and Joseph Nicholson's evaluation of 609 urban churches in twelve cities (seven southern) and 169 rural churches in four counties (all southern). Almost "all of the Churches . . . have cooperated with other churches, or with community institutions and agencies, through ministerial alliances and associations; in religious educational activities; in cooperative humanitarian movements; in social welfare, poor relief, and the like," they declared.[37] Decades before that survey, churches did much to furnish a safety net. Congregations consistently fed the hungry, housed the homeless, and comforted the sick. Denominations financed homes for girls, orphans, and the aged; nurseries; mission and fraternal charities; home health and Bible classes; and employment assistance.

Those supportive services benefitted North Carolinians Lillie Fenner and Walter Cavers. Fenner, a Halifax County farmhand, grew up in humble circumstances. "We never had no land of our own. We'd sharecrop with the white people," she muses. Blacks toiled "on the farm" and "in the log woods. . . . That's the way they made their living." They also created protective and cooperative associations. Belonging to the church and lodge, her parents both gave and received help. "My daddy was a member of the lodge called the Knights of Gideon, and they would go to the lodge at night, he and my mama. It was some kind of meeting. They would meet and discuss different things. When somebody would pass in the family they would always give . . . a certain portion of money to help them. Then they would fix food and carry to the house," she continues. "Won't no insurance or nothing. So different ones would pitch in and help them." They helped Lillie after she married and bore six children. Cavers, a Charlotte minister, was a sick stranger when someone at Charlotte's First Baptist Church rescued him. Fleeing white men in Alabama on a northbound train, he jumped off in Charlotte, was staying outdoors, and nearly died from the exposure. "They put me to bed and I had pneumonia." The lady who took him in "used one of her home remedies [and] the Sunday School department sent me thirteen dollars," he remembers. "First Baptist Church that I am now a member of, the pastor there saw to it that I got food. And I didn't know nobody, and I've been here ever since."[38] Fenner and Cavers show us that churches and fraternal orders were crucial in blacks' effort to overcome poverty and caste.

Dora Dennis, a domestic from Forrest City, Arkansas, shares a similar anti-poverty story. Her mother left a Baptist church with her children and joined an Episcopal church. "And we all was confirmed" there. The rector, Father King, ministered to the entire community. "Anybody, you didn't have to belong to the church, anybody that needed help, our church would help them," she divulges. Father King began "what they called the sale room, clothes in there and shoes that the children could wear. The diocese would send them down to him." Shoes, secondhand and some new clothes, coats, and other clothing were sold cheaply to those with means but generally given away. "Some children would come to school with no coats or sweaters, and Father King would tell their mothers to come and see could they find clothes in the sale room. . . . But anybody that wasn't able to buy clothes, [he] would give them to them so the children could go to school and church. That's the way that it was."[39] Dennis invokes the church's various initiatives to furnish relief. Spiritual support came in congregation—at church, home, or work. It was in these places that religion served to affirm oneself and as a shelter amidst life's maelstrom. Durham secretary Theresa Lyons found its assurance. "For a long time I had a terrible inferiority complex, I guess because I had come up so poor," she submits. "I visited a lot of churches but I kept going back to that one [Baptist church on Cheek Road] because the people were warm." The good "preaching, gospel singing, praying, testifying . . . would give me hope, something that I could live from this week to that week." Assuring each other, members would "be in the field talking about religion, anywhere," Elizabeth Pitts exclaims. "Them old people get together they wouldn't have to be at church. They go to talking about it and shout at home." Church was a "very strong institution in a family's life," Anthony Farmer makes clear. "And, so, after you went to church and, you know, told God all of your troubles, that kind of led them and gave them strength right on into the next week. And, then, boom, back to the fuel pump again." The process of refueling was continuous. "When things was bad, they prayed, and when things was wrong.... They was really sharing in all kinds of ways with each other," Cleaster Mitchell avers of her parents and neighbors. In fact, "if anything went wrong, somebody would go to the church and ring the bell.... That was how we got the news out." The children were mentored to be strong. "We were taught not to hate" but to be proud of our color, she emphasizes.[40] Church infused them with resiliency; they not only tolerated Jim Crow but mentally defied it.

Faith is the fourth theme in the reminiscences. Hebrews11:1 denotes it "the substance of things hoped for, the evidence of things not seen." It affirmed the black community, its elites and masses "of tenants and renters, unskilled and semiskilled workers, the more secure domestic and personal servants, train and store porters, day laborers, and others in similar occupations," wrote Charles S. Johnson in *Patterns of Negro Segregation* (1943). They "have little education but are anxious about the education of their children. A common boast is that they 'stay out of trouble' or 'stay out of jail.' They generally seek the associations and consolations of the church and, in religious language, condemn the social and religious looseness of the lower class."[41] Though the condemnation of sinners, intemperance, and immorality was customary, BTV informants appear to digress from that pattern, as they seldom condemn the "unsaved" or speak condescendingly of them.

Rather, they give voice to an introspective, empathetic, and redemptive faith—in creed and practice. Elders inspired and instructed children to live by its commands. Youths ordinarily did, whether due to adults' push or the stigma of eternal damnation. Mary Dulin had "a good talking" to by her grandmother. "If you should die, something happen to you and you should die, you'll go to hell. You're twelve years old and accountable for your sins," Dulin comments. "Even as a child, I can remember thinking that when I was small that my grandmother was just too good. You know, she talked about the Lord so . . . She'd talk about the Lord will take care of this and the Lord will do this. In the church, you hear the other people talking about the Lord." Heeding such devout witnesses, many children, normally during revivals, flocked to the "mourners bench" to join the church. For radio broadcaster Aurie Flowers of Baker City, Georgia, revival "would last a period of two weeks . . . in which we went to the church and we just sang and prayed and then the next week would be when the minister would come and preach."⁴²

Congregations celebrated newcomers to the faith. The singing "seemed like it was more spiritual," Indianola, Mississippi, laborer William Davis muses. "It seemed like the people, you know, like the Negro, I mean hymns and things, church hymns. Seems like they were just belting them out, louder and everything." A neighbor, domestic Annette Clayborn, thinks: "That was a very special time for us . . . because that was when most of all the kids joined the church during that time. No other time, except in revival." Baptizing was memorable. "That's a coming out thing for the individual that be involved in the baptizing," she mulls. "Well, we call it debutante and all this good stuff back at that time that I was coming out." Willie Harrell came out "when I was a boy going to church there. Call myself, you know, turning on the mourning and professing religion, you know. I was baptized in the pool where horses and mules were drinking water on the plantation."⁴³ Baptism, by immersion or by sprinkling, was the rite of passage into the circle of the faithful.

Indeed, many informants portray faith as a lasting value. Theresa Lyons attributes hers to her grandmother. She "was a very strong person. I think any values that I learned I got from her. She was very religious, and as I was growing up, being from a single mother, my mother was . . . just 18– so she was still dating. So my grandmother was really my mother." Lyons acknowledges that "when I got old enough to start going out, she would always tell me. 'You cannot go to the movies unless you go to church.'"⁴⁴ Kathleen Daise, an educator from St. Helena Island, South Carolina, honors forefathers and mothers' faith, declaring that "they depended on the Lord for everything." Mostly illiterate, they had "dreams and the Lord would show them a teacher, somebody to lead them." She adds: "I came [up] that way too but later on when I had a better understanding, could read the Bible and understand for myself, I understood what it was really like. You would have to accept Christ by faith and then let the church and pastor know."⁴⁵

Faith not only tied one generation to the next; it also linked individuals. "But back there during that time, whatever the man was, and the woman married him . . . she went into the faith that he believed in," Tolbert Chism explains. "Well, my father was a Baptist and my mother was a Methodist, and they courted . . . and when they got married and started a family, she joined the Baptist church." Domestic Ruth Davis, from Brunswick County, North Carolina, saw a different situation: Baptist mother and Methodist father. "We would go to church with my dad on the first and third Sundays. . . . Then on the fourth Sunday there was church at my mother's church and I would go there," she reports. "One thing about it my mother never pushed me to be a Baptist and my father never pushed me to be a Methodist. We grew up between the two churches and we'd choose whatever denomination we wanted after we were old enough to decide for ourselves."[46]

Above all, faith strengthened personal and racial identities, enabling believers to withstand what Du Bois calls "double-consciousness, this sense of . . . two-ness—an American, a Negro; two souls, two thoughts, two unreconciled strivings; two warring ideals in one dark body, whose dogged strength alone keeps it from being torn asunder." That tenacity anchored black Christian universalism, the belief that God "hath made of one blood all nations."[47]

Compare these voices. In an interview with the Open Minded Seniors of Halifax County, North Carolina, Susan Weathersbee, age ninety-three, expresses forgiveness. In tears, this widow, mother, and ex-sharecropper, recalls a murder. "Miss Hattie White had a son. I don't know what Keifers had done. He got away and got down here to Spring Hill somehow or another. And they come and shot him. Took a flashlight and hold that light on him and shot that boy and killed him. And they didn't find him until the next day." He spoke up for his mother, who had a dispute with the white storekeeper in Tillery. "Cause he like his ma, he didn't take nothing off' n nobody and she got mad with 'dem folks . . . they had a store and she wouldn't go in that store and buy nothing."

Notwithstanding, Weathersbee clings to faith and forgives: "I know how to treat people. I don't care what race they is, I know how to treat them, how to love them. And if I can do anything for you, to help you, I will." A voice within the Veil, she evokes, quoting Du Bois, "the passion of its human sorrow, and the struggle of its greater souls." Mildred Page and

Cleaster Mitchell echo faith-based black identity and resilience. "It was a funny thing that white people would come to our church to a funeral but I know my family never went to a white church," Page says. "I doubt very seriously that any other black people went to the white church." The black church exhorted self-respect. Mitchell appreciates elders' approach to protecting children. Often, when injustices happened "they would say 'Well, don't worry about it. The Lord will fix it. Vengeance is God,'" she reflects. "They meant you couldn't pursue it. They knowed. We didn't know" the possible consequences.[48] Protecting hearts, minds, and lives, they forwarded the stride toward freedom.

Suffice it to say that oral history is a critical tool that helps us recover, rethink, enlarge, and understand black churches' roles in the Jim Crow South. They offered sanctuary for members to seek Christian salvation and power to engage their struggles for freedom. Clearly, they provided ministries of moral uplift and redemption, of social endurance and resistance. A primary goal of *The Negro Church* was to refute the inferiority of African Americans promoted by historians and white society through empirical facts on the Negro's intelligence, morality, worth to be a citizen. Du Bois warned: "People who are thoroughly fitted . . . and who show by their conduct that they have the disposition and purpose to be good citizens are not going to be permanently excluded in any part of this country from . . . citizenship." He invoked what Evelyn Higginbotham terms "the politics of respectability" to combat anti-black racism and press the struggle for equality.[49] At the same time, in its denominational structures, parishes, and auxiliaries, the black church marshaled a language of human dignity, justice, and hope that helped to sustain a sense of common purpose; a black culture of aspiration and education; care for the disadvantaged; and a transcendent faith. Behind the Veil narrators indeed offer a lens on how the church dignified and empowered blacks, foreshadowing not only the Montgomery Bus Boycott but also the church's centrality in the civil rights movement.

Notes

1. Raymond Gavins, email to editors, November 7, 2015.
2. Cf. William R. Beardslee, *The Way Out Must Lead In: Life Histories in the Civil Rights Movement* (Atlanta: Center for Research in Social Change, Emory University, 1977);

William H. Chafe, Raymond Gavins, Robert Korstad et al., eds., *Remembering Jim Crow: African Americans Tell About Life in the Segregated South* (New York: The New Press, 2001); Michael Keith Honey, *Black Workers Remember: An Oral History of Segregation, Unionism, and the Freedom Struggle* (Berkeley: University of California Press, 1999); Kim Lacy Rogers, *Life and Death in the Delta: African American Narratives of Violence, Resilience, and Social Change* (New York: Palgrave Macmillan, 2006); Anne Valk and Leslie Brown, *Living with Jim Crow: African American Women and Memories of the Segregated South* (New York: Palgrave Macmillan, 2010).

3. "Behind the Veil: Documenting African American Life in the Jim Crow South" Collection, Franklin Research Center for African and African American History and Culture, Rubenstein Rare Book and Manuscript Library, Duke University, Durham, NC (hereafter, BTV). Sponsored by the Center for Documentary Studies, project graduate assistants worked at twenty-three community sites in eleven southern states (summers, 1993–95). They interviewed 1,248 individuals (born 1894–1947) and collected thousands of their papers, pictures, and objects. Most interviews are on tape, some with transcripts; all NC interviews and one hundred others are on-line.

4. W. E. B. Du Bois, ed., *The Negro Church: Report of a Social Study made under the direction of Atlanta University; together with the Proceedings of the Eighth Conference for the Study of the Negro Problems* (Atlanta, GA: Atlanta University Press, 1903), ii; Henry Louis Gates, Jr., and Terri Hume Oliver, eds., *The Souls of Black Folk: Authoritative Text, Contexts, Criticism/W.E.B. Du Bois* (New York: W. W. Norton, 1999), 50.

5. Gates and Oliver, eds., *The Souls of Black Folk*, 5.

6. African Methodist Episcopal Church, 1816; African Methodist Episcopal Zion Church, 1822; Christian Methodist Episcopal Church, 1870; National Baptist Convention, U.S.A., Inc., 1895; National Baptist Convention of America, 1915; Progressive National Baptist Convention, 1961; and Church of God in Christ, Holiness, 1897, are the historically black denominations. See C. Eric Lincoln and Lawrence H. Mamiya, *The Black Church in the African American Experience* (Durham: Duke University Press, 1990), 1, 18.

7. Cf. Yvonne V. Jones, "Kinship Affiliation through Time: Black Homecomings and Family Reunions in a North Carolina County, *Ethnohistory*, 27 (Winter 1980): 49–66; and William H. Wiggins, *O Freedom! Afro-American Emancipation Celebrations* (Knoxville: University of Tennessee Press, 1987), 79–80.

8. In order, quotes are in John M. Giggie, *After Redemption: Jim Crow and the Transformation of African American Religion in the Delta, 1875–1915* (New York: Oxford University Press, 2008), 60; Albert J. Raboteau, *Slave Religion: The "Invisible Institution in the American South* (New York: Oxford University Press, 1978), ix; W. E. B. Du Bois, *Black Reconstruction in America 1860–1880* (1935; New York: Atheneum, 1970), 638; and Gates and Oliver, eds., *The Souls of Black Folk*, 5.

9. First three quotes from Raymond Gavins, "The Meaning of Freedom: Black North Carolina in the Nadir, 1880–1900," in Jeffrey J. Crow et al., eds., *Race, Class, and Politics in Southern History: Essays in Honor of Robert F. Durden* (Baton Rouge: Louisiana State University Press, 1989), 204; the fourth from Frenise A. Logan, *The Negro in North Carolina 1876–1894* (Chapel Hill: University of North Carolina Press, 1964), 149.

10. In order, quotes from Ray Gavins, "Recasting the Black Freedom Struggle in Wilmington,

1898–1930," *Carolina Comments*, 48 (November 2000): 144; Walter B. Weare, *Black Business in the New South: A Social History of the North Carolina Mutual Life Insurance Company* (Urbana: University of Illinois Press, 1973), 26, 31; and Gavins, "The Meaning of Freedom," 207.

11 Gavins, "The Meaning of Freedom," 175, 212; Raymond Gavins, "Behind a Veil: Black North Carolinians in the Age of Jim Crow," in Paul D. Escott, ed., *W. J. Cash and the Minds of the South* (Baton Rouge: Louisiana State University Press, 1992), 26, 30.

12 Gavins, "Behind a Veil," 26.

13 William R. Reaves, *"Strength Through Struggle:" The Chronological and Historical Record of the African-American Community in Wilmington, North Carolina 1865–1950*, ed. Beverly Tetterton (Wilmington: New Hanover County Public Library, 1988), 6, 15, 17, 200–202; Gavins, "Recasting the Black Freedom Struggle," 146–147.

14 W. Fitzhugh Brundage, *Lynching in the New South: Georgia and Virginia, 1880–1930* (Urbana: University of Illinois Press, 1993), 262–264, 281–283; Charles S. Johnson, *A Statistical Atlas of Southern Counties: Listing and Analysis of Socio-Economic Indices of 1104 Southern Counties* (Chapel Hill: University of North Carolina Press, 1941), 254.

15 Celestyne Porter interview, BTV.

16 Porter interview; Jacqueline Goggin, *Carter G. Woodson: A Life in Black History* (Baton Rouge: Louisiana State University Press, 1993), 113–118.

17 Porter interview; Wiggins, *O Freedom!*, 86.

18 Porter interview.

19 Ann Pointer interview, BTV.

20 Pointer interview.

21 Booker Federick interview, BTV.

22 Federick interview.

23 Lincoln and Mamiya, *The Black Church*, xi.

24 Tolbert Chism, Katherine Hinton, Anthony Farmer interviews, BTV.

25 Mary Dulin, William Zepherin, William Malone, Daisy Livingston, Manuel and Myrtle Crockett interviews, BTV.

26 Willie Harrell, Wilhelmina Baldwin, Ernestine Clemmons interviews, BTV.

27 Josephine McCray, Ida Belle interviews.

28 Du Bois, ed., *The Negro Church*, 72; Gates and Oliver, eds., *The Souls of Black Folk*, 50; Cleaster Mitchell, interview, BTV.

29 Du Bois, ed., *The Negro Church*, 72–73; David Matthews interview, BTV.

30 Matthews, Leamon Dillahunt interviews, BTV.

31 Emily Herring Wilson, *Hope and Dignity: Older Black Women of the South* (Philadelphia: Temple University Press, 1983), 87–92; York Garrett, Jr., interview, BTV.

32 George P. Rawick, ed., *The American Slave: A Composite Autobiography*, 19 volumes, series 1 (Westport, CT: Greenwood Publishing Co.), vol. 14: *North Carolina Narratives*, Part 1: 449–452 (Isabell Henderson); William Childs interview, BTV.

33 Childs, McCray interviews.

34 Baldwin, Mildred Page interviews, BTV.

35 Du Bois, ed., *The Negro Church*, 171; Dillahunt, Dorcas E. Carter interviews, BTV.
36 Dillahunt, Baldwin, Mitchell, Crockett, Elizabeth Pitts, James Lewis interviews, BTV.
37 Benjamin E. Mays and Joseph W. Nicholson, *The Negro's Church* (New York: Institute of Social and Religious Research, 1933), 157.
38 Lillie Fenner, Walter Cavers interviews, BTV.
39 Doris Dennis interview, BTV.
40 Theresa Lyons, Pitts, Farmer, Mitchell interviews.
41 Charles S. Johnson, *Patterns of Negro Segregation* (New York: Harper & Brothers, 1943), 234.
42 Dulin, Aurie Flowers interviews, BTV.
43 William Davis, Annette Clayborn, Harrell interviews, BTV.
44 Theresa Lyons, Pitts, Farmer, Mitchell interviews.
45 Lyons, Kathleen Daise interviews, BTV.
46 Chism and Ruth Davis interviews, BTV.
47 Gates and Oliver, eds., *The Souls of Black Folk*, 11; Acts 17: 26.
48 Susie Weathersbee, Page, Cleaster interviews, BTV.
49 Du Bois, ed., *The Negro Church*, 197; Evelyn Brooks Higginbotham, *Righteous Discontent: The Women's Movement in the Black Baptist Church, 1880–1920* (Cambridge: Harvard University Press, 1993), 187.

2

From the Old to the New

Speculations on a Southern Place, 1850–1890

RANDOLPH D. WERNER

When I first read The New South Creed *many years ago I was struck by one sentence in particular. On page 42, Paul wrote that by 1886 the New South was on "the verge of achieving the hegemony once enjoyed by the creed of the Old South."*[1] *While perhaps parsing Paul's verb choice too finely, it struck me that if this ideology was so ubiquitous, it must have also influenced, to some degree, even the "agrarian" rebels of the 1890s who clearly had little sympathy for the "boosterism" of New South partisans.*

While the idea of a New South had an agricultural component, historians generally have interpreted the southern political conflicts of the 1890s as a clash of world views, with the farming masses rejecting the predominantly commercial and industrial orientation of New South Democrats in favor of a more traditional "producer" culture. Certainly, the South became a poorer, more rural, less developed place than the nation as a whole; but that outcome was unknown to those of the generation that came to maturity during the 1870s and 1880s.

The essay that follows is a speculative rumination on the idea of ideological hegemony raised in The New South Creed. *It attempts to describe how many of the intellectual tenets later associated with the creed, earlier had become commonplace truisms accepted by all southerners regardless of residency or occupation. The commercial expansion and rise of small retail centers that marked life across the countryside during the 1870s and 1880s, it suggests, provided the infrastructure that not only brought many of these tenets to the "verge" of intellectual hegemony, but rendered them "facts" of life for the generation that led the agrarian insurgencies of the 1890s. If so, it may be that* The New South Creed *underestimated the pernicious influence of this ideology.*

～

The American South in 1860 was a culture defined by slavery and cotton, one that generated untold wealth for many southerners of European descent.[2] But the Civil War of 1861–1865 obliterated this world. In the aftermath new realities overturned many of the social verities that had organized southern life for generations. Raised as the masters of worlds large and small, European-heritage southerners now answered to a conquering army and, soon, to representatives of their former chattel. It seemed, one survivor lamented, that the entire world had "turned topsy turvey."[3] Nor was she far wrong. Could any "white" southerner in 1861 have imagined "black" people as American citizens, soldiers, judges, and legislators? Surely not; the very idea was absurd, or worse. Yet four years later, it was a reality.

All southerners struggled across the post-war generation to make sense of this and other new realities. Some proved intolerable. European-heritage southerners, for example, refused to surrender their mastery over the newly freed. In this they were successful, through terrorism, legal manipulations, and federal indifference.[4] But a more intransigent reality persisted: the destruction of a slave-based cotton economy. Southern nationalists had staked their cause upon the belief that the entire world would bow before the economic might of "King Cotton." In this they were wrong.

From the first days of the new post-war era, many ex-Confederates lamented their pre-war enthusiasm for cotton production. Once "we produced nothing but cotton and with that great staple we fancied, in our foolish self-sufficiency, that we had a mighty monarch," bemoaned one wartime survivor.[5] In hindsight, others concluded that the erstwhile king was actually a "demon" that fed an overweening arrogance among its retainers; or as another put it, the pre-war enthusiasm for cotton was nothing but a "species of idolatry" that "led us into the pit of ruin."[6] We must "LET COTTON ALONE" insisted the *Augusta Daily Constitutionalist* in 1866.[7]

"The simplest dictate of common sense must teach us," opined "Georgian," that cotton culture and large plantations were not viable in the new era of free labor.[8] Emancipation had caused a "revolution of our ancient system of labor" that necessitated "great agricultural changes."[9] The ex-chattel were "disinclined" to work, remarked another writer from Augusta, Georgia; if you plant cotton, "the mules and the Federal government and the niggers will eat all the meat and give you the polished bone."[10] But if not cotton, what was to be the basis for an economic recovery?

Alternative strategies to restore southern prosperity abounded early in the new era. In the main, these de-emphasized the role of commodity agriculture in favor of industrial and commercial growth; an approach variously termed a "new departure" or a "new South." The enthusiasm for this "new" economy was concentrated in a "relatively small group of merchants and planters," many of them located in southern towns and cities.[11] These men envisioned a future profoundly different from that of the past, one in which industrial and commercial development would replace commodity crop agriculture as the keystone of economic prosperity. Agriculture remained important, but in a subsidiary role as the food provider to an ever more urban, industrial workforce.

While this approach ultimately enriched a few, it did little to enhance the well-being of the rural masses, even after the return of "home rule" under the leadership of Redeemer Democratic leaders during the 1870s. Impoverished and ignored, the southern masses finally erupted during the 1890s in a series of agrarian political insurgencies against ruling Democratic parties across the South. But through fraud, violence, and intimidation, these insurgencies were crushed. In the aftermath, New South strategies devolved from programs of action into an ideological creed that buttressed the financial reign of a fortunate few over the impoverished rural masses, regardless of race, for generations.[12]

Most histories of the post-war era are premised upon an underlying assumption that the ideas inherent in the "New South" ideal were dramatic, or even radical, departures from southern cultural traditions.[13] In the main, these new ideals were rejected by the rural masses among whom a more traditional "agrarian" or "producer" ethos prevailed, one defined by older "republican" mores that privileged communal bonds of kinship, barter, and reciprocity over commercialism and industrial development.[14] We know from the recent work of Edward Baptist and others, however, that capitalist impulses were not alien to antebellum southern plantation culture, nor were rampant commerce or capital accumulation.[15] In some parts of the pre-war South central features later associated with the idea of a new South were well established prior to the Civil War defeat. Indeed, in some places, manufacturing and industrial development were viewed as critical, albeit supplementary, components of an independent southern economy. The up-country town of Augusta, Georgia, was one such place.

Augusta began as an eighteenth-century fur trading station, becoming by the 1850s the commercial center for an extensive hinterland that stretched across the rich cotton growing "black belt" lands of Georgia and South Carolina.[16] Located at the fall line on the Savannah River dividing Georgia from South Carolina, the town was a major inland river port and a terminus for three of the South's most important railroads, the Georgia, the South Carolina, and the Central; and, owing to its telegraphic connections, the southern headquarters of the nation's dominant overland express company, the New York-based Adams Express Company.[17] Augusta was a thriving commercial entrepôt by the late 1850s, deserving, as one South Carolinian remarked, "an overflowing patronage from the two States."[18] But the town was more than a commercial hub; it was also an embryonic manufacturing center.

Construction of a power generating canal through Augusta during the late 1840s was directly responsible for a five-fold increase of the capital invested in manufacturing between 1840 and 1850 coupled with a comparable increase in the number of factory workers, mostly immigrants.[19] New factories, large and small, emerged throughout the 1850s, each having a local "multiplier effect" that created additional job opportunities.[20] Flour, for example, was an imported staple in 1850. But a decade later, local mills were exporting multiple grades of flour and other milled products to Europe and the North.[21] Textile mills were the largest employers, however, with the Augusta Manufacturing Company employing over three hundred. Other significant manufacturers included the Augusta Paper Manufacturing Company, the Eagle Foundry, the Bellville Factory, the Augusta Iron and Brass Foundry, the Iron and Steamboat Company, machinery manufacturers, and numerous smaller enterprises.[22] In addition, twenty-five miles to the east, along the Horse Creek, resided one of the best known manufacturing enterprises in the cotton South, the Graniteville Mill Company, and a companion mill downstream at Vaucluse.[23]

While industrial production and employment expanded steadily across the 1850s, cotton remained the keystone of local prosperity. But as southern political leaders moved ever more aggressively to defend sectional "rights" from northern intrusions, some Augustans worried that a cotton-based economy, while an engine of sectional economic prosperity, might be inadequate as the foundation of an independent southern nation.[24] How, for instance, was a plantation economy to contend with the industrial might of New England, should the need arise? For some, the answer was obvious.

We must "develop all the resources of our section, and give those who engage in them a liberal patronage" if we are to be free from northern interference, the *Augusta Daily Constitutionalist* opined in 1859. "We will then be better able to talk of independence and rights of the South, than we are at this time."[25] The continual presence of northern trade representatives in Augusta, noted another townsman, while it inspired "a pleasing consciousness of the power of our resources," also reflected the "unpleasant feature" that southerners sent their cotton "fifteen hundred miles to be worked up, when we might manufacture it at home, and divide these benefits among ourselves."[26] Leading Augustans readily echoed a complaint from Macon that

> we send our cotton to Manchester and Lowell, our sugar to New York refineries, our hides to down-east tanneries and our children to Yankee colleges, and we are ever ready to find fault with the North because it lives by our folly. We want home manufactures and these we must have, it we are ever to be independent.[27]

"Anything which looks to the advancement of our manufacturing interests we go in for most heartily," the *Augusta Chronicle* declared in 1860.[28] "We have the water power, the raw material of every kind on hand, and a climate far more genial than the North."[29] But natural resources and manufacturing alone could not guarantee economic independence. Agricultural reform was vital if the South were to be independent of northern manipulations.

From the correspondent in the *Constitutionalist* who believed an economically independent South must be self-sufficient in foodstuffs, to an oft-repeated dictum that the most prosperous families raised their own corn and meat, the rhetoric of self-sufficiency was a constant theme of public discussion during the 1850s.[30] "All our food must be produced at home, both for man and beast," if the South was to be truly independent, went the refrain.[31] Sorghum, grains, Irish potatoes and "southern peas" were but a few of the crops proposed as alternatives to cotton.[32] True independence demanded that southerners "plant less cotton and endeavor to produce more of the real substantials of life."[33] The "undue absorption" of our "productive wealth" by "the culture of cotton," noted one writer early in the decade, was shortsighted.[34]

Farming should be "emphatically an experimental art and science;" plantation innovation and industrial development the dual *sine qua non* of an independent plantation regime.[35] Nearby planters and townsman alike embraced the catechism of diversification and industrial development.[36] Farm diversification combined with foundries, manufacturers, machine works, and other industrial establishments were the vital "elements of prosperity which need but patronage" to guarantee the success of our new nation, noted the *Daily Constitutionalist* soon after secession.[37] But as U. S. Senator James Hammond had once noted, in order for planters to de-emphasize cotton production, "there must be a *pinch* of some sort, & with cotton at 10c & negroes at $1000 the South will know no *pinch*."[38] In the moment, there was no "pinch."

Military defeat and the obliteration of the slave-based plantation economy provided the penultimate "pinch." But initially it pressed less heavily upon Augusta than upon other places.[39] While black belt Georgia and South Carolina were ravaged and burned, the town and nearby countryside escaped untouched by the conflagrations common elsewhere.[40] While the town was occupied by Federal troops after the Confederate surrender, it was never attacked and re-entered the Union with the local power structure intact, the manufacturing infrastructure undamaged, and warehouses bursting with stored cotton.⁴¹ As other places struggled to rebuild, Augustans looked to the future, hoping to enhance their manufacturing infrastructure and railroad connections.

Manufacturing and the exploitation of the section's abundant natural resources, not commodity agriculture, were expected to be the main drivers of future prosperity. The pre-war urgency to diversify agriculture redoubled as southerners confronted the reality of northern reconstruction demands. Remember, "Isundiga" told *Constitutionalist* readers, radical New Englanders hated the South and intended to use their military victory to "keep us forever hewers of wood and drawers of water for her."⁴² These people took "a devilish pride in backing the menial against his master," all for "the aggrandizement of their section."⁴³ In New England, one Augustan raged

> Negro suffrage is manifestly wrong and improper, but in the South it is eminently just and absolutely necessary. Is not the animus plain? Hatred of the South; jealousy of its growth and prosperity, combined with a determination to hold the reigns [sic] of power in their own hands. It is not that they really love Cuffee and Sambo.... Thirst for power and place, hatred of the South, are the controlling motives of Negro agitation.

All efforts to empower the ex-chattel were "sectional, vindictive, fanatical," he continued. "Philanthropy for the Negro was the pretense. Vengeance upon the white [was] the motive."⁴⁴

While our "political vassalage is bad enough," remarked another townsman, "it is the worst kind of bondage to depend upon others for bread."⁴⁵ Every "true patriot, who loves his State and desires its welfare" should strive to develop and "increase consumption" of home enterprises.⁴⁶ Had earlier generations "lived within themselves, diversified their crops or resisted the temptation of the cotton fever," southerners would not be at the mercy of radical New Englanders.⁴⁷ "Real independence," required men to abandon "the delusion of maintaining mammoth plantations."⁴⁸ These were but symbols of a "false pride," an ancient ideal "irretrievably broken" by the faithlessness of free labor.⁴⁹

"Real independence" it now seemed, came not from political insurrection but from creating a South that was "financially, commercially, and otherwise, independent of the North."⁵⁰ A strategic re-orientation of agriculture from extensive plantations to smaller farms utilizing the most modern "scientific" or "intensive" agricultural methods was critical to this independence. Agricultural diversification was no longer a supplement to the empire of cotton; it was instead an economic imperative, a strategy unblemished by wartime defeat that seemed to "fit" with post-war realities. If implemented successfully, farm innovation and reform along with expanded manufacturing would restore sectional economic parity, empower political leaders to limit the "devilish" intrusions of New England Yankees, and, perhaps, even redress the humiliations of military defeat and federal occupation.

Emancipation had forever altered the economics of cotton production. If only the "polished bone" remained for growers, was it logical for farmers to rely upon the "demon" staple? Yet, most farmers refused to "let cotton alone." Most had no choice. The sharecropping and tenancy systems soon prevalent across the region forced renters and croppers to plant cotton. But even as a robust demand for the staple both domestically and internationally during much of the post-war decade supported prices above historic averages, the traditional dynamics of the cotton trade were soon upended.⁵¹

Initially, the frenzy of railroad construction that marked the new era seemed likely to enhance Augusta's position as a dominant regional cotton market.⁵² Moreover, the rapidly expanding rail network was accompanied by a series of enabling innovations followed these new rail lines—expanding telegraph systems, new shipping techniques, and mechanical enhancements. But railroad expansion and the attendant innovations soon negated the advantages once enjoyed by antebellum river and ocean port mercantilists. Instead, they provided men at interior railroad depots with access to timely commercial information and the ability to ship cotton directly to distant markets without interruptions.⁵³ Within a decade of the Confederate surrender, an expanding coterie of interior men had replaced antebellum Augusta mercantilists as the primary marketers of inland cotton.⁵⁴

The transfer of cotton marketing to the interior sparked the emergence of numerous small interior railroad settlements where newly empowered men not only purchased cotton, but also assembled, distributed, or supplied goods and services to the surrounding farm population.⁵⁵ These places, previously unnoticed or barely existent backcountry settlements, became the fulcrum of communal social interactions during the later 1870s. Credit arrangements, roads, education, court systems, public gatherings, tax collections, recreation, shops, stores, and political power all gravitated toward centralized local settings and increased the necessity for people to visit these places regularly.

This trend catalyzed and energized new behaviors, notably embryonic patterns of consumption for goods and services in these places. Backcountry farmers, only a few at first, but in greater numbers over time, purchased an expanding variety of products and services during regular and frequent visits to retail places where they collected mail, bartered, transacted business, and sought recreation. Across the post-war generation, these places evolved into a rough hierarchy of hamlets, villages and towns linked to Augusta, the hub of regional commerce.⁵⁶

Thomson, Georgia, for example, located some thirty five miles west of Augusta and a station on the Georgia Railroad, barely existed before the war. It was "in the woods," one visitor remarked. "There were two stores but a yoke of oxen could have pulled all the goods for sale in them in one load."⁵⁷ During the 1870s, however, Thomson became the seat of a new county, home to a new brick courthouse, two high schools, and boasted a population approaching 1,000 residents. It was a substantial cotton market with a newly built warehouse and, soon, the site of a brick "business row" that housed dry goods dealers, druggists, lawyers, and other retailers.⁵⁸ Aiken, South Carolina, located on the slightly cooler, drier Sand Hills plateau twenty five miles east of Augusta, was also a new county seat and a nationally known resort town by 1880.⁵⁹ Owing in part to the winter influx of affluent northern visitors, Aiken was the largest retail center in the backcountry, reportedly home to forty-four stores.⁶⁰ Farther north, Johnston became "unquestionably the chief commercial town in Edgefield County" with thirty-three retailers in 1880.⁶¹

The transfer of cotton marketing to men at railroad depots like Thomson or Johnston increased the cash and credit available to backcountry residents. While the expansion of supply was modest, it nonetheless generated and sustained emerging retail behaviors. Many items that antebellum families had produced themselves or did without—leather goods, tailored clothing, household implements, or commercial medicines—now were acquired with cash or credit. Across the post-war generation, retail consumption became an ever more ordinary activity and a critical variable in the economic growth of backcountry towns.[62] Diverse retail offerings increased customer traffic to a town, which, in turn, supported increasingly specialized retailers.[63] Consequently, improvements and expansions to the transportation infrastructure, primarily rail lines and wagon roads, were vital for the growth of retail trade.

The more numerous and better maintained the roads, the more frequent and regular were visits to town.[64] As roads improved during the post-war years, specialized retail offerings previously found only in Augusta became available at backcountry rail towns.[65] Larger interior towns were "gradually drawing to themselves the commercial traffic of their respective counties," reported "Phacks" in 1881, with Augusta serving primarily as a "wholesale mart" where "only a few wealthy planters" traded.[66] A generation after the war, Augusta mercantilists were primarily wholesale distributors and suppliers to increasingly specialized backcountry retailers. This was a fundamentally new pattern of economic integration that created continuous interactions among people within the region and, increasingly, with those in more distant places.[67]

The regular and frequent interactions at backcountry places like Thomson or Johnston fundamentally altered the rhythms of life across the countryside during the post-Reconstruction years. While many "white" adults lamented the "chaotic perplexity" of this new era, for their children the new era was merely ordinary.[68] For the younger generation, the interactions of daily life occurred ever more frequently in small town squares and courthouse steps, not on semi-autonomous plantations or farms. In these town squares, amidst the humdrum of regular visits, whether daily, weekly, or bi-weekly, young people encountered a multitude of ideas, perceptions, understandings, beliefs, claims, conclusions, judgements, assumptions and attitudes, some new, some familiar.

Those tenets that "fit" or resonated with personal experiences or communal norms tended to be internalized as "common sense" truisms, "facts" so obvious as to require neither consideration nor comment, everyone just knew them. This was, in the main, an emotive, not an intellectual process. The integration of new ideas into broadly accepted intuitive understandings occurred across the years in the course of a multitude of interactions and conversations, often punctuated by the tilt of a head, a skeptical glance, the shrug of a shoulder, or an affirming nod. The effects of this cultural process were cumulative. Twenty years on, it led the poet Hamilton Hayne to lament from his home near Augusta that "we of the '*Old South*,' have need, God knows, to stand by each other *staunchly*. The *new Generation* hardly comprehends us."[69]

Who were the men and women of this "*new Generation*?" They were born between 1850 and 1870 into a world unlike that of their parents.[70] Those of European descent likely recalled slavery and the war only as childhood memories and most were too young to participate actively in the post-war white racial terrorist campaigns. Still, they surely imbued the cultural loyalties and proto-nationalistic sentiments deeply resonant among their parents. They likely carried these childhood sentiments into their adulthood and despised the triumphant "Yankees;" for, as one Augusta mother remarked, it was "part of the religion I have taught our children, to dislike the Yankees."[71]

But even as they internalized such devotions, the new generation grew up amidst the world of backcountry towns. What was new, confusing, or innovative to their elders likely seemed merely ordinary to them. Telegraphs, telephones, bicycles, electricity, and refrigeration were familiar features of their adolescence, if not yet commonplace.[72] Moreover, the intellectual innovations forced upon white southerners by wartime defeat—free labor, universal male suffrage, the expansion of Federal powers—were lifelong realities for the new generation, even if they learned to be contemptuous of such realities. But in the new era, it was an older medium that perhaps most directly shaped conversations in newly energized backcountry town centers and by extension the perspectives of a new generation.

Newspapers were an important supplement to the regular and frequent interactions of the retail marketplace; in traditional societies, a harbinger of modernization.[73] While Augusta had a rich newspaper history, virtually no newspapers were published in the backcountry prior to the Civil War.[74]

Antebellum advertising revenues were virtually non-existent; subscribers were few and scattered, delivery was slow and burdensome. After the war, however, newspapers became ubiquitous across the backcountry. Aiken, Edgefield, Johnston, Harlem, and Thomson all had at least one weekly by the early-1870s, with others to follow.[75]

The emergence and survival of town newspapers was an indicator of retail specialization and a catalyst for disseminating understandings about life in the new era. If a settlement had only a few general dry goods merchants, frequent advertising was unnecessary. Specialized retailers, however, advertised constantly to generate awareness and demand, providing a critical mass of consistent newspaper revenue. Not surprisingly, local editors were enthusiastic advocates of nearly any scheme, no matter how far-fetched, that promised to expand commercial opportunities and generate economic growth.

But these ebullient boosters were also trusted interpreters of the world. Regional editors functioned, in effect, as an "intelligentsia" influencing how people comprehended their world.[76] Historian Francis Butler Simkins, reminiscing about his childhood in early twentieth century Edgefield, recalled that an editor wielded "a mighty influence among his townsmen." He was simultaneously "a social arbiter, a political guide, an agricultural and household adviser and the village's single source of news of the world at large."[77] Another Edgefield historian described local editors as "backwoods intellectuals who wielded mighty influence among town and country subscribers."[78] These men framed and explained new mores, interpreted events, and ascribed logic to happenings in the larger world. They visited each other, editorialized about their brethren, and reprinted items from nearby papers. Editors of the larger Augusta dailies were not aloof from this process; they reported consistently about local activities on both sides of the river, visited backcountry editors, had same day delivery to nearby railroad towns, and published weekly "country" editions.[79]

Local news and opinions gathered from weekly newspapers undoubtedly influenced and leavened the conversations that occurred as farmers and others gathered in town squares or courthouse steps. Backcountry editors shared with their Augusta brethren the belief that a new "era of prosperity" would only commence when farmers "let exclusive cotton planting alone and turn[ed] their attention to small crops."[80] The editor of the *Thomson Advertiser* spoke for many when he concluded in 1870 that "experience has demonstrated the folly of cultivating cotton to the exclusion of corn." True, he continued, "once in ten years more money will be realized by that course, [but] in the other nine years all the profits of the cotton crop will be consumed in the purchase of plantation supplies."[81]

The South would never be truly independent so long as men relied upon cotton, insisted John White of the *McDuffie Weekly Journal*. Farmers must "'throw cotton to the dogs'. . . and raise sufficient provisions to supply the country, then will we becom[e] independent in spite of all the dark powers of Radicalism that can be arrayed against us." A "true and permanent independence for the South" was impossible so long as farmers grew "all-cotton."[82] White, like his editorial brethren, insisted that only a diversified farm economy responsive to market conditions and demands would restore southern prosperity, "impoverish New England," and "bankrupt the entire North."[83] "Young men" must adapt to the "new order of things," others believed, and consider their land as "Capital," and "produce from its employment the greatest amount of profit."[84]

The connection between "cotton fever" and political "vassalage" was a truism, a common sense "fact" in the new generation. "Extensive" cotton plantations were anathema, too speculative, an Aiken editor concluded, employed too much labor, and led to extravagant debt.[85] Smaller farms, utilizing the most modern "scientific" or "intensive" agricultural methods were central to the redemption of southern honor and pre-eminence in the restored Union. "Intensive" farming enabled owners to more easily alter planting decisions based upon market demands, apply new farming techniques, and adopt other innovations to generate the greatest possible yield and profit per acre. The proper use of fertilizers, crop diversification, efficiency, improved labor systems, better livestock and poultry care, an understanding of soil chemistry, market analysis, and creation of agricultural organizations were all aspects of a new professionalism necessary for farm prosperity. John E. White of the *McDuffie Weekly Journal* was typical in urging efficiency and the utilization of modern business methods.[86] "What a farmer most needs, is a thorough knowledge of his profession, and in no pursuit is knowledge more indispensable."[87]

But the farming masses lacked the resources for "intensive" farming. Most were welded to the crop by the sharecropping and lien finance systems, regardless of race.[89] In the early years of the new era, the consequences of this dependency were muted. Cotton prices remained high, in most years trading above the costs of production. In Thomson, for example, cotton merchants paid 17 cents per pound for middling cotton during 1872, a price that held through the 1873 harvest season.[90] At these prices, cotton farming, even within the confines of an evolving lien system, perhaps was a rational decision.[91] There was little urgency to abandon the crop.

But as prices trended downward after the nationwide financial panic and depression of 1873, the more successful landowners began to de-emphasize cotton in favor of foodstuffs and grains. This was the beginning of a bifurcation that soon defined local agriculture in the new era. Initially, a small number of established landowners, many of them Confederate veterans, operating smaller farms, often little more than a hundred acres, began utilizing commercial fertilizers and experimenting with the alternative crops applauded by the regional intelligentsia. These innovative farmers continued to grow cotton as a supplementary crop while increasingly re-deploying their cotton profits into plantings of corn, oats, fruit, and other foodstuffs marketed at expanding retail center.

John E. Smith, for example, was a well-known pre-war landowner near Thomson who began growing cotton in 1867. Soon after, he was termed one of the area's "most successful planters," by the *McDuffie Weekly Journal*, a "scientific" farmer who harvested an exceptional yield of nineteen bales from nineteen acres in 1872.[92] When cotton prices declined after 1873, Smith reduced his cotton acreage and planted oats, which he found easier to grow and more successful than corn. He planted thirty-five acres of "thin land" in oats during 1874, harvested thirty bushels per acre for a total crop worth $1,050, leaving him a profit of $785 on his oats. Smith urged other farmers to augment their income in a similar fashion for "then the proceeds of his cotton crop will be his own and not go to the western corn producers."[93]

Other like-minded older men managed similarly successful "intensive" farms near Thomson. A. E. Sturgis, a vocal exponent of scientific farming, harvested eleven bales from ten acres in 1872, along with the exceptional yield of 560 bushels of corn from thirty acres.[94] William S. Smith harvested even better oat crops than his brother John on a renovated plantation where soil erosion was repaired.[95] Two years later, he concluded that grains were more profitable than cotton even at 15 cents per pound.[96] John H. Scott likewise produced excellent grain crops averaging twenty-two bushels per acre in 1879 while another farmer near Thomson produced over forty bushels of corn per acre a year earlier through the judicious use of fertilizer and other "intensive" techniques.[97] Similar examples abounded. Thomas A. Hamilton and A. R. Stother had exceptional grain harvests in 1876, John Langford produced a profitable "brag" oat crop in 1877, John Lambert was lauded for his oat and wheat harvests in 1879, while closer to Augusta, Thomas Cumming and William Printup harvested excellent wheat crops in 1878.[98] Carolinians, too, moved toward alternative crops, primarily among farm owners on the better lands north of the South Carolina Railroad, near the towns of Aiken, Trenton, and Johnston.[99]

Prosperous diversified farmers were of course exceptions, but they were also, in modern parlance, local "movers and shakers." They stood as men to be emulated, respected in their communities, and examples of what might be achieved if one embraced scientific practices and diversified his crops. For them, scientific practices and crop diversification became almost a patriotic mantra by the late 1870s. Farm reform stood almost as a test of communal loyalty, a means of reversing the humiliations of military defeat. Those of the new generation likely looked to emulate the successes of men like William Smith or A. E. Sturgis. Importantly, many also experienced and perhaps benefited from an exceptional confluence of events in 1882 that seemingly demonstrated the financial benefits of crop diversification.

The 1881 cotton harvest was a disaster for growers across the Augusta backcountry. The summer was marked by an intense drought that devastated local cotton crops. The harvest not only fell by 25 percent but drought also damaged the quality of the crop causing market prices to plummet.[100] Tenant farmers suffered disproportionately with large numbers reportedly surrendering leased lands and resuming work as day laborers.[101] Retail merchants were affected as well. Farm families had little cash, and with credit difficult to obtain, many were forced to "economize."[102] Amidst widespread anxiety and despair, local editors redoubled their long standing call for farm diversification.

It was now self-evident, declared the *Augusta Chronicle* that

> the day that the South learns to live largely within herself and invest her savings in substantial and not speculative property [i.e. cotton], she will be the richest country in the world. . . . Plenty of money worse than wasted . . . could have been used for southern independence in a commercial way. . . . Let our people put their money in home development and not fling it away on Northern sharpers. . . . We need good milk and butter. People clamor for and are willing to pay for them . . . is it not better for the South to supply herself than to send the profits abroad.[103]

Whether from necessity or by choice, many farmers reduced their cotton acreage, planting foodstuffs, corn, wheat, and oats instead.

Across the nearby countryside cotton acreage declined during the 1882 planting season, by some 9,000 acres in Aiken and Edgefield counties while wheat and oat plantings increased by 27,000 acres.[104] Similarly, a "small grain mania" reportedly swept McDuffie during the spring planting season. A. E. Sturgis reported optimistically in April that "the prospect for a fine oat crop is wonderful."[105] In many years such early season prospects were overturned by the weather. But this year the corn and grain plantings benefitted from a near perfect combination of rain and sun along with the extensive use of commercial fertilizers.

While the autumn cotton harvest was large, the quality was uneven, and market prices failed to rebound.[106] In contrast, the harvest of grains and foodstuffs in 1882 was unprecedented. The oat crop reportedly was the best ever; farmers had "corn to sell and keep," all food crops were "bountiful."[107] Across the region, farmers reportedly ended the year in better financial condition than at any time since the war. They reportedly borrowed less money in advance of the 1883 planting season. The volume of goods purchased on credit in Aiken County between 1881 and 1883, for example, declined by

17 percent. Statewide in South Carolina, farm advances in 1883 declined by nearly $3.0 million.[108] No longer, it seemed, were the benefits of crop diversification an abstraction. Indeed, there was now a broad-based demonstrable "fit" between experience and common sense assumptions about the proper path to prosperity.

Local farmers finally recognized, remarked one Augustan, that smaller, more diversified farms managed on business principles "pay better than large ones."[109] Tellingly, fruit crops, vegetables, oats, and wheat plantings reportedly were more popular than ever in the spring of for 1883.[110] Moreover, these years coincided with the beginning of what one scholar later termed Augusta's "golden age."[111] A plethora of new enterprises located along the Augusta canal during these years, from boiler repair shops to chemical companies. Three massive new textile mills opened between 1881 and 1883, spurring an influx of poor sharecroppers and tenants from the countryside seeking new opportunities.[112] Regional growers seemed poised to reap the benefits of a rapidly expanding urban market for grains and foodstuffs. The path to future farm prosperity seemed clear.

Intent upon ending their vassalage to "Northern sharpers" regional farm leaders joined together in new agricultural clubs. Thirty-five local farmers established the Richmond County Agricultural Club in 1883, hoping to increase professionalism by sharing information about agricultural innovations and efficient management practices. As with other regional clubs, members were exclusively white landowners, merchants, and professionals operating diversified farms managed for profitability. Member C. H. Phinizy, for example, ran a prosperous "model farm" noted for large oat and wheat crops, in addition to being President of the Georgia Railroad.[113] Nor were his fellow members any less prominent. Thomas P. Branch was an Augusta cotton merchant and financier, scion of a prominent Virginia mercantile family. James L. Gow and Patrick Walsh, editors of Augusta's two leading daily papers were active members, as were Mayor Robert May, County Sheriff Wilberforce Daniel, and City Court Judge W. Frederick Eve, longtime owner of a "fine farm" in Richmond County.[114]

Similarly, the Edgefield Agricultural Society was organized by mid-1884 to promote agriculture along with "the business interests and resources . . .

that are connected with and kindred to agriculture."[115] Organizers bemoaned the "anomaly" of men "claiming to be sensible, ruining their farms and impoverishing themselves to raise cotton, while buying their supplies." It was time, they insisted, for "a new departure. Let us go raising something else as a surplus, besides freedom. . . . We live in the nineteenth century, let us show that we realize it and intend to keep abreast of the times."[116] Until men recognized that agriculture was a "progressive science" requiring "brain as well as muscle work," a member later warned, the average farmer would remain "a mere drayer [sic] of water or hewer of wood."[117] Much like their brethren in the Richmond County, society members were farm owning townsmen, physicians, and lawyers, as well as "progressive" farmers operating model farms near railroads that provided easy access to Augusta markets. Member Ben Tillman, for example, was a leading regional horticulturalist noted for five thousand grape vines and a successful dairy at his "Highview" farm near Trenton on the C. C. & A. Railroad.[118] The disparity between these widely praised prosperous "intensive" farmers and their cotton dependent brethren became ever greater during the 1880s, perhaps nowhere was the fissure more visible than on "the Levels."

The Levels was a nine mile wide flat plateau of sandy soils near Aiken. It was home to a group of families operating farms widely admired for their close attention to business methods, good management, and "the fact that they raise their own bread and meat."[119] While these families grew some cotton, they concentrated on other crops. Like their Georgia brethren, these "intensive" farmers limited cotton to a few acres, from which they produced extraordinary yields. Thomas Whatley, for example, devoted most of his lands to grape vineyards and apple orchards, his primary crop. But Whatley also produced fifteen bales of cotton from only six acres whereas many of his neighbors consistently harvested nearly two bales per acre.[120] County Sheriff M. T. Holley had the largest dairy herd on the Levels, raising cotton only as a supplement, while nearby the Michigan-born Aiken lawyer, Henry M. Dibble, grew some cotton on his model dairy farm, the "Vale of Montmorenci."[121] Levels farmers were highly visible practitioners of those farming practices, ranging from fruit production to crop rotation to better livestock care, perceived as engines of regional prosperity. Their successes stood in stark contrast to plight of most Sand Hill farmers, who struggled to survive in the declining cotton market of the 1880s.

Privileged regional farmers and their intelligentsia brethren cared little about the motivations that led men to grow "all-cotton." But the apparent disregard by the masses of the importance of regional self-sufficiency was infuriating and seemingly counter-intuitive. The seemingly illogical commitment to cotton among the "majority of our people" rendered these people "mere 'hewers of wood and drawers of water'," for distant northern interests.[122] This vast "majority," comprised primarily of ex-slaves, their children, and the most "ignorant" white men, had never learned "to farm instead of plant."[123] They were dupes, virtually accomplices, of those "Northern sharpers" intent upon perpetuating a dishonorable vassalage. Worse still, were those who financed their "stupidity." Ben Tillman, for one, raged often about the lords of "extensive" plantations, many the heirs of antebellum planter families, who "ignored the simplest dictate of common sense" by perpetuating "the delusion of maintaining mammoth plantations." They were complicit in southern humiliation, he later lamented, for not "progressing and keeping abreast of the times." They continued "as our fathers did fifty years ago and aggravate their butchery" to the land "by renting to ignorant lazy negroes," while "vainly" striving "to keep up the fertility of the lands by commercial fertilizers."[124]

Tillman, like others who led the political insurgencies that roiled Georgia and South Carolina during the early 1890s, was frustrated by the slow pace of commercial growth and stagnant farm income, incensed by the continuation of an "all-cotton" economy. Like him, most insurgent leaders in the Augusta region lived in or near retail towns and were prosperous, diversified farmers of the new generation.[125] They had little tolerance for the struggles of the all-cotton masses. Tillman, for example, believed that Edgefield farmers were poorer in 1887 than they had been ten years earlier because of their apparent refusal to abandon cotton. Even now, he insisted, when "we are clamoring for the new South," the intransigence of the farming masses resulted in our "getting nothing of the new South."[126] "Ignorance," he maintained earlier, was responsible for the "insane system" of farming that prevailed in South Carolina.[127]

But local frustrations eased during the late 1880s. After several disappointing years, crop harvests rebounded sharply in 1887, an upturn coupled with the emergence of the Farmers' Alliance, not as a protest organization, but as an engine of farm reform.[128] Wherever the Alliance "has a foothold," noted one local leader in 1888, "one-third more corn is planted than last year."[129] The Order's "principle [was] good and its objects grand" remarked the *Augusta Chronicle* a year later. It was "on the right line" in demonstrating that farmers must diversify their crops and give their farms "the same close, everyday, personal attention that a merchant gives to his business."[130] This message seemed to take hold across the next two years. Cotton acreage was reduced during 1889 and 1890 while the harvests of fruits, grains, and foodstuffs during these years were extraordinary, outstripping even the harvest of 1882.

But the anticipated financial windfall vanished as southern railroads, now owned entirely by northern corporations, imposed skyrocketing freight rates that devoured profits on the fruits and vegetables central to the income of diversified growers.[131] Soon after, leading men of the new generation rebelled against these continued northern intrusions, harnessing their outrage over the destruction of their commercial expectations in an assault against those northern "plutocrats," and their Democratic retainers. But within Augusta's retail region, these insurgencies were led by men embracing commercial capitalism, not the "republican" ethos prevalent elsewhere; here, the "wool hat boys" were not agrarians.[132]

The idea for a new South was, as David Blight once put it, the "mythos" that facilitated sectional reconciliation in the aftermath of the Civil War. It was central to a "new religion of nationhood" that enabled Americans to make sense of wartime carnage and a failed reconstruction; "the 'new' demanded an 'old' counterpoise for emotional fuel and sustenance."[133] It may be that while the "old" world was obliterated and discredited, central features of the "new" had also been integral to the "old," present as subsidiary strands in a culture defined by the ideal of plantation slavery. Unsullied by wartime defeat, these tenets perhaps entered seamlessly into post-war understandings about the future. Rather than being on "the verge of achieving the hegemony once enjoyed by the creed of the Old South" in 1886, as Paul Gaston once noted, the common sense understandings that underlay the idea of a New South were already triumphant.¹³⁴ If so, then the insurgencies of the 1890s might have failed not from the ability of Democratic partisans to defraud, intimate, or distort the goals of the insurgents but rather in part because the "agrarian" protesters could not envision a future outside the parameters of a New South.¹³⁵

The desire to achieve "real independence" from the North fostered intuitive understandings among the first new South generation that became common sense truisms, the "natural facts," that they carried into their adulthoods. This sensibility continued long after any possibility of "real independence" had vanished because the underlying precepts were experienced "as laws of nature rather than political judgments."¹³⁶ Unable to question the natural facts that circumscribed their world, the white southerners of this generation were left, perhaps, with only the fantasies of a Lost Cause and racial tyranny to assuage their sense of failure. In the end, insurgent leaders across the Augusta region, and perhaps beyond, turned their anger at the South's continued economic struggles first against "northern sharpers" and their southern Democratic minions, before ultimately rounding against the pre-dominantly African-heritage "all-cotton" farmers, that "majority" perpetuating southern "vassalage."

NOTES

1   Paul M. Gaston, *The New South Creed: A Study in Southern Mythmaking* (New York, 1970), 42.
2   Sven Beckert, *Empire of Cotton: A Global History* (New York, 2014).
3   Quoted in Lee Ann Whites, *The Civil War as a Crisis in Gender: Augusta, Georgia, 1860–1890* (Athens, GA, 1995), 111.
4   See for example Elaine Frantz Parsons, *Ku Klux: The Birth of the Klan During Reconstruction* (Chapel Hill, 2015); Allen Trelease, *The Ku Klux Klan Conspiracy and Southern Reconstruction* (Baton Rouge, 1971); George C. Rable, *But There Was No Peace: The Role of Violence in Reconstruction Politics* (Athens, 1984).
5   *Augusta Daily Press*, March 6, 1866. The development of factories, foundries, and schools, he continued, will "give us more real independence than a dozen wars." Similarly, see the column by "State Rights," March 27, 1866.
6   *Augusta Daily Constitutionalist*, May 15, 1866; *Augusta Daily Press*, March 16, 1866. See also Carter, *When the War Was Over*, 112, 114, citing *Augusta Chronicle*, June 28, 1865.

7 *Augusta Daily Constitutionalist*, May 15, 1866.
8 "Georgian" in *Augusta Daily Constitutionalist*, December 1, 1867; November 28, 1866.
9 *Augusta Daily Constitutionalist*, January 9, 1866.
10 *Augusta Daily Constitutionalist*, May 16, 1866.
11 Gaston, *New South Creed*, 219.
12 Gaston, *New South Creed*, 189–214.
13 C. Vann Woodward, *Origins of the New South, 1877–1913* (Baton Rouge, 1951) esp. 175–204 remains the classic statement. See also Edward Ayers, *The Promise of the New South: Life after Reconstruction* (New York, 1992).
14 This ethos is perhaps most clearly defined in Steven Hahn, *The Roots of Southern Populism: Yeoman Farmers and the Transformation of the Georgia Upcountry, 1850–1890* (New York, 1983), 252–254, 282–283.
15 Edward Baptist, *The Half Has Never Been Told: Slavery and the Making of American Capitalism* (New York, 2014); Beckert, *Empire of Cotton*; Tom Downey, *Planting a Capitalist South: Masters, Merchants, and Manufacturers in the Southern Interior, 1790–1860* (Baton Rouge, 2006).
16 J. William Harris, *Plain Folk and Gentry in a Slave Society: White Liberty and Black Slavery in Augusta's Hinterlands*, (Baton Rouge, 1998 edition), 5.
17 S. Walter Martin, "Henry B. Plant," in Horace Montgomery, ed., *Georgians in Profile: Historical Essays in Honor of E. Merton Coulter* (Athens, 1958), 263–264; Alden Hatch, *American Express: A Century of Service, 1850–1950* (New York, 1950), 27; G. Hutchinson Smythe, *The Life of Henry Bradley Plant . . .* (New York, 1898), 42–55.
18 *Edgefield Chronicle* quoted in *Augusta Daily Constitutionalist*, November 10, 1859.
19 John R. deTreville, "The Little New South: Origins of Industry in Georgia's Fall-Line Cities, 1840–1865," (Unpublished Ph. D. dissertation, University of North Carolina, 1986), 133. The capital invested increased from $145,000 in 1840 to $700,000 after the canal was completed in 1848 while the number of manufacturing laborers grew from 238 in 1840 to 995 by 1850. By 1860, Richmond County had the state's largest capital investment in manufacturing. Mary DeCredico, *Patriotism for Profit: Georgia's Urban Entrepreneurs and the Confederate War Effort* (Chapel Hill, 1990), 14. The Irish were the most numerous of these new residents, exceeding 1,500 in 1850, but Augusta also home to a significant number of German artisans, as well as small but influential Jewish and French communities. Edward Cashin, *The Story of Augusta* (Augusta, 1980), 106; David Gleeson, *The Irish in the South, 1815–1877* (Chapel Hill, 2001), 33, 77–80. Augusta's Jewish community was composed largely of merchants from Savannah families who migrated up river early in the century and retained strong commercial and family ties in in the ocean port. Charles C. Jones, Jr., and Salem Dutcher, *Memorial History of Augusta, Georgia . . .*, (Spartanburg, S.C., 1980 reprint of 1890 ed.), 384–385.
20 Since Georgia was settled late, nearly a century after New England, economic development perhaps lagged the North as much from the late start as from ideological issues. deTreville, "Little New South," 158–167. State-wide the capital invested in manufacturing increased by nearly $5.0 million during the decade. Mary DeCredico, "'War is Good Business': Georgia's Entrepreneurs and the Confederate War Effort," *Georgia Historical Quarterly* 73 (Summer 1989): 231–249. Moreover, the 1850s were the years

when state government adopted an aggressive strategy for economic development that played out primarily in the area of state-owned railroad construction. Jonathan Wells, *Origins of the Southern Middle Class, 1800–1860* (Chapel Hill, 2004), 168–174; Peter Wallenstein, *From Slave South to New South: Public Policy in Nineteenth-Century Georgia* (Chapel Hill, (1987), 32–39; Donald DeBats, "An Uncertain Arena: The Georgia House of Representatives, 1808–1861," *Journal of Southern History* 56 (August 1990): 441–456.

21 *Augusta Daily Constitutionalist*, April 15, 23, 1859.

22 Edward Cashin, *The Story of Augusta* (Augusta, 1980), 96; Jones and Dutcher, *History of Augusta*, 429; deTreville, "Little New South," 164; *Augusta Evening Dispatch*, March 4, 1859.

23 The Horse Creek was a ready source of manufacturing power that ran through a rugged valley stretching some twenty five miles east of Augusta. On the history and importance of this valley see Tom Downey, "Riparian Rights and Manufacturing in Antebellum South Carolina: William Gregg and the Origins of the 'Industrial Mind'," *Journal of Southern History* 65 (February 1999): 107–108. Similarly see Bess Beatty, "Lowells of the South: Northern Influences on the Nineteenth-Century North Carolina Textile Industry," *Journal of Southern History* 53 (February 1987): 37–62; Chad Morgan, "Progressive Slaveholders: Planters, Intellectuals, and Georgia's Antebellum Economic Development," *Georgia Historical Quarterly* 86 (Fall 2002): 398–422.

24 *Augusta Daily Constitutionalist*, December 23, 29, 1859; *Augusta Evening Dispatch*, February 19, 1859.

25 *Augusta Daily Constitutionalist*, August 18, 1859. Another townsman similarly noted that "while we talk flippantly and boastfully of our independence, we are compelled to acknowledge that we are *not* independent." Quoted in Florence F. Corley, *Confederate City: Augusta, Georgia, 1860–1865* (Columbia, S. C., 1960), 28 (emphasis in original). Long before construction of either the canal or railroads one townsman lamented the cultivation of "cotton, cotton, cotton." Such a course, he feared "will inevitably terminate in our ultimate poverty and ruin. Let us manufacture, because it is our best policy." An 1827 editorial quoted in J. G. Johnson, "Notes on Manufacturing in Ante-Bellum Georgia," *Georgia Historical Quarterly* 16 (September 1932): 219. See also Harris, *Plain Folk and Gentry*, 32.

26 *Augusta Evening Dispatch*, January 24, 1859.

27 Quoted in Emory Thomas, *The Confederacy as a Revolutionary Experience* (Columbia, SC., 1991 reprint), 79.

28 Quoted in Whites, *Civil War as a Crisis in Gender*, 42.

29 *Augusta Evening Dispatch*, October 16, 1859 (quoting *New Orleans Picayune*).

30 deTreville, "Little New South," 69, 131, 237–238; Harris, *Plain Folk and Gentry*, 25; John Solomon Otto, "The Migration of the Southern Plain Folk: An Interdisciplinary Synthesis," *Journal of Southern History* 51 (May 1985): 197–198; Drew Gilpin Faust, *James Henry Hammond and the Old South: A Design for Mastery*,(Baton Rouge, 1982), 118–119; George B. Crawford, "Cotton, Land, and Sustenance: Towards the Limits of Abundance in Late Antebellum Georgia." *Georgia Historical Quarterly* 72 (Summer 1988): 215–247.

31 Quoted in Whites, *Civil War as a Crisis in Gender*, 42.
32 James C. Bonner, *A History of Georgia Agriculture, 1732–1860* (Athens, 1964), 83–89.
33 Quoted in Crawford, "Cotton, Land, and Sustenance," 245.
34 Harris, *Plain Folk and Gentry,* 32, quote from an 1851 editorial.
35 John D. Fair, "The Georgia Peach and the Southern Quest for Commercial Equity and Independence, 1843–1861," *Georgia Historical Quarterly*: 86 (Fall 2002): 376 (quote); *Augusta Daily Constitutionalist*, January 5, 1861 (citing *Southern Field & Fireside*), May 11, 1861.
36 We must "infuse more of the manufacturing and commercial spirit" into these impoverished white people, James Hammond wrote a friend from his Beech Island plantation near Augusta in 1850. He later gloated that manufacturing would insure the allegiance of white workers to a regime that controlled the factories upon which their livelihood depended. Harris, *Plain Folk and Gentry,* 32–33 (quote); Faust, *James Henry Hammond,* 275.
37 *Augusta Daily Constitutionalist*, May 11, 1861.
38 Quoted in James L. Huston, *The Panic of 1857 and the Coming of the Civil War* (Baton Rouge, 1987), 123. Hammond's comment, made in a journal entry dated July 12, 1855, accurately captured the economics of the Augusta slave trade across the decade when slaves sold for from $950 to nearly $2,000 per person. See Virginia Ingraham Burr, ed., *The Secret Eye: The Journal of Ella Gertrude Clanton Thomas, 1848–1889* (Chapel Hill, 1990), 131; *Augusta Daily Constitutionalist*, October 1, December, 25, 1859.
39 When the Confederacy was formed, Augusta bid fair to become a dominant industrial center in the new nation. A massive powder works was built on the canal during 1862 that supplied gunpowder for all southern forces east of the Mississippi throughout the war. In addition, the military effort generated scores of ancillary small factories and cottage industries. Firearms, uniforms, foundries, locomotive parts, and military paraphernalia from shoes to tents were but a few of the items manufactured by Augustans. Corley, *Confederate City,* 46–56.
40 General William T. Sherman's Union Army swept thirty miles west of the town in route to Savannah in 1864 and then within twenty miles to the east as it moved toward Columbia, South Carolina, in early 1865.
41 "Seldom, if ever," had Augustans "enjoyed a summer trade so lucrative as the last," the *Chronicle* noted at years end. December 21, 1865 quoted in John R. deTreville, "Reconstruction in Augusta, Georgia, 1865–1868," (Unpublished M. A. Thesis, University of North Carolina, Chapel Hill), 12. Augusta was largely recovered from the effects of the war by 1866. Alan Conway, *Reconstruction of Georgia*, 27–28.
42 *Augusta Chronicle*, July 20, 1867.
43 *Augusta Chronicle*, March 10, 1867 (first quote) and "Junius Brutus", March 7, 1867 (second quote). Similarly see February 7, March 20, 27, April 18, 1866. The attempt of New England to "arrogate to itself the common name of all," was a clear violation of constitutional principles. April 20, 1866.
44 *Augusta Chronicle*, March 4, 1866.
45 *Augusta Chronicle*, February 16, 1866.
46 *Augusta Daily Press*, March 16, 1866, p. 2, c. 1.

47 *Augusta Daily Constitutionalist,* December 11, 1867 (first quote); Letter of "Isundiga" in July 20, 1867 (second quote). Similarly, see May 6, June 20, 1866. Or, as the *Edgefield Advertiser* concluded a few years later, "the people of the South are simply nothing more than serfs for the New England States." January 9, 1873.

48 *Augusta Daily Press,* May 7, March 14, 1867; *Augusta Daily Constitutionalist,* March 15, 1867. See also *Augusta Daily Constitutionalist,* November 9, 1866, where the desire for large plantations was termed "a false pride."

49 *Augusta Daily Constitutionalist,* November 9, 1866 (first quote), September 30, 1866 (second quote).

50 *Augusta Banner of the South,* November 11, 1868.

51 Beckert, *Empire of Cotton,* 274–292; Harold D. Woodman, *King Cotton and His Retainers: Financing and Marketing of the Cotton Crop of the South, 1800–1925* (Lexington, Ky., 1968), 269–294.

52 The pre-war Columbia and Augusta Railroad was extended to Charlotte, North Carolina, an important hub of traffic bound for the Mid-Atlantic States. Re-christened the Charlotte, Columbia and Augusta Railroad, this line provided important direct access to the northeast, in contrast to the southern and western orientation of the town's existing roads. Jones and Dutcher, *History of Augusta,* 507; *Augusta Chronicle,* December 29, 1880. The new Port Royal and Augusta offered cheaper access to European ports than either the Central or South Carolina lines, roads long believed to discriminate against Augustans. *Augusta Chronicle,* September 2, 1879; James Doster, "The Georgia Railroad and Banking Company in the Reconstruction Era," *Georgia Historical Quarterly* 48 (March 1964): 1–5, 14; John Martin Davis, Jr., "'Black an' Dusty, Goin' to Agusty': A History of the Port Royal Railroad," *South Carolina Historical Magazine* 105 (July 2004): 198–226.

53 These post-war innovations ranged from the mundane, such as acceptance of "through bills of lading," to the rapid dispersal of powerful new cotton presses at interior railroad depots and junctions. By the early 1870s, the factorage system of the antebellum South had all but disappeared. See Woodman, *King Cotton,* 269–279; Alfred Chandler, Jr., *The Visible Hand: The Managerial Revolution in American Business,* (Cambridge, 1977), 121–123.

54 Woodman, *King Cotton,* 288.

55 People and wealth tend to collect at the intersections of transportation routes, railroad settlements typically became the dominant backcountry retail centers. Railroads facilitated the interchange of goods by frequently interrupting the transit of goods. All the major market towns that emerged around Augusta during the post-war years were local transportation hubs. Since these settlements functioned at least in part as service centers, their location at transportation intersections encouraged the continuous exchange of goods and services necessary for expansion. See Amos Hawley, *Human Ecology: A Theory of Community Structure* (New York, 1950), 216, 242–243, for a concise statement of the importance of transportation intersections.

56 A useful introduction and overview of this conceptualization is found in Leslie J. King, *Central Place Theory,* (London, 1984). The expansion of commercial activity necessitated the creation of new counties and courthouse repositories. Both McDuffie County in Georgia and Aiken County in South Carolina were established during the early 1870s.

57 Quoted in Leila B. McCommons and Clara Stovall, compositors, "History of McDuffie County, Georgia," (Unpub. mss., 1932), 96. See also Alice Massengale, "Old Wrightsboro," manuscript in File No. 2—McDuffie County, Georgia State Archives, Atlanta.

58 McCommons and Stovall, "History of McDuffie;" 245; *McDuffie Weekly Journal,* October 30. November 6, 13, December 18, 1872, January 15, 1873, September 2, 1874.

59 With construction of the large and fashionable Highland Park Hotel in 1870, Aiken became a well-known winter haven for prosperous northerners. W. H. Geddings, *Aiken As A Health Station* (Charleston, 1877); George Sala, *America Revisited...*, I (London, 1883), 277; *Augusta Banner of the South,* October 2, 1869; *Edgefield Advertiser,* March 3, 1872; *Augusta Evening News,* November 21, 30, 1877.

60 Harry Hammond, *South Carolina, Resources and Population. Institutions and Industries* (Charleston, 1883), 697. "The old general store . . . has become a thing of the past in Aiken," the *Aiken Journal and Review* remarked on October 5, 1887.

61 Hammond, *South Carolina Resources,* 707; *Edgefield Chronicle,* August 24, 1881. The paper noted a few days earlier that Johnston's growth was "something unparalleled in this region," August 10, 1881. The railroad passed through Johnston in 1869. As early as 1873, it was home to nine dry goods stores, a drug store, and other retailers. *Edgefield Advertiser,* January 30, February 6, July 31, 1873.

62 The variety of available goods and services remained limited during the early 1870s. Specialized goods and services such as banks, photographers, tailors, larger farm implements, furniture, specialty lumber, and bricks remained available only in Augusta. Acquiring them required a considerable investment of time and effort. At some distance, the time, cost, and inconvenience outweighed the value of an item.

63 The greater the diversity of goods and services offered, the greater the likelihood that those with longer ranges, like large farm equipment or banks, would "pull" distant customers to a settlement. While the success of Thomson retailers in "attracting the patronage of the surrounding county" held out the promise that "at no distant day" it would be a "place of no mean importance," continued growth depended upon further specialization and improving roads that made it easier for a family to "choose" Thomson over another settlement. *McDuffie Weekly Journal,* October 16, 1872; Brian J. L. Berry and William Garrison, "A Note on Central Place Theory and the Range of a Good," *Economic Geography* 24 (October 1958): 304–311; Harold Carter, *The Study of Urban Geography* (London, 1972), 71–72.

64 Road maintenance was a preeminent local concern. During the late 1860s, most regional roads were described as being "in very bad condition," "deplorable," and "awful." Imagine, one resident wrote, the skill required to travel roads "skirted by deep gullies, and abounding in rocks of large and small dimensions, over and through which" one had to navigate. *The Daily Press,* January 6, February 12, 13, 1867; Charles Stearns, *The Black Man of the South, and The Rebels . . .* (New York,1969, reprint of 1872 edition), 34. After a generation of effort, roads were often filled with clay, some were macadamized, and most were maintained by "chain gangs." *McDuffie Weekly Journal,* December 10, 1873; *Augusta Chronicle & Constitutionalist,* January 22, 1886.

65 By way of illustration, the *Thomson Advertiser* had no local advertisers in a March 1871 issue, eight from Augusta, and twenty-four from distant places. But by 1875, nine

Thomsonites advertised in a local weekly, along with nine Augusta firms and twenty-one from outside the region. Five years later, an issue listed twenty-three Thomson advertisers, thirty-nine Augustans, and only two from elsewhere. Noteworthy was the increase in advertisements by dealers in non-perishable specialty goods, machinery, marble, pianos, bricks and furniture. From none in 1871, two in 1875, to ten in 1880. *McDuffie Weekly Journal*, March 27, 1871; March 17, 1875; December 22, 1880.

66 Letter of "Phacks" in *Augusta Chronicle & Sentinel*, April 13, 1881. Similarly, South Carolina backcountry towns were "drawing around them small but growing communities." Hammond, *South Carolina, Resources and Population*, 659–660.

67 Rather than compete for retail trade in the backcountry, city merchants were urged to become wholesalers. See the letter of "N'Importe" in the *Augusta Chronicle & Sentinel*, November 18, 1880 and similar communications on August 14, 1879; August 29, September 9, 1880; January 29, 30. February 6, 1881.

68 Harry Hammond, Beech Island, South Carolina, to William Courtenay, November 27, 1883. William A. Courtenay Papers, South Caroliniana Library, University of South Carolina, Columbia. Beech Island township was five miles southeast of Augusta.

69 Paul Hamilton Hayne, to unidentified correspondent, February 4, 1885, Paul Hamilton Hayne Papers, Perkins Library, Duke University. (emphasis in original.) Hayne lived in Columbia County Georgia near Augusta.

70 "Generation" is an amorphous concept. The most widely used time period seems to be twenty years, the time frame used in this essay. While some of those born around 1850 likely participated in the war, most did not. Older children of this generation remembered the wartime, and experienced emotional engagement with the conflict, but not actual participation as soldiers or guerillas. For a more detailed and comprehensive use of the generational approach to the post-war South see Jane Turner Censer, *The Reconstruction of White Southern Womanhood, 1865–1895* (Baton Rouge, 2003). Michael Healey and Brian Ilbery, *Location and Change: Perspectives on Economic Geography*, (New York, 1990), 114–117, found that opportunities for innovation adoption are unequally distributed with younger, better educated men operating specialized farms being more likely to embrace agricultural innovations. While the main sources of information are friends, neighbors, and relatives, increased forms of communication is an important catalyst for adoption. With an expanding information infrastructure, a regional network of individuals in towns and villages communicate with each other, intersecting with a multitude of overlapping smaller communication networks evolving from individual locales.

71 Burr, ed., *Secret Eye*, 285–287 (September 20, 1866). Southerners, regardless of their age, retained a "widespread and tenacious devotion to the Confederate nation." Gary W. Gallagher, *The Confederate War* (Cambridge, MA, 1997), 71–73, 96–97 (quote on 72); Similarly, Mayilyn M. Culpepper, *All Things Altered: Women in the Wake of Civil War and Reconstruction* (Jefferson, NC, 2002), 135, concluded that a "hatred of the Yankees was almost universal among southern women." See also James Marten, *The Children's Civil War* (Chapel Hill, 1998), 24–25, 141 and on the broad-based support for southern nationalism see Drew Gilpin Faust, *The Creation of Confederate Nationalism: Ideology and Identity in the Civil War South* (Baton Rouge, 1988).

72 Telegraph lines came early to the Augusta, backcountry, erected along the Georgia

Railroad during 1848–1849. A web of new lines emanated from railroad towns into the countryside during the post-war decade. Beginning with an office at Thomson in 1873 that placed local residents in "direct communication with all the world," the Southern & Atlantic Telegraph opened offices in every rail town near Augusta by decade's end. *McDuffie Weekly Journal,* February 5, 1873. *City Directory of Augusta,* (Augusta, 1880), 45–46. An early telephone network was operating in Augusta by 1879 with seventy-eight subscribers. By 1881, telephone connections were available to any city residence. Aiken resorts were linked by telephones in 1877, and service from Aiken to Augusta began in 1883. Thomson, too, had telephone lines to nearby Mesena by that date. Aiken *Courier Journal,* December 13, 1877; *Aiken Journal and Review,* May 2, 1883, August 20, 1884; *McDuffie Weekly Journal,* March 15, 1882. Electric lights were installed in Augusta in 1881; refrigeration was in commercial use by 1879. *Augusta Chronicle & Sentinel,* November 5, December 17, 1881.

73 Richard D. Brown, *Modernization: the Transformation of American Life, 1600–1865* (New York, 1976), 117–118. On this and other aspects of the transformations that occurred during the 1870s with particular relevance to the interior South see Robert J. Gordon, *The Rise and Fall of American Growth: The U. S. Standard of Living Since the Civil War* (Princeton, 2016), esp. 39–43, 47–61, 66, 77, 123, 133–163.

74 Antebellum Edgefield village was an anomaly, connected to Augusta by a well-maintained, twenty-six mile plank road, virtually the only easily traveled road in the entire region. The village was a political mecca among antebellum Carolina politicians, home to the well-established *Edgefield Advertiser* and Arthur Simkins, an influential political editor. More typically, the Thomson *Herald* began publication in August 1859 with a local physician as editor. It survived less than two years. *Augusta Daily Constitution,* August 20, 1859; June 25, 1861.

75 These weeklies included the Aiken *Journal and Review, The Aiken Press,* the Johnston *Weekly Monitor,* the Harlem *Columbian,* the *McDuffie Weekly Journal,* and the *Thomson Advertiser.*

76 As used here, "intelligentsia" differs from "intellectuals." The regional intelligentsia was comprised of men, often journalists but also political, economic, and farm leaders, who advocated for a ideas and strategies that looked to achieve an economic triumph over "the North." They were "activist" thinkers in pursuit of a cultural ideal, as opposed to the more analytical orientation of intellectuals. Richard Pipes, *The Russian Revolution* (New York, 1990), 120–128, contains a concise discussion of the differences.

77 Francis Butler Simkins Notes, Southern Historical Collection, University of North Carolina, Chapel Hill. Simkins wrote an unpublished essay about the *Advertiser* in 1947.

78 Orville Vernon Burton, *In My Father's House Are Many Mansions: Family and Community in Edgefield, South Carolina* (Chapel Hill, 1985), 68. Similarly see his "Race and Reconstruction: Edgefield County, South Carolina," *Journal of Social History* 12 (Fall 1978): 33.

79 See for example, May 8, 1873, where editor Thomas Adams of the *Edgefield Advertiser* remarked that the *Augusta Chronicle* was as popular in Edgefield as in Richmond County, or the comment by the *Chronicle's* editor that "we, on this side of the river, are very naturally interested in the affairs of our neighbors on the other." March 26, 1880. The

network of new regional newspapers was synergistic with the expanding commercial traffic. Traditionally, southerners were "little given to reading. Our education is ... derived chiefly from conversation and verbal discussion," one editor had noted during the war. But new backcountry weeklies, much like printed sermons and songs during the war, had a "multiplier effect" among their readers. Faust, *Creation of Confederate Nationalism*, 16. Faust also makes the important point that the Civil War saw the rise of the "functional precursors" of mass communication. This trend intensified during the post-war years. 5–6, 17–18.

80 *Edgefield Advertiser*, November 12, 1879.
81 *Thomson Advertiser*, January 22, 1870.
82 *McDuffie Weekly Journal*, May 29, 1872.
83 *McDuffie Weekly Journal*, October 29, 1873. Earlier, editor White wrote that if farmers would but "plant and thoroughly cultivate five acres of corn, three of wheat and three of oats for every acre planted in cotton, one season will produce such a revolution in farming interests as will astound the most incredulous." August 13, 1873.
84 *Augusta Banner of the South*, May 21, 1870.
85 Aiken *Courier Journal*, February 7, 1878. His solution was draconian, urging farmers to "take charge of the Negro ... and reduce the cost of his living to the lowest rate," in addition to crop rotation.
86 William S. Smith expressed similar sentiments, believing local farmers lacked "energy, perseverance, industry and economy." Many of these shortcomings derived from the fact that "we, as parents, are not raising our children for leading business lives." *McDuffie Weekly Journal*, March 28, 1877.
87 *McDuffie Weekly Journal*, February 14, 1872.
88 Omitted.
89 Edward Royce, *The Origins of Southern Sharecropping* (Philadelphia, 1993); Harold Woodman, *New South, New Law: The Legal Foundations of Credit and Labor Relations in the Postbellum Agricultural South* (Baton Rouge, 1995).
90 *McDuffie Weekly Journal*, October 30, 1872, September 17, 1873. During the summer, quoted prices had been over twenty-one cents per pound. See issue of July 17, 1872.
91 Contemporaries estimated that the cost of raising a pound of cotton ranged from 8 cents to 10 cents, and in some places for as little as 6 cents a pound. R. H. Loughridge, "Report on the Cotton Production of the State of Georgia . . ., in Eugene Hilgard, ed., *Report on Cotton Production in the United States. . .*, 1880 Census, Vol. VI (Washington, D. C., 1884), 175; Harry Hammond, *South Carolina. Resources and Population*, 162. It may be that during the post-war decade those living near towns devoted all their land to cotton, instead of growing corn or other crops, thereby reaping the benefits of high prices for the staple while purchasing corn and grains.
92 *McDuffie Weekly Journal*, November 27, 1872.
93 *McDuffie Weekly Journal*, June 17, 1874.
94 *McDuffie Weekly Journal*, November 20, 1872. Sturgis continued to produce exceptional yields throughout the decade. In 1880 he harvested 610 lbs. of lint cotton (1.2 bales) an acre on lands involved in a state fertilizer experiment. See Georgia Department of Agriculture, "Results of Soil Tests of Commercial Fertilizer . . . 1880" circular no. 14,

new series (Atlanta, 1880), 62. In contrast, the U. S. Census reported that in 1879 cotton growers in the counties surrounding Augusta averaged less than 1/3 of a bale per acre.

95 "Observer" in *McDuffie Weekly Journal,* July 22, 1874.
96 *McDuffie Weekly Journal,* June 21, 1876.
97 *McDuffie Weekly Journal,* July 17, 1878, June 25, 1879. On Scott's similar success in 1876 see issue of June 28, 1876.
98 *McDuffie Weekly Journal,* June 19, 1878; May 17, 1876; June 27, 1877; June 25, 1879; Thomas W. Cumming to Mrs. Emily C. Hammond, November 30, 1878, Hammond, Bryan, Cumming Family Papers, South Caroliniana Library, University of South Carolina, Columbia.
99 Like their Georgia brethren, "intensive" farmers across the Savannah limited cotton to a few acres, from which they produced extraordinary yields. The successes of these men stood in stark contrast to plight of most farmers, tenants and sharecroppers struggling to survive in the declining cotton market of the 1880s. *Aiken Journal and Review,* May 14, 1884, August 12, 1885, July 1887; *Augusta Chronicle & Sentinel,* August 22, 1885.
100 *Augusta Chronicle,* September 7, October 7, 19, 1881.
101 *Augusta Chronicle,* October 5, 1881, February 24, 1882. Similarly see a letter from "One of the Sufferers" in *Edgefield Advertiser,* November 17, 1881.
102 *Augusta Evening News,* September 18, 1881.
103 *Augusta Chronicle,* May 10, 1882. See similar editorials on April 4, June 22, 1882.
104 "Report of the Commissioner of Agriculture," *Reports and Resolutions of . . . South Carolina . . . 1882* (Columbia, 1882), tables following 347.
105 Georgia Department of Agriculture, *Commonwealth of Georgia* "Crop Report for . . . April, 1882," Circular no. 26, new series (Atlanta, 1882), 18–19. Sturgis also noted that cows and sheep came out of winter quarters in better condition than at any time during the past decade. A month later, he predicted that the oat crop would double from 1881. "Crop Report for . . . May, 1882," Circular no. 27, new series (Atlanta, 1882), 13. A traveler through Thomson in March was struck by the extensive grain plantings. Letter of "M" in *Augusta Chronicle & Sentinel,* March 29, 1882.
106 "Crop Report for . . . May, 1882," Circular no. 27, new series (Atlanta, 1882), 325; "Supplemental Report of the Department of Agriculture . . . 1882," Circular no. 34, new series (Atlanta, 1882), 8.
107 *Edgefield Chronicle,* August 16, 1882; *Augusta Chronicle & Sentinel,* January 26, 1883; *McDuffie Weekly Journal,* February 15, August 9, 1882. Corn yields per acre doubled in Aiken County compared to 1881, from five bushels to ten bushels, while in Edgefield the yield jumped from six to eleven bushels per acre.
108 "Report of the [South Carolina] Commissioner of Agriculture," *Reports and Resolutions . . . 1882,* 347–363; "Report of the [South Carolina] Commissioner of Agriculture," *Reports and Resolutions . . . 1886,* Vol. 1, 158.
109 *Augusta Chronicle,* January 31, 1883.
110 Georgia Department of Agriculture, "Crop Report . . . April, 1883 . . ." Circular No. 42, new series, (Atlanta, 1883), 26, 34, 38–39; Georgia Department of Agriculture,

"Crop Report for June, 1883," Circular no. 44, new series, (Atlanta, 1883), 22; Paul F. Hammond in "Minutes of the Beech Island Club, August 4, 1883," South Caroliniana Library, University of South Carolina, Columbia. Beginning in 1883, backcountry farmers had access to refrigerated freight cars an innovation that dramatically expanded the markets for local fruit and vegetable growers.

111 William Whatley, "A History of the Textile Development of Augusta, Georgia, 1865–1883," (Unpublished M.A. thesis, University of South Carolina, 1964), 14–16. Augusta town leaders sought to enhance manufacturing infrastructure after the war in hopes of accelerating economic growth. The antebellum canal was enlarged and improved. Begun in 1872, the $1,000,000 canal expansion was financed by a municipal bond and private funds. Across the following decade, it had the desired effect.

112 Richard German, "Queen City of the Savannah: Augusta Georgia during the Urban Progressive Era, 1890–1917," (Unpublished Ph.D. dissertation, University of Florida, 1971), 21–25; Earl Bell and Kenneth Crabbe, *The Augusta Chronicle: Indomitable Voice of Dixie, 1785–1960* (Athens, Ga., 1960), 98–99; Whatley, "Textile Development of Augusta," 47; *Augusta Chronicle*, February 3, 1880.

113 *Augusta Chronicle*, September 11, 1883.

114 *Augusta Chronicle*, June 3, 1883, July 23, 1885, October 12, 1888.

115 *Edgefield Chronicle*, June 25, September 3, 1884.

116 *Edgefield Chronicle*, October 8, 1884.

117 Washington H. Timmerman, a physician and farmer, in *Edgefield Chronicle*, July 29, 1885. Similar agricultural societies were formed in Aiken and Columbia counties.

118 Tillman was a frequent visitor to Augusta where he marketed dairy products, delivering eighty pounds of butter to regular customers every Saturday. *Augusta Chronicle*, July 21, 1889; Diane Neal, "Benjamin Ryan Tillman: The South Carolina Years, 1847–1894," (Unpublished Ph. D. dissertation, Kent State University, 1976), 16, 48–49; Stephen Kantrowitz, *Ben Tillman & the Reconstruction of White Supremacy* (Chapel Hill, 2000), 82, 88. Similarly, society leader R. B. Watson was a prominent owner of extensive peach orchards, while A. J. Norris was a lawyer in Edgefield village, a successful farmer, and soon to be President of the Bank of Edgefield.

119 *Aiken Journal and Review*, May 28, 1884.

120 *Aiken Journal and Review*, May 14, 1884, August 12, 1885; *Augusta Chronicle & Sentinel*, August 22, 1885.

121 *Aiken Journal and Review*, July 1887.

122 *Edgefield Advertiser*, October 9, 1884.

123 Letter of Ben Tillman, *Augusta Chronicle*, March 5, 1886.

124 *Edgefield Chronicle*, June 24, July 1, 1885. Here was one source of Benjamin Tillman's strident animosity toward the low-country plantation elite typified by Wade Hampton, his gubernatorial opponent in 1890.

125 On the Georgia insurgent leaders see Randolph Werner, "The New South Creed and the Limits of Radicalism: Augusta, Georgia before the 1890s," *Journal of Southern History* 67 (August 2001): 586–588.

126 *Augusta Chronicle*, November 2, 1887. See also *Edgefield Chronicle*, May 18, 1887

where he lambasted local cotton growers for the fact that Edgefield was at the "tag end" of the state in terms of "agricultural and mechanical progress." Edgefield village, he concluded, lagged behind similar places where there was "abundant evidence of progress and thrift in their Courthouses, brick stores and buildings generally, and in the fact that they had banks."

127 Letter of Ben Tillman, *Augusta Chronicle*, March 5, 1886. Southerners, he continued, needed to "learn as a people to farm instead of plant."

128 The best history of the Alliance remains Robert C. McMath, Jr., *Populist Vanguard: A History of the Southern Farmer's Alliance* (Chapel Hill, 1975).

129 *Augusta Chronicle*, May 29, 1888; *Edgefield Chronicle*, May 30, 1888.

130 *Augusta Chronicle*, June 18, 1889.

131 Werner, "Limits of Radicalism," 593–594.

132 In contrast see, Barton Shaw, *The Wool-Hat Boys: Georgia's Populist Party* (Baton Rouge, 1984), 7–44.

133 David Blight, *Race and Reunion: The Civil War in American Memory* (Cambridge, 2001), 221–222.

134 Gaston, *New South Creed*, 42.

135 It is notable that antebellum southerners equated agrarianism with the forced allocation of land among the landless. Harris, *Plain Folk and Gentry*, 37. Agrarianism continued to be a term of opprobrium in the new era; hurled first at northerners advocating land distribution among freedmen, later at political insurgents during the 1890s. See for example *Augusta Daily Constitutionalist*, March 17, June 22, 1867; *Augusta Chronicle and Constitutionalist*, May 11, 1890. Not until the grandchildren of the post-war generation reached maturity during the 1920s did agrarianism take on a more appealing, laudatory tenor.

136 The quote is from Elizabeth Fox Genovese and Eugene Genovese, *Fruits of Merchant Capital: Slavery and Bourgeois Property in the Rise and Expansion of Capitalism* (New York, 1983), 135, who were referring to the hegemony of a pre-civil war ideology.

3

Virginia on the Cusp of Change

James H. Hershman, Jr.

My first meeting with Paul Gaston in September 1971 set the course of my graduate study and gave me the subject of the history I subsequently wrote. It was not, however, to be the history I thought I would write when I went to Charlottesville. Paul's then recently published book, The New South Creed, *brought me to Virginia for the chance to work with him. The author of this eloquently written, thought provoking study of the late nineteenth century South would be the right mentor for the study I had in mind. My just completed master's thesis at Wake Forest was on biracial politics in post-Reconstruction North Carolina; for my dissertation, my thought was to continue on that topic. We started talking and within minutes I was sure I had made the right choice for an advisor. Our conversation quickly revealed that during the previous year both of us had a common focus on school desegregation in the South. Paul had been in Atlanta supervising a study for the Southern Regional Council on desegregation. I had worked in a federally funded school desegregation project in North Carolina. As we recounted our experiences, Paul picked up on my interest and enthusiasm, and soon we were discussing Virginia's troubled and turbulent history after the* Brown *decision. Perhaps I might consider looking into that story, especially at the people who opposed the segregationists. That sounded just right—thus began my study of the opponents of Virginia's massive resistance.*

Paul's style as mentor was to use the light touch. Nonetheless, he frequently put me on the right track and always made me think. The sources for my new topic were quite different from those I had used earlier. Particularly helpful was the fact that Paul himself had been present and active in the events that I was opening for research. He had specific suggestions on sources, and he sent me to other people, such as his friend Staige Blackford, who had additional ideas.

Since the period had little historical coverage, it needed an interpretative shape. Paul encouraged me in my attempts to give it form. On the fundamental issue, the great moral wrong of racial oppression, we were in complete agreement. At times there were some differences of opinion on interpretation. Affected by the reigning social science ideas of the day, I offered the view that social structure and institutions were the dominant elements for the historian. Paul disagreed and, in his soft Alabama accent, reminded me that it was people inside those structures who made history. Even when I criticized the limitations of the southern liberalism with which Paul was affiliated, he encouraged me saying that my point had merit and the future might prove me right. Though delivered in a soft voice, his assessments were clear and direct. When he said of a chapter that it was alright but it lacked the depth of research and richness of detail of my previous work, I knew it needed renewed effort. His praise was not easily dispensed; thus his enthusiastic approval of my final product was all the more valuable to me.

Throughout our time at the university and for years afterward, my wife and I came to know Paul and Mary Gaston and to enjoy their warm and gracious hospitality. It remains a fond memory of my stay at Virginia. There was, however, one addition that Paul wanted me to add to my work: an interpretative essay summing up the period I covered. Over the years, he has brought up that suggestion several more times. The essay that follows is an attempt to fulfill that request and an expression of my gratitude for Paul's mentorship and friendship.

∼

The July 1959 Democratic primary in Virginia received press coverage that was rare for a mere state legislative election. The *New York Times* declared, "Moderation Wins in Virginia," while *Time* magazine headlined its article, "Virginia Moral Victory." *The Economist* put the election in a French revolutionary context. Noting the primary occurred on the 14th, *The Economist*'s reporter wrote: "On Bastille Day voters in Virginia had their first chance to choose between Governor Almond's moderate (and therefore revolutionary) stand on racial segregation and a return to the *Ancien Regime*, with its policy of shutting the tax-supported schools for white children when the courts require the admission of Negroes." The voters, the writer noted with approval, gave their backing to the governor.¹

What accounted for the outsized national and international attention focused on this election? It was, after all, only a Democratic primary for the Old Dominion's all-white, almost all-male (two women delegates) General Assembly, albeit one where Democrats held 132 of the 140 seats and nomination was tantamount to election. Although less than a third of the seats were contested, it was the most acrimonious campaign in recent memory and certainly the most expensive. The obvious explanation is that the primary was the closing act in a drama that began three years earlier. In 1956, Virginia's political leadership embarked on a campaign to defy the 1954 and 1955 U.S. Supreme Court rulings outlawing public school segregation. The state's plan, called massive resistance, had several aspects, but its centerpiece was the threat to close white public schools rather than admit even one black student. The state made good its threat when it closed nine schools in three communities in the fall of 1958, locking out nearly 13,000 white students to block the entry of fewer than fifty African Americans. The school closing crisis caused stirrings that produced long-lasting consequences among the state's white and black citizens. In January 1959, when the state's highest court and a federal district court declared the school closing law unconstitutional, Virginia Governor J. Lindsay Almond—unexpectedly—backed down, permitting twenty-one black students to enroll in Norfolk and Arlington schools. Almond appointed a legislative commission to devise a new, moderate plan that tightly limited desegregation, provided tuition grants for private education, and allowed localities to modify their systems, an opening that Prince Edward County later used to close its public schools. Amid a furious backlash from supporters of massive resistance, the governor pushed his plan through a special legislative session by the closest of margins. Massive resisters vowed to return to a program of defiance by defeating Almond's moderate supporters in the July Democratic primary. Since Virginia had served as a pace setter for other southern states in the desegregation crisis, the national press avidly covered the July campaign. In the end, Almond's moderates prevailed, preserving his slim majorities.

Assessing and interpreting these events—putting them in the larger context of change, determining what the capacious term moderation meant (and how anyone could consider it revolutionary?)—has proved a challenge for historians. Even the initial 1959 desegregation presents a paradox. Though only a token, it did breach the wall of Jim Crow segregation and was perceived as an infuriating defeat by defenders of the legal, rigid structure of white supremacy. At the same time, for school desegregation it was indeed a modest victory: a year later, out of the state's more than 200,000 black students, only 103 were in formerly white schools; large scale desegregation did not come until 1969. While change in the schools was glacial, other aspects of the state's society were moving faster. Virginia, in fact, was poised to begin a decade in which national and home-grown forces would mesh to produce the most sweeping change in the twentieth century. In an influential interpretation, historian Numan V. Bartley termed the 1959 events "A Thermidorean Reaction." It marked a turn away from the reactionary radicalism of massive resistance, but it was, he said, "a shift that was conservative rather than reformist, that sought social stability rather than social change."[2] What unfolded in Virginia, where change was gaining momentum, did not stay in the simple confines of continuity Bartley outlines. Broadly speaking, the shift could be termed conservative because full racial equality was not the outcome and in a fluid time social stability prevailed. A more accurate and precise description, however, is social change managed through pro-corporate, conservative reform.

Without question discrimination and a host of legacies from the racial caste system stubbornly outlived massive resistance and the civil rights gains that followed it. The racial regime, the rules and norms concerning race, however, had changed markedly. Gone by 1970 was the overt discrimination of the 1950 legal code that mandated racial separation in all aspects of life, replaced by a covert discrimination that mixed race with socio-economic status and justified it under the rubric of "Freedom of Choice." The daily indignities of Jim Crow were gone, and African American participation in political life greatly expanded—highly significant, meaningful achievements. But there was a major shortcoming: the gains of 1959 and after brought legal rights without the means to give them fulfillment. Three centuries of economic exploitation and discrimination coupled with educational deprivation went unacknowledged and unaddressed. A relatively small proportion of black Virginians had the resources needed to take full advantage of the hard won new rights, but the great majority did not. Moreover, in the two decades from 1950 to 1970, residential patterns of racial separation grew far more pronounced in the metropolitan areas where the majority of Virginians were choosing to live. Race combined with socio-economic class to define the new social landscape: middle class suburban whites surrounding mostly low income blacks in urban centers with Virginia's peculiar system of local government—independent cities—exacerbating the separation.

The black challenge to massive resistance, though the driving force, was not the only element pushing for change in 1959. A rift emerging within the white elite in the 1950s became entwined with the school desegregation struggle. Virginia's elite was dominated, in a way perhaps unique among American states, by a single political grouping: the Democratic Party faction headed by U.S. Senator Harry F. Byrd, known as the Byrd Organization. In the post-World War II years, an urban-based, younger generation of its adherents began to take exception to the Organization's static, rural-oriented governing policies. Historians have noted that this group found the Byrd policies inadequate in addressing the state's modern social service needs. Less noted is that the businessmen and bankers within the group saw the Organization's rule as stifling Virginia's economic future. They wanted to make major, transformative changes in banking laws, in industrial development policy, in land use policy, and provide greater spending on infrastructure and government services, especially education. In the end, they had more success achieving their goals than African Americans did in reaching full equality.

Massive resistance and the school closing crisis created a broad de facto coalition for change united only by opposition to the state's radical defiance of federal authority. A disparate, loose-knit, and short-lived alliance, it ended after the mid-1960s; nevertheless, it was the harbinger of the metropolitan society Virginia was to become in the last third of the twentieth century. The coming together of all those forces made 1959 an inflection point when the pace of change accelerated. University of Virginia political scientist Ralph Eisenberg touched on the dynamic when he later wrote: "massive resistance was significant in Virginia political history not only for resurrecting [Byrd] organization preeminence but also for crystallizing opposition to the organization and its leadership."[3] As the next decade would prove, the Byrd Organization would not go down easily. The events of 1959 did not mark its demise, but they were the beginning of the end.

I

Throughout most of the long period from the American Revolution until the Second World War, Virginia was an overwhelmingly rural state. In 1900, using U.S. Census definitions, its population was 81.7 percent rural; in 1920, 70.8 percent remained in that category. At mid-century it still had a bare rural majority of 53 percent, but the pace of urban growth was quickening: to a majority of 55.6 percent in 1960; and a decisive majority of 63.2 percent by 1970. By the 1920s there were some large industries—shipbuilding, textile and tobacco manufacturing, and coal mining—but they were concentrated in a few areas. The state's political leadership reflected that reality, effectively enshrining rural values and views into state law and government. When Harry F. Byrd won office as governor in 1925, he took over a conservative Democratic political machine created over three decades earlier to wrest power from a political movement of white farmers and black Republican voters. Byrd gained a reputation as a reformer, but his reformism was distinctly conservative, designed to make the state government and his Democratic organization more efficient and effective. He sponsored constitutional amendments drawing power from the localities into the state government, hence into the Byrd Organization that controlled that government. He acted, too, to ensure the perpetuation of the low tax, low service government he and his supporters favored. Another constitutional amendment banned the state from issuing general obligation bonds. Expenditures on infrastructure or any other state initiative would be "pay-as-you-go" from current revenue. Coupled with the Organization's strong aversion to tax increases, it imposed a fiscal and policy straitjacket on the commonwealth. Byrd earned his place as a leading Southern Business Conservative in the 1920s.[4] Virginia's few big businesses fared well on taxes and labor law, but the state's rural elite was then and would remain until 1959 the dominant interest in Byrd's regime.

Of all the aspects of rural Virginia life the single most important for maintaining Byrd Organization rule concerned race—the maintenance of white supremacy. While the Organization enjoyed majorities in all rural counties, except a few in the Valley of Virginia and in the far Southwest region, its greatest support came from whites who lived in counties with a high proportion of African Americans. In 1920, almost a third of white Virginians lived in black belt counties, where 40 percent or more of the population was black; 24 of the state's 100 counties had a black majority that year. Through a poll tax and difficult registration requirements, Byrd's predecessors in the 1902 state constitution removed virtually all blacks (and many poor whites) from the voter rolls. They also gave racial segregation constitutional sanction. The state's commitment to white supremacy reached its apogee in the 1924 Racial Integrity Act. In Byrd's gubernatorial term, segregation laws were extended and the 1924 Act enforced. At the same time, Byrd endorsed legislation striking at lynching and at the Ku Klux Klan. The Klan, it was true, could damage Virginia's national image, but a more tangible threat was its potential as an independent political force beyond Byrd's control. By its actions, the Byrd Organization assured the white electorate that the state government was the protector of white supremacy, obviating the need for any vigilante action. Over the next three decades, Byrd made certain that no one could get to the right of his Organization on race.

The Byrd Organization and the white elite it led fostered an image of thoroughly paternalistic race relations. Their narrative was one of genteel interactions between the races, of "the Virginia Way" that differentiated the Old Dominion from the far less refined Deep South states. It was a story that visiting journalists, even academics doing state studies, found persuasive and the great mass of white Virginians accepted as an accurate description. As a depiction of a surface reality, it had plausibility, but behind that surface mask was the blunt reality of a well-developed system of white supremacy. Virginia's highest court proclaimed in a 1932 decision that "the preservation of racial integrity is the unquestioned policy of this state" and that the policy was "sound and wholesome" was beyond doubt. The racial integrity statute banning interracial marriage was relentlessly enforced, strict segregation was extended to every aspect of life, and capital punishment for the crime of rape, or attempted rape, was reserved for, and frequently applied to, black men for attacks on white women—the most basic of white supremacist fears. Beneath the Old Dominion's cloak of paternalism was the strong arm of state power to ensure that blacks "stayed in their place."[5]

From the beginning of Byrd's time in office until the fall of massive resistance, his organization's political strength in the tightly restricted electorate was undergirded by large voter majorities in black belt counties. With that structure in place, little opportunity existed for a serious opposition to develop. Republicans could claim majorities in a few mountain counties but had only a small presence in state politics. Organized labor, hampered by several factors including the state's anti-union legislation, was a marginal presence. Similarly, more liberal, anti-Organization Democrats, while periodically mounting a challenge, posed little sustained threat. Byrd's power, however, was of a kind that surpassed that usually exercised by a "political machine." The Organization did indeed have a strong hold over virtually every local government—their officials constituted its operatives—but its reach extended beyond the courthouse to encompass the power structure, the leading attorneys, bankers, insurance brokers, and other businessmen and large landowners in nearly all the counties and cities of Virginia where it held sway. Byrd served, in effect, as chairman of the state's unified elite capable of marginalizing any dissenting figure or group. The Organization's grip on the state was so strong, its ability to ignore rather than adapt to change, that in time its strength turned into its weakness—and the crisis of massive resistance exposed it.

II

For all their dominance of the state, Byrd's coterie had limited control over two forces that threatened its comfortable status quo: population growth combined with economic development; and the emerging attack of black Virginians on the racial caste system. Population grew over 48 percent from 1940 to 1960, increasing from 2,677,773 to 3,966,949. The Northern Virginia suburbs of Washington, D.C., and the cities surrounding Hampton Roads accounted for the largest share, much of it spurred by federal government spending on military bases or the expansion of the Washington bureaucracy. Military personnel were transients with little significant political impact, but they did not account for all the growth. Richmond and other cities also grew.[6] The new urban and suburban residents had different expectations of government services than Byrd's rural and small-town base. Just as the growing urban middle class found its needs unaddressed, urban business interests also found their attempts to adapt to the changing circumstances thwarted. Thomas Boushall (who emerged later as a critic of massive resistance), President of the Bank of Virginia, advocated branch banking which would bring convenience to customers and allow greater concentration of bank capital to meet the needs of the growing areas. In response, the Byrd-controlled 1948 General Assembly enacted a law protecting the state's small-town banks by strictly limiting branch banking. Similarly, the areas beginning to experience suburbanization found their tentative efforts at zoning laws challenged in court based on nineteenth-century property rights concepts. Though the principle of land use zoning was affirmed in a 1947 case, its use as a tool of suburban development was questionable under a rural oriented state government.[7]

In 1949, the urban stirrings gave a hint of political threat when a few anti-Organization candidates won assembly seats in the growth areas and, though unsuccessful, one drew strong urban support in the gubernatorial primary. A group of mostly city-based young legislators who considered themselves aligned with the Organization began questioning the state's spending priorities. Dubbed the "Young Turks," they staged a fight over appropriations for schools and mental hospitals in 1954 and won a partial victory. As a rebellion, it was a mild one, though one of the "Young Turk" leaders, Armistead L. Boothe, went considerably further by advocating racial desegregation in public transportation and proposing modifications in the state's "Right-To-Work" law. The Organization responded to this in-house dissent by giving the legislators poor committee assignments and denying the promise of political advancement. In a move to bolster their overall control, senior Organization leaders chose not to recognize population changes in the legislative re-apportionment following the 1950 Census, thus ensuring their rural base was over-represented at the expense of the proliferating metropolitan regions.[8]

In Virginia's rural and urban black communities a more deep-seated demand for change—one that would shake the existing social order to its foundations—was taking shape. There had been black protest and challenge to segregation laws since their enactment in the early twentieth century, but the most sustained challenge began in the mid-1930s. Using the legal precedent of "separate but equal," attorneys for the NAACP began demanding that the egregiously unequal educational facilities for African Americans be made equal—in transportation, teacher pay, buildings, and curriculum. The campaign won some court victories in the late 1930s, was largely suspended during World War II, then resumed at an increased pace in the late 1940s. Success in several federal court suits highlighted the twofold strategy of the NAACP lawyers: to win better schools for their clients and to make operation of the separate systems more expensive for the white authorities. For some western Virginia counties, the financial and legal pressure was leading to the conclusion that only desegregation could bring equalization. Though the indirect attack through equalization had some notable gains, the national NAACP decided in 1950 the time had come to make a direct attack.[9] The change in strategy soon produced a case in Virginia. When students at the overcrowded and inadequate black high school in Prince Edward County staged a protest strike in April 1951, NAACP attorneys told them they could not bring an equalization action, that they could only challenge the segregation law outright. With the agreement of the local NAACP chapter and the parents of the striking students, the attorneys filed suit in federal court in May.[10]

Within days after the Prince Edward court filing, talk among leading whites was about the need to create a publicly-subsidized "private" school for whites if the court should rule against segregation. Quietly the state government began to explore the idea, first testing the concept to see if the federal court would allow private contractors to operate state parks on a segregated basis. If the courts permitted "privatized" parks, the practice logically could be extended to public schools; at the same time, the attempt would draw far less publicity than talk involving the schools. In 1952, when a state senator from Appomattox County in southern Virginia introduced bills to allow private contractors to operate public schools, the leadership buried the legislation, saying it was "premature" to take such action.[11] While the Virginia case and those from three other states made their way on appeal to the U.S. Supreme Court, other southern states passed legislation that would allow the ending of public education in the event of a desegregation ruling. In contrast, the message coming out of Richmond seemed to be: stay calm, let the Byrd Organization handle it.

By the early 1950s, when the school case reached the U.S. Supreme Court, Virginia's racial demographics were changing. The state was becoming whiter: as a component of the total population, African Americans had dropped from 35.6 percent in 1900 to 22.3 percent in 1950. The number of counties with black majorities had declined from twenty-four in 1920 to seventeen by 1950. Similarly, the number of whites living in black belt counties fell from a bit over 30 percent in 1920 to 10.5 percent by 1950. Virginia's black/white ratios were closer to those of Ohio than of Mississippi, but racial attitudes did not change as quickly as population statistics. The movement of black Virginians out of the state occurred over just a few recent decades; many whites in areas no longer black belt retained the racial consciousness instilled in them at an earlier time. Many of the whites streaming into Northern Virginia and to a lesser extent the Tidewater cities were non-Virginians who, while not free of racial prejudice, had less commitment to the caste system. Many others were Virginians leaving rural counties and smaller cities for the Richmond and Norfolk metropolitan areas.[12] Post-war suburbanization was burgeoning, and with it came greater spatial separation of the races. Because of their greater wealth, middle class whites had more automobiles to commute from the suburbs, and the new housing developments sprouting there were segregated by the practices of realtors and mortgage lenders, and by Federal Housing Administration rules. Fairfax County, for example, experienced spectacular growth, increasing from 95,557 in 1950 to 275,000 in 1960, with the non-white portion falling from 10 to 5.4 percent. Henrico County bordering Richmond had a 104.6 percent growth rate from 1950 to 1960, rising from 57,340 to 117,339, with the non-white portion staying at 5 percent. A decade later, Henrico's numbers would surge to 154, 364 with whites constituting 93.5 percent of the total.[13] As massive resistance fell in 1959, the demographic shifts started to be felt and would play a key role in Virginia's transition from a racial regime of legal segregation to one of "Freedom of Choice."

III

When the U.S. Supreme Court declared school segregation unconstitutional in 1954, it came as a shock to most white Virginians. During the next year and a half, the question of how to deal with it was uncertain, but, as he had done since the 1920s, Byrd eventually moved to ensure that no one could get to his right on race among voters in his base. Initially, Virginia's governor and attorney general urged calm while Senator Byrd denounced the Court's action as gross judicial overreaching. The Court had deferred an implementation ruling until the next year, allowing time for opposition to mobilize. The governor appointed a study commission of thirty-two General Assembly members headed by state Senator Garland Gray. The Byrd Organization stalwarts predominated—all-white, all-male, and nineteen represented rural counties with substantial black populations. At the same time, state and federal legislators representing the region south of the James River declared that desegregation was totally unacceptable, and local officials from across the region, meeting in Blackstone, Virginia, formed a segregationist pressure group, The Defenders of State Sovereignty and Individual Liberties. The Defenders, as they came to be known, had close ties to the Byrd Organization—most of its officers were county officials aligned with it, and its legal counsel, Collins Denny, Jr., was a longtime Byrd operative. For the aging chairman of Virginia's white elite, the sentiments they represented carried the most weight.

The High Court's ambiguously worded implementation decree issued on May 31, 1955, brought an array of responses from Virginia conservatives. James J. Kilpatrick, influential young editor of the *Richmond News-Leader*, denounced the Court's action in his editorial, "Now It's the South's Move." He called for new pupil assignment laws and repeal of compulsory attendance rules and for efforts to "give fresh stimulus to the formation and operation of private schools." He also said that segregation statutes should be repealed since "these provisions are dead letters now and only a hindrance." There were, he noted, several localities—34 counties and 10 cities with black populations below 10 percent—that might want to desegregate, and they should be permitted to do so. The Defenders, on the other hand, took a more hardline stance. On repeal of attendance laws and permitting the state to fund private education, they agreed, but they also called for the more drastic step of ending state funding for any desegregated public schools. Reliance on pupil assignment, the Defenders contended, would "do nothing more than delay for a short while the full integration of the Schools." "What difference," they asked, "does it make as a matter of principle whether it comes in 1955 or 1956? Each means the ultimate mongrelization of the races." Moreover, all public officials and candidates for office should make known their position on the question.[14] Clearly, for the Defenders there was no middle ground or compromise. Support for the idea that the state could do anything it chose with the schools came in the decision of a Circuit Court judge in Hanover County. Ruling on the legal validity of bonds voted for segregated schools, Judge Leon M. Bazile issued a twenty-one page opinion, extensively excerpted in the *New York Times*, arguing that the clauses of the Virginia Constitution requiring the state to maintain a system of "public free schools" and the mandate that they be segregated were not separable: invalidating one, removed the other. The state, according to Bazile, was under no obligation to operate public schools. It was a contention that became a key part of the thin constitutional defense of massive resistance.[15]

The Gray Commission recommended an approach that took note of the diversity of the state's regions. As shaped by the commission's counsel, Richmond attorney David J. Mays, the plan relied on pupil assignment by local school boards to limit desegregation. For parents wishing to avoid any desegregated education, it would allow localities to remove attendance laws and for state tuition grants to students for non-sectarian private education. Because the state constitution barred expenditure of public funds for private education, the tuition grant proposal required removing that prohibition. The plan certainly limited desegregation, but it would not block it everywhere. Before it was made public in early November, Senator Byrd, who was on a visit to U.S. military bases in Europe, received an advance copy. He is said to have commented, "This won't do," and upon his return began the push for a harder line. University of Virginia President Colgate

Darden later remembered that Byrd told him, "Nobody ever need plan to run for public office in Virginia that's not on the segregated side of that issue." Congressman William M. Tuck, a former governor and close Byrd confidant, indicated what the senator had in mind: a state law denying funds to any desegregated school.[16] The Organization's leaders did favor the Gray Plan's proposal to make tuition grants constitutional and called a special legislative session to accomplish that goal. The legislators set a January 9, 1956, referendum to be followed by a March constitutional convention, if the yes vote prevailed. But tuition grants were only one element in the evolving plan to defy the U.S. Supreme Court; it would be months before it was enacted. In the meantime, James J. Kilpatrick would formulate the ideological rationale for it.

The thirty-five-year-old Kilpatrick had gained the editorship of the *News-Leader* in 1951 based upon his skill as an editorial writer. Though he was from Oklahoma, "he quickly became," in the words of *Washington Post* columnist Ben Muse, "more Virginian than Virginia," and "flourished because he fitted congenially" with the Byrd Organization. Though he would return to it in November 1958, he dropped the tolerance for letting some communities desegregate in favor of Senator Byrd's position. He would, moreover, convince white Virginians that their opposition to desegregation was not a matter of racial prejudice but instead a constitutional argument over State Rights. During late November 1955, he ran a series of long editorials claiming that Virginia had the right to "interpose" its state sovereignty to block the enforcement of a federal court ruling. He drew mainly upon the discredited pre-Civil War political doctrines of South Carolinian John C. Calhoun, garnished with ample quotes from the 1798 Kentucky and Virginia Resolutions of Thomas Jefferson and James Madison.[17] The referendum on tuition grants carried by more than a two to one margin, though scattered voices in the urban areas opposed it as a threat to public education. When the General Assembly convened, it brought up an "Interposition Resolution" along the lines advocated by Kilpatrick and adopted it by a margin of thirty-six to two in the State Senate and ninety to five in the House of Delegates. With opposition to desegregation surging in his political base, Senator Byrd chose in late February 1956 to issue his call for a campaign of "massive resistance" to the Supreme Court decision.

In late August 1956 a special session of the General Assembly enacted the legal structure of massive resistance amid a public clamor to preserve segregation. A majority of Gray Commission members renounced their earlier proposals in favor of a plan to prevent any desegregation anywhere in the commonwealth. Centralizing all pupil assignments in a special state panel was the first protection of the color line. Should that fail, the governor was mandated to seize and close any public school under a desegregation order. State and local funds from that closed school were to be issued as tuition grants to the affected students for use in (segregated) private schools. Other statutes sought to intimidate the NAACP by demanding their membership rolls and threatened their legal counsels with disbarment and prosecution for illegally fomenting lawsuits. With passage of this legislation, massive resistance was in flood tide among white Virginians. The atmosphere carried over into the 1957 gubernatorial election. Attorney General J. Lindsay Almond, who convinced massive resisters in southern Virginia that he would not "give one inch" while hinting to northern Virginians that he might accept some "enforced integration," won 63 percent of the vote in the governor's race against a GOP opponent championing a pupil assignment plan.[18] Even as Almond defended state rights with oratorical flourish in his 1958 inaugural address, state appeals of federal court desegregation orders affecting four localities were running out—a reckoning with federal power was only months away.

IV

The threat of school closings produced a wave of independent organizing unprecedented in the tightly controlled Old Dominion. For middle-class white parents, the motivating concern was to save the public schools; for some of the state's leading businessmen, saving and strengthening public education was an important goal, but they had others, too. An elite group of bankers, lawyers, and business executives saw the inevitable crisis over school closing as pitting Byrd's traditional Virginia against an emerging new Virginia. It might well end by tipping the balance of power toward the changes they favored. Shaped themselves by Virginia customs, most members of this upper-class group were not keen to desegregate; in fact, their industries and banks had long conformed to the racial caste system in hiring and lending practices, but they wanted economic growth and knew that grow required change. The first move came when state Senator Eugene B. Sydnor, a Richmond department store executive active with the state chamber of commerce, got a resolution through the General Assembly to create an industrial study commission. The governor appointed Richmond banker J. Harvie Wilkinson, Jr., and eleven other business executives and public officials—virtually all from urban areas—to serve on Sydnor's panel. Issued at the very end of 1957, the Sydnor Commission report found Virginia woefully deficient in its efforts to recruit industry. Investment in plant and equipment in 1956 fell at least two-thirds short of what it should have been, and the problem was not new—it ran throughout the Byrd years. Virginia "industrial payrolls in 1929 provided 17.5 percent of our civilian income, and by 1956 this proportion had increased to 20.9 percent," which was well short of the national average of 31.3 percent. The state government's economic development effort needed new emphasis with an agency dedicated to it. In addition, the state needed to create an industrial development corporation empowered to issue revenue bonds to finance growth and expansion. It cited "the current uncertainty over the question of segregation and integration in the public schools" as a deterrent in the effort to attract more investment.[19]

With Sydnor's report in hand, ninety leaders in Virginia's economic life joined together in an organized push for implementation of its recommendations. Impetus for formation of the Virginia Industrialization Group came from Richmond attorney (later U.S. Supreme Court Justice) Lewis F. Powell. Other leading figures were railroad president Stuart T. Saunders and banker J. Harvie Wilkinson, Jr. Membership included the executive officers of the state's major industries, big retail merchants, bankers, and the publishers of the Norfolk and Richmond daily newspapers.[20] At a dinner meeting in December 1958, a critical point in the school closing crisis, members of the group sought to sway Governor Almond's thinking. The school crisis, they emphasized, was a serious threat to the state's economy—massive resistance drove away investment. At the time, Almond appeared to rebuff their warning, though barely a month later he took their advice. Even before the dinner, on their editorial pages several large Virginia newspapers had advocated dropping massive resistance. Most notable was the *Richmond News Leader* where the fiery James J. Kilpatrick was returning to his original position of permitting a little desegregation with a lot of private education using state grants.[21]

Organizing among urban and suburban middle class whites began in Arlington in April 1958. Community leaders in the Washington suburb facing a federal desegregation order anticipated that their schools would be closed in the fall. They formed a group, the Arlington Committee to Preserve Public Education (later shortened to Arlington Committee for Public Schools), whose purpose in the coming crisis was to keep the schools open. By focusing on protecting public education, they sought to shift public thinking from the polarizing concept of segregation versus integration to the more pragmatic open or closed schools, though obviously keeping schools open would mean accepting some desegregation. Although the organizers favored desegregated schools, they decided to limit the group's membership to whites as a tactical measure. In the racially charged atmosphere, interracial groups could draw only a small membership; the school committee organizers wanted to enlist a massive membership ahead of an expected referendum on public education. The Arlington group grew to over 4,000 members by summer and other communities in the state facing school closing emulated the Arlington model.

When six secondary schools in Norfolk were closed by the governor in September, the Norfolk Committee for Public Schools swelled to 7,500 members. It financed a federal court challenge to the school closing laws and blocked a move by city council to close the city's remaining secondary schools, most of which served African Americans. In early December 1958, the local committees formed a state-wide organization—the Virginia Committee for Public Schools (VCPS).[22] In addition to attracting parents, the VCPS made a wider appeal to the middle class based on the economic value of public education. Useful in this regard was a widely publicized study on the economic impact of school closings by University of Virginia economist Lorin Thompson. Dr. Louis Rader, who represented the General Electric

Company in the state, made the case directly in speeches and written pieces. He told his audiences that General Electric, which had opened three large plants in Virginia in 1955–56 (drawn by its anti-union laws), would not have come to the state had it known public education was threatened. By spring 1959, VCPS had fifteen local committees with 25,000 members.[23]

All the organizing was necessary to meet the coming political storm. Despite his earlier blustering rhetoric, Governor Almond—to the surprise and chagrin of the massive resisters and the unforgiving ire of Senator Byrd—yielded to the federal courts and allowed desegregation to occur in Norfolk and Arlington on February 2, 1959. The forty-member legislative commission he appointed, headed by state Senator Mosby G. Perrow, had a majority from areas not supportive of massive resistance. Its recommendations—a pupil assignment plan, state tuition grants for private education, repeal of compulsory attendance—resembled the Gray Plan. It would permit some desegregation, albeit on a limited, very gradual basis. What marked it as different was that the commission and Almond seized upon an idea promoted by retired newspaper executive Leon Dure as an attractive new rationale. Dure's argument was that the constitutional right of association carried the equal corollary not to associate. He called his new "right" the "Freedom of Choice of Association" that was shortened to "Freedom of Choice." Critics noted that it ignored the context of discrimination and was a justification for segregation (the U.S. Supreme Court agreed in a 1968 decision), but at the time it was an attractive dodge. For whites moving into the new suburbs, it carried the popular consumer phrase "choice," and gave the impression that simple economic choice, not morally questionable racial prejudice, was behind the segregation in their communities.[24]

Supporters of the plan were called moderates, a loose term covering a spectrum on desegregation that ran from a grudging to a welcoming acceptance, all united by their opposition to the school-closing massive resisters. The moderates' answer to the racial problem was that economic growth and expansion of the black middle class would solve it. Almond's moderate coalition consisted of the urban-suburban wing of the Byrd Organization and the General Assembly's handful of anti-Organization Democrats and Republicans. Less noted amid the intense focus on the debate over tolerance for desegregation was the moderate backing for the reform agenda advocated by the businessmen, a fact made evident in 1960 and 1962. After turning back a massive resister proposal to end the state's commitment to public education, moderates in the April 1959 special session passed the Almond-Perrow plan by a margin of seven votes in the House of Delegates and by a single vote in the State Senate. Unyielding segregationists were furious at what they regarded as an act of betrayal; a "Bill of Rights Crusade" rally of 5,000 at the state capitol cheered speeches attacking Almond and his supporters. At their annual convention in May, the Defenders demanded a return to massive resistance and vowed to punish the moderates. In the convention's keynote speech, former Georgia Governor Marvin Griffin (introduced by Kilpatrick) ridiculed moderates as slow-motion integrationists. Other speakers pointed to the thin margins that passed Almond's plan. Those numbers, they declared, needed to be changed—the upcoming July Democratic primary would be a time of testing for the moderates.[25]

The massive resisters targeted the moderates in their urban base: the Defenders ran their own slates of House candidates in Norfolk and Newport News and strongly endorsed pro-massive resistance challengers to several moderate state senators and one of the few rural ones. The pro-public school side countered by backing challenges to massive resister House incumbents in Portsmouth and Fredericksburg and backing senate challengers in Hampton and Newport News. National attention focused on the senate races in Norfolk and, particularly, Alexandria, where a leading moderate, Armistead Boothe, was challenged by a former mayor who was Senator Byrd's cousin.[26] The VCPS urged its members to pay their poll tax and provided voter registration information. Black leaders, too, urged their community to vote, warning that much was at stake. The moderates, they noted, made statements of preference for segregation (they could not get elected otherwise), but their stands on public education and economic policy were far better than the massive resisters. Black voter registration and participation had been rising in Virginia's cities since the 1940s, and their impact was felt in the primary.[27] Similarly, organized labor devoted resources to the pro-public school side. Labor's membership had risen to about 12 percent of the state's workforce, with much of it concentrated in the Tidewater cities.²⁸ The pro-public school mobilization worked—moderates prevailed in all the crucial state Senate races. In the House races, a few supporters of the Almond plan were defeated, but the public school forces also picked up seats. A coalition of angry white parents, labor, and black voters had elected two liberal independent Democrats in Norfolk and defeated a strong massive resister in Portsmouth. On balance, moderates were strengthened in the Senate and had a small net loss in the House.²⁹ Power had tipped in the Old Dominion.

V

Black Virginians saw the 1959 desegregation, minimal as it was, as proof that even the most powerful segregationists could be overcome. The impulse to attack the entire structure of legal segregation was rising, especially among the young who found the progress of lawsuits too slow. Speaking to the 1959 state NAACP convention, Oliver W. Hill, Virginia's leading civil rights attorney, agreed with that sentiment: court cases were not enough to achieve equality; African Americans must take actions as citizens in their communities. At a large Richmond rally, Dr. Martin Luther King, Jr., declared that "attempting to resist integration today is like standing against a tidal wave . . . it is an unstoppable movement." And the tidal wave was not long in coming: shortly after the initial February 1960 lunch counter sit-in in Greensboro, North Carolina, direct action spread to the Old Dominion, with sit-ins at lunch counters and public libraries.³⁰ "The irony of *Brown*," legal scholar Paul Finkelman writes, "is that it led to the destruction of segregation virtually everywhere in our country except the schools."³¹

What happened in the all-white 1960 General Assembly on race? The moderate mobilization had produced a slim majority backing the governor. Other than some grumbling about "nullification," there was no attempt to revive massive resistance. Although massive resisters were outraged that it permitted any desegregation, "Freedom of Choice," the governor's plan, was in no objective sense liberal or pro-integration. Nothing was done, for example, about Prince Edward County which had defunded its public school system to avoid desegregation. In fact, the tuition grant program which supported private education was strengthened and the grant amounts increased. Now in the minority, the massive resisters were still there and not reluctant to express their racist views. Richmond state Senator Ed Haddock, a racial liberal, encountered an ugly example of that expression when he introduced a bill to create a Human Relations Commission. At a Rules Committee hearing on Haddock's bill, a black minister testifying in support rhetorically posed the question, "Don't you think there will be Negroes in heaven?" The reply from one of the Senators was "why, of course they will—who would wait on the tables, otherwise?"[32]

By contrast, there was intense activity on the moderates' economic issues and decisive victory after a hard legislative fight. Economic development measures—such as the Industrial Development Corporation—advocated by the businessmen in 1958 were enacted and funded. The governor's budget boosting spending on education, social services, and infrastructure backed by increased alcohol and tobacco taxes passed by a close margin. A sales tax of 3 percent, Almond's signature item, was blocked by the Byrd Organization's old guard in an act of revenge. Senator Byrd's son, state Senator Harry Byrd, Jr., killed it in the committee he chaired.[33] An anonymous legislative supporter of Almond explained to Claude Sitton of the *New York Times* that the split stemmed from the social and economic changes brought by urbanization and industrialization. Almond's faction, he said, wanted to adapt to those changes while "those closest to Senator Byrd had insisted on adherence to 'stand pat conservatism' and, failing to win the argument, had adopted 'a rule or ruin' attitude."[34]

A year later, even so stalwart a massive resister as Harry Byrd, Jr.'s brother-in-law, Alexandria Delegate James Thomson, concluded that "our only course will be to minimize the effect of integration" through pupil assignment.[35] In the 1961 Democratic gubernatorial primary, Byrd loyalists were challenged by backers of the Almond program, but it was not a clear contest of massive resisters versus moderates. Even the more conservative candidate slate recognized the shift in voter sentiment and took moderate stands on racial and economic policy. "Freedom of Choice" was the common solution, though there was disagreement, particularly between the lieutenant governor candidates, over the Prince Edward schools. Using "race-neutral" criteria, it would be the state's policy in pupil assignment and awarding tuition grants until ended by the federal courts in 1968 and 1969.[36] The conservative slate's victory enshrined that racial policy, but it also gave the green light to make keynote moderate economic reforms.

Paramount for the 1962 General Assembly session was passing a law encouraging bank mergers and consolidations. Proponents of the legislation contended it would create larger banks with increased capital to fund economic development; its opponents said it was "just one more means of eliminating the small country banks and concentrating financial power in a few locations." Delegate James Thomson offered an amendment to restrict mergers but it was removed in the State Senate. The legislation passed, transforming the state's financial institutions. A wave of mergers ensued followed by the creation of massive state-wide bank holding companies.[37] In recognition of the Old Dominion's growing suburbs, a unified zoning code was passed. The state's highest court to which zoning cases were appealed reflected the shift in power in its make-up: from a rural majority of five of its seven justices in 1955 to an urban majority of six out of seven by 1965. A change to twentieth-century land use legal concepts was in the offing.[38]

The genie of change was fully out of the bottle when federal legislation and court rulings between 1964 and 1966 ended legal segregation, threw out the poll tax, and reapportioned the General Assembly on a population basis. In a true touch of irony, after a conversion to moderation Mills Godwin, an architect of massive resistance, was elected governor in 1965 by appealing to black voters, labor, and urban whites—the 1959 pro-public school coalition.[39] Godwin's administration enacted every element of the moderate economic reform agenda. In the late 1960s and early 1970s, liberal figures in both political parties sought to turn the change in a more liberal direction—and failed. But make no mistake: change, urban pro-business oriented change, had come. The locus of power had shifted from the courthouses to the boardrooms of banks and corporations, from country squires to Richmond bankers and Northern Virginia developers. The key to political success became winning suburban voters. That change's dynamic added an element of racial and gender diversity to the state's elite, expanded the black middle class modestly, and further concentrated poverty among the urban black underclass. Just as in the rest of the country, inequality had a new structure and a new rationale—and was growing wider. In that way, the "revolutionary" changes that followed 1959 accomplished what the Civil War did not: they made Virginia more closely resemble the nation of which it was a part.

Notes

1. *New York Times*, July 19, 1959, E10 (hereafter cited as *NYT*); *Time*, July 27, 1959, 14; *Economist*, August 1, 1959, 287. According to Benjamin Muse, the anonymous columnist for the *Economist* was J. Keith Kyle, who had sought his advice on Virginia matters, Interview with Benjamin Muse, March 10, 1982.
2. Numan V. Bartley, *The Rise of Massive Resistance: Race and Politics in the South During the 1950s* (Baton Rouge: Louisiana State University Press, 1967), 320–327. In a later article focused on events in Georgia, Bartley's interpretation agrees with that advanced in this essay, see "Another New South?" *Georgia Historical Quarterly*, 65 (Summer 1981):133. James W. Ely, Jr., *The Crisis of Conservative Virginia: The Byrd Organization and the Politics of Massive Resistance* (Knoxville: University of Tennessee Press, 1976), 203–207, views the events of 1959 as only a "shift in tactics" followed by continuity in policy.
3. Ralph Eisenberg, "Virginia: The Emergence of Two-Party Politics," in *The Changing Politics of the South*, ed. William C. Havard (Baton Rouge: Louisiana State University Press, 1972), 54.
4. On the Byrd Organization, see the series of articles by Edward T. Folliard in *The Washington Post and Times Herald* (hereafter cited as *WP*), June 9–19, 1957. Ronald L. Heinemann, *Harry Byrd of Virginia* (Charlottesville: University Press of Virginia, 1996) is the best overall biography of Byrd. On Byrd's gubernatorial career, see Raymond Pulley, *Old Virginia Restored: An Interpretation of the Progressive Impulse, 1870–1930* (Charlottesville: University Press of Virginia, 1968), 176–183. On Byrd's political methods, see Brent Tarter, *The Grandees of Government: The Origins and Persistence of Undemocratic Politics in Virginia* (Charlottesville: University of Virginia Press, 2013), 281–304.
5. J. Douglas Smith, *Managing White Supremacy: Race, Politics, and Citizenship in Jim Crow Virginia* (Chapel Hill: University of North Carolina Press, 2002); *Wood v. Commonwealth*, 159 Va. 963 (1932); Donald H. Partington, "The Incidence of the Death Penalty for Rape in Virginia," *Washington & Lee Law Review* 22 (Spring 1965): 43–75.
6. William J. Serow, "Population Change in Virginia, 1960–1970," *University of Virginia Newsletter* 47 (May 15, 1970). The state's net population increase from in migration in the 1950s was 2.6 percent and increased to 23.4 percent in the 1960s.
7. Charles O. Meiburg, "Changes in Virginia Banking: 1948–1964," *University of Virginia Newsletter* 41 (June 15, 1965); John H. Wessells, Jr., *The Bank of Virginia: A History* (Charlottesville: University Press of Virginia, 1973), 95–96. For land use cases, see *County of Fairfax v. Parker*, 186 Va. 675 (1947) and *Board of Supervisors v. Carper*, 200 Va. 653 (1959).
8. "Byrd Party Foes Gain in Virginia," *NYT*, March 21, 1954, 50; James Latimer, "Virginia

General Assembly, Then and Now," *University of Virginia Newsletter*, 36 (January 15, 1960); George M. Kelley, "The Changing Style of Virginia Politics," *University of Virginia Newsletter*, 45 (February 15, 1969). For Boothe's labor proposal, see Richard Morris, "Bill Proposes Union Shops in Virginia," *WP*, January 31, 1952, B2.

9   Interview with Oliver W. Hill, October 5, 1976; Doxey A. Wilkerson, "The Negro School Movement in Virginia: from 'Equalization' to 'Integration,'" *Journal of Negro Education*, 29 (Winter 1960): 17–29; Larissa M. Smith, "A Civil Rights Vanguard: Black Attorneys and the NAACP in Virginia," in *From the Grassroots to the Supreme Court*, ed. Peter Lau (Durham: Duke University Press, 2004), 129–153; Brian J. Daugherity, *Keep On Keeping On: The NAACP and the Implementation of Brown V. Board of Education in Virginia* (Charlottesville: University of Virginia Press, 2016).

10 Christopher Bonastia, *Southern Stalemate: Five Years without Public Education in Prince Edward County, Virginia* (Chicago: University of Chicago Press, 2012); Jill Ogline Titus, *Brown's Battleground: Students, Segregation, & the Struggle for Justice in Prince Edward County, Virginia* (Chapel Hill: University of North Carolina Press, 2011).

11 Benjamin Muse, "Abrupt Halt of Segregation Feared," *WP*, June 3, 1951, B6; "Parks Lease Considered by Virginia," *WP*, August 16, 1951, B6; "Run-off Vote Bill Adopted By Va. House," *WP*, February 1, 1952, B2; William J. O'Brien, "State Parks and Jim Crow in the Decade before *Brown v. Board of Education*," *The Geographic Review*, 102 (April 2012): 172–175.

12 See James H. Hershman, Jr., "A Shrinking Black Belt and Virginia's Massive Resistance: A Note," *Virginia Social Science Journal*, 20 (Winter 1985): 93–97.

13 For Richmond's suburbanization, see *Bradley* v. *School Board of City of Richmond, Virginia*, 338 F. Supp. 67 (1972); John V. Moeser and Rutledge M. Dennis, *The Politics of Annexation: Oligarchic Power in a Southern City* (Cambridge, MA: Schenkman Publishing Company, 1982). Matthew D. Lassiter, *The Silent Majority: Suburban Politics in the Sunbelt South* (Princeton: Princeton University Press, 2006), 1–18, gives a wider view of the process.

14 *Richmond News Leader* (hereafter cited *RNL*), June 1, 1955, 1; "To the People of Virginia," paid advertisement, *RNL*, June 14, 1955, 14. A copy of the Defenders' eleven page pamphlet, "A Plan for Virginia," can be found in J. Segar Gravatt papers, box 2, #11584, Albert and Sydney Small Collection, University of Virginia.

15 "Virginia Court Bars Bonds," *NYT*, June 3, 1955, 1. For the state's use of the argument and its rejection by the Virginia Supreme Court of Appeals, see *Harrison* v. *Day*, 200 Va. 439 (1959). On the bonds case, see James H. Hershman, Jr., "Public School Bonds and Virginia's Massive Resistance," *Journal of Negro Education*, 52 (1983):398–409.

16 On Mays and the Gray Plan, see *Race, Reason, and Massive Resistance: The Diary of David J. Mays, 1954–1959*, ed. James R. Sweeney (Athens, GA: University of Georgia Press, 2008); Guy Friddell, *Conversations with Guy Friddell* (Charlottesville: University Press of Virginia, 1978), 161–162 (quotes);"Va. Segregation Woes Told," *WP*, November 20, 1955, B3.

17 Benjamin Muse, "Why Virginia Took on the Court," *WP*, March 11, 1956, E1. For Kilpatrick's editorial series, see: *RNL*, November 21–23, 28–29, 1955, and his article "The Right to Interpose," *Human Events*, December 24, 1955. Kilpatrick drew the idea of interposition from an undated pamphlet authored by a local attorney, William Old,

"The Segregation Issue: Suggestions Regarding the Maintenance of State Autonomy." A copy of Old's pamphlet can be found in a packet marked October 20, 1955 in box 47, folder 47.06, C. Harrison Mann, Jr., papers, Collection #C0094, Special Collections and Archives, George Mason University Libraries.

18 For Almond's statements, see "Almond Tells Southsiders Not to Yield," *WP*, July 4, 1957, B2; Paul Sampson, "Almond Sees Some Integration," *WP*, October 7, 1957, A1.

19 Senate Document no. 10, *Report of the Commission to Study Industrial Development in Virginia* (Richmond: Commonwealth of Virginia, Division of Purchase and Printing, 1957); "Industrial Hearing Set For Jan. 22," *WP*, January 13, 1957, J6; "Virginia Urged to Pep up Program For State's Industrial Development," *WP*, January 4, 1958, C14; James H. Hershman, Jr., "Massive Resistance Meets Its Match: The Emergence of a Pro-Public School Majority," in *The Moderates' Dilemma: Massive Resistance to School Desegregation in Virginia*, eds. Matthew D. Lassiter and Andrew Lewis (Charlottesville: University Press of Virginia, 1997), 112. William K. Klingaman, *J. Harvie Wilkinson, Jr.: Virginian, Banker, Visionary* (Richmond: Sterling Printers, 1994).

20 Charles H. Ford and Jeffrey L. Littlejohn, "Reconstructing the Old Dominion: Lewis F. Powell, Stuart T. Saunders, and the Virginia Industrialization Group, 1958–65," *Virginia Magazine of History and Biography* (hereafter cited as *VMHB*) 121, No.2 (2013): 147–168; Hershman, "Massive Resistance Meets Its Match," 112; John C. Jeffries, Jr., *Justice Lewis F. Powell, Jr.: A Biography* (New York: Charles Scribner's Sons, 1994), 150–153; Klingaman, *Harvie Wilkinson*, 87–88.

21 "To Win This War," *RNL*, November 12, 1958, 10; Robert E. Baker, "Shift Seen in Virginia Resistance," *WP*, November 12, 1958, AI; Benjamin Muse, "Some Basis for Solving the Problem," *WP*, November 23, 1958, E2. Muse notes Kilpatrick's changing positions from 1954 to 1959 in "How to Box the Compass Editorially," *WP*, June 21, 1959, E2.

22 Susanna McBee, "Arlington Movement Mobilizing to Resist Shut-down of Schools," *WP*, June 1, 1958, B1; Lester Tanzer, "School Shutdown: It Nears on Virginia Plan to Shut Schools to Avert Integration," *Wall Street Journal* (hereafter cited as *WSJ*), July 26, 1958, 1; Interview with Edmund and Elizabeth Campbell, August 27, 1972; Hershman, "Massive Resistance Meets Its Match," 107–117.

23 Robert E. Baker, "Economic Peril Cited In Closing of Schools," *WP*, December 11, 1958, A17; Josephine Ripley, "Public Schools Important to Industry," *Christian Science Monitor*, June 26, 1959, 22.

24 For Dure's argument and criticism of it, see Leon Dure, "Individual Freedom v. State Action," and Hardy Cross Dillard, "Freedom of Choice and Democratic Values," *Virginia Quarterly Review* 38 (Summer 1962): 400–419. For "color-blindness" in the suburbs, see Nancy MacLean, *Freedom Is Not Enough: The Opening of the American Workplace* (Cambridge: Harvard University Press, 2007), 230.

25 Warren Strother, "Defenders Appeal for School Fight," *Richmond Times-Dispatch* (hereafter cited as *RTD*), May 25, 1959, 1; "Griffin Addresses Defenders Session," *RTD*, May 25, 1959, 1; Susanna McBee, "Defenders Urge General Assembly to Assume Pupil Placement Power," *WP*, April 5, 1959, B3.

26 Robert E. Baker, "School Issue Is Tied to Ballot," *WP*, June 22, 1959, B2; interview with Armistead Boothe, September 14, 1974.

27 "Back Almond in Primary, Group Urges," *WP*, July 10, 1959, A14. For the endorsements of black leaders, see *Norfolk Journal and Guide*, July 11, 1959, and Gene Littwin, "Letter Asks Negroes to Support Incumbent Delegates and Wilson, Noncommittal in 2nd Senate Race," Newport News *Daily Press*, July 10, 1959. For the impact of black voting, see Robert E. Baker, "Negro Vote Activity Spurs Rise in Turnout in the South," *WP*, July 20, 1959, A12.

28 Interview with Henry Howell, August 22, 1974; Alan Draper, *Conflict of Interests: Organized Labor and the Civil Rights Movement in the South* (Ithaca, NY: ILR Press, 1994), 105–106.

29 "Moderation Wins In Virginia," *NYT*, July 19, 1959, E10; "The Tide Turns," *Norfolk Virginian-Pilot* July 16, 1959, 4; Benjamin Muse, "'Phenomenon of Major Proportions,'" *WP*, July 19, 1959, E2.

30 "More Legal Attacks Seen on Virginia Segregation," *WP*, October 11, 1959, A12; "King Sees Integration As Modern Tidal Wave," *WP*, January 2, 1960, A9; Peter Walllenstein, *Cradle of America: Four Centuries of Virginia History*, 2nd ed., rev. (Lawrence, Kansas: University Press of Kansas, 2014), 388–402. Edward H. Peeples describes the rising pace in Virginia of civil rights activity in his memoir, *Scalawag: A White Southerner's Journey through Segregation to Human Rights Activism* (Charlottesville: University of Virginia Press, 2014), 77–85, and Thulani Davis captures it in her novel, *1959* (New York: Grove Press, 1992).

31 Paul Finkelman, "The Centrality of *Brown*," in *Choosing Equality: Essays and Narratives on the Desegregation Experience*, eds. Robert L. Hayman, Jr., and Leland Ware (University Park: Pennsylvania State University Press, 2009), 241.

32 Dr. E.E. Haddock to the author, March 31, 1975 (copy of the bill with commentary on the hearing, including the quote). The bill was killed in the Senate committee chaired by Garland Gray.

33 Robert E. Baker, "Virginians Turn to New Problems," *WP*, July 19, 1959, A1; "Industrial Loan Plan Offered in Richmond," *WP*, January 28, 1960, B4; Paul Duke, "Byrd's Virginia, Land of Balanced Budgets, Torn by Fiscal Feud," *WSJ*, February 16, 1960, 1; Elsie Carper, "New Taxes Are Voted in Virginia," *WP*, March 13, 1960, A1; Ralph F. Reikowsky, "Byrd Machine Spanked By Backers of Almond," *WP*, March 13, 1960, B6; John F. Daffron, "Almond Hits Byrd 'Minority,'" *WP*, March 15, 1960, A17.

34 "Byrd Forces Seen Aiming at Almond," *NYT*, February 7, 1960, 52.

35 "Thomson Sees No Hope of Halting Desegregation," *WP*, April 26, 1961, B4.

36 William Chapman, "Delegates Uphold Tuition Grant Plan," *WP*, February 5, 1964, B1; "Va. Denies Segregation Is Plan's Aim," *WP*, October 13, 1964, B1; "Negroes Attack Virginia Tuitions," *NYT*, December 15, 1964, 48. The two federal cases were: *Green v. New Kent County*, 391 US 430 (1968), and *Griffin v. State Board of Education*, 296 F. Supp. 1178 (1969).

37 Robert E. Baker, "Larger Virginia Banks Asked to Attract Industries," *WP*, January 19, 1962, B2; Baker, "Va. House Ready to Pass Banks Merger Bills Today," *WP*, February 14, 1962, B5; "Bill to End restrictions on Banking Approved," *WP*, February 28, 1962, B3; Meiburg, "Changes In Virginia Banking"; Wessells, *Bank of Virginia*, 133–137; Klingaman, *Harvie Wilkinson*, 89–144.

38 "Unified Virginia Law Proposed on Zoning," *WP*, November 17, 1961, B6; W.L. Gibson, Jr., "Land Use Problems and Rural Zoning in Virginia," *University of Virginia Newsletter*, 36 (May 15, 1960); Robert J. Austin, "The Virginia Supreme Court of Appeals: Career Patterns and the Selection Process," *University of Virginia Newsletter*, 45 (December 15, 1968).

39 See James R. Sweeney, "Bridge to the New Dominion: Virginia's 1965 Gubernatorial Election," forthcoming in *VMHB*.

4

Publicity and Prejudice

The *New York World*'s Exposé of 1921 and the History of the Second Ku Klux Klan

JOHN T. KNEEBONE

I arrived at the history department's building at the University of Virginia in August 1973, expecting to study with Willie Lee Rose, but, unknown to me, she had moved that summer to Johns Hopkins University. The kind people in the department's office suggested that I should talk with Paul Gaston, who was in his office right then. I knocked, we talked, and I left committed to studying the history of the American South with him.

That first semester at Virginia I took Paul's history of the South course and his graduate readings course on the New South. He also taught us about his own heritage at Fairhope, Alabama, and the utopian ambitions of his grandfather and father. We were the rare students of southern history who knew from the beginning of our studies about the influence of Henry George and the single tax on the region, I suspect, but Paul's larger teaching was that alternatives were possible, that the future was open. For students of history, I think that what he taught was to view the past as open, too. If the present and future were not inevitable, then even more do we need historical analysis and understanding.

The South's history could offer warnings aplenty of wrong directions was my first thought, but Paul Gaston taught me another lesson. By that time I had begun work on my dissertation about southern liberal journalists prior to the civil rights movement. He invited me to present to a class he was then teaching on southern liberalism. I spoke that day about the journalists' editorials against the Ku Klux Klan, against religious intolerance, against the exploitation of sharecroppers, against lynching, and so on. Paul waited for me to pause, and then he asked, "John, what were they for?"

That question stayed with me, through the dissertation and the subsequent book. Not only did Paul make the original suggestion that I look into southern liberal journalists, back in my first seminar class with him, but he also subsequently talked up the manuscript with editors at the University of North Carolina Press. I am grateful for his assistance along the way, but I am most grateful for that question. Not what were they against, he asked, but what were they for? Speaking up in opposition was valuable, the question seemed to say, but how will you make things better?

Paul Gaston seemed little interested as a teacher, scholar, and activist in merely pointing out the villains. He taught us about the people who held and exercised power, of course, but he devoted little class time to such groups as the Ku Klux Klan, in all of its incarnations. In retrospect, his influence may explain why I gave little attention to the Klan in my dissertation/book even though the southern liberal journalists I studied had written fierce editorials against the hooded order in the 1920s. When I later came to investigate the Klan (thanks to the fortuitous opening of the American Civil Liberties Union's clipping files at Princeton University while I was there), what aroused my interest was the drumbeat of anti-Catholicism in Klan sources, when I expected to find a roar of racism.

This essay, about the New York World's *well-known exposé of the Knights of the Ku Klux Klan in fall 1921, is an attempt to explain how a distinctly southern organization, paying homage to the white terrorists of Reconstruction (and the film* The Birth of a Nation*), became a national organization waving American flags and attacking Roman Catholics. More important, in the tradition taught by Paul Gaston, the essay contends that the* World's *exposé, and the NAACP's protest that engaged the* World *in the Klan fight, had good effect, contrary to historians' past conclusions. As he always taught, no accomplishments in history are complete or permanent, but the effort to make better alternatives a reality does matter.*

∽

"Secrets of the Ku Klux Klan Exposed By The World." So read the headline atop the front page of the *New York World* on September 6, 1921. Twenty days and twenty front-page stories later, the *World* concluded its exposé with a proud headline declaring "Ku Klux Inequities Fully Proved." By then more than two dozen other papers across the country were publishing the *World*'s exposures, and, as Rodger Streitmatter puts it, "the series held more than 2 million readers spellbound each day." The Knights of the Ku Klux Klan, Inc., had become national news. Most contemporary observers agreed with the *World* that the now-visible Invisible Empire would not survive the attention.[1]

Predictions of the Klan's demise proved premature. Three years later, its leaders claimed a membership of more than two million white, Protestant, native-born, 100 percent Americans. Even if the figures were inflated, by 1924, the second Ku Klan had become, in Kenneth T. Jackson's words, "the most powerful fraternal and nativistic organization in American history."[2]

Historians of the Klan of the 1920s agree, with remarkable unanimity across nearly a century's writing, that a cause-and-effect relationship exists between the *World*'s exposé and the Klan's later prominence. Although rarely giving more than cursory attention to the exposé, they see it and the limited and inconclusive congressional investigation that followed as crucial windfalls of publicity that advertised the Klan to potential recruits across the nation. Such an assumption fits well with new interpretations of the Klan put forward across the past quarter century that have proposed a "populist" Klan, present throughout the nation and largely composed of everyday citizens concerned with prohibition enforcement, public schools, and good government. These scholars argue that local conditions decisively shaped the histories of local units—Klaverns, in Klan parlance—and the *World*'s exposé serves well as the necessary cause to bring the Klan to the locality under study.[3]

There is a matter to be explained, though. The most recent Klan historians do agree with their predecessors that anti-Catholicism was the dominant theme of Klan recruiters, of the Klan press, and of the Klan's political agenda (to the extent that it had one). Yet, the second Klan's origin as a fraternal order that commemorated the Ku Klux Klan of Reconstruction hardly predicts an eventual central theme of anti-Catholicism. Moreover, a main impetus for the *World*'s exposé was an epidemic in summer 1921 of vigilante violence in Texas and other states where the Klan had already spread, yet the "populist" Klan according to recent scholarship was relatively peaceful and, in some places, more often the target of violence than the perpetrator. A reconsideration of the *World*'s exposé is in order, for the exposé and its consequences do help to explain how the racist, vigilante Klan of 1921 became national, anti-Catholic, and political.[4]

There is another and related reason that the exposé deserves closer attention. Historians also agree that expansion strained the Klan's incompetent and corrupt leaders, who, after struggles for power and profit, watched helplessly as the second Klan collapsed as swiftly as it had emerged. As David M. Chalmers put it, "The decline of the Klan as a mass movement in America was its own fault, and nobody else's." Thus, if the *World*'s exposé enabled the Klan to become a mass movement but its own leaders brought it down, the narrative is self-contained. Historians need not devote much attention to the Klan's presumably ineffective, even counter-productive opponents. Indeed, the exposé might serve as a warning to the present. Better to let sleeping bigots lie, the Klan's history seems to say.[5]

The purpose of this essay is not to argue that we should awaken sleeping bigots, but examination of the *World*'s exposé does suggest a more complex and less pessimistic conclusion. The exposé did make the Klan known to the nation, but not as Klan leaders would have preferred. The result was nearly a decade of controversy and debate over the Klan. That controversy is the proper focus for study of the Ku Klux Klan of the 1920s. The Klan survived, and even thrived for a short time, but the exposé was more significant and more consequential than the historians' superficial treatment of it suggests.

To begin, a distinction must be made. As Stetson Kennedy, the man who exposed the Klan after World War II, explained, "publicity and exposure are two very different things." Both do involve making a person, organization, or other commodity known to the public, but publicity seeks to present that commodity in a flattering light, serving the interests of the publicity seeker but not necessarily the public interest. An exposé, on the other hand, exposes to public scrutiny, by means of facts and other pertinent information, and does so with the intention of discrediting the object of scrutiny.⁶

The distinction is important. Long before the exposé, the Knights of the Ku Klux Klan, Inc., employed publicity to attract new members. From the first news story about the founding of the Klan, atop Stone Mountain a century ago, to the hand-drawn advertisement for the Klan, in the *Atlanta Constitution*, as the film *The Birth of a Nation* played there two weeks later, the Klan's leaders set out to make the Invisible Empire visible. Arriving in theaters as the commemorations of the fiftieth anniversary of the Civil War ended on a sustained note of sectional reconciliation, the movie completed the story by eliminating blacks from citizenship. It made the Klan known to white audiences in a positive light, but it slandered African Americans, and they fought back. Someone passed along the Klan's advertisement to James Weldon Johnson, of the NAACP, then at war with *The Birth of a Nation*, who published a column in the *New York Age* warning of this evil fruit of the movie. From the beginning, the Klan's publicity efforts alerted its enemies, too.⁷

Thanks to *The Birth of a Nation*, when Americans thought of vigilantes defending the community they thought of the Ku Klux Klan, and, thanks to World War I, many Americans came to believe that defense of the community justified vigilante violence. Campaigns to eliminate "hyphenated Americans," the disloyal, the slackers, and others deserving of censure resulted in acts of vigilante violence across the United States, with news reports often using the name Ku Klux Klan as a synonym for the patriotic vigilantes. That atmosphere inspired at least two other fraternal orders employing the Klan name to organizing after the war, and in 1918 and 1919 the Imperial Wizard sought aid from the press in distinguishing his incorporated group from both the vigilantes and the copycat organizations.⁸

Then, as most accounts have it, fate took a hand: the Klan's founder and Imperial Wizard, William Joseph Simmons, signed a contract on June 7, 1920, with the Southern Publicity Association to propagate his Klan. The Klan's connection with Edward Young Clarke, partner in the Southern Publicity Association with Elizabeth Tyler, probably came earlier. Clarke and Tyler contracted in January 1920 with the Anti-Saloon League, the pressure group behind the enactment of the Eighteenth Amendment banning the commerce in alcohol, to raise money in the southeastern states to help pay for enforcement of the amendment. Among the numerous organizations in Atlanta signing up to support Prohibition was Simmons's Klan, and it is irresistible to speculate that Clarke saw potential in selling the Klan to the nation's Prohibitionists as a private enforcer of the new law. Nonetheless, Clarke and Tyler waited until the rejection of their proposal to do publicity for the Republican Party in that year's presidential campaign before contracting with the Klan.[9]

Through the summer of 1920, salesmen—Kleagles in Klan parlance—received on-the-job training in Georgia. Clarke then sent the most talented salesmen out to other states in September as King Kleagles, or state sales managers. To publicize the expanded sales campaign, Klan leaders appeared in Houston for the Confederate Veterans' Reunion in early October, where, at a press conference, the Imperial Wizard proclaimed the Klan "a bulwark of loyalty to the flag and the nation." He returned that fall for another address, repeating one he had made to a large audience in Atlanta, as the Klan took off like wildfire in the Lone Star state, with the recruitment pattern suggesting grassroots demand rather than a centralized sales campaign. In late November, Clarke and Tyler produced press releases that met growing interest (and concern) about the Klan with positive publicity.[10]

The Klan's new visibility caused the NAACP to respond with a campaign of negative publicity depicting the Klan as a revival of the anti-Negro terrorist organization of Reconstruction. The black press was the main medium for this campaign, but the NAACP also found an ally in the *New York World*. Walter White, of the NAACP, contacted his friend, Herbert Bayard Swope, the *World*'s executive editor, and Swope arranged for a front-page story on October 10, 1920, reporting the opposition of southern blacks and Catholics to the Klan. Aiding the NAACP's case was the shocking victory in September in the Georgia senatorial primary for Thomas E. Watson, notorious for anti-Catholicism and anti-Semitism, with both Watson and the Klan presented as Georgia products.[11]

The NAACP stepped up the campaign. In December, White wrote to Klan headquarters in Atlanta, describing himself as a former resident of Atlanta interested in becoming a member. He not only received a membership application, but also a personal letter from Edward Young Clarke proposing that he become chief Klan organizer in New York City. White released the correspondence to the newspapers, of course, but Clarke's plans to recruit Klansmen outside the South set off alarms. White and James Weldon Johnson began meeting privately with leaders of Catholic and Jewish organizations to enlist their aid, and passed information along to sympathetic members of New York City's police department. Such a coalition of blacks, Catholics, and Jews was something new, birthed by the Klan. What only a few months earlier had been a bizarre report from the deepest South was also becoming a news story of local interest in New York.[12]

In response, the Klan shifted its publicity strategies. In New York City and other places where opposition existed, the Klan went underground, relying on secrecy and informal recruitment to avoid criticism. Elsewhere, the Klan still employed carefully controlled publicity to shape its image. The same sequence of events recurred in town after town. An attention-getting stunt—a parade of robed Klansmen or a letter mysteriously delivered to the local newspaper—would precede the appearance of an Imperial Lecturer, who, the advertisements declared, would give the truth about the Klan. With local interest aroused but with the Klan controlling all the information, the Kleagle then reaped the harvest of his publicity campaign.[13]

During the first eight months of 1921, the Klan's sales force spread across the nation. Recruitment went well, and on July 2, 1921, Clarke formed a national sales organization, dividing the country into ten Realms under the direction of Grand Goblins, or regional sales managers. By the end of August, Klan membership approached 100,000, and the sky seemed the limit.[14]

In Atlanta, the Klan used its national success to claim respectability. The first annual Klonvocation, or convention, took place on May 6, 1921, and the newspapers reported the presentation of a new house to the Imperial Wizard. Major C. Anderson Wright was there to announce that Simmons had agreed to head an aviator's Klan, the Knights of the Air. Through the summer, local newspapers reported regularly on the Klan's wonderful national expansion and the order's impressive plans for property purchases. When the Klan dedicated Simmons's new house, Klankrest, early in August, Governor Thomas Hardwick himself was there to applaud the hooded order.[15]

By then, investigators from the *New York World* were hot on the trail of the Knights of the Ku Klux Klan, Inc. The *World* had already established itself as an enemy of the Klan, but Herbert Bayard Swope found an exposé attractive for other reasons, too. The newspaper lacked the resources to compete with the *New York Times* for comprehensive news coverage, and the new tabloid *Daily News* had cornered the market on sensation. Swope made the best of the situation with a frugal policy of "selective" news coverage through feature stories on a leading issue of the day. When a disenchanted former Kleagle from Tennessee offered his files to the *World* in early July, Swope jumped at the opportunity. An exposé of the Klan would attract readers, fit the paper's editorial policies, and was within its means.[16]

Despite the financial constraints, the exposé rested on a firm foundation of facts, gleaned, as the *World* proudly declared, from investigation "in more than forty cities in a score of different states." Rowland Thomas, the editor in charge, obtained cooperation and files from the NAACP, and H. E. C. Bryant, a North Carolina native and the *World*'s Washington correspondent, did the same in Atlanta with the Commission on Interracial Cooperation. Charles P. Sweeney, a freelancer who had been covering anti-Catholicism in the South, assisted Bryant, and Thomas also solicited copies of stories, editorials, and other information from anti-Klan papers across the country.[17]

As the publication date neared, the *World* offered its exposé to other papers. Seventeen of them purchased the series of articles, and several others joined after publication began. For some historians, the syndication, the widespread advertising, and the circulation manager's happy report that the *World*'s daily circulation jumped "almost 100,000" seem to contradict the paper's claim of disinterested public service. If profit had been the main motive behind the exposé, the *World* failed to take advantage of its opportunities. When no Atlanta paper seemed willing to carry the exposé, Julian LaRose Harris, of the *Columbus (Ga.) Enquirer-Sun*, requested permission to publish the series if the cost were not too great. The *World* gave its articles to Harris at no charge, as it also did when the *Baltimore Afro-American* made a similar inquiry.[18]

As the Klan became the hottest news story of the day in New York City, William Randolph Hearst's *New York American* began its own exposé, featuring Major C. Anderson Wright, of the Klan's aeronautical auxiliary, the Knights of the Air. Except for what he gleaned during his short stay in Atlanta in May, Wright knew little about the Klan, secret or otherwise. Blazing headlines announced wildly improbable accounts of Klan activities every day for two weeks. Hearst's series had plenty of sensation but almost none of the documentary evidence that made the *World*'s exposé convincing.[19]

The *World* organized its evidence to prove three charges against the Klan. First, it charged that the Klan was a "dangerous secret agency of super-government" and as proof printed the order's oaths of total, secret allegiance and reported dozens of recent acts of vigilante violence by bands of masked men. Second, the *World* charged that the Klan was an agent of religious bigotry and, third, that it incited racial hatred. As evidence of both, it cited the exclusion from membership of all but native-born white Protestants and reprinted the anti-Catholic and anti-immigrant tracts sent to Kleagles for distribution to prospective members. For these reasons, the Klan was "a menace to American life and institutions."[20]

As the exposé began, Swope sent telegrams to "leading men and women . . . prominent in the business and social life of the nation," including every governor, asking for comment on the Klan. Replies, condemning the Klan and praising the *World*, soon accompanied the exposé. The *World* also reprinted boasts from the Klan's publicity literature that various public officials had joined the order, and those reports provoked denials—some less convincing than others—from every person identified. Local papers began reporting the charges and denials, too. As the *World* marshalled opposition to the Klan and stripped away its claims to respectability, the exposé changed from a syndicated series of feature articles into a national investigation of the Klan.[21]

The Klan's salesmen, in particular, found themselves under uncomfortable scrutiny. The *World* published an official roster of the national Klan salesforce on September 9, 1921, and the repercussions were immediate. Nervous Grand Goblins and King Kleagles tried unsuccessfully to avoid the reporters begging for interviews, and the Kleagles headed for cover. On September 11, the *World* reported that the Klan's Midwestern office in Chicago—only a month before, the fastest growing Domain of all—was "almost deserted."[22]

Two weeks after the exposé began, the story suddenly exploded onto the front pages of newspapers everywhere. On September 19, the *World* and the *Atlanta Georgian* reported that two years earlier, Edward Young Clarke and Mrs. Elizabeth Tyler, heads of the Klan's sales force and the forces behind the Imperial Wizard's throne, had been arrested together late at night and charged with disorderly conduct and violation of the liquor laws. Headlines shouted the scandal: "Clarke and Mrs. Tyler Arrested While In House of Ill Repute."[23]

The *Houston Chronicle* refused to publish the syndicated article, explaining that its opposition to the Klan was "based solely on the issues involved and not on the personal acts of Klan officials."[24] The revelation did not advance the themes of the exposé, but nor did it violate its nature. From the beginning, the "issues involved"—the illegitimacy of vigilante violence and the exploitation of prejudice for profit—were bound up with the exposure of Klan secrets. The *World*'s intention to discredit the Klan then reinforced and justified exposure for the sake of exposure. Publication of Clarke's and Tyler's troubles with the law served that purpose, even though it did not contribute directly to educating the public on the main issues involved.

In fact, an exposé, by its nature, is not a straight forward vehicle for changing mass opinion. With the goal of branding the object of scrutiny a deviant, an exposé implicitly champions presumed community standards that the deviant has violated. For example, when the *World* condemned the Klan's prejudices, it condemned attitudes omnipresent in American culture, yet the strategy of exposé led the *World* to assume general condemnation of the bigotry, rather than trying to change those attitudes directly.

Instead, the exposé primarily mobilized elite opinion against the Klan. Developments in Atlanta measure the *World*'s achievement. Well into September, the city's newspapers ignored the exposé but reported every statement issued from Klan headquarters. A *World* correspondent interviewed "at least fifty leading citizens" and reported they were afraid of the Klan. "They will talk in confidence," he wrote, "but they dare not come out in the open." The silence in Atlanta outraged the editors of the *Columbus (Ga.) Enquirer-Sun*, who had been attacking the Klan for more than a year. Advertisements appeared in the Atlanta newspapers, announcing that the *Enquirer-Sun* would carry the *World's* exposé. "Back numbers sent on request, if desired," the ad said, "and sent *free* if you don't want the truth any other way."²⁵

The story grew larger. Reporters discovered that someone at police headquarters had destroyed all records of the arrests of Clarke and Tyler. That evening Klan supporters on the city council passed a resolution petitioning the *World* to investigate the Knights of Columbus because the Catholic fraternal order was a much greater menace to the nation. Then, the *Searchlight*, the Atlanta Klan's weekly newspaper, hit the streets with a bloodthirsty, front-page editorial exhorting patriotic Protestants to unleash the dogs of war to stop the Catholic conspiracy against the Klan. The *Atlanta Georgian* decided to carry the exposé, too.²⁶

The appeal to anti-Catholicism was the Klan's last resort (but soon to be its main focus). At first, Klan leaders brandished threats of libel suits against all the newspapers involved, but the *World* continued publishing and dared the Klan to sue. Then the Imperial Wizard announced that when the *World* finished the Klan would answer all charges with its own series of articles. Finally, as it became clear that the Klan could not dispute the accuracy of the *World's* articles, Klansmen began making the charge that the exposé was the product of a Roman Catholic conspiracy. In Texas, the *Houston Chronicle* and the *Dallas News* received so many letters making this accusation that their editors felt compelled to report the religious affiliations of their editorial staff members.²⁷

The nation's anti-Catholics—organized before World War One through the Guardians of Liberty and the Knights of Luther, and with newspapers like the *New Menace* and the *Rail Splitter* urging on the Klan—became the second Ku Klux Klan's core constituency. Indeed, Otis L. Spurgeon, anti-Catholic lecturer and organizer prior to the war, appeared on the *World's* list of Klan salesmen as King Kleagle of Minnesota. Will W. Alexander, of the Commission on Interracial Cooperation in Atlanta, was a close observer of the Klan. In June 1922, he explained to a friend that "the Ku Klux Klan would have collapsed after the New York World exposé but for the fact that they almost completely changed their appeal from the anti-Negro and anti-foreign appeal to an anti-Catholic appeal."²⁸

As the Klan's anti-Catholicism came to the fore in Atlanta, that city's silent elite finally spoke up. "Intolerance and prejudice is harming Atlanta," the *Georgian* warned, and the *Atlanta Journal* declared that "it is high time to end this harmful intolerance." On Sunday, September 25, several prominent local ministers delivered sermons against religious bigotry, and soon thereafter the Evangelical Ministers' Association passed a resolution to the same effect. Civic associations, including the Rotary, Civitan, Kiwanis, and Lions Clubs, similarly condemned intolerance. These were conservative editorials and resolutions, expressing concern that that Klan, and the notoriety brought by the *World*'s exposé, threatened the city's economic and social stability. The *Constitution*, for example, appealed to "the conservative, thinking people" with the story of a local Catholic manager for "one of the great business concerns of America," who intended to close the Atlanta branch office because of anti-Catholicism.[29]

This turn against the Klan in Atlanta was in keeping with the purpose of the *World*'s exposé. As indicated by Swope's telegrams asking prominent persons to comment on the Klan, the *World* sought to mobilize opinion leaders, the nation's elite, against the Klan. By doing so, despite its claim to be a defender—and outside the law, if needed—of the community's values, and despite its recruiters' claims that the "best citizens" joined the Klan, the *World* pushed the hooded order outside the bounds of respectability. The recent local studies of the Klan, all with starting points after the *World*'s exposé, agree that local elites did not join the Klan. Moreover, they find a "populist" spirit within these local Klans that often challenged the power of those local elites.[30] It is irresistible to propose that the absence of local elites from local Klan membership rolls stemmed at least partly from the exposé's effects.

The inconclusive congressional investigation that followed proved an anti-climax. Declaring that Klan violence—the main danger from the hooded order, according to the exposé—fell under state and local jurisdiction, the House Rules Committee rejected a "wide field of discovery" and limited the hearings primarily to the question of whether the Klan had violated Post Office regulations. Then Major C. Anderson Wright repeated his exaggerations from the *New York American*'s exposé. His testimony, contradicted by other witnesses, tainted the sounder testimony of the *World*'s Rowland

Thomas and weakened the case against the Klan even before the Imperial Wizard took the stand. In the performance of his life, Colonel Simmons denied everything, denounced his enemies, and dramatically ended his statement by collapsing to the floor in a faint. The congressmen than closed their investigation without recommending any action against the Klan. The hearings fizzled out, and the Klan survived.[31]

On his return to Atlanta, the Imperial Wizard declared himself "entirely satisfied with the result from a Klan standpoint."[32] His statement raises history's final question about the *World*'s exposé. Newspapers everywhere, including at least a dozen from Georgia, published editorials condemning the hooded order, and yet Klan leaders continued to issue brave statements insisting that the exposé was excellent advertising and that applications for membership were pouring in. Did the *New York World*'s exposé backfire? Did it help the Klan by giving publicity to prejudice?

In fact the exposé had come at a most vulnerable time in the Klan's short career. The Klan actually consisted of several hundred local Klaverns, scattered across the country, linked together only by the Kleagles, King Kleagles, and Grand Goblins of Edward Young Clarke's sales force. Clarke's notoriety in the wake of the *World*'s revelations made him the Klan's greatest liability at the same time that his propagation department was necessary for its survival.

Klansmen elsewhere disagreed that Clarke was indispensable, and soon a revolt broke out. It began among Chicago's twenty thousand Klansmen (nearly a quarter of the order's total membership) when the Grand Goblin of the Great Lakes Domain tried unsuccessfully to oust Clarke. As recruitment and income lagged, Grand Goblins in four other Domains soon joined the rebellion, and telegrams of support from Klansmen across the Midwest and Northeast testified to its seriousness. The Grand Goblins' revolt reshaped the Klan. Before the exposé, the Klan had reported swiftest expansion north of the Mason-Dixon line; the exposé stalled that expansion, and the revolt brought it to a dead halt.[33]

Nine months after the exposé, in June 1922, the *New York Herald* reported on the "waning strength of the Klan," with capsule descriptions of the Klan's health in twenty-six states, including several where the Klan later did grow strong. In the rebellious Great Lakes Domain, the Illinois

Klan was "unimportant and inactive," and the Indiana Klan "inconsequential and decaying." In the rebellious Atlantic Domain, Pennsylvania had "unimportant, sporadic activity," New Jersey was "weak and lapsing," and in New York, the Klan was "negligible or non-existent." Reports of local Klan activities—some twelve hundred of them—published during 1922 in the *Searchlight*, the Atlanta Klan weekly, elaborate the same pattern. In the Midwest and the Northeast, the Klan experienced a difficult year after the exposé.[34]

Most of the reports of Klan vitality came from the Western Domain, especially from Texas, one of the few states where Klan organizing had passed beyond the initial stages before the *World's* exposé. Nonetheless, there are indications that the exposé had effects there, too. Texas Klan leaders tried to halt the vigilante violence that had figured so prominently in the exposé, as they turned to state politics. As the Klan itself became the issue in Texas politics, the Klan press there displayed the anti-Catholicism characteristic of the post-exposé Klan. By embracing anti-Catholicism, the Klan also entered into politics, taking up issues such as Prohibition enforcement and Bible reading and prayers in public schools that anti-Catholic activists had long favored. For example, the passage in fall 1922 of legislation by referendum in Oregon making attendance to the public schools mandatory was credited to the Klan's influence, even though the Oregon Federation of Patriotic Societies first brought the issue forward.[35]

The relationship between the exposé in 1921 and the Klan's large membership in 1923–1924, therefore, must be judged an indirect and complicated one at best. The immediate effect of the exposé was to stall recruitment in areas where the Klan later grew strong. Moreover, beginning with the revolt of the Grand Goblins after the exposé, leadership changes and struggles for power continually plagued the hooded order, dismaying Klansmen and discrediting their leaders.

The constant turmoil also ensured that the Klan would remain highly localistic, as recent studies have shown. The Klan of the 1920s did grow powerful in some places at some times, but it never became the potent national organization that its leaders sought and its opponents feared. Finally, the *World's* exposé shows that understanding the Klan controversy of the 1920s is impossible without closer attention to the Klan's opponents. Publicity and prejudice is not the whole story.

Notes

1. *New York World*, September 6, 1921; Rodger Streitmatter, *Mightier than the Sword: How the News Media Have Shaped American History* (Boulder, CO: Westview Press, 2016), 90–104 (the quoted phrase is on page 93). Streitmatter follows the historians in assessing the consequences of the exposé: "the *World* soon discovered that its bold campaign had backfired" (94). He rates the later anti-Klan campaigns of the *Memphis Commercial Appeal* and the *Montgomery Advertiser* as more successful, both of which also won Pulitzer Prizes. A Wikipedia site, https://en.wikipedia.org/wiki/New_York_World_Expos%C3%A9_of_the_Ku_Klux_Klan#cite_ref-NYW_1-18, provides a synopsis of each day's articles.
2. Kenneth T. Jackson, *The Ku Klux Klan in the City, 1915* (New York: Oxford University Press, 1967), 251.
3. On the supposed direct connection between the exposé and the Klan's large membership, see, for example, John Moffat Mecklin, *The Ku Klux Klan: A Study of the American Mind* (New York: Harcourt, 1924), 10–13; Emerson H. Loucks, *The Klan in Pennsylvania: A Study in Nativism* (Harrisburg, Pa.: Telegraph Press, 1936), 21–23; Arnold S. Rice, *The Klan in American Politics* (Washington: Public Affairs Press, 1962), 7–8; Charles C. Alexander, *The Klan in the Southwest* (Lexington: University of Kentucky Press, 1965), 9–10; David M. Chalmers, *Hooded Americanism: The First Century of the Ku Klux Klan, 1865–1965* (Garden City, N.Y.: Doubleday, 1965), 38; Jackson, *Klan in the City*, 11–12; Wyn Craig Wade, *The Fiery Cross: The Ku Klux Klan in America* (New York: Simon and Schuster, 1987), 160–162; Richard K. Tucker, *The Dragon and the Cross: The Rise and Fall of the Ku Klux Klan in Middle America* (Hamden, Conn.: Archon Books, 1991), 25–26; Shawn Lay, "Introduction: The Second Invisible Empire," in Lay, ed., *The Invisible Empire in the West: Toward a New Appraisal of the Ku Klux Klan of the 1920s* (Urbana: University of Illinois Press, 1992), 8; Nancy MacLean, *Behind the Mask of Chivalry: The Making of the Second Ku Klux Klan* (New York: Oxford University Press, 1994), 5; Rory McVeigh, *The Rise of the Ku Klux Klan: Right-Wing Movements and National Politics* (Minneapolis: University of Minnesota Press, 2009), 21–23; Craig Fox, *Everyday Klansfolk: White Protestant Life and the KKK in 1920s Michigan* (East Lansing: Michigan State University Press, 2011), 45; Thomas R. Pegram, *One Hundred Percent American: The Rebirth and Decline of the Ku Klux Klan in the 1920s* (Chicago: Ivan R. Dee, 2011), 9–10; Dale W. Laackman, *For the Kingdom and the Power: The Big Money Swindle That Spread Hate Across America* (Chicago: S. Woodhouse Books, 2014), 227–228; and William Rawlings, *The Second Coming of the Invisible Empire: The Ku Klux Klan of the 1920s* (Macon: Mercer University Press, 2016), 130–135. John Craig, *The Ku Klux Klan in Western Pennsylvania, 1921–1928* (Bethlehem: Lehigh University Press, 2015), 5, dissents from this consensus, concluding that if the exposé was invaluable publicity for the Klan, evidence for that conclusion is lacking in western Pennsylvania (5).
4. Of anti-Catholicism, David M. Chalmers says, "it was this more than anything else which made the Klan" (*Hooded Americanism*, 33). See also, for instance, discussions

in Mecklin, *Ku Klux Klan*, 157–158; Stanley Frost, *The Challenge of the Klan* (Indianapolis: Bobbs-Merrill Company, 1924; reprint: New York: AMS Press, Inc., 1969), 102–103; Richard K. Tucker, *The Dragon and the Cross: The Rise and Fall of the Ku Klux Klan in Middle America* (Hamden, Conn.: Archon Books, 1991), 3–5; MacLean, *Behind the Mask of Chivalry*, 95–97; Shawn Lay, *Hooded Knights on the Niagara: The Ku Klux Klan in Buffalo, New York* (New York and London: New York University, 1995), 77–78; Pegram, *One Hundred Percent American*, 69–78. On the Klan violence in Texas in summer 1921, see, for instance, William G. Shepherd, " A Nightgown Tyranny," *Leslie's Weekly*, 133(10 September 1921): 331. The most important statement of the "populist" interpretation of the Klan is Leonard J. Moore, "Historical Interpretations of the 1920s Klan: The Traditional View and Recent Revisions," in Lay, ed., *The Invisible Empire in the West*, 17–38 (the essay originally appeared in *Journal of Social History*, 24[Winter 1990]:341–357). Nancy MacLean developed a different conception of the Klan's "populism" in "The Leo Frank Case Reconsidered: Gender and Sexual Politics in the Making of Reactionary Populism," *Journal of American History*, 78 (December 1991): 917–948. Dissenters on the issue of relative Klan non-violence include McLean, *Behind the Mask of Chivalry*, and Craig, *Klan in Western Pennsylvania*, xiii-xiv.

5   Chalmers, *Hooded Americanism*, 299.

6   Stetson Kennedy, *The Klan Unmasked* (Tuscaloosa: University of Alabama Press, 1990; originally published in 1954), 188.

7   "Klan Is Established With Impressiveness," *Atlanta Constitution*, November 28, December 7, 9, 1915; James W. Johnson, "Where Will It All End?" *New York Age*, December 16, 1915. MacLean, *Behind the Mask of Chivalry*, notes that Henry Lincoln Johnson, black Republican leader in Georgia, on December 9, 1915, "begged the governor to make the order change its name, on the grounds that the Klan's re-establishment would encourage 'mob outlawry'" (13).

8   Contemporary observer Walter Lippmann wrote in *Public Opinion* (New York; Harcourt, Brace, and Company, 1922), 92: "the Ku Klux Klan, thanks to Mr. Griffiths [sic], takes vivid shape when you see the *The Birth of a Nation*. Historically it may be the wrong shape, morally it may be a pernicious shape, but it is a shape, and I doubt whether anyone who has seen the film and does not know more about the Ku Klux Klan than Mr. Griffiths, will ever hear the name again without seeing those white horsemen." Actions by patriotic vigilantes, which received the generic label of Klan in press reports, occurred throughout the nation during 1917 and 1918: Cincinnati (October 29, 1917, *Quincy (Ill.) Daily Journal*); Tulsa (November 10, 1917, *New York Journal*); Altus, Okla. (March 20, 1918, *Fort Worth Record*); Wisconsin (March 22, 1918, *Chicago Tribune*); Tulsa (April 11, 1918, *Pittsburgh Sun*); Salinas, Cal. (April 12, 1918, *San Francisco Chronicle*); Oakland, Richmond, and San Jose, Cal. (May 3, 1918, *New York Times*); Duval County, Fla. (June 18, 1918, *New York Age*); Gadsden, Ala. (July 25, 1918, *El Paso Herald*). The reports of vigilante actions are discussed in Littell McClung, "Ku Klux Klan Again In The South," *New York Times*, September 1, 1918. Two of the fewer than a dozen Klaverns of the Knights of the Ku Klux Klan, Inc., were located in Birmingham and Montgomery, Alabama, and Klansmen in both cities struggled publicly to distinguish themselves from the local patriots in robes (on Birmingham, see *New York Tribune*, May 9, 1918; *Atlanta Constitution*, May 9, 12, 1918; on Montgomery, see *Montgomery Advertiser*, September 22, October 13, November

23, 1918). One Klan group, the Soveren Klan of the World, Columbian Union, was founded by Jonathan B. Frost, a former Klan organizer, and legal conflicts with Frost established W. J. Simmons's copyright ownership of the name and imagery of the Klan and forced Frost to drop the Klan references from his fraternal beneficiary order, but not before his organizers had aroused African Americans to fight the Klan (see, for instance, *Richmond Planet*, July 15, 1919, and *Washington Post*, July 31, 1919; the legal battle with Frost was finally settled in October 1920, as Simmons's Klan began to organize, see *Tulsa Daily World*, October 17, 1920). The other Klan, the Loyal Order of Klansmen, was founded in North Carolina by A. B. Ritchie, a vaudeville strongman and organizer, in 1919 but it received a harsh reception from Governor Thomas W. Bickett and soon disappeared [see "Loyal Order of Klansmen—A Very Foolish and a Very Wicked Order" (June 30, 1919), in R. B. House, ed., *Public Letters and Papers of Thomas Walter Bickett, Governor of North Carolina, 1917–1921* (Raleigh: Edwards and Broughton Printing Company, 1923), 289–291].

9   Historians of the public-relations profession have given some attention to Clarke, Tyler, and the Southern Publicity Association. See Scott M. Cutlip, *The Unseen Power: Public Relations: A History* (Hillsdale, NJ: Erlbaum Associates, 1994), 372–413, and Laackman, *For the Kingdom and the Power* ("a story of two brilliant marketing executives who, in the early days of the twentieth century, used their collective genius to spread hate across America" [i]). Simmons and Clarke had opportunities in Atlanta to meet prior to 1920. For example, in 1916 Clarke organized a local "preparedness parade," where Simmons's Klan made an early public appearance, by which, the *Atlanta Constitution* reported on July 5, 1916, "they showed just what they think 'preparedness' means." Clarke was in charge of raising funds in the southeastern states for the Anti-Saloon League to use for enforcement of the new Prohibition laws, as neither Congress nor the states had appropriated moneys enough to stop illegal commerce in booze. "Last Rites of Late John Barleycorn Thursday Night," *Atlanta Constitution*, January 11, 1920. See also *Edgefield (S.C.) Advertiser*, January 7, 1920; *Laurens (S. C.) Advertiser*, January 14, 1920; *St. Petersburg (Fla.) Independent*, January 23, 1920). On the lack of funding for Prohibition enforcement, see Thomas R. Pegram, *Battling Demon Rum: The Struggle for a Dry America, 1800–1933* (Chicago: Ivan R. Dee, 1998), 150–161, and Daniel Okrent, *Last Call: The Rise and Fall of Prohibition* (New York: Scribner, 2010), 109–114, 131–145. On Clarke's and Tyler's negotiations with the Republican Party, see Marion Monteval, *The Klan Inside Out* (Claremore, Okla.: The Monarch Publishing Co., 1924; reprint Westport, Conn.: Negro Universities Press, 1970), 161–166 (Tyler may have been active in the party on her own, too. See "Progressive Stand Worries G. O. P. Here," *Atlanta Constitution*, February 3, 1920).

10 *Houston Post*, October 9, 1920; *Houston Observer*, October 9, 1920; *Atlanta Constitution*, October 10, 1920; *Dallas Express*, October 16, 1920; *Atlanta Constitution*, November 8, 1920; *Houston Post*, November 27, 1920; *New York Tribune*, November 27, 1920; *New York World*, November 27, 1920; *Washington Post*, November 29, 1920; *New York Tribune*, December 15, 1920; *Washington Herald*, December 28, 1920. On early organizing in Macon, see *Atlanta Constitution*, August 14, 1920; in Savannah, see *Christian Recorder*, September 2, 1920; in Florida, see *Washington Bee*, September 11, 1920.

11 "Ku-Klux Klan Is Resurrected in Nine States of South under Charter from Georgia

Court," *New York World*, October 10, 1920. See also, E. J. Kahn, Jr., *The World of Swope* (New York: Simon and Schuster, 1965), 240–241, and James Boylan, *The World and the 20's: The Golden Years of New York's Legendary* Newspaper (n.p.: The Dial Press, 1973), 61. The venerable news weekly, *The Outlook*, opined after Watson's victory that "his success does not promise much for progress in his state" ("The Primary Results in Georgia," *The Outlook*, September 22, 1920, p. 130).

12 Report of the Field Secretary, for December 1920 meeting of the Board, NAACP Papers, Library of Congress, I, R4, F120; Walter White, *A Man Called White: The Autobiography of Walter White* (New York: The Viking Press, 1948), 53–55.

13 J. Q. Nolan, of Atlanta, was an early and popular Imperial Lecturer, who lectured throughout North Carolina in spring and summer 1921 on the themes of white supremacy and the Klan's role in preserving it. In North Carolina, in May 1921, his theme was white supremacy, and the NAACP, he thundered, was the nation's greatest menace. (*Durham Morning Herald*, May 22, 1921. In July, at Hickory, North Carolina, Nolan inspired the unidentified reporter: "Col. Nolan, besides bringing a message, had a flow of oratory that ascended into the uttermost limits of the starry horizon, placing an apostrophe here, another there. . . . He shed oratory." Nolan told his audience that the Klan favored white supremacy, Americanization of all immigrants, and public offices open only to white, Protestant, gentiles. (*Hickory Daily Record*, July 13, 1921).

14 "Clarkes' Own Roster Shows 'Kleagles' In Nearly All States," *New York World*, September 9, 1921.

15 "Big Parade Held by Ku Klux Klan," *Atlanta Constitution*, May 7, 1921; "Hardwick Lauds Klan Principles," *Atlanta Constitution*, August 7, 1921.

16 Alfred Allen Lewis, *Man of the World: Herbert Bayard Swope* (Indianapolis: The Bobbs-Merrill Company, 1978), 82, 92–94. The Kleagle subsequently told his story in book form: Henry P. Fry, *The Modern Ku Klux Klan*, (New York: Negro Universities Press, 1969; orig. published 1922).

17 On Bryant, see http://ncpedia.org/biography/bryant-henry-edward-cowan. On Sweeney, see Charles P. Sweeney, "Bigotry in the South," *Nation*, 112 (November 24, 1920):585–586; "Bigotry Turns to Murder," *Nation* 113 (August 31, 1921): 232–233. Louis M. Spaulding, secretary of the NAACP chapter in Newport News, Virginia, sent a purloined roster of the Klan there to NAACP headquarters in New York, and White sent it on to the *World* to use in the exposé. The paper did not publish the list and returned it to White, who then (unfortunately) returned it to Spaulding. See Spaulding to James Weldon Johnson, September 25, 1921; Spaulding to Johnson, October 2, 1921; White to Clarence Snyder (*New York World*), October 14, 1921; White to Spaulding, October 24, 1921, NAACP Papers, 312, group I, series C, administrative file.

18 "Klan Exposé Wins Readers," *Editor and Publisher*, 54 (September 17, 1921): 15. Newspapers in the following states carried the exposé: CA, GA (2), IN, LA, MA, MN, MO, NY (2), OH (4), OK, PA, TX (3), WA, WI. See *Columbus Enquirer-Sun*, September 10, 1921; *Baltimore Afro-American*, September 16, 1921.

19 "Headquarters Goblin Exposes Ku Klux Klan! Sensational Developments! See Later Editions of the American," *New York American*, September 15, 1921.

20 The first quoted phrase is from the *World*'s statement of its purpose in the exposé, as

printed in *Syracuse (N.Y.) Herald*, September 7, 1921. Second phrase, *Syracuse Herald* and *Galveston News*, September 18, 1921, and *Fort Wayne News Sentinel*, September 19, 1921.

21   See, for example, telegram, Swope to Governor Westmoreland Davis, September 22, 1921, Governor's Office Papers, box 18, "Newspaper Interviews" file, Library of Virginia.

22   *New York World*, 9, September 11, 1921.

23   The *Atlanta Georgian*. September 21, 1921, reported that on their arrival in Atlanta all 500 copies of the *World* with the story about the arrests had been immediately purchased by parties unknown. Clarke's initial statement, quickly retracted, had it that his estranged wife caused the arrests to harm him. It does seem likely that the arrests, whether inspired by vengeance or to provide a cause for a divorce, reflected Clarke's marriage woes and not a sexual relationship between him and Tyler. (See *Atlanta Constitution*, September 20, 1921.)

24   "2 Imperial Offices of Klan Resign; Deny Misconduct Charges," *Houston Chronicle*, September 22, 1921.

25   "Secrets of Ku Klux Klan To Be Exposed in Enquirer-Sun, Which Will Publish New York World Articles on the 'Masked Menace' in Full, Beginning Sunday," *Columbus Enquirer-Sun*, September 10, 1921.

26   "Council Asks Investigation Of The Knights Of Columbus," *Atlanta Constitution*, September 20, 1921; "Mutilated Record Probed; Klansmen Allege Attempt To Steal Mailing Lists," *Atlanta Constitution*, September 22, 1921; "Article in Searchlight Written by Hutcheson Claimed To Be 'Treason'," *Atlanta Constitution*, September 24, 1921; "Georgian Joins Enquirer-Sun in Publishing World Exposure of Simmons' Ku Klux Klan," *Columbus Enquirer-Sun*, September 25, 1921. Carl Hutcheson, a member of the Atlanta School Board, and his law partner, J. O. Wood, operated the *Searchlight*. Issues from the paper's first year no longer exist, but at late as June 1921, the paper's focus was on white supremacy. By September 10, 1921, the paper was defending the Klan and embracing anti-Catholicism. See *Atlanta Constitution*, June 2, 1921; *Searchlight*, September 10, 1921.

27   *Dallas Morning News*, September 15, 1921; *Houston Chronicle*, October 9, 1921 (the *Chronicle* also stated that the majority of letters received opposed the Klan). A self-described charter member of the Klan in Norfolk, Virginia, wrote to Louis I. Jaffe, editor of the *Norfolk Virginian-Pilot*, accusing the paper of attacking the Klan while supporting the Catholic Knights of Columbus (Letter, "A Member of the K.K.K." to Jaffe, September 18, 1921, Louis I. Jaffe Papers, 9924-e, box 1, University of Virginia).

28   Letter, W. W. Alexander to Dr. Worth M. Tippy, Birmingham-Southern College, June 12, 1922, Papers of the Commission on Interracial Cooperation, microfilm edition, 1:4, frames 646–647. On pre-World War One anti-Catholicism, see Washington Gladden, "The Anti-Papal Panic," *Harper's Magazine*, July 18, 1914, and Justin Nordstrom, *Danger on the Doorstep: Anti-Catholicism and American Print Culture in the Progressive Era* (South Bend: University of Notre Dame Press, 2003). On Spurgeon, see "Rev. O. L. Spurgeon in Lime Light Again; Tells Ku Klux Secrets," *Cedar Rapids (Iowa) Evening Gazette*, September 26, 1921.

29   "Intolerance and Prejudice Is Harming Atlanta," *Atlanta Georgian* September 24, 1921; "It Is High Time To End This Harmful Intolerance," *Atlanta Journal*, September 25,

1921; "Intolerance Is Deplored by Ministers," *Atlanta Georgian*, September 26, 1921; "Clubs of Atlanta Denounce Spirit of Intolerance," October 5, 1921; "A Challenge to Atlanta's Good Name!" *Atlanta Constitution*, September 25, 1921.

30 See Moore, "Historical Interpretations of the 1920s Klan."

31 Constance Corry, "The Klan Hearings of 1921: A Triumph of One Interpretation of Americanism," *Melbourne Historical Journal*, 15 (1983): 86–107.

32 "Simmons Satisfied With Result of Probe," *Atlanta Constitution*, October 21, 1921. Despite promises of libel suits and a series of articles responding to the exposé, the Klan finally issued a full-page advertisement in a few newspapers declaring victory in "a national fight on this organization by un-American forces." See, for example, *Searchlight*, December 24, 1921.

33 See, for example, "Deposed Goblins Say Klan Is Broken / One of Four Domain Chiefs Who Tried to Oust Mrs. Tyler and Clarke Tells of 'Smash' / Says 18,000 Quit in Chicago / And 3,000, or Entire Membership, Resigned in Philadelphia—Simmons Upholds Clarke," *New York Times*, December 3, 1921. The Klan, on November 26, 1921, distributed a letter in response to the Chicago Klan leaders' open letter, which went to Klans across the country, written by General A. B. Booth, a leader of the United Confederate Veterans in New Orleans, a supposed member of the Reconstruction Klan, and a member of Old Hickory Klan No. 1. (See A. B. Booth to Robert A. Gunn, et al, November 21, 1921, copy dated November 26, 1921, W. D. Robinson Papers, series 1, folder 1, Southern Historical Collection, University of North Carolina.)

34 "Waning Strength of the Ku Klux Klan," *New York Herald*, June 19, 1922. Rory McVeigh, *Rise of the Ku Klux Klan*, used a similar compilation of data from articles in the *Imperial Night-Hawk*, the official Klan magazine that replaced the *Searchlight* after 1923. He writes: "Because the *Imperial Night-Hawk* fulfilled its mission to keep readers informed about Klan events taking place throughout the country, systematic coding of the magazine's content can provide a valuable measure of state-level variation in Klan activity" (11). The same logic should apply to the *Searchlight's* coverage.

35 On Texas, see Alexander, *Klan in the Southwest*, and Norman D. Brown, *Hood, Bonnet, and Little Brown Jug: Texas Politics, 1921–1928* (College Station: Texas A. & M. University, 1984); on Oregon, see Malcolm Clark, Jr., "The Bigot Disclosed: Ninety Years of Nativism," *Oregon Historical Quarterly*, 75 (June 1974): 109–190 (especially 168–172). Mark N. Morris, in "Saving Society Through Politics: The Ku Klux Klan in Dallas, Texas, in the 1920s," (Ph.D. dissertation, University of North Texas, 1997), shows that even though the Klan was well-established in that city, after the exposé, which the *Dallas Morning News* carried, the order became subject to local opposition, and the Klan's newspaper, *The Texas American*, which first appeared in February 1922, devoted its columns, when not filled with anti-Catholicism, to defending the Klan against attacks (107).

5

Triangles of Change

The Southern Regional Council in the Civil Rights Movement

ROBERT J. NORRELL

I dare say that Paul Gaston has had as large an impact on my life as he did over any of the hundreds, maybe thousands, of other students he influenced over his long career at the University of Virginia. I first met him when I took Paul's class in the history of the South in the fall of 1972, my third year at the University. I had discovered my keen interest in history during the previous year and thought that I might have a particular curiosity about Paul's subject. I had grown up in Alabama in the 1950s and 1960s amid the constant conflict of the civil rights movement. My parents argued about it, and I identified more with my liberal-minded mother against my bigoted father. But I did not know exactly what to think about the many race issues of my childhood.

I recall the handsome, well-dressed fellow in his early forties who spoke in a mellow drawl to a large class in Wilson Hall. As I look back over my notebook from Paul's class, I see that his lectures were learned and detached, not didactic or political in the way that I might have expected had I known more about his background at that point. What Paul did for me that fall—a fateful time in my life—was to engage my imagination with the past. I think I was a historian all along, but watching Paul so eloquently explain the nature of slavery, the failings of white attitudes toward African-Americans, the diversity of opinion among people from my part of the world—brought to my consciousness a reality that I wanted to think about and study intensively. Paul's lectures provided me with a model for what I might aspire to with my own mind, morality, and energies.

During that first class, I read The New South Creed, *a relatively new book at the time, and began to appreciate the power of elegant and morally weighted prose. Paul directed me in an individual course of readings in the spring of 1973. I loved writing critical essays for him, because he told me that I wrote well and then reeled off a series of "do's and don'ts" that have guided my prose ever since. When he agreed to oversee my honors thesis, I found my vocation. I wrote about Alabama politics and race in the 1950s, and Paul was so generous in his criticism and praise about it that he gave me consent to pursue an academic career, something that no one in my family had ever attempted or really could imagine. Paul advised me about the prestigious graduate programs in southern history, but then broke the news gently that, while I had been a good undergraduate, I probably wouldn't be accepted into any of them. The consolation was that he could get me into the Virginia program, which was what I wanted all along.*

In the spring of 1974, he and I collaborated on the creation of a twentieth-anniversary commemoration of the Brown decision, for which he arranged the presence of many civil rights activists, all friends of his, to visit the Grounds and talk about the movement and the change it had wrought. It was thrilling for me to meet folks who had made history and talked so brilliantly about it. By the end of this conference, I had spent several evenings in Paul's home on Winston Road, gotten to know the wonderful Mary, and acquired not just a mentor but a hero in Paul Gaston.

I was a mediocre graduate student, but here the consolation was that Paul said I might think about doing a community study of the civil rights movement. For my undergraduate honors thesis, he had sent me to Tuskegee to meet his Southern Regional Council friend Charles Gomillion whose experience in fighting for voting rights in the famous little Alabama town had fascinated me. When I told Paul that Tuskegee was the community I wanted to write about, he shrugged and said it was hardly a typical place but obviously there was a story there. Gomillion turned out to be my next great hero.

I went to Tuskegee in 1977 and took five years to write a short dissertation. When Paul finally got to read most of the manuscript in early 1983, he was complimentary—and relieved that it did not need a lot of line editing. He contacted his great friend Ashbel Green at Knopf, who accepted it for his list six weeks after I defended the dissertation in the spring of 1983. Would that my later publications, none of which had Paul's active sponsorship, had come so easily.

In the ensuing years, Paul has been my great friend, advisor, and confidant. He had changed my life, and he continued to watch over me. He remains my model for the use of the intellect to tell the truth about our world and to use it to make a better place.

The following paper is a tribute to Paul's long commitment to the Southern Regional Council. It attempts to set a framework for thinking about the whole history of the SRC, going from its original purposes through its evolution as the organization responded to events in the 1950s and 1960s. To do that I must spend some brief time on matters related to its founding and then move rapidly through about three decades of SRC's history. Given time and space limits, this paper is more suggestive than authoritative, though it is based on extensive study of the Council's files through 1970.

~

Historians have tended to deal rather harshly with SRC, mainly because of the organization's handling of the segregation issue at its founding. Morton Sosna wrote that for its first five years "SRC maintained a nebulous stand on segregation in the hope of drawing support from people with differing views on the issue" but that it "finally adopted a clear position" in 1949. Patricia Sullivan is similarly critical about the segregation question and characterizes SRC as a continuation of "traditional" southern liberalism whose leaders had become "apologists for the segregation system." Sullivan insisted that there was a new and improved southern liberalism that had "abandoned the notion of 'self-reconstruction'—a defining principle of traditional liberals—as legally, politically, and tactically flawed." When Sullivan discusses a southern liberalism that operated "exclusively within the parameters of a caste system" and that was "mired in fatalism and doomed to powerlessness," she clearly is referring to SRC, in contrast to the politically-active and class-oriented Southern Conference for Human Welfare (SCHW).[1]

Both Sosna and Sullivan fail to consider adequately how the wartime white hysteria and red-baiting inhibited many SRC liberals—and indeed led to the demise of what Sullivan calls the SCHW's "new" southern liberalism. Most whites at the center of SRC's founding believed a public rejection of segregation would doom the organization. This belief was shaped by the intense escalation of racial tensions in the South, the result in large part of growing black protests and willingness to challenge whites in many new contexts. Howard Odum had been struck by this rising tension and had captured it in his 1944 book *Race and Rumors of Race*. He believed the problems that presently concerned SRC were quite specific: "First, we must do something to help in the race problem that will be good for the Negro and, second, we must if possible stem this sure tide of bloodshed that is coming." Virginius Dabney, the Richmond newspaper editor and a longtime liberal, believed that all race relations were "fraught with explosive issues." The black founders of SRC were also divided over whether to condemn segregation openly. Gordon Hancock, a black Virginia college professor, declared that he was more interested in getting "something done than in getting something said." Carter Wesley, the Houston publisher, counseled that "we must be realistic if we are going to accomplish anything in the South," and suggested that SRC's emphasis should be on equalizing opportunities.[2]

The expectation of violence after World War II was based on the memories of 1919 and 1920, when riots swept the nation and lynchings surged. That violence had brought about the original Commission for Interracial Cooperation (CIC), and thus the current, larger war was expected to have a proportionally more violent postwar outcome. Even before the war was over, the Council published a pamphlet, *After the War*, which began with the question, "Do you remember what happened after World War I?" It gave this response: "Unless people of good will are on guard and act vigorously, history may repeat itself after the present war." Accordingly, much of what SRC planned for its postwar effort was aimed at defusing or preventing violence. In 1946 it appeared for a time that the fears of racial violence were warranted. That year the staff investigated the lynching of four African Americans in Monroe, Georgia, and a race riot in Columbia, Tennessee. But in fact such violence soon subsided, and the years after World War II represented a far more peaceful time than the South experienced after the Civil War or World War I.

If the segregation question was left officially unsettled in SRC's early years, the organization moved in its earliest days to work against the main forms of racial discrimination that composed segregation. In late 1945 Guy Johnson listed program matters that focused on improving conditions in black schools, protecting rights for black veterans, obtaining fair employment voting rights for blacks. If the SRC leadership was not willing to set a firestorm over segregation, it was no less committed to addressing the various ways that white supremacy was enforced. SRC still concerned itself with violence that enforced white supremacy. The criminal justice system warranted close scrutiny: In 1947 SRC began a study of the hiring of—and failure to hire—black policemen in southern cities. It published a booklet, *Race and Law Enforcement*, which described proper practices for policemen in dealing with blacks and distributed thousands of copies throughout the region. SRC's focus on the racial aspects of policing would continue for the next two decades.[3]

A movement for inter-racialism had emerged to prevent violence during the war and after. In communities across the United States there had been a big push to establish local interracial councils in the aftermath of the tense summer of 1943. After the riot in Columbia, Tennessee, the Council announced it was "convinced that if there had been a genuine, functioning interracial committee in Columbia the tragedy would never have happened." In each state SRC organized councils of blacks and whites that created connections across the racial divide and expanded the outreach possibilities of the Council's efforts. Interracial work among women, carried forward primarily by white churchwomen, continued in the tradition of the Association of Southern Women for the Prevention of Lynching. In 1949 Dorothy Tilly, a veteran of the anti-lynching crusade, formed a new organization, the Fellowship of the Concerned. The Fellowship made personal appeals to southern authorities for fair treatment to blacks. For example, members would visit the chief of police in their town and give him the Council's booklet, *Race and Law Enforcement*.[4]

The Council recognized from its inception that democratic processes were used to enforce white supremacy. Here it departed from the CIC and took positions that, except for the SRC's leaders general wariness of Henry Wallace and Clark Foreman, were not much different from the SCHW's. Black voting rights had emerged during the war as a primary civil-rights issue. The Council staff monitored the response to *Smith v. Allwright*, both the further attempts of whites to keep blacks out of the Democratic Party and the stepped-up efforts of blacks to get registered. Starting with a 1948 report on black voter registration by the Virginia political scientist Luther P. Jackson, the Council kept close touch with the progress of voter registration throughout the region. Indeed, it was the main source for the situation with black voters until the United States Civil Rights Commission caught up about 1960.[5]

By 1948 the Council had come to embrace the notion that change in southern race relations would probably be imposed from outside. As a result of the war, the role of the federal government in American life was obviously much larger, and thus SRC by 1948 was far more concerned with events in Washington than southern liberals had been earlier. The SRC staff provided assistance to the President's Committee on Civil Rights, appointed by Harry Truman in late 1946. Dorothy Tilly was one of the two southerners on the committee. Guy Johnson briefed the Committee on what his organization thought were the main concerns in the South. Despite intense opposition to the report from most white southerners, the Council publicly endorsed the report and produced a pamphlet that summarized the Committee's findings and recommendations. Thus began SRC's commitment to federal intervention in civil rights, a position that set the organization well outside the white mainstream.

The signs of impending federal intervention only got clearer: On June 5, 1950, the United States Supreme Court delivered three smashing blows against school segregation in the *Sweatt*, *McLaurin*, and *Henderson* decisions. Two months later, George Mitchell told the Council's executive committee that the organization should face the race question squarely and exclusively: "We should be less sweeping in our pretended area of inquiry and action and admit that the thing we can do well is to aid in the unraveling of the knots and cords of racial jealousy that hamper the growth in the South of the modem society." At that point the SRC leadership, and most others committed both for and against civil rights, began looking toward a Supreme Court order overturning school segregation.

Most historians have failed to acknowledge that SRC's more careful positions in the mid-1940s allowed it to survive, whereas SCHW went out of existence in 1948. Indeed, new or not, the only southern liberalism of any significance in shaping events in the 1950s was SRC's. In 1946 and 1947, the Southern Conference for Human Welfare had been a much stronger organization than SRC—more money, more members, and a higher national and regional profile. But by the end of 1948 it had disbanded, a victim of anti-communism and the defeat of its intensively political approach. SRC struggled through that time because it had kept as much distance as it could from radical politics and because it had avoided inflaming enemies over the segregation question. By 1948 SRC had become just as committed as the soon-to-be-defunct SCHW to federal intervention to change race relations, and in three years it would still be in existence when it did take as firm a stand as any white southerner against segregation.

Why did it matter that SRC had survived? The organization stood as a symbol that some whites in the South rejected white supremacy and embraced freedom and equality for black people. The organization's very existence represented an affront to all those who loudly insisted all white southerners supported segregation. SRC's contradiction to that most basic faith of the white-supremacists' creed was in many ways its signal achievement in the coming decade.

That such an organization could exist, that it could survive in the South as an opponent of segregation gave encouragement to important constituencies who would be crucial in overthrowing segregation. First among these constituencies were white southerners, who in order to stir courage needed to be shown that some of their fellows were committed to fundamental change. Second, black southerners were spurred to greater activism by the sense that some whites would support their cause. Third, the white public outside the South was inspired to support forcing change on the South by evidence that some whites already had a true sense of democratic values. Fourth, for much the same reason, philanthropists who wanted to support reform in the South had a dependable, reputable place to invest. Fifth, the national media had in SRC both an anti-segregation source of information and opinion and an example that southerners were not all of one mind in supporting Jim Crow. Sixth, agents of the national government found in

SRC reliable guidance on how to use government constructively to improve human relations in the South.

From its creation through the 1960s, SRC created connections among these constituencies that advanced the cause of civil rights. Although the Council's work was often done in one-on-one consultation between an SRC staff person and a scared liberal in some small town or a foundation executive or a newspaper reporter, its achievement represented larger connections of groups of Americans interested in changing race relations. Think of SRC as the point that closed triangles of thought and action on behalf of civil rights that joined necessary constituencies to bring about a massive change in human relations. The Southern Regional Council functioned as a kind of surveyor of the South in the 1950s that used its own position to draw lines to other groups in order to measure spaces within which a more humane region could be created.

SRC only barely survived during the late 1940s and early 1950s. An attempt to become a broad-based membership organization like the NAACP, to which several hundred thousand persons contributed a dollar every year, brought in only a tiny fraction of what the organization needed to survive. The significant early support came from the General Education Board and the Rosenwald Foundation, the oldest and most reliable funders of race reform in the South. When Rosenwald gave away its assets and closed its operations in 1948, the Council lost its chief benefactor. By then severe financial problems had already hit. By mid-1947 SRC was having difficulty meeting its payroll. In early 1948 SRC was existing in part on borrowed money. George Mitchell cut staff, though one laid-off worker continued to work. In 1949 SRC engaged a professional fundraiser, but with little apparent success. Times were so hard in the summer of 1949 that Mitchell doubted he would make payroll in August, but he stood up to the board when it voted to lay off Dorothy Tilly. In October 1949 SRC did not meet its payroll, and several people were paid and then laid off. In late 1949, Mitchell reported dire conditions to the SRC president: "We had $88.00 in the bank this morning, today is pay day, and the payroll is somewhere around $900.00. We found $40.00 we could deposit; and I took out of my bank the money I was going to use to pay taxes on my house—$200.00. That let us pay the most needed persons, but did not reach the higher salaried ones." In the summer of 1950 Mitchell reported that "we got everybody but me paid August 31," but that "we will be far short of enough to pay out the next thousand September 15."[6]

These difficulties occurred despite heroic efforts on the part of SRC loyalists to find money. Mitchell and Dorothy Tilly always sought financial help as they traveled extensively in their various tasks. Through the late 1940s Will Alexander gave much effort to fundraising, especially among foundations. Virginius Dabney regularly called on potential supporters of the organization. Paul Williams, the Richmond businessman who became SRC president in 1946, traveled constantly for the Council seeking support from religious groups, foundations, and corporations in the Northeast and Midwest.[7]

Several obstacles blocked the best fundraising efforts. SRC's precarious financial situation hurt with potential funders. About the Rockefeller Brothers Fund in 1949, Williams wrote to Mitchell that "they are not keen on giving money to an outfit that might be going out of business." The concern about radicalism in civil rights activism undermined the efforts in other places. In 1949 a corporation executive asked Williams about Clark Foreman and Louis Burnham, two original SRC board members who had been often red-baited for their leadership roles in the Southern Conference for Human Welfare and the Civil Rights Congress. Williams encountered another businessman in Baltimore who "clearly demonstrated his contempt for the Sou. Conf. For Human Welfare."[8]

The more fundamental obstacle was the overall inability to find support in the South. Despite much effort, SRC had little success with southern foundations. Aside from relatively small contributions from religious groups, labor unions, and a few individuals, all the significant support came from outside the South. The Council leadership was convinced by 1950 that anything that addressed race relations would only happen with support from outside the South. Grace Hamilton, the Atlanta Urban League director and SRC board member, declared in early 1951 that a proposed human-relations education was "never going to be carried locally." The Atlanta lawyer Morris Abram agreed that "all our experience shows that you can't" get local support for race-betterment efforts.⁹

By late 1951 the SRC leadership believed its future rode on the Ford Foundation. The death of Henry Ford in 1947 led to the settlement of some $500 million on the Ford Foundation, which made it by the far the largest foundation in the United States at the time. In 1949 George Mitchell was asked his views on what the foundation ought to support, and he gave them a version of his economic and human geography of the South with a strong appeal for help to develop human resources throughout the region. In 1950 he got directly to the point in a letter to the foundation: SRC was "an established southern interracial organization working effectively in the field of human relations within the South," and governed by "the cream of the leadership of both races." With only "the greatest struggle" was the Council able to get $15,000 from within the region and it took $50,000 to $60,000 "to do even as much as we have been doing." He asked Ford for $15,000 for each of three years. The foundation was encouraging but not forthcoming. In late 1951 Mitchell was reluctant even to schedule the SRC annual meeting in the absence of a Ford decision, out of concern that it would become a "liquidation" meeting, because he doubted that Ford would make a decision by the fall. The meeting did go forward, but many SRC leaders feared it would be the last one.¹⁰

As the Council waited on Ford, the foundation spun off a new entity, the Fund for the Republic (FFR), established in 1953, and gave it $15 million and a responsibility to uphold American freedom in the face of the rising tide of McCarthyism. Although many foundations would have a reputation for liberalism and social activism in the late 1960s, in the early 1950s most of the larger ones were extremely cautious about what they would support in the way of social reform. They felt more comfortable funding medical and education activities. But Ford had so much money to give away that it could support many things, and some of its advisers believed strongly some money should go to help uphold political freedom. The Fund for the Republic, which soon came under the direction of Robert Hutchins, the former president of the University of Chicago, was established as a kind of anti-communist opponent of Joseph McCarthy and those who practiced his ruthless style of political conformism. The Fund for the Republic underwrote a number of studies of American radicalism in order to develop a more realistic picture than McCarthy was promoting. But it also began to examine the abuses of power in the congressional hearings process, and it funded human rights and civil rights activities around the country. The Southern Regional Council became the main southern and civil-rights beneficiary of the FFR's largesse when in April 1954 the foundation granted SRC $240,000 to establish a network of state human-relations councils.

Patricia Sullivan interprets SRC's alliance with the Fund for the Republic as its cozying up to McCarthyism, which conclusion she draws by noting the foundation's support of investigations into communism. This completely misconstrues the purpose of FFR, which was in fact attempting to bring some factual understanding about radicalism into the Red Scare. Sullivan missed entirely the larger purpose of FFR in countering McCarthyism. Thus she misinterprets entirely SRC's position with regard to the uses of anti-communism. SRC was in fact saved financially by the one philanthropic endeavor in the United States created to challenge McCarthyism. It was indeed a delicious irony that McCarthyism was the indirect cause of SRC's salvation by instigating the funding source for which the organization had been desperately searching for years.[11]

The Cold War and McCarthyism were otherwise great obstacles to civil-rights activism, as the Council experienced all too frequently in the 1950s. White southerners who opposed segregation had been subject to red-baiting since the 1930s, as the destruction of SCHW and the continuing harassment of the Southern Conference Education Fund and the Highlander Folk School demonstrated throughout the 1950s. After the 1951 declaration against segregation, the Southern Regional Council drew hot fire from segregationists who insisted that the Council was a communist-front group like the SCHW allegedly had been. In 1953 *One Methodist Voice*, a Georgia newspaper, declared that SRC was "honey-combed with leftists, radicals, Communist frontiers"—singling out in particular George Mitchell and Dorothy Tilly, both of whom were staunch Cold Warriors—for their "stubborn program of racial mixture which is obnoxious to Southern Methodists." The next year, with the announcement of the Fund for the Republic grant, Senator Herman Talmadge's newspaper mouthpiece declared that SRC "espouses ideologies completely foreign to the South." The constant reiteration of the charge and the institution of an investigation by the Georgia attorney-general led the Council to require a loyalty oath from its staff in December 1954.[12]

The hostility got even more intense after the *Brown* decision, because any organization that could be associated with the National Association for the Advancement of Colored People (NAACP) was subject to the kinds of harassment that was in fact stopping NAACP activities in many southern places. The White Citizens' Councils in Alabama and Mississippi threatened the Ford Motor Company with boycotts for its support of "integrationism" through the Fund for the Republic. In 1956 the Hearst newspapers reported that virtually the entire roster of the Council's leadership were communists or fellow travelers. The reports clearly were libelous, but to sue the newspapers meant creating more publicity about the communist allegations and making even more precarious the existence of white integrationists in the South. The forces of massive resistance to desegregation heaped scorn on SRC. In 1956 the regional newspaper of the citizens' council movement condemned the Council for accepting money from the "race-mixing" Fund for the Republic. In 1957 the American Legion publication *Firing Line* ran a story under the headline "Red Front" reporting on accusations that SRC was a communist-led organization made by a professional communist hunter before the Louisiana legislature. That same year Thomas Waring of the *Charleston News and Courier* repeated the charge of communism against SRC, and James J. Kilpatrick of the *Richmond News Leader* echoed it. In 1958 and 1959 a professional communist hunter made similar charges to the legislatures of Arkansas and Mississippi.[13]

SRC's connection to the Fund for the Republic turned the organization's history in crucial ways. SRC might well have folded but for the support, especially if one imagines the difficulties of weathering the white-supremacist backlash of 1955–57 without the foundation money. Now SRC had a high-profile foundation that was thus invested in SRC's success. Because FFR had made a major investment, and because this was widely reported in the many stories about FFR's conflict with the pro-McCarthy forces in 1954 and 1955, other foundations were much more likely to be interested in helping SRC. The FFR staff commonly made suggestions to the SRC about other foundations that should be contacted for support—the FFR having already spoken on behalf of SRC to potential new funders. FFR staff would go on to other foundations that would later fund SRC. Out of connections made in the mid-1950s through the Fund for the Republic, SRC executive directors and presidents were able to establish relations with the Field, Stern, Taconic, and Rockefeller Brothers foundations. These would be the main supporters of SRC from about 1958 to 1965.

SRC's connections to philanthropy were often the most important of its triangles because they provided the lifeblood for action. Two examples are most important. The state human-relations councils would not have developed as they did once FFR funding paid full-time staff members in every state. Had they not been viable operations, Harold Fleming and Leslie Dunbar probably would not have found new sources after FFR stopped funding them in the late 1950s. Had they not been established and continually supported, isolated white liberals and black activists would have been far more lonely in segregated southern towns than they were already.

The other good example of the philanthropy triangle was the Voter Education Project (VEP), which was funded initially by the Taconic Foundation, a new and quiet institution that apparently emerged about 1958 when Audrey and Stephen Currier decided to use most of her vast Mellon inheritance for social reform causes. Recommended to the Curriers by the director of another foundation, Harold Fleming established a warm relationship with Stephen Currier and advised his giving until the couple died in a plane crash in 1967. Taconic funded the state councils, SRC operations, and other projects. Stephen Currier was the initial supporter of the Voter Education Project when it was conceived in 1961. Once up and going, Leslie Dunbar persuaded the Field Foundation, the Stem Family Fund, and finally the Ford Foundation to help. The VEP represented a very powerful SRC triangle, because starting in 1962 and continuing through the 1960s, it funded activism in hundreds of southern communities by the Student Nonviolent Coordination Committee, the Congress of Race Equality, SCLC, and the NAACP.

Another of the crucial triangles made connections among the Council, black-run civil rights organizations, and the media. The links had been established as early as 1947. Council membership believed that new ideas and new information could improve the racial attitudes of southerners. SRC emphasized research and dissemination of those findings through its regular publications, first *Southern Frontier* and, starting in 1946, *New South*. In these publications appeared the latest developments on the region's racial front. The most prominent message in *New South* during the postwar years was the march of progress in southern race relations. The editors kept up the refrain that the South had changed, was changing, and would continue to change. It did this, of course, to promote acceptance of change while white-supremacists denounced any change as a threat to the timeless social order of the South.

Under Harold Fleming, SRC adopted a policy of service to the national press on its coverage of race and the South. Fleming made a special effort to provide information to *Time* and *Newsweek* and to assist the Associated Press, which often relied on SRC in stories that were carried widely by southern newspapers. This strategy also worked because in 1947 the *New York Times*, the nation's most influential newspaper, assigned its first full-time correspondent, John Popham, to the South. A Virginian with much affection for the region but with large experience outside the South, Popham immediately began reporting on what he saw as the emerging liberalism of the South. He quickly fastened on to Fleming, like him a World War II veteran with liberal race views, as a source for information and interpretation. Popham began citing the Council as "the South's leading interracial organization" or as "the most effective interracial organization in the South." Fleming recognized that these national media outlets had a positive effect on SRC's influence with the southern newspapers. "It became impossible," he said later, "for the Atlanta papers and other Southern papers to ignore our statements and other publications when they were appearing on the front page of the *New York Times*."[14]

SRC's media triangle served many purposes. It kept the organization's name in front of funders, and it revealed SRC's commitment to racial progress. It helped to encourage the attention of the northern public on southern race relations, especially during the long periods in the 1950s when there was little "breaking" news but when there was a continuing awareness that the South represented a "problem" to the national creed of democratic values. SRC functioned as a kind of think tank for the national media, providing facts and figures as well as analysis of what they meant. Johnny Popham counted on simply to re-write SRC reports in the *Times*. In a less apparent way, SRC served similar functions for the Associated Press, the news magazines, the *Wall Street Journal*, the *Christian Science Monitor*, and a wide variety of other daily newspapers. For all these outlets, SRC was there as an already-established authority on southern race matters when a crisis or big event emerged. When the *Brown* decision was announced, the *Times* quoted three white southerners—Herman Talmadge, Jimmy Byrnes, and Harold Fleming.

The media triangles would become even more important when sit-ins of 1960 sparked five years of sustained direct-action protest. Especially during 1960, when the sit-ins startled most observers, SRC provided crucial interpretation for the national media, much of it through the *Times*'s reporter Claude Sitton. Through much of the 1960s, SRC served as a regular stopping point for many media representatives covering the civil rights movement, because it had the closest approximation to comprehensive information and it was judged to be pro-civil rights but one independent of the protest organizations.

The media triangles were crucial for encouraging observers of the civil rights movement, both North and South, to see the civil rights movement in a positive light. Through its media influence, SRC communicated its assessment that the civil rights protest was a constructive force, when few whites North or South believed that in the early 1960s. Again, SRC affirmed to blacks and northern white liberals that the South could be redeemed. The SRC leadership, like the CIC inter-racialists before them, assumed that race reform would depend on changing how whites thought about human relations. Its media effort contributed to the large transformation that did take place.

SRC served as a vital connection among human-rights organizations. Not much has been written about the civil rights work of the American Friends Service Committee, the American Jewish Committee and Jewish Congress, the Anti-Defamation League of B'nai B'rith, or the American Civil Liberties

Union. All of these groups coalesced with SRC from the late 1940s into the 1960s at some level. It should be noted that the Jewish groups were far more active in their commitments than the Christian denominations, where support for segregation, even among Mrs. Tilley's Methodists and George Mitchell's Presbyterians, far outweighed any help for civil rights. To SRC, the Jewish groups provided money and fundraising advice, information, and fierce determination to help the southerners who were willing to take stands against bigotry. There is a remarkable story in the lengths to which the American Jewish Committee and the Anti-Defamation League, working through Harold Fleming, went to save *The Petal Paper* and its colorful editor P. D. East from the oblivion and bankruptcy intended for him by the White Citizens' Council of Mississippi. Jews North and South seemed especially to understand the fundamental truth that, when it was made clear that not all southern whites were ready to die for segregation, the Jim Crow system was doomed.

The last important triangle to mention was the connection that SRC provided among the federal government and the protest organizations. The organization worked with the newly formed United States Civil Rights Commission from its earliest days in 1958. It advised the Kennedy Administration on what it should do on civil rights as soon as they came to power. SRC's role was crucial in planning the VEP, with which the Kennedy Administration was closely involved. When in 1961 Stephen Currier and Harold Fleming set up the Potomac Institute to shape federal policy on civil rights, SRC's influence was enhanced as Fleming used his years of SRC experience to advise the Kennedys on what to do next. But its position was not as supplicant to federal power. Having been a consistent patriot up to the Albany movement, Leslie Dunbar lambasted the Kennedys for not supporting the pro-civil rights cause in the southern Georgia city. The triangular relationship perhaps helped to elicit a stronger response from the Kennedys after the Birmingham demonstrations in 1963.[15]

The early 1960s marked special years for SRC, as they did for most southerners. SRC's role in establishing the VEP and advising on federal policy decisions and civil-rights protest strategies had so enhanced SRC's position that its function may have changed fundamentally from triangulator—arranger, connector, and interpreter—to being a more central participant in events. Leslie Dunbar believed that by the time he became executive director in 1961 SRC's role had changed from mainly influencing how southerners thought to playing a role in the activism, the protest itself. Paul Gaston, in looking back on events he participated in with the Council, uses the metaphor of the cockpit, as in SRC was the cockpit of the civil rights movement.[16]

The surge of federal action from late 1963 through 1966 kept the Council staff busy advising on new policies. "Our office is a meeting-place of men, organizations, ideas, and programs, Leslie Dunbar, SRC executive director, wrote in late 1964. The signing of the Civil Rights Act of 1964 marked a moment of triumph for SRC, a vindication of the anti-segregation position that the Council had taken, and held to, in 1951. Harold Fleming continued to connect the Council's views to federal policymakers; he became head of the U.S. Community Relations Service and helped to organize the Equal Employment Opportunity Commission. Starting in 1965, the Council addressed President Lyndon Johnson's anti-poverty efforts and the growing emphasis on economic justice from Martin Luther King, Jr. Also starting about 1965, SRC stepped up its concern with school desegregation, which a decade after the *Brown* decision remained very much an unresolved problem. The Council studied the various desegregation issues including busing, the rise of private schools, the inequitable funding of public schools in the Black Belt, and separation by "tracking" of black children in desegregated schools.[17]

In October 1965 the Ford Foundation granted $972,000 to SRC for "evaluation of Federal and state-government programs in the South and technical aid to community groups through affiliated state and local human-relations councils." At the same time, under the leadership of McGeorge Bundy, Ford became heavily focused on programs for inner-city redevelopment in many places in the U.S., all of which represented a ninety-degree turn toward social reform that the main Ford philanthropy had theretofore avoided. Ford announced that the SRC grant would underwrite "studies of federal programs in city planning, fair employment, antipoverty, housing, and school integration, and a second group of studies dealing with state welfare programs, rehabilitation of criminals, penal administration, and unemployment caused by technological change." And it would provide "technical assistance and training to Negro and other groups trying to help themselves through community organizations, credit unions, and agricultural cooperatives; will support training in human relations within Southern labor unions; and will help carry out a program of voter registration."[18]

The 1965 Ford grant represented the beginning of almost a decade of institutional prosperity. More large grants came in succeeding years. The Council embarked on a program of research and project development that emphasized fair employment, fair housing, humane welfare, and the encouragement of cooperatives, credit unions, and labor organizations. Much of the initial emphasis would be on hunger and the failure of welfare programs to provide adequately for the South's poor. The Council staff investigated health issues and discovered a plethora of problems endemic among poor southerners. By 1969 SRC was focused heavily on economic questions in a way it had not been since 1946 when it was still thinking in terms of Howard Odum's regionalism framework. The areas of action were on housing policies and assistance to groups planning low-cost housing; serving as a watchdog over governments; organizing cooperative, economic development groups, community action, and the Appalachian Regional Commission; and manpower issues, especially employment discrimination.[19]

The Ford Foundation's perspective clearly shaped the SRC agenda. In 1971 the foundation announced that it was committed fundamentally to strengthening the black community, which goal was often shortened simply to "empowerment." Its objectives were leadership development, which essentially meant increasing the number of black lawyers, public administrators, journalists, cooperative managers, Ph.D. students, and business school students. In the South that meant development of such new black institutions as the Federation of Southern Cooperatives, Southeast Alabama Self-help Association, and many economic development groups in the Mississippi Delta, at the same time that it continued to fund existing institutions including VEP, American Friends Service Committee, the Lawyer's Committee for Civil Rights, and SRC. Ford declared that the "basic continuing problem in every phase of Southern life" was still discrimination in employment, education, public services, governmental participation, housing, legal services, and justice. In 1971 the federal government actions for civil rights lacked the force of moral leadership and indignation to destroy the sophisticated harassment and re-segregation had taken the place of the formal barriers of segregated schools. "The middle-class Southerner cannot be appealed to rationally as easily today as five years ago," Ford said, "for the rhetoric of the militant young black man, free of his father's inhibitions, frightens white Southerners, and so they close their ears."[20]

The Ford perspective in SRC was intensified more in 1972 when George Esser, a North Carolina political scientist, was named executive director of the Council. Esser had headed the North Carolina Fund, a state-level effort to address poverty that actually operated as a kind of southern branch of the Ford Foundation. In the late 1960s, he became Ford's main representative in the South. He brought to SRC Ford's values and perspective—as well as its money—and pushed the organization toward becoming a missionary outpost of the foundation. To be sure, the Council still received significant funding from the Field and Rockefeller foundations, but the large majority of its support came from Ford. With the advent of President Richard Nixon's "New Federalism" in the early 1970s, the Council undertook, at Ford's encouragement, to monitor the use of federal block grants to states and local governments. The Southern Governmental Monitoring Project examined the administration of the revenue sharing programs; housing program, especially Nixon's 1973 freeze on subsidized housing programs; health programs, including administration of Medicaid and Hill-Burton funds; administration of welfare programs including food-stamp eligibility. The monitoring project would, however, be the last large, Ford-financed project.[21]

In February 1975, Esser reported to the SRC executive committee that an auditor had found that the budget was $382,000 short. Esser explained that the deficit came from failure to be reimbursed from foundations. Apparently he had been using grant funds earmarked for projects to cover general operating expenses, in the full expectation that future grants, from Ford especially, would cover the shortfall. In fact, however, Ford and other foundations were cutting grants as a result of the current recession that was reducing foundation income. Esser reported to the executive board at about the same time that basic operating expenses had doubled in the past two years and that total expenditures were by "500 percent in the two-year period." Also at the time there was an $80,000 deficit from the creation of the new Council's new publication *Southern Voices*. The 1975 financial crisis forced the resignation of Esser, a reduction of other staff, and a curtailment of activities. *Southern Voices* was discontinued. All this resulted in a sharp drop in morale, though at the time the SRC staff was deeply divided over race, gender, and class issues. There was a strong belief that discrimination existed within the staff, and apparently dissension had been a problem for several years.[22]

After years of struggle and then triumph, SRC had lost its clear sense of purpose, and natural divisions and long-muted conflicts came into the open. By this time SNCC and CORE had disappeared, and SCLC and the NAACP were far less potent than they had been in the 1960s. By the 1970s, some questioned whether the South needed an interracial organization like the Southern Regional Council, especially one that had been based so much on the authority of its idealism. As a motivating force for reform, moral idealism depended on contrasting democratic ideals with racial practices, but with improvements in race relations, disagreement arose about what was reality in the South. For every example of poverty or powerlessness or ignorance, someone could offer other examples of new African American achievement. For every person who argued that much work remained to be done to overcome past and continuing injustice, there were others who claimed that our society had been made fair to all in the 1960s and that those who still suffered lacked the character to succeed. To many of those who denied that race remained a problem, reformers in the 1970s and 1980s were not idealists but special pleaders.

The civil rights movement had indeed taken away the most fundamental reason for SRC to exist—to show that some whites opposed segregation in order that integration could come. Now most blacks were registered to vote, and in many states they had cast their ballots for "New South" governors who had publicly disavowed segregation and preached a politics of racial inclusion. What was interracial organization supposed to do in the new, integrated South? Some people believed that SRC should turn from race to matters of gender discrimination. Others thought the Council should become a consumer advocacy organization for the South. Clear and persuasive answers did not emerge soon.[23]

One way to think of SRC's problems is to see that after 1965 the geometry of race reform had changed. Instead of triangles of change, now there were more straight lines of influence that did not always need SRC's participation. So much of its work after 1965 was implementing "empowerment" that the Ford Foundation wanted implemented or enforced—the money came from New York to Atlanta and from there to project to improve economic benefits or political influence for African Americans, or to check whether federal money was being spent correctly. These activities required far less of the mediating influence that established new and better human relations than it did of unilateral aid to empowerment or hard-nosed scrutiny about how federal money was being spent. One of the fundamental things about empowerment for black people was that they did not have to listen to or coalesce with whites, and many simply refused to do so.

SRC had made fateful decisions in the late 1960s that undermined its ability to continue to make triangular connections with its constituencies in the southern states. In about 1969 SRC resolved not to continue supporting state councils. At about the same it separated the VEP from SRC because of concerns that a new tax law had meant that participation in voter registration would endanger the Council's tax-exempt status. Both of these decisions, made at the encouragement of Paul Anthony, the executive director, cut the organization off from its broader regional constituency.[24]

Triangulation may have been less necessary because government was doing so much more, but most of the tripartite connections were occurring in Washington, D.C., not Atlanta. The historian Hugh Davis Graham has described the emergence of a regulatory "subgovernment" of civil rights composed of the Office of Federal Contract Compliance and the Equal Employment Opportunities Commission, which enforced Title VII of the Civil Rights Act; the Commission on Civil Rights, which frequently reported on the efforts, and especially the failures, to enforce civil rights laws; the Civil Rights Division (CRD) of the Justice Department—and the Voting Rights Section within the CRD—which enforced the Voting Rights

Act of 1965; the Office of Civil Rights within the Department of Health Education and Welfare, which implemented school desegregation; and the corresponding offices for civil rights in the Defense Department, Housing and Urban Development, and soon in all eleven cabinet departments.

Outside the executive branch, but monitoring and working with this civil-rights sub-government, were two other concentrations of power. One was the civil rights organizations that represented constituents to be protected by the agencies-the NAACP, the Urban League, and the Leadership Conference on Civil Rights, which was a broad consortium of pro-civil groups including organized labor and foundations. The other concentration existed in Congress. It included congressional oversight and funding subcommittees like the House Judiciary Subcommittee on Civil Rights Oversight. In 1971 the Congressional Black Caucus was formed. Graham asserts that by 1972 an "iron triangle" of power connected executive agencies that ran programs and enforced policies with the congressional committees that oversaw and funded them and the constituent groups that benefited from the policies and campaigned for their continuation and expansion.[25]

Changes in the national media also made more difficult the Council's ability to connect to broader constituencies. The rising influence of television led the Council staff to attempt to develop relationships with network television reporters only to discover that bureaus changed personnel so often that building relationships with reporters was virtually impossible. Even the print media became less helpful to Council purposes. With the concentration of newspapers into large chains, reporters were less able to identify for themselves what were the important issues. National offices were much more likely to tell southern bureaus what was newsworthy, and they showed little respect for a regional approach to problems; news and interpretation of news were either national or local, but not regional. This meant that the Council was less able to influence from Atlanta whether, and how, the national media understood a southern problem. This represented a great change from the time when Harold Fleming had discussed an issue with John Popham and effectively shaped how that matter was reported in the nation's media.[26]

In the years after 1975, a new director, Steve Suitts, restored order and financial stability to a much smaller but more independent Council staff. Suitts pointed the Council toward several main purposes that would advance the organization's values in the post-civil rights South. The new purposes presumed the need for connections that the Council's triangles of change had so successfully relied upon in the past. The first was to make sure that the right to vote did in fact result in real and effective political power for people historically disfranchised. This meant examining, and sometimes challenging, electoral forms and voting districts so that at-large elections and legislative districts did not simply preserve entrenched power, and providing information and other support services to newly-elected black legislators. Second, the Council promoted public policies aimed at improving working conditions for people in low-wage jobs. Third, the organization continued its longstanding commitment to public education by developing projects to improve leadership and encourage curriculum innovation in rural, Black Belt schools, the areas where public support for education was weakest. Finally, through its publications, the Council remained true to the belief that information and ideas could improve human relations.[27]

Paul Gaston, a Council veteran who can remember the days when the Council's view on the South was cited by the *New York Times* with almost Biblical authority, and the times when the executive director jumped on an airplane to Washington to tell John Kennedy what a civil rights bill ought to look like, observed in the 1990s that since the mid-1970s Council activities sometimes had seemed like drops of water on a vast desert. But perhaps the truth of southern history is that only rarely do we stride toward freedom. Most of the time we step slowly, not very far, uncertain even if we are going in the right direction, not knowing whether our connections will finally result in real and lasting change. The history of the Southern Regional Council leaves us with a powerful example of how sustained effort, and faith in a vision of a better society, did in fact prevail for a time.[28]

NOTES

1   Morton Sosna, *In Search of the Silent South: Southern Liberals and the Race Issue* (New York, 1977), 153–66; Patricia Sullivan, *Days of Hope: Race and Democracy in the New Deal Era* (Chapel Hill, 1996), 166–7.
2   Gavins, *Hancock,* 150; Odum to Guy Johnson, June 20, 1944, in SRC/Gaston files,

in possession of Paul M. Gaston, Charlottesville, Virginia; Sosna, *Search,* 154; John Egerton, *Speak Now Against the Day: The Generation Before the Civil Rights Movement* (Chapel Hill, 1995), 461.

3   Johnson to Paul Williams, November 29, 1945, Southern Regional Council papers, microfilm set, series I, reel 74, frame 2213. The last two dealt with operations matters—improving distribution of publications and getting new members.

4   See *New South* 1946–49.

5   *New South* (January 1948).

6   Julia Anne McDonough, "Men and Women of Good Will: A History of the Commission on Interracial Cooperation and the Southern Regional Council, 1919–1954," (unpublished Ph.D. dissertation, University of Virginia, 1992), 401–03; Mitchell to Williams, May 17, 1948; Mitchell to Williams, April 20, 1949; Mitchell to Williams, July 27, 1949; Mitchell to Williams, October 20, 1949; Mitchell to Williams, December 2, 1949; Mitchell to Williams, September 11, 1950, SRC I, 74, 2213.

7   George Mitchell to Paul Williams, August 14, 1947; Mitchell to Williams, November 26, 1947; Williams to Mitchell, January 3, 1948; Williams to Mitchell, December 4, 1948; March 31, 1949; SRC I, 74, 2213

8   Williams to Mitchell, April 4, 1949; Williams to Mitchell, April 5, 1949; Williams to Mitchell, September 26, 1949, I, SRC 74, 2213.

9   Williams to Mitchell, January 26, 1949; Mitchell to Williams, May 2, 1949, SRC 74, 2213.

10 George S. Mitchell to the Ford Foundation February 9, 1950, SRC, I, 20, 843. To the Ford Foundation, Morris Abram suggested, the argument should be that "the South still remains the nation's number one political, economic, and moral problem" and that "the solution can never be in terms of indigenous money, but has to be in terms of indigenous people" who "are not within the economic structure and are not going to be, so the money has to come from outside, and it has to be private and not government money." Abram insisted that the points to emphasize with the Ford Foundation was that "the will of the whole nation remains stymied because of these recalcitrants which the South puts into Congress" and that because "millions are being spent for bad causes in the South; some money should be spent for good ones." Minutes from meeting on Ford Foundation Appeal, February 23, 1951, SRC, I, 20, 843; Mitchell to Williams, August 21, 1951, SRC I, 74, 2213.

11 Sullivan, *Days of Hope,* 274. Sullivan writes: "Northern foundations inclined to support civil rights efforts, such as Ford and Rockefeller, steered clear of groups tainted by any association with the Progressive Party. The Ford Foundation established the Fund for the Republic specifically to undermine alleged communist influence on blacks. In the South, the largely nonpolitical Southern Regional Council was the primary beneficiary of the fund's support."

12 Gordon Hancock to Mitchell, February 9, 1948, in Gaston personal papers; McDonough, "Good Will, 556–70.

13 McDonough, "Good Will," 556–570.

14 See, for example, *New York Times,* October 17, 1955; Edwin Lee Plowman, "Analysis of Selected Strategies Used by the Southern Regional Council in Effecting Social Change

in the South," (unpublished Ph.D. dissertation, Boston University, 1976), 142.

15 Leslie Dunbar interview, Southern Oral History Project (SOHP) at UNC Southern History Collection, December 18, 1978. SRC consulted extensively with Harris Wofford, Burl Bernhard, and Adam Yarmolinsky, all involved in setting civil-rights policy in the Kennedy Administration. SRC's benefactor Stephen Currier was close to Burke Marshall, Kennedy's chief of civil rights. The Potomac Institute became the after-work meeting place for the Kennedy Justice Department. Dunbar told Fleming that his chief function in the civil rights efforts was "dispensing liquor."

16 Leslie Dunbar interview, SOHP; Paul Gaston to author, September 2003.

17 *New South* issues for 1963–66; SRC Annual Reports, 1963–66; Plowman, "Selected Strategies," 217–273.

18 "News from the Ford Foundation," press release, October 26, 1965, SRC 25, 848.

19 1970 SRC Annual Report, George Esser Papers, UNC Southern Historical Collection, box 16.

20 Ford memorandum [1971], Esser Papers, box 18.

21 Christopher F. Edley to Anthony, December 3, 1965, SRC 25, 848; Dunbar interview, UNC; Memo, Peter Petkas to Harry Bowie, May 8, 1974, Esser Papers, 21. Leslie Dunbar was later critical of his successors at SRC for allowing foundations to set the agenda for SRC. "I didn't take direction from foundations. I think SRC has got into a lot of trouble since by doing that, especially with Ford and Rockefeller." Once Ford starting funding SRC it kept "shoving money down there."

22 Esser and Bowie memo to staff, February 10, 1975; Esser to executive board, February 14, 1975; Esser to executive committee, March 6 1975; Esser to executive committee, March 8, 1975, all in Esser Papers, UNC, box 21; Esser report on staff evaluations, no date, 1975, Esser Papers, box 2. Ford agreed to loan money to cover the deficit.

23 SRC Annual Report, 1975; author's interview with Paul M. Gaston, February 19, 1994; author's interview with Steve Suitts, February 21, 1994.

24 Leslie Dunbar interview, UNC, (SOHP), December 18, 1978. Dunbar believed that Anthony could not control Vernon Jordan and wanted to be free of him.

25 Hugh Dave Graham, *The Civil Rights Era: Origins and Development of National Policy* (New York, 1990), 362–3, 343.

26 Author's interview with Steve Suitts, February 21, 1994.

27 SRC Annual Reports, 1979–1993.

28 Gaston interview; SRC Annual Report, 1979.

6

Reparations and History

The Emancipation Generation's Ethical Legacy for the 21st Century

LYNDA J. MORGAN

I entered the graduate program in American history at the University of Virginia in 1978, after earning an M.A. at Western Carolina University and spending the summer in Washington, D.C., as a Peace Corps/VISTA intern. I had not settled on a concentration, but I leaned toward African American history. The year was demanding. I had no funding and worked three work/study jobs. The courses were difficult, the curriculum less than progressive. Cultural dissonance was intense for me, a first-generation college student. The male-dominated department, save one woman hired that year, was stuffy and aloof. Eight years had passed since the university first admitted women and African Americans, but the atmosphere felt unwelcoming, particularly for someone of my class background. I navigated this environment uncertainly—apprehensive that I would fail not only because I felt like an outsider, but also because of my alienation from the history being taught. I thought that if this was what it meant to be a historian, I would never make it. When I finally opened up to someone, I was told that I should wait until next year, when Paul Gaston returned from sabbatical. Could I endure that long? Who was this Paul Gaston? Was I being told the truth?

Paul spent that year in his hometown of Fairhope, Alabama, with his wife Mary and son Gareth. He grew up in this utopian single-tax community that his Populist grandfather, Ernest Berry Gaston, established in 1894. His father, Cornie Gaston, later directed this colony of dissenting freethinkers. Paul had returned for the first time in a quarter century to begin work on a history of Fairhope. The result became part memoir because of how fundamentally Fairhope shaped his moral compass, defined his scholarship and activism, and helped craft him into an extraordinary teacher who exercised profound influence on the lives and works of students and many others. Coming of Age in Utopia: The Odyssey of an Idea *(2010) showcased Paul's commitment to employ rigorous history in the service of social justice, his empathy with the downtrodden, his patient determination in pursuing progressive changes, his playful, subtle irony, and his elegant prose. From it I learned that a far stodgier UVA had jolted him too when he arrived in 1957: "I felt small. My stomach churned, a sign of both my eagerness and my sense of inadequacy."*[1]

I wish he had shared that with me when I screwed up the courage to go to his office that second year. I think I blurted out something awkward about how people had told me that I needed to meet him. I am more certain that he greeted this declaration with characteristic charm and his captivating chuckle. I would learn that my informants knew whereof they spoke. This remarkable professor, along with the late Armstead L. Robinson, understood my discontent and taught me to produce disciplined, useable, and ethical history. Paul recruited Armstead in 1980 to establish a viable African American curriculum and improve black faculty recruitment. With Armstead's leadership, they founded the Carter G. Woodson Institute for African and African American Studies, devoted to the support of pre- and post-doctoral scholars. Between 1984 and 1986, I was privileged to be a Woodson fellow, which enabled me to finish Emancipation in Central Virginia, 1850–1870, *and earn my degree.*

A delightful aspect of participating in this Festschrift *was the opportunity to review Paul's body of scholarly work. I began with his classic* The New South Creed: A Study in Southern Mythmaking *(1970), which won the Lillian Smith Book Award. Here Paul analyzed the intellectual inventions and damaging legacies of some key architects of segregation in the late nineteenth century, dishonorable if successful men whose efforts fueled the Supreme Court decision of* Plessy v. Ferguson *in 1896. Still in print, what struck me about* The New South Creed *nearly a half-century after its appearance was the degree to which its method and approach inform many recent and excellent works in the field. What Paul termed "mythology" in 1970, when such studies were few and far between, is now "historical memory," routinely employed by myriad historians. In southern history, its use is perhaps best exemplified in the work of David W.*

Blight, whose 2001 Race and Reunion: The Civil War in American Memory *proved how a racist version of Civil War and Reconstruction history had sunk deep roots in the American public's interpretation of these events, much to the detriment of public policy and race relations. Most contemporary historians readily connect the dots between slavery, the war, Reconstruction, and segregation with the present day. In 1970, however, such practices were revolutionary. Paul forcefully addressed this durability in the epilogue, "The Enduring Myth." He stressed that these New South ideologues gave a gift that kept on giving long after their deaths: "Efforts to cope with its mythology persist seventy years after the original movement reached its climax." No other group of like spokesmen replaced them: "There was no need for one so long as the mythology created by the first one endured."*[2] *Today there is a consensus that these mythologies continue to shackle many minds despite a thorough academic refutation of them. Douglas R. Egerton recently argued, for example, in* The Wars of Reconstruction: The Brief, Violent History of America's Most Progressive Era *(2014), that "[w]e study history . . . not as a quaint exercise in antiquarianism, but to understand the present. History, properly understood, is a series of meandering roads that all converge on the modern day. If we consciously ignore unpleasant parts of that journey, or seek to redraw that map, so that the country's first era of progressive reform instead resembles a tragic era of corruption and bad government, then we fail to understand the contemporary world."*[3]

Here, then, lies the essence of what made Paul a unique force when The New South Creed *appeared: his ability to harness his powerful intellect to the grassroots activism of his day, activism that was critical to the assault against such ideologies in the modern civil rights era, at least within the academy. As I appreciate this feature of his work anew, I am more conscious of the degree to which my own work follows this pattern. At the conclusion of* Coming of Age in Utopia, *Paul reminds us of the ongoing nature of this struggle:*

> *There is a phrase in the Talmud that says this much better: "It is not given to us to complete the task. Nor may we remove our hands from the plow." Charles Gomillion, the hero of the Tuskegee freedom movement, put it this way: "Keep everlastingly at it." And Ned Cobb, the Alabama sharecropper who could make the language sing, said simply, "It takes many a trip to the*

river to get clean." I speak for multitudes, past, present, and future, when I thank you, Paul, for guiding us on those river trips, and for helping me learn to go on them with others.[4]

∼

[A version of the article below was published in the Journal of African American History *99, Fall 2014, pages 403–426. It appears here with permission.]*

Historian John Hope Franklin often insisted that "if the house is to be set in order, one cannot begin with the present. He must begin with the past."[5] How might we best use the long history of reparations efforts to bolster recent reparations demands and establish greater economic equality by acting on the blueprints that the emancipation generation, and their descendants, laid down? What follows is an effort to link together some past efforts at reconciliation and reparations, and to explore the worldview out of which they grew, specifically highlighting an ethos rooted in stolen labor that put a premium on both political and economic democracy. The emancipation generation's broad democratic vision of economic and political equality has yet to reach fruition, but it continues to hold salience for the reparations debates, at both the national and global levels.

In many respects, contemporary debates swirl around the very problems that animated African American thought and action in the emancipation era. Today, heated arguments revolve around the form proper redress should take, debates the emancipation generation would find familiar. Some call for individual payments based on the value of lost labor and stunted wealth accumulation. A therapeutic model underscores the need for a keener historical consciousness about the many profound legacies slavery left for the present, largely in the truth and reconciliation tradition. Others support policies designed to launch a wholesale class-based attack on economic and political inequality, perhaps funded from a national trust or "Reparations Superfund."[6] This last and most visionary approach for a thorough democratic housecleaning emanates from principles the emancipation generation articulated. They knew that setting matters aright for freedpeople could not occur without a national redemption, which required establishing economic as well as political equality. They made substantial inroads on political equity, at least for a time, but economic justice has loomed as a far more difficult quest with formidable opponents.

From Social Revolution to Counterrevolution

Frederick Douglass observed in 1850 that "only when we contemplate the slave *as a moral and intellectual being* . . . can [we] adequately comprehend the unparalleled enormity of slavery, and the intense criminality of the slaveholder."[7] He thereby condensed the fundamental ethical principles borne of the collective historical experience of two and a half centuries of slavery. Slavery's most enduring intellectual legacy for enslaved African Americans and their descendants—the central pursuit of freedom and equal rights—derived from their experience and analysis of bondage itself. After the revolution of emancipation was achieved, that ethos sensitized the bulk of a heterogeneous population to the pressing need for democratic and humanistic social reform. Their agenda was on full display during Reconstruction. It was a vision so egalitarian as to provoke consistent violent opposition at the time and ultimately an implacable terrorist counterrevolution that required political disfranchisement and legal segregation. These reactionary measures were designed to silence threats against capitalistic excess, and they paved the way for decades of extraordinary exploitation of black, poor white, and immigrant labor as well.[8] This period of counterrevolution between the 1890s and the early decades of the twentieth century was so vicious that it has become known as "the nadir" of post-emancipation African American history.[9] Despite the counterrevolution's pitiless ferocity, the democratic visions of the emancipation generation continued to inform African American resistance strategies throughout the twentieth century. To preserve and transmit the history, lessons, and meanings of slavery and Reconstruction to subsequent generations, thereby providing them with intellectual and moral armament, was a vital imperative for the emancipation generation.

When we consider the oft-posed question about slavery's continued influence on the present, typically the answers focus on the many deleterious effects that the institution has had on interracial relations and economic disparities. It also remains common to hear arguments that posit long-term residual effects that slavery had on African American cultures—alleged poor work ethics, indifference to education, or disordered family lives.[10] Rarely do we acknowledge the rich ethical legacy the enslaved workers bequeathed to not just their descendants but to the nation, and which fueled one of the most radical democratic and egalitarian movements in U.S. history.

The basis of the freedpeople's ethical views pivoted on the interdependence of political economy and morality, which to them meant the universal human responsibility to work for the common good. In the era of enslavement, African Americans employed this foundational nexus they identified between work and ethics as the springboard for multifaceted deliberations about human nature, oppression, liberation, fairness, justice, and opportunity. Their moral economy was not a derivative or a simple assimilation of "white" or "American" beliefs, though American they surely were. Numerous similarities with the cosmologies of other Americans, especially the nascent antebellum working class and small landholders, existed.[11] But on balance, the very experience of enslavement itself formed the primary material context out of which emerged free and enslaved African Americans' ethical values. "Slavery" had been no abstract metaphor for the freed-people, as it often was for the emerging working class; the lessons of human bondage were unique and visceral.[12]

This egalitarian ethos had long permeated African American religious consciousness and rhetoric. By the early nineteenth century African American religions were the syncretized products of West and Central African animistic religions, West African Islam, the experiences of slavery, and a redefined Christianity. Many pre-colonial West and Central African religions, particularly among lineage societies, were profoundly egalitarian, communal, and spiritualistic—and blurred the sacred and the secular. These ethics survived the Middle Passage intact, establishing the foundation for the eventual Africanization of Christianity, which began to take shape in the mid-eighteenth century and matured in the early nineteenth century.[13] Africanized Western religions were noted for their refutation of proslavery ideology, firm embrace of equality and humanism, and rejection of racial determinism. Slavery was a sin and therefore most whites were sinful and immoral; slaveholder Christianity was "slaveholding priestcraft." Pre-Civil War African Americans generally believed that salvation and emancipation were both spiritually and temporally feasible, and they identified closely with the ancient Israelites and the biblical story of the Exodus. When emancipation occurred in 1865, many took it as a fulfillment of prophecy.[14]

A central feature of Africanized Christianity was its insistence that religion was as much or more concerned about life on earth as in heaven, and should be used to address injustices in the here and now. Regarded by many scholars as fundamentally a liberationist faith, Africanized Christianity placed stress on "honest labor"—the divine imperative for all to labor toward the common good. Freedman John Quincy Adams reflected the views of many when he observed that living off the labor of others constituted a violation of Divine imperatives. "Who ever heard of such a thing," he asked, "as a man working for another for nothing and he sitting down doing nothing, but only violating the laws of God and the just laws of the land, and then say it is right."[15] Born into slavery in Delaware in 1760, Bishop Richard Allen, founder of the African Methodist Episcopal Church in Philadelphia in 1816, preached a gospel and led a life that exemplified the connections between activism, morality, and religious faith. Among his many political pursuits, Bishop Allen helped organize the first National Convention of Colored Persons, which took place in Philadelphia in 1830, championed the anti-slavery movement, and condemned the racial discrimination against free people of color inside and outside the South. Allen was a prominent supporter of the Free Produce Society, which joined moral to economic arguments in its attack on goods produced by slave labor. Allen's was a liberation Christianity that posited that the United States could be rescued from social and economic immorality by recognizing African Americans' experiences as revolutionary and redemptive, capable of creating a true democracy. Allen thus utilized religion to generate a moral critique of the state that subsequent generations continued to venerate.[16] Throughout the period of enslavement, political disfranchisement, and Jim Crow segregation, African Americans' critiques of the United States as a "Christian" nation were theologically based. Frederick Douglass, Frances E. W. Harper, Ida B.

Wells, W. E. B. Du Bois, and others defined legal segregation and lynching as moral and spiritual matters and believed that they were extending the antebellum religious legacy of public protest against earthly injustices.[17]

This widespread and durable cultural ethos did not mean that African American political views were homogenous or static, nor that enslaved and free African Americans possessed innate goodness or were ethically infallible or uniformly humane. What it did mean was that their intellectual debates about a better future were grounded in the experience of slavery and their role in the economic advancement of American society. As with any group that shares a common experience, African Americans' analysis of their predicament posed particular questions, and spawned multiple answers, including some widely recognized truths about freedom and justice. By the late 1880s and 1890s, debates about the nature of the relationship between work and morality in the changing social and political circumstances became more contentious. Industrial capitalism advanced, along with campaigns for disfranchisement and legal segregation. Under these conditions some African Americans came to believe that the nation's racial sins were beyond redemption and embraced emigration from the United States to Africa as the only guarantee of their freedom. Still others, Frederick Douglass notably among them, vigorously opposed such plans and insisted on claiming the United States as African Americans' legitimate home, but that it was greatly in need of repair.[18] Divergent approaches to how to use (or not use) the memories and legacy of slavery fostered divisions about how best to resist the counterrevolution against emancipation.[19] But irrespective of approach, the enduring philosophical position remained that there was a fundamental connection between work and an ethical existence; that labor was central to individual and collective advancement; and that it was necessary to repair the damage slavery and legal segregation had wrought.

Upon acquiring the franchise in 1867, African American politicians and their constituents identified common goals, though they did not always agree on specific policies and approaches. Overwhelmingly they united to promote free, universal public education and legislation guaranteeing their civil rights. It was African Americans in the South who demanded the establishment of public school systems, although they faced uphill battles in gaining and maintaining funding for black public schools.[20] They supported public responsibility for the poor and infirm through the opening of orphanages, insane asylums, and relief for the poor. African Americans rejected laws allowing public whippings; property qualifications for voting, holding elective office, or jury service; and incarceration for debt. Reconstruction governments scaled back the list of crimes qualifying as capital offenses, and voting districts were redrawn along fairer lines. In South Carolina, the Reconstruction legislature passed its first divorce bill and removed limitations on married women's property rights. Formerly enslaved African Americans sought equal access to public accommodations—ratified in law in the 1875 Civil Rights Act—and tried unsuccessfully to decriminalize interracial marriage. They eschewed revenge and rejected calls for ex-Confederate disfranchisement. They recognized the importance of installing African Americans in certain official positions such as sheriff because of their importance in protecting the freedpeople from violence and fraud.[21]

But political rights alone would not bring full equality. Economic opportunity was critical to full freedom, and African American politicians strongly supported measures to promote fairer tax codes and railroad and industrial development, as well as a variety of measures to ensure that businesses contributed responsibly to public interests. Reconstruction legislators invalidated usury statutes, capped interest rates, and battled against attempts to assume the Confederate war debt.[22] And while many supported some form of ex-slave reparations demands—typically the redistribution of slaveholders' lands confiscated during the Civil War— masses and leaders also sought laws that guarded workers' rights to the fruits of their labor and protected equal economic opportunity. Radical Republicans left an impressive democratic mark on the emerging legal and economic landscape, and their progressive values and legislation embodied unambiguously the reparatory goals of newly freed African Americans and their allies.[23]

The enemies of these Reconstruction-era gains became determined to rein them in, if not destroy them. The federal government, under Republican administrations, either withdrew or refused to enforce legal and military protection for the freedpeople, and focused on the commercial objectives of industrial capitalists. The conditions for U.S. labor worsened, especially for southern black agricultural workers. White supremacists at the state and local levels grew in power and influence and violently repressed African Americans and their allies. The freedpeople's setbacks resulted directly from the extent to which they had used political power to try and check the mounting capitalist excesses, safeguard the rights of workers, and promote democratic rights.[24] W. E. B. Du Bois made perfectly clear the dynamics of the counterrevolution: "It must be remembered and never forgotten," he opened his chapter on this topic in *Black Reconstruction in America,* "that the civil war in the South which overthrew Reconstruction was a determined effort to reduce black labor as nearly as possible to a condition of unlimited exploitation and build a new class of capitalists on this foundation. . . . This program had to be carried out in open defiance of the clear letter of the law."[25] These economic and political changes laid the groundwork for a thoroughgoing ex-slave reparations movement.[26]

EMANCIPATION WITHOUT COMPENSATION

Africans' and African Americans' demands for reparations stretch back at least to the era of the American Revolution. In Boston, Massachusetts, in 1783, a free woman around 80 years of age named Belinda sued her former owner, loyalist Isaac Royall, for compensation for a near-lifetime of slavery. Belinda's petition to the state legislature explicitly justified the suit on the basis of her labors that had filled Royall's pockets. When the revolution forced Royall to flee to England, Belinda sued his estate for an annual allowance for herself and her invalid daughter. In the suit Belinda argued that she had been "denied one morsel of that immense wealth, a part whereof hath been accumulated by her own industry and the whole augmented by her servitude." Hers was not the first such effort. Indeed, beginning in 1770, petitions for reparations appeared regularly before Massachusetts legislators, often successfully, though enforcement proved lax. For example, the legislators granted Belinda's petition, but the estate only made one of the annual payments the Commonwealth mandated.[27]

One could argue that enslaved workers appropriated slaveholder property, not as robbery, but by "taking" what was morally justified, given the theft of their labor. Some elevated such appropriation to a fine art. In July 1841 the members of the Henderson Gang—Madison Henderson, James Seward, Amos Warrick, and Charles Brown—were hanged in St. Louis, Missouri, for the murder of two bank clerks in the course of a failed robbery. Henderson was a fugitive, and Warrick was a free black who had been kidnapped into slavery. Seward and Brown were freeborn, but militant, egalitarians who bristled under racial injustices. Seward, well educated and an acquaintance of abolitionist Gerrit Smith, felt it perfectly justified to "cheat the world as much as possible" and to "support [himself] in an easy life." The gang had a reputation for generosity in the free black community, spending freely on pleasure and recreation. The gang targeted "bankers, shopkeepers, plantation owners, and merchants" and were experienced river workers on the Mississippi between St. Louis and New Orleans. They aided fugitives, traded illegally, and killed to defend themselves. While the clever and flamboyant Henderson Gang might seem unusual, historian Thomas C. Buchanan argues that they were representative of a widespread African American river culture that condoned such actions that led to the redistribution of the wealth. When the gang members were finally captured, city officials in St. Louis had their heads mounted on poles to sow fear among those who contemplated following their example.[28]

Formal calls for redress and compensation abounded during the nineteenth century. In his *Appeal to the Colored Citizens of the World*, David Walker argued in 1829 that African Americans should demand that whites "raise us . . . to [the status] of respectable men, and . . . make a national acknowledgment to us for the wrongs they have inflicted on us."[29] Free black Hosea Easton, in his 1837 *Treatise on the Intellectual Character and Civil and Political Condition of the Colored People,* called for reparations payments to African Americans in the North who had gone through the process of "gradual manumission."

> The emancipated must be placed back where slavery found them and restore to them all that slavery has taken away. Merely to cease beating the colored people, and leave them in their gore, and call it emancipation, is nonsense. Nothing short of an entire reversal of the slave system in theory and practice—in general and in particular—will ever accomplish

the work of redeeming the colored people of this country from their present condition.

Likening slavery to thievery, as most African Americans did, Easton stressed that "the work of emancipation is not complete when it only cuts off some of the most prominent limbs of slavery, such as destroying the despotic power of the master, and the laying by of the cow-hide." Emancipation without compensation only left behind people who were "half dead, without proscribing any healing remedy for the bruises and wounds received by their maltreatment."[30]

In the early nineteenth century, African Americans had some white allies in making demands for reparations. In 1810 Yale University president Timothy Dwight addressed the matter of collective historical responsibility, still a contentious issue in the modern debates.

> It is in vain to allege that *our ancestors* brought them hither, and not we. . . . We inherit our ample patrimony with all its incumbrances; and are bound to pay the debts of our ancestors. *This* debt, particularly, we are bound to discharge: and when the righteous Judge of the Universe comes to reckon with his servants, he will rigidly exact the payment at our hands. To give them liberty, and stop here, is to entail upon them a curse.[31]

Solomon Northup, the free New Yorker kidnapped in 1841, was sold into slavery in southern Louisiana, and spent twelve years enslaved before he was released. Upon regaining his freedom, Northup became involved in one of the earliest attempts to obtain reparations from the federal government. Arguing that both he and his family had suffered economically during his enslavement, Northup, with the support of abolitionist Frederick Douglass and Congressman Gerrit Smith (Liberty Party), petitioned Congress directly for recompense. A more widespread petition campaign subsequently developed. Although Congress tabled all of these petitions, Northup's efforts proved inspirational for later attempts, some by whites, to target the federal government for financial redress for enslavement.[32] Numerous examples exist of people who compensated manumitted workers with land, money, and supplies, and some religious and abolitionist groups supported material redress for the emancipated.[33]

During the Civil War and Reconstruction, Congressman Thaddeus Stevens of Pennsylvania and Senator Charles Sumner of Massachusetts were vocal proponents of land redistribution. In 1867 Stevens warned the House of Representatives about the long-term social effects should House Resolution (HR) 29, the "Slave Reparation Bill," fail to pass. He argued that economic independence through landholding would benefit not only the freedpeople, but whites as well, because land redistribution would reinvigorate the southern economy. Stevens pointed out that when Russian serfs were emancipated, the Czar "did not for a moment entertain the foolish idea of depriving his empire of their labor or of robbing them of their rights. He ordered their former owners to make some compensation for their unrequited toil by conveying to them the very houses in which they lived and a portion of the land which they had tilled." Stevens cited the biblical injunction that required Egyptians to compensate Jews after Moses led them to freedom: "There was no blasphemer then to question God's . . . decree of confiscation. . . . If we refuse to extend to this downtrodden and oppressed race the rights which Heaven decreed them, and the remuneration which they have earned through long years of hopeless oppression, how can we hope to escape still further punishment if God is just and omnipotent?"[34] Even Union General William T. Sherman, no friend of formerly enslaved African Americans, established a plan to set aside lands from Georgia to Florida for black settlement.[35] Some writers even consider the educational efforts of the federal government's Freedmen's Bureau as its most positive, if temporary, endeavor to provide a form of reparations.[36]

ORGANIZING FOR REDRESS AND RESTITUTION

In the post-Reconstruction era and into the twentieth century, Ida B. Wells-Barnett, Bishop Henry McNeil Turner, W. E. B. Du Bois, T. Thomas Fortune, Monroe Trotter, Marcus Garvey, and other leaders spoke out in favor of compensation and reparations. Fortune, for example, argued in 1886 that "the crime of holding property in man" meant that whites were "responsible to the African people of this country for the principal and compound interest thereupon of the wages of each such slave, or his descendant, for at least the time covered by the adoption of the Federal Constitution (1787) and the manumission of the slave (1865); and that, until such principal and interest are paid to the last penny, the American white man should cease to reproach us because of our poverty, ignorance, or mendacity."[37] In 1898 Callie House, a former slave from Tennessee and a laundress, became a leader of the National Ex-Slave Mutual Relief, Bounty, and Pension Society, founded in 1896. The society sought compensation chiefly for elderly and desperately poor black southerners, and for this reason House endured federal harassment for years prior to her conviction for mail fraud and imprisonment for a year in Missouri.[38] Between 1901 and 1907, the National Industrial Council, organized by Stanley P. Mitchell of Dallas, Texas, sought congressional legislation to establish an ex-slave pension fund. Although Mitchell met with President Theodore Roosevelt about the bill, like House, he was accused of mail fraud for soliciting funds for his ex-slave pension campaigns.[39]

Paul Robeson, Mary McLeod Bethune, and lawyer William Patterson announced their support for reparations in the 1930s and 1940s; and A. Philip Randolph, Queen Mother Audley Moore, Malcolm X, Dr. Martin Luther King, Jr., Huey Newton, and Stokely Carmichael made their cases for reparations in speeches, books, and articles in the 1950s and 1960s. In 1969 former Student Nonviolent Coordinating Committee (SNCC) executive director James Forman interrupted services at New York's Riverside Church to issue the "Black Manifesto," a $500 million reparations plan to be financed by white Christian and Jewish congregations. Forman organized the National Black Economic Development Conference to coordinate this effort. Forman's demands focused on educational and labor strategies, as well as a southern land bank and a plan for cooperative businesses in the United States and Africa. "We seek," Forman underscored, "legitimate and modest reparations for our role in developing the industrial base of the Western world through our slave labor."[40] Three years later, eight thousand people attended the National Black Political Convention held in Gary, Indiana, which had recently elected the first black mayor of a large city, Richard Hatcher. The convention called for the establishment of nationwide health centers, national health insurance, the elimination of capital punishment, an urban "Homestead Act," a guaranteed minimum wage and annual income, a black "United Fund," and enforcement of anti-trust legislation.[41]

One of the leading organizations in the recent reparations movement in the United States has been the National Coalition of Blacks for Reparations in America (N'COBRA), founded by Imari Obadele in 1988.[42] Utilizing a Pan-African approach, N'COBRA supports a variety of means of redress.

Reparations can be in as many forms as necessary to equitably (fairly) address the many forms of injury caused by chattel slavery and its continuing vestiges. The material forms of reparations include cash payments, land, economic development, and repatriation resources particularly to those who are descendants of enslaved Africans. Other forms of reparations for Black people of African descent include funds for scholarships and community development; creation of multi-media depictions of the history of Black people of African descent and textbooks for educational institutions that tell the story from the African descendants' perspective; development of historical monuments and museums; the return of artifacts and art to appropriate people or institutions; exoneration of political prisoners; and, the elimination of laws and practices that maintain dual systems in the major areas of life including the penal system, health, education and the financial/economic system. The forms of reparations received should improve the lives of African descendants in the United States for future generations to come; foster economic, social and political parity; and allow for full rights of self-determination.

N'COBRA also embraces the tenets of the therapeutic model, stressing that acknowledgment of abuses would leave "the nation as a whole . . . stronger. Truth and atonement are essential ingredients for a just and peaceful society. Although some may assert that reparations will increase racial divisiveness, this does not have to be the result. Indeed, it should decrease racial divisiveness because it is an acknowledgment that allows us to go forward rather than remain stuck in the pain of the present that is caused by the unresolved pain of the past."[43]

Harvard Law School professor Charles J. Ogletree has acted as long-time counsel for N'COBRA, and he participated in the federal lawsuit brought against the city of Tulsa, Oklahoma, in 2003, seeking reparations for the 1921 riot that left some three hundred dead, forty blocks of property destroyed, and more than eight thousand people homeless. Although some white leaders in the local municipal government acknowledged the need for reparations payments to the victims of the Tulsa riot, and in 2001 the Oklahoma Committee to Investigate the Tulsa Riot of 1921 concurred, the state legislature declined to support the recommendations, citing a lack of constitutional power. When the case was brought before federal courts, the statute of limitations was invoked to avoid paying some forty surviving victims.[44] This use of the statute of limitations defense, legally called "remoteness" in common law, has hindered numerous reparations lawsuits.[45]

Reparations efforts have also made their way to, though not through, the U.S. Congress. In 1989 Democratic Congressman John Conyers of Michigan introduced House Resolution 40 (HR 40), a proposal to establish a congressional investigative commission to study reparations proposals. Conyers chose "40" in reference to the "forty acres" promised, but never distributed, to freedpeople in the aftermath of the Civil War. Conyers has reintroduced the bill each year since 1989, but HR 40 has never made it to a floor vote. HR 40 itself does not call for reparations, but merely seeks "to further a national dialogue on the plight of African Americans in the context of slavery, Jim Crow, and other legally sanctioned discriminations." A commission would "acknowledge the fundamental injustice, cruelty, brutality, and inhumanity of slavery in the United States" and determine if remedies were appropriate. Conyers modeled HR 40 on the restitution process outlined in the Civil Liberties Act of 1988 that made payments to Japanese Americans incarcerated during World War II.[46]

Should the members of Congress elect to address reparations, they would find no shortage of investigations into the racial wealth gap, in both the longer term—reaching back to slavery and Jim Crow segregation—and in the current era. Estimations of the amount of money lost to slave labor, legal segregation, and discrimination range widely, based on varied methods of calculation, but the sums involved and the ongoing wealth gap estimations are always eye-opening. They range in the trillions of dollars, from a low of $5 trillion to $24 trillion to more than $100 trillion. The methods of payment, to whom, and for what—lost labor only, or including other factors like physical and psychological health— have also been calculated and debated in myriad ways. Most investigators concede that these levels of restitution, particularly if directed to individuals, are unlikely.[47]

In 2005 a team of health policy professionals made an explicit effort to support Conyers's congressional investigative initiative by analyzing health and wealth disparities by race and over time. Their analysis of the intergenerational impact of slavery, segregation, and discrimination concluded that "time alone does not change" the demonstrable gaps in black-white wealth, much of which emerged from inherited wealth differentials worsened by discriminatory policies. While the removal of obstacles to racial wealth parity might mitigate or, less often, eliminate barriers to equality, this study found that such an approach could not correct for historical—that is, generational—damages. These injuries are measured in terms of human capital, especially in terms of health, a creator of wealth. African Americans have lower life expectancies and higher death rates than whites. They suffer more from diabetes, coronary disease, breast cancer, and hypertension. Slavery and legal segregation have played key roles in these disparities that have persisted over generations. Better education alone, they argue, cannot reverse these longstanding differences. These health professionals argue for policies that bring an end to skewed access to health care, provide for insurance coverage tailored to the specific problems facing African Americans, and an attack on residential segregation, which many scholars recognize as the central factor in ongoing racial discrimination. These researchers also support wealth transfers, particularly when directed towards the eradication of these ongoing causes of inequality.[48]

While the Civil Liberties Act of 1988, the basis of the Conyers initiative, is the most compelling legal precedent, reparations advocates point to numerous others that have occurred both nationally and internationally. A few have resulted in modest levels of restitution, though most have come in the form of apologies or, more often, acknowledgments or statements of regret. In 1993 Congress apologized for the invasion of Hawaii. In 1994 Florida established a $1.5 million fund to compensate survivors and descendants of the 1923 Rosewood massacre. Nine people who could either prove that they had resided in Rosewood at the time of the massacre, or whose ancestors lost property in the attack, eventually received settlements. The state also established the Rosewood Family Scholarship Fund for descendants of victims, and in 2004 designated the town a Florida Heritage Landmark. Germany, along with a number of private businesses, paid $65.2 billion to survivors of the Holocaust, and Germany has also compensated the state of Israel. In the 1990s Argentina and South Africa launched investigations into the victims of military dictatorship and the apartheid regime respectively.[49] In 1997 the U.S. House of Representatives condemned sexual enslavement of Chinese and Korean women—"comfort women"—by the Japanese during World War II and ordered the Japanese government to pay each victim $40,000.[50]

Timothy Pigford and some four hundred other black farmers filed two class action suits against the Department of Agriculture in 1999 for having either denied or delayed loans to African American farmers. In 2010 *Pigford v. Glickman II* recognized these claims, and President Barack Obama signed the compensation into law. About $1.25 billion has been paid to some eighteen thousand farmers, although investigations of the application process have revealed substantial fraud, chiefly among law firms pressing additional claims.[51] In 2005 the South African government paid $85 million in reparations to nineteen thousand apartheid victims who testified before the Truth and Reconciliation Commission, amounting to $3,900 per person, which fell far short of the requested $360 million.[52]

British Prime Minister Tony Blair fell shy of a full apology in November 2006 and instead expressed "deep sorrow" for his nation's involvement in the slave trade.[53] But the British have recently put some money where their mouth is. In June 2013, Britain apologized for torturing Kenyans fighting in the 1950s Mau Mau uprising against British colonial rule, agreeing to pay $30 million to over 5,000 victims.[54] North Carolina plans to compensate fifteen hundred living victims of a state sterilization program that was in place between 1929 and 1977. This eugenics policy chiefly targeted black, poor, and disabled women. The state has established a fund of $10 million for this purpose, and those eligible will be compensated starting in 2015.[55]

Ambitious and ongoing efforts at the international level have added considerable but hard-won momentum to the reparations movement. In late August and early September 2001, the United Nations sponsored the World Conference against Racism, Racial Discrimination, Xenophobia, and Related Intolerance (WCAR) held in Durban, South Africa, where activists struggled to get reparations issues on the agenda. By the end of the conference, the governments of Senegal and Nigeria had joined with the United States and the European Union to thwart the call for reparatory justice, with United Nations Secretary General Kofi Annan's tacit blessing. The United States dispatched Secretary of State Colin Powell and national security adviser Condoleezza Rice to safeguard the nation from reparations demands. But these opponents were unable to squelch either the legal or historical basis for reparations, or the determination of reparations activists. Their efforts live on today in the suits currently being pursued against Britain, France, the Netherlands, and other former slave-trading European nations by the Caribbean Community and Common Market (CARICOM), a coalition of fourteen Caribbean nations that formed in 1973, and a group that had been at the forefront of the WCAR reparations efforts. Should these suits fail, the group has pledged to take its case to the International Court of Justice.[56]

A key issue in the failed attempts at WCAR was a debate over whether slavery and slave trading had been crimes against humanity at the time they were committed. Reparations opponents maintained that since national governments had no legal sanctions against slavery and the trade—indeed, had them enshrined in law—they could not be considered crimes retrospectively. The final document that resulted from the conference stated that slavery and the trade "were appalling tragedies" and acknowledged that they were "*crimes* against humanity and *should* always have been so." Dismayed CARICOM members opposed the use of "should" in the final document, and used their dissent as the fulcrum on which to keep future reparations efforts alive. It is within that context that CARICOM cited the exhaustive and detailed work presented by historian Hilary McD. Beckles in *Britain's Black Debt: Reparations for Caribbean Slavery and Native Genocide* (2013), which demonstrated that slavery and slave trading were initially illegal, but once the practices became lucrative, they were made legal. On that basis CARICOM launched a renewed effort through the European courts that perhaps will ultimately be brought to the international court of law for reparations payments. Beckles was a pivotal member of the Durban conference, and he has been a key figure in pressing CARICOM's renewed efforts forward.[57]

In the United States, repeated attempts to sue the federal government for reparations have failed because of the principle of sovereign immunity, which allows such suits only with the government's permission. Activists therefore chose new strategies. In the late 1990s, when the modern reparations movement gained momentum, advocates began to target corporations to establish compensatory funds. The results fell far short of demand. Lawyer Deadria Farmer-Paellmann of the Restitution Study Group brought suits against various corporations with the intent of proving how extensively they profited from slavery and Jim Crow. In 2002 she brought suit against several corporations with the intent of proving how extensively they profited from slavery and Jim Crow. Among the targeted companies were FleetBoston Financial, Richmond, Virginia, transportation company CSX, and Aetna Insurance Company, with the suit calling for an estimated $1.4 trillion in reparations, the amount then estimated to have been stolen in terms of labor costs from four million slaves, not including interest.[58] This ambitious effort failed. But in 2005, J. P. Morgan-Chase Bank established a $5 million scholarship fund for African Americans in Louisiana after admitting having profited from slavery. Forced by a 2003 Chicago ordinance that made businesses disclose their historic ties to slavery, J. P. Morgan-Chase acknowledged that between 1831 and 1865, two of its predecessor banks in Louisiana accepted around 13,000 slaves as collateral and owned 1,250 of them through defaults. Many critics of the settlement denounced the amount placed in the fund as an insulting pittance, and Farmer-Paellmann and others argued that corporations should have no authority over how reparations dollars are spent.[59]

The preferred response to reparations demands by most public and private officials has been an embrace of the therapeutic model. Since the late 1990s a veritable cottage industry of apologies, near apologies, and "statements of regret" about slavery, legal segregation, and lynching had sprouted, with state and federal legislatures, colleges and universities, corporations, church groups, a U.S. President, and a British Prime Minister all chiming in. Many of these statements acknowledge the foundational contributions slave labor made to national economies, certainly something that the emancipation generation and their descendants would applaud. But the phenomenon of "statements of regret" emerged because authentic apologies, with their connotations of guilt, are more vulnerable to reparations suits. For example, President Bill Clinton led the pack with his May 1997 apology for the Tuskegee Project, in which 399 poor African American men in Alabama infected with late-stage syphilis between 1932 and 1972 were denied treatment in the interest of studying the effects of the disease. In 1998 Clinton issued another apology—some say a semi-apology—for the Atlantic slave trade.[60]

In 2004 the University of Alabama apologized for slavery. In 2006 the Virginia legislature issued a "statement of regret" about slavery that acknowledged that slave labor had built much of value in the Old Dominion. This document appeared just as the state was about to embark on the four hundredth anniversary commemoration of the establishment of Jamestown, where the first people of African descent were sold to British colonists. The University of Virginia, Thomas Jefferson's creation, soon issued another statement of regret. U.S. Representative Steve Cohen of Tennessee proposed a congressional apology for slavery in February 2007. The North Carolina Senate passed its statement of regret in April 2007, as did the Alabama and Maryland legislatures, which preferred to express "profound regret." New Jersey followed suit in 2008. New York, Missouri, and Georgia considered making statements but failed to do so.[61]

On March 15, 2007, one month before the state's statement of regret was issued, the North Carolina General Assembly passed house bill 751, a remarkable—and accurate—acknowledgment of the 1898 Wilmington Riot that overturned biracial political power in that city and left twenty-two African Americans dead. Hundreds of African American residents were then forced to leave, losing their property and turning Wilmington into a majority white city. The assembly acted after having commissioned a 464-page report. They issued the following statement:

> Political leaders and other members of a white elite were directly

responsible for and participants in the violence of November 17, 1898; engineering and executing a statewide white supremacy campaign in order to win the 1900 elections that was vicious, polarizing, and defamatory toward African Americans and that encouraged racial violence.... [T]he effects of... the Wilmington Riot lasted far beyond 1898, paving the way for legislation that disfranchised African Americans and poor white citizens, for lynching and violence against African American citizens, and for Jim Crow segregation.... [The state] is saddened by the full extent of leaders' involvement in the Wilmington Riot of 1898.... The General Assembly... on behalf of the people of North Carolina, acknowledges that the violence of 1898... was a conspiracy of a white elite that used intimidation and force to replace a duly elected local government, that people lost livelihoods and were banished from their homes without due process of law, and that government at all levels failed to protect its citizens.[62]

Such statements and investigations have not been limited to university presidents and politicians. On July 10, 2008, the American Medical Association (AMA) apologized to African American physicians for "past wrongs" dating back to the 1870s, when the AMA refused to admit African American delegates to their conferences, prompting the formation of the separate National Medical Association in 1895. They also cited the establishment of separate and usually inferior hospitals, the closing of all but two African American medical schools in 1910, and the bans against African American patients in white hospitals as reasons for their contrition. Not until 1968 did the AMA take a constitutional stand against racism in the medical profession.[63]

Colleges and universities in the United States have been active in scrutinizing their ties to slavery, the slave trade, and legal segregation. Such investigations have occurred at Yale, Harvard, and Princeton universities, and a growing list of other institutions have or are currently undertaking like efforts, including William and Mary, Duke, Amherst, and the Universities of North Carolina, South Carolina, Virginia, Alabama, and Maryland. In 2006 Ruth J. Simmons, president of Brown University, spearheaded efforts to detail the university's connections to the Atlantic slave trade through the

Brown brothers, who made their fortunes in the trade in the eighteenth century and then gave generously to the founding of the university. The consequent report, "Slavery and Justice," acknowledged the controversies over economic redress and focused instead on a therapeutic process. The university would preside over community discussions that allegedly would foster a more equitable future by promoting "truth telling" about "traumatic histories." Brown has since established the Ruth J. Simmons Postdoctoral Fellowship in Slavery and Justice, which calls for applicants to investigate "questions concerning the historical formations of slavery in global or comparative terms; issues concerning contemporary forms of indentured servitude; or philosophical, historical, and theoretical questions concerning slavery, justice, and freedom."[64]

In February 2011 Emory University organized a conference on "Slavery and the University" and will publish its findings in a forthcoming volume. In the fall of 2013 historian Craig Steven Wilder published *Ebony and Ivy: Race, Slavery, and the Troubled History of America's Universities,* a wide-ranging and exhaustive analysis of slavery and the founding of American colleges and universities from the colonial era to the antebellum period. Not surprisingly, those major southern institutions that existed, such as the College of William and Mary and the University of Virginia, had multiple direct ties to the wealth that slavery generated. But so did the Ivy League colleges in New York, Connecticut, Massachusetts, and New Jersey, whose leaders actively courted wealthy slaveholders and slave traders for donations and who either held slaves themselves or were invested personally in the slave economy. In the nineteenth century, the faculty at these colleges became distinguished for their "scientific" arguments about racial hierarchies and the social dangers that Africans and indigenous peoples represented. "The academy," Wilder concluded, "never stood apart from American slavery—in fact, it stood beside church and state as the third pillar of a civilization built on bondage."[65]

The current crop of apologies and statements of regret at least recognize that slave labor built the nation—a comfortable enough admission for those who could be found liable. And indeed, some reparations proponents, like N'COBRA, insist that apologies accompany any restitution that might transpire. But shorn of compensation, these statements seem defensive and ring hollow because they fail to address the economic legacies of slavery and legal segregation in concrete terms. As formerly enslaved African Americans knew well, specific policies addressing political as well as economic injustices are essential to achieving a lasting social harmony. As they well understood, morality and behavior can be changed through law and the power of the state. What occurred when these protections were either not in place or went unenforced remain bluntly plain historical lessons.

In April 2007 a local independent newspaper in Chapel Hill and Durham, North Carolina, interviewed John Hope Franklin on his reactions to the recent spate of apologies, as well as the North Carolina legislature's report on the 1898 Wilmington Massacre. "It's going to become epidemic now," Franklin presciently observed:

> People are running around apologizing for slavery. What about that awful period since slavery—Reconstruction, Jim Crow and all the rest? And what about the enormous wealth that was built up by black labor? If I was sitting on a billion dollars that someone had made when I sat on them, I probably would not be slow to apologize, if that's all it takes. I think that's little to pay for the gazillions that black people built up—the wealth of this country—with their labor, and now you're going to say I'm sorry I beat the hell out of you for all these years? That's not enough. . . . How large is the black population now living in abject poverty in this country? How large is the population of blacks who have poor health? Sometimes they inherited the poor health right from their forebears who were beaten and treated like they were animals all over this country. It's simply not enough. And I'm impatient with the piety that goes along with it. They're so syrupy in their apologies. What does it cost? Nothing.

Franklin found the North Carolina report on Wilmington "commendable," particularly if it led to more instruction in the public schools about the event. But he remained pessimistic about monetary reparations. "The American government, whatever its needs are to equalize opportunity and to provide justice for all," he observed, "is probably not responsible for making up the defects of slaveholders and shareholders in Virginia or Maryland or North Carolina. . . . I really expect though, that the government would not tolerate any continued discrimination and any continued defects in the relationship between one group of citizens and another. That if it is not in the position to make amends for everything that has happened, it can certainly see that it doesn't continue to happen. And I would settle for the government doing that."[66]

"When I was chairman of the president's [Bill Clinton's] advisory board on race," Franklin continued, "I found very few groups that wanted to acknowledge that they had made mistakes in the past, and that it would be well to reconsider them and apologize for them—very seldom did I find any group that was willing to do that. I'm not at all certain that we can find any groups that want to give up any property or any resources that they've gained through the years as a result of the way in which they acquired these properties and so forth. They simply don't want to think about it or to do anything about it."[67] Polls reflect the accuracy of Franklin's assessment. A majority of white Americans oppose reparations by margins of two-thirds and greater while African Americans support reparations at the corresponding level.[68] The most demagogic opponents quail particularly over the individual payment approach. They lack all sense of the collective historical benefits to whites, preferring instead to argue that they had no direct personal or individual role in slavery or Jim Crow.[69]

But some reparations proponents frame the issues more comprehensively and systemically, emphasizing community-oriented, sometimes class-based, rehabilitation and educational programs. Some refer to these as forward-looking, rather than backward-looking, plans. Improvements in public education are always high on list, which is President Barack Obama's preferred solution. Many would equalize public education by eliminating property taxes as the basis for funding and providing free higher education for all citizens. Jobs programs, stronger and better protected Affirmative Action programs, single-payer health care, reforms in drug offender sentencing, extensive penal reforms, effective education of the electorate—these, they argue, would combat the corruption of democracy caused by greed and generations of wealth redistributed from African Americans and other exploited people to financial elites. Many believe that expanding economic opportunity and democracy by establishing political protections for the most vulnerable would be vastly more effective than individual reparations payments, which would doubtless be meager, inadequate, and fleeting, benefitting chiefly the companies where such relatively small sums would likely be spent.[70] Law professor Charles Ogletree's observations reflect this approach.

> The reparations movement should not, I believe, focus on payments to individuals. The damage has been done to a group—[enslaved] African-Americans and their descendants—but it has not been done equally within the group. The reparations movement must aim at undoing the damage where that damage has been most severe and where the history of race in America has left its most telling evidence. The legacy of slavery and racial discrimination in America is seen in well-documented racial disparities in access to education, health care, housing, insurance, employment, and other social goods. The reparations movement must therefore focus on the poorest of the poor—it must finance social recovery for the bottom-stuck, providing an opportunity to address comprehensively the problems of those who have not substantially benefited from integration or affirmative action. The root of "reparations" is "to repair." This litigation strategy could give us an opportunity to fully address the legacy of slavery in a spirit of repair.[71]

Were these broadminded and collectivity-oriented visions put into operation, they would reflect much of what freedpeople and their descendants in the United States called for in the name of reparations and greater democracy in the emancipation era and subsequent decades. Many indeed rejoiced in the promise of land redistribution. In the aftermath of redistribution's bitter failure, they called at least for political protections—exercise of the ballot so as to influence laws that governed economic opportunity. While they exercised political power, they attacked greed and fraud. They widened educational access and called for improved health care, job growth, and wage equity. They gave us the draft for a better future that aimed to limit confrontation and establish mutual respect, the stated aims of modern reparations activists.[72] They understood that opponents directed their attacks at African American families and communities in order to compromise if not destroy their ethical pasts and presents, assaults that had formidable public policy implications. We of the 21st century should heed these ethical legacies of the freedpeople and their descendants, people who experienced slavery and legal segregation and passed on wisdom that still speaks to policies that continue to debilitate the individual and common good and thereby imperil national integrity. Such an initiative would be a fitting commemoration of the 150th anniversary of emancipation.

Notes

The author wishes to thank the anonymous reviewers for the *Journal of African American History*, whose comments greatly strengthened another version of this essay, and V. P. Franklin for his comments and support.

1. Paul M. Gaston, *Coming of Age in Utopia: The Odyssey of an Idea* (Montgomery: NewSouth Books, 2010), 170.
2. Paul M. Gaston, *The New South Creed: A Study in Southern Mythmaking* (New York: Alfred A. Knopf, 1970), 218–19, 221.
3. Douglas R. Egerton, *The Wars of Reconstruction: The Brief, Violent History of America's Most Progressive Era* (New York: Bloomsbury, 2014), 346–47.
4. Gaston, *Coming of Age in Utopia*, 341.
5. Franklin first made this statement in a September 8, 1968, *New York Times* article, "Rediscovering Black America: A Historical Roundup."
6. V. P. Franklin, "Introduction: African Americans and Movements for Reparations: From Ex-slave Pensions to the Reparations Superfund," *Journal of African American History* 97, nos. 1–2 (Winter–Spring 2012): 1–12.
7. Frederick Douglass, "What Is a Slave?" in *African-American Social and Political Thought*, ed. Howard Brotz (New Brunswick, 1996), 217. Emphasis added.
8. The literature on the exploitation of black labor during the nadir is voluminous, but an excellent entry would be the detailed analysis of how that process unfolded in the Mississippi delta. See Nan Elizabeth Woodruff, *American Congo: The African American Freedom Struggle in the Delta* (Cambridge, 2003); Douglas A. Blackmon, *Slavery By Another Name: The Re-enslavement of Black Americans from the Civil War to World War II* (New York, 2008); Pete Daniel, *The Shadow of Slavery: Peonage in the South, 1901–1969* (Chicago, 1972); and Ronald W. Walters, "The Impact of Slavery on 20th and 21st Century Black Progress," *Journal of African American History* 97, nos. 1–2 (Winter–Spring 2012): 110–30.
9. The widely employed term "the nadir" used to describe the disfranchisement and segregation years as the worst since emancipation originated with historian Rayford

Logan's *The Negro in American Life and Thought: The Nadir, 1877–1901* (New York, 1954). In this seminal work Logan emphasized economic exploitation, violence, the perfidy of presidents Hayes, Cleveland, Harrison, and McKinley, and of the Supreme Court, and the northern press on civil rights issues as the chief perpetrators of the counterrevolution. Logan's work shifted historiography on these issues.

10 I. A. Newby, *Jim Crow's Defense: Anti-Negro Thought in America, 1900–1930* (Baton Rouge, 1965).

11 See Eric Foner, *Free Soil, Free Labor, Free Men: The Ideology of the Republican Party before the Civil War* (1970; repr., New York, 1995), ch. 1; Daniel T. Rodgers, *The Work Ethic in Industrial America, 1850–1920* (Chicago, 1978), passim.

12 As one student of politics stressed, "Slavery was not mere background or prologue; it was formative and foundational." Steven Hahn, *A Nation Under Our Feet: Black Political Struggles in the Rural South, From Slavery to the Great Migration* (Cambridge, MA, 2003), 6; David Roediger, *Wages of Whiteness: Race and the Making of the American Working Class* (1991; repr., New York, 2007).

13 Sylvia R. Frey, "The Visible Church: Historiography of African American Religion Since Raboteau," *Slavery and Abolition* 29, no. 1 (March 2008): 83–110; Mechal Sobel, "The West African Sacred Cosmos," in *Trabelin' On: The Slave Journey to an Afro-Baptist Faith* (Westport, CT, 1979), 3–21; Frey and Betty Wood, *Come Shouting to Zion: African American Protestantism in the American South and British Caribbean to 1830* (Chapel Hill, 1998), xi–xiii, 1–62; Thomas L. Webber, *Deep Like the Rivers: Education in the Slave Quarter Community, 1831–1865* (New York, 1978), 118–30; V. P. Franklin, *Black Self-Determination: A Cultural History of African American Resistance* (Brooklyn, 1992), 27–68.

14 Kathryn Gin, "'The Heavenization of Earth': African American Visions and Uses of the Afterlife, 1863–1901," *Slavery and Abolition* 31 (June 2010): 207–31; Webber, *Deep Like the Rivers*, 63–70, 87; Franklin, *Black Self-Determination*, 51–67; Albert J. Raboteau, *A Fire in the Bones: Reflections on African-American Religious History* (Boston, 1995), 28–36.

15 John Quincy Adams, *Narrative of the Life of John Quincy Adams, When in Slavery, and Now as a Freeman* (Harrisburg, 1872): 16–17, 21–22, available from *Documenting the American South*, University Library, UNC–Chapel Hill, http://docsouth.unc.edu/neh/adams/adams.html.

16 Richard Newman, *Freedom's Prophet: Bishop Richard Allen, the AME Church, and the Black Founding Fathers* (New York, 2008), 1–26, 266–68, 291–99.

17 Edward J. Blum, "'O God of a Godless Land': Northern African American Challenges to White Christian Nationhood, 1865–1906," in *Vale of Tears: New Essays on Religion and Reconstruction*, ed. Edward J. Blum and W. Scott Poole (Macon, 2005), 93–111.

18 Kevin Gaines, *Uplifting the Race: Black Leadership, Culture and Politics in the Twentieth Century* (Chapel Hill, 1996); August Meier, *Negro Thought in America, 1880–1915: Racial Ideologies in the Age of Booker T. Washington* (Ann Arbor, 1963), 46–7, 149–57, 187.

19 David W. Blight, *Race and Reunion: The Civil War in American Memory* (Cambridge, 2001); Mitch Kachun, *Festivals of Freedom: Memory and Meaning in African American*

Emancipation Celebrations, 1808–1915 (Amherst, 2003), ch. 4 and passim; Thavolia Glymph, "'Liberty Dearly Bought': The Making of Civil War Memory in Afro-American Communities in the South," in *Time Longer Than Rope: A Century of African American Activism, 1850–1950*, ed. Charles M. Payne and Adam Green (New York, 2003), 111–39; Kathleen Ann Clark, *Defining Moments: African American Commemoration and Political Culture in the South, 1863–1913* (Chapel Hill, 2005), especially ch. 1, "The Vanguard of Liberty Must Look into the Past: Celebrations of Freedom," 13–55.

20 See, for example, Christopher M. Span, *From Cotton Field to Schoolhouse: African American Education in Mississippi, 1862–1875* (Chapel Hill, 2009).

21 Leon Litwack, *Been in the Storm So Long: The Aftermath of Slavery* (New York, 1979); Eric Foner, *Reconstruction: America's Unfinished Revolution, 1863–1877* (New York, 1989); Hahn, *Nation Under Our Feet;* James Dance Cawthon, "A Caddo Parish Sheriff During Reconstruction Times," *Northern Louisiana Historical Journal* 20 (1989): 3–19.

22 Jane Elizabeth Dailey, *Before Jim Crow: The Politics of Race in Postemancipation Virginia* (Chapel Hill, 2000).

23 Foner, *Reconstruction*; Hahn, *Nation Under Our Feet.*

24 Litwack, *Been in the Storm So Long;* Hahn, *Nation Under Our Feet;* Ida B. Wells-Barnett, *Crusade for Justice: The Autobiography of Ida B. Wells*, ed. Alfreda M. Duster (Chicago, 1972).

25 W. E. B. Du Bois, *Black Reconstruction in America: An Essay Toward a History of the Part Which Black Folk Played in the Attempt to Reconstruct Democracy in America, 1860–1880* (1935; reprt., Cleveland, 1964), 670.

26 See Barbara J. Fields's critique of such arguments in "Slavery, Race, and Ideology in the United States of America," *New Left Review* 181 (May–June 1990): 95–118.

27 Roy E. Finkenbine, "Belinda's Petition: Reparations for Slavery in Revolutionary Massachusetts," *William & Mary Quarterly* 64 (January 2007): 95–104.

28 Thomas C. Buchanan, "Rascals on the Antebellum Mississippi: African American Steamboat Workers and the St. Louis Hanging of 1841," *Journal of Social History* 34 (Summer 2001): 797–817.

29 Peter P. Hinks, ed., Introduction, *David Walker's Appeal to the Coloured Citizens of the World* (University Park, 2000), 70–71.

30 Hosea Easton, "Treatise on the Intellectual Character and Civil and Political Condition of the Colored People," in *To Heal the Scourge of Prejudice: The Life and Writings of Hosea Easton*, edited with an introduction by George R. Price and James Brewer Stewart (Amherst, 1999), 118–19.

31 Quoted in Finkenbine, "Belinda's Petition," 104.

32 Roy E. Finkenbine, "We Need to Include Reparations in the Story of Solomon Northup," *History News Network,* 20 January 2014, http://hnn.us/article/154463#sthash.fYN9xE09.dpuf.

33 See, for example, Jean R. Soderlund, *Quakers and Slavery: A Divided Spirit* (Princeton, 1985).

34 Thaddeus Stevens, speech on Section 4 of H.R. 29, *Congressional Globe,* 40th Cong., 1st sess., March 1867, 203, 205.

35   William T. Sherman, *Memoirs of General W. T. Sherman*, Vol. 2 (New York, 1891), 250–52; Foner, *Reconstruction*, 70–1.

36   Mary Frances Berry, "When Education Was Seen as Proper Reparations for Slavery," *Journal of Blacks in Higher Education* 48 (Summer 2005): 102–03.

37   T. Thomas Fortune, "Civil Rights and Social Privileges," *AME Church Review* 2 (1886), reprinted in *T. Thomas Fortune, the Afro-American Agitator: A Collection of Writings, 1880–1928*, ed. Shawn Leigh Alexander (Gainesville, 2008), 123–24.

38   Mary Frances Berry, *My Face Is Black Is True: Callie House and the Struggle for Ex-Slave Reparations* (New York, 2005), 200–11.

39   Mitchell and his colleagues formed the National Liberty Party in 1903 and nominated a presidential candidate in 1904. The presidential candidate was George Edwin Taylor from Alabama and his running mate was Virginian W. C. Payne. James M. Davidson, "Encountering the Ex-Slave Reparations Movement from the Grave: The National Industrial Council and National Liberty Party, 1901–1907," *Journal of African American History* 97, nos. 1–2 (Winter–Spring 2012): 13–38.

40   James Forman, "Black Manifesto," in *Redress for Historical Injustices in the United States: On Reparations for Slavery, Jim Crow, and Their Legacies*, ed. Michael T. Martin and Marilyn Yaquinto (Durham, 2007), 593–99; see also Walter Johnson, "Slavery, Reparations, and the Mythic March of Freedom," *Raritan* 27 (Fall 2007): 56–59, and Elaine Allen Lechtreck, "'We Are Demanding $500 Million for Reparations': The Black Manifesto, Mainline Religious Denominations, and Black Economic Development," *Journal of African American History* 97, nos. 1–2 (Winter–Spring 2012): 39–71.

41   "National Black Political Agenda: The Gary Declaration," 1972, reprinted in *Redress for Historical Injustices in the United States*, ed. Martin and Yaquinto, 600–05. For more information on the movement in the 20th century, see "Epilogue: The Movement Still Lives," in Berry, *My Face Is Black Is True*, 230–51; the essays and documents in Martin and Yaquinto, eds., *Redress for Historical Injustices in the United States*; Special Issue: "African Americans and Movements for Reparations: Past, Present, and Future," *The Journal of African American History* 97, nos 1–2 (Winter–Spring 2012): 1–173; and James T. Campbell, "Settling Accounts? An Americanist Perspective on Historical Reconciliation," *American Historical Review* 114 (October 2009): 963–77. Campbell's work focuses on the truth and reconciliation efforts that fall into the therapeutic category of redress initiatives. The article was part of an international forum on reconciliation initiatives and whether accurate historical accounts of abuses can reduce social conflicts. Campbell argued that such efforts can "at least narrow the range of permissible lies," which he regards as "no small achievement."

42   Adjoa A. Aiyetoro, "The National Coalition of Blacks for Reparations in America: Its Creation and Contributions to the Reparations Movement," in *Should America Pay? Slavery and the Raging Debate on Reparations*," ed. Raymond A. Winbush (New York, 2003), 209–25.

43   National Coalition of Blacks for Reparations in America, newsletter, www.ncobra.org; see also "National Coalition of Blacks for Reparations in America (2000): The Reparations Campaign," in *Redress for Historical Injustices in the United States*, ed. Martin and Yaquinto, 625–28.

44   Charles J. Ogletree, "Repairing the Past: New Efforts in the Reparations Debate,"

Harvard Civil Rights–Civil Liberties Law Review 38 (2003): 302–03; Ogletree, "Tulsa Reparations: The Survivors' Story," in *Redress for Historical Injustices in the United States*, eds. Martin and Yaquinto, 452–68.

45 Hilary McD. Beckles, *Britain's Black Debt: Reparations for Caribbean Slavery and Native Genocide* (Kingston, Jamaica, 2013), 168–70.

46 See www.congress.gov/bill/114th-congress/house-bill/40/all-info.

47 See the summary in Joe R. Feagin, "Documenting the Costs of Slavery, Segregation, and Contemporary Racism: Why Reparations Are in Order for African Americans," *Harvard Black Letter Law Journal* 20 (2004): 49–81; for recent figures, see Thomas M. Shapiro, Tatjana Meschede, and Laura Sullivan, "The Racial Wealth Gap Increases Fourfold," Institute on Assets and Social Policy, *Research and Policy Brief*, May 2010, iasp.brandeis.edu; Thomas M. Shapiro, *The Hidden Cost of Being African American: How Wealth Perpetuates Inequality* (New York, 2004); William Darity, Jr., "Forty Acres and a Mule: Placing a Price Tag on Oppression," in Richard F. America, ed., *The Wealth of Races: The Present Value of Benefits from Past Injustices,,* Contributions in Afro-American and African Studies no. 132 (New York: Greenwood Press, 1990), 3–13; Larry Neal, "A Calculation and Comparison of the Current Benefits of Slavery and an Analysis of Who Benefits," in ibid., 91–106; James Marketti, "Estimated Present Value of Income Diverted during Slavery," in ibid., 107–24.

48 Darrell J. Gaskin, Alvin E. Heaten, and Shelley I. White-Means, "Racial Disparities in Health and Wealth: The Effects of Slavery and Past Discrimination," *Review of Black Political Economy* 32 (Winter 2005): 95–110.

49 Martha Biondi, "Rise of the Reparations Movement," *Radical History Review* 87 (Fall 2003): 8–9.

50 Joe R. Feagin, "Documenting the Costs of Slavery, Segregation, and Contemporary Racism: Why Reparations Are in Order for African Americans," *Harvard Black Letter Law Journal* 20 (2004): 64.

51 Charles J. Ogletree, "Litigating the Legacy of Slavery," *New York Times,* March 31, 2002; "U.S. Opens Spigot After Farmers Claim Discrimination," *New York Times,* April 25, 2013.

52 Ginger Thompson, "South African to Pay $3,900 to Each Family of Apartheid Victims," *New York Times,* April 16, 2003.

53 David Smith, "Blair: Britain's 'Sorrow' for Shame of Slave Trade," *Guardian,* November 2006.

54 Alan Cowell, "Britain to Compensate Kenyan Victims of Colonial-Era Torture," *New York Times,* June 6, 2013.

55 In April 2012 Democratic Governor Bev Perdue initially recommended $11 million in reparations. A total of 7,600 people were sterilized through the eugenics program. The legislature complied with the request, but reduced the amount to $10 million in July 2013. "Truth and Atonement in North Carolina," *New York Times,* 29 April 2012; "N.C. Legislature Approves $10 Million for Victims of Forced Sterilization," upi.com, 26 July 2013; "Eugenics Compensation Amendment Continues to Leave Some Victims Out," *North Carolina Health News,* May 29, 2015, northcarolinahealthnews.org.

56 Beckles, *Britain's Black Debt,* 5–7.

57 Ibid., xi–xiv, and especially ch. 13, "'Sold in Africa'": The United Nations and Reparations in Durban," 172–93; V. P. Franklin, "Commentary—Reparations as a Development Strategy: The CARICOM Reparations Commission," *Journal of African American History* 98 (Summer 2013): 363–66; Laurent Dubois, "Confronting the Legacies of Slavery," *New York Times*, 28 October 2013.

58 John Torpey, *Making Whole What Has Been Smashed: On Reparations Politics* (Cambridge: Harvard University Press, 2006), 107–8, 110, 123–24, 125. Also named in the suit were Brown Brothers Harriman and Company, New York Life Insurance Company, Norfolk Southern Corporation, Lehman Brothers Corporation, Lloyd's of London, Union Pacific Railroad, J. P. Morgan-Chase, R. J. Reynolds Tobacco Company, Brown and Williamson, Liggett Group, Inc., Canada National Railway, Southern Mutual Insurance Company, American International Group (AIG), and Loews Corporation. Numerous investigations into the actual monetary value of lost labor exist, some ranging as high as 24 trillion dollars, with hundreds of millions in interest annually. See, for example, Feagin, "Documenting the Costs of Slavery, Segregation, and Contemporary Discrimination."

59 Ken Magill, "From J. P. Morgan Chase, An Apology and $5 Million in Slavery Reparations, *New York Sun*, February 1, 2005. Edward E. Baptist, *The Half Has Never Been Told: Slavery and the Making of American Capitalism* (New York: Basic Books, 2014), 274, found that one of these predecessor banks, Citizen's Bank of Louisiana, left inventories of more than five hundred mortgaged slaves in the years leading up to the Panic of 1837, a practice the bank followed for the remainder of the antebellum era.

60 "The White House—Apology for Tuskegee Experiment," in *Redress for Historical Injustices in the United States*, eds. Martin and Yaquinto, 638–41; see also Charles P. Henry, *Long Overdue: The Politics of Racial Reparations* (New York, 2007), 1–8.

61 "Remarks by the President in Apology for Study Done in Tuskegee," White House Press Release, May 16, 1997, http://www.edc.gov/tuskegee/clintonp.htm; Alison Mitchell, "Clinton Regrets 'Clearly Racist' U. S. Study," *New York Times*, May 14, 1997; Henry Louis Gates, Jr., "The Future of Slavery's Past," *New York Times*, July 29, 2001; Damien Cave and Christine Jordan Sexton, "Florida Legislature Apologizes for State's History of Slavery," *New York Times* March 27, 2008; Jeremy Peters, "A Slavery Apology, But the Debate Continues," *New York Times* January 13, 2008; Jamon Smith, "Slavery Marks University's Past," TuscaloosaNews.com April 7, 2006; *UVA Today*, April 24, 2007; Krissah Thompson, "Senate Backs Apology for Slavery," *Washington Post*, June 19, 2009.

62 General Assembly of North Carolina, session 2007, house bill 751, "Wilmington Race Riot Acknowledgement,"1–2. See www.history.ncdcr.gov/1898-wrrc/report/report.htm for the full commission report, *1898 Wilmington Race Riot: Final Report, May 31, 2006*. See also David Cecelski and Timothy Tyson, eds., *Democracy Betrayed: The Wilmington Race Riot of 1898 and Its Legacy* (Chapel Hill, 1998).

63 Harriet A. Washington, "Apology Shines Light on Racial Schism in Medicine," *New York Times*, July 2008.

64 Andy Guess, "Facing Up to a Role in Slavery," *Inside Higher Education* 25 (April 2007): n.p.; *Slavery-and-Universities*, wikispaces.com/Harvard; Kate Zernike, "Slave Traders in Yale's Past Fuel Debates on Restitution," *New York Times*, August 13, 2001; *Slavery*

and Justice: Report of the Brown University Steering Committee on Slavery and Justice, 2003, www.brown.edu/Research/Slavery-Justice; Johnson, "Slavery, Reparations, and the Mythic March of Freedom," 61–63; Adolph Reed, in "The Case Against Reparations," *Progressive* 64 (December 2000): 15–18, deems such approaches "a politics of psychobabble" and argues that class-based "access to quality health care, the right to a decent and dignified livelihood, affordable housing, [and] quality education for all" is the only possible way to redress historical grievances. Race-based solutions, according to Reed, only undermine the chances of multiracial solidarity. See a similar argument in John Torpey, *Making Whole What Has Been Smashed: On Reparations Politics* (Cambridge: Harvard University Press, 2006).

65 *Slavery and the University: Histories and Legacies*, Emory University Conference, February 2011; program and podcasts available at https://slavery-and-universities, wikispaces.com/Conference2011; Craig Steven Wilder, *Ebony and Ivy: Race, Slavery, and the Troubled History of America's Universities* (New York, 2013), 10–11, 289–90, and passim.

66 olofunke moses, "John Hope Franklin: Apologies Aren't Enough," *IndyWeek* April 18, 2007; indyweek.com.

67 Steven F. Lawson, ed., *One America in the Twenty-first Century: The Report of President Bill Clinton's Initiative on Race* (New Haven, 2009).

68 See, for example, the findings in Alfred L. Brophy, *Reparations: Pro and Con* (New York, 2006), 3–5, where two polls from 2002 and 2003 indicated that between 60 and 65 percent of whites opposed reparations from the federal government, whereas 67 percent of blacks favored reparations.

69 David Horowitz presented a particularly vitriolic and ahistorical case against reparations in "Ten Reasons Why Reparations for Blacks Is a Bad Idea for Blacks—And Racist Too," *Front Page,* 3 January 2001. Horowitz even argued that black people owed America a debt for having emancipated them. For a rebuttal, see Ernest Allen, Jr., and Robert Chrisman, "Ten Reasons: A Response to David Horowitz," *The Black Scholar* 31 (2001): 49.

70 See, for example, the findings summarized in William Darity, Jr., "Forty Acres and a Mule in the 21st Century," *Social Science Quarterly* 89 (September 2008): 658–60.

71 Charles J. Ogletree, "Litigating the Legacy of Slavery," *New York Times,* March 31, 2002. In his recent article "The Case for Reparations," *The Atlantic,* May 21, 2014, Ta-Nehisi Coates covered the history of reparations, going into depth on the contract buying system for residential housing that targeted African Americans in Lawndale, a Chicago suburb. Through contract buying, residents did not actually own or acquire equity in their homes, and could be evicted and lose their entire investment. Coates argued that such practices should be considered in any reparations investigation, such as Conyers's congressional proposal. Responses to the article have ranged from supportive to condemnatory, the latter category focusing on such themes as how reparations would undermine work ethics and the difficulty in designating the "proper" recipients of a reparations plan. For a positive evaluation of Coates's article, see Manuel Roig Franzia, "With Atlantic Article on Reparations, Ta-Nehisi Coates Sees Payoff for Years of Struggle," *Washington Post,* June 18, 2014. For negative responses, see Kevin D. Williamson, "The Case Against Reparations," *National Review,* May 24, 2014, and David Frum, "The Impossibility of Reparations," *The Atlantic,* June 3, 2014. Coates

responded in "The Radical Practicality of Reparations: A Reply to David Frum," *The Atlantic,* June 4, 2014.

72 Today, even political influence has come under attack with Supreme Court's assault on the Voting Rights Act of 1965. In 2013, the Court struck down the preclearance requirement of the act, permitting nine states and numerous counties and municipalities to change election laws without prior federal approval. In the wake of that decision, gerrymandering, stricter voter identifications laws, and suspension of early voting have occurred with growing regularity, demonstrating that black political power remains a threat to the ruling elite. John Lewis, "John Lewis and Others React to the Supreme Court's Voting Rights Act Ruling," *Washington Post,* June 25, 2013; Beckles, *Britain's Black Debt,* 22.

7

Bending Toward Injustice

The Election of Barack Obama, the Political Legacy of the 1865 Voting Rights Act, and the Myth of a Post-Racial America

ROBERT A. PRATT

In the fall of 1980 I enrolled in graduate school at the University of Virginia with a desire to study civil rights history. Unlike today's graduate students who peruse university websites and faculty rosters and know exactly with whom they wish to study well in advance of applying, I was totally clueless as to who would supervise my course of study. I met Paul Gaston upon arriving in the history department and was immediately impressed with his quiet, dignified southern charm and was elated when he agreed to serve as my major professor.

As I became more curious about this southern gentleman who had agreed to be my mentor, I learned that this son of Fairhope, Alabama, had a long history of civil rights activism. He had been active in the Charlottesville sit-ins in the 1960s and had been a powerful and persistent voice for progressive change at the lily-white University of Virginia and within the larger Charlottesville community. It just so happened that my arrival at the University of Virginia coincided with that of the late Armstead Robinson, who had joined the history faculty the same year and who had been recruited from the University of California Los Angeles (UCLA) to found the Carter G. Woodson Institute for African American and African Studies. Armstead and I bonded immediately, and he soon became a mentor and would eventually become co-director of my dissertation along with Paul. As director of the Woodson Institute, Armstead frequently brought in nationally-known scholars and civil rights activists, most of whom at some point during their stay in Charlottesville would be entertained at the home of

Paul and Mary Gaston. Being in the enviable position of studying under both Paul and Armstead, I was always invited to attend these "five-star occasions" (as Paul liked to refer to them), during which time he served the finest vintage from his impressive wine cellar. It was during these occasions that I would have the opportunity to meet some of the nation's foremost scholars and activists, many of whom would later influence my own work in civil rights history.

It was Paul who suggested that I write my master's thesis on school desegregation in Richmond, Virginia. Paul was well-versed on the subject in part because of his long friendship with Henry L. Marsh, a veteran civil rights attorney who for many years had been in the forefront of the fight to dismantle school segregation in that city. Marsh was also a member of Richmond's city council, a partner in the law firm of Hill, Tucker, and Marsh, and, in 1977, would become the city's first black mayor (I had the pleasure of interning in his office during my senior year at Virginia Commonwealth University). But there was an interesting backstory to Henry Marsh's historic election as Richmond's first African American mayor—one that came about as a consequence of a series of political maneuvers and electoral shenanigans, and one that in future years would help influence the direction of my own scholarly work.

The city of Richmond witnessed some dramatic demographic shifts during the 1960s; in short, the city's black population was increasing while the white population was rapidly declining—which to some extent reflected the exodus of whites from the city in order to avoid school desegregation which was looming on the horizon. Richmond's white political leaders no doubt saw the handwriting on the wall and realized that within a few years their control of city politics would be threatened by a new black electoral majority. In 1970, in an attempt to forestall the inevitable, the city annexed twenty-three square miles of land formerly belonging to Chesterfield County. Richmond's pre-annexation population was 202,359, of which 104,207, or 52 percent, were black. The annexation added to the city 47,262 new residents, of whom 1,557 were black and 45,705 were white. The post-annexation population of the city was 249,621, of which 105,764, or 42 percent, were black. Overnight, the city of Richmond went from majority black back to majority white. Since the city used an at-large voting scheme where all candidates had to run in a city-wide election, it was virtually impossible for blacks to win seats on city council in a majority white city.

Although Richmond's white politicians maintained that the annexation was necessary to expand the city's tax base, blacks charged that the annexation was racially motivated, and that its sole purpose was to dilute black voting strength. (Richmond's white city leaders had conducted negotiations in secrecy with Chesterfield officials for six years, and Richmond's white mayor was quoted as saying "I don't want niggers to take over the city.")[1] When the case finally reached the United States Supreme Court some years later, the justices were neither amused nor persuaded by the city's argument. The Court allowed the annexation to stand, but ordered the city of Richmond to move from at-large to single-member district elections. When the city's electoral map was reconfigured, nine districts were created: four would have black majorities, four would have white majorities, and the ninth would be a swing district, almost evenly balanced. But by the time the elections were held in 1977, the swing district had become majority black, and for the first time blacks held a 5–4 majority on city council. The mayor is chosen from among the council members, and by a vote of 5–4, Henry Marsh became the city's first black mayor. I witnessed those developments firsthand, and that was my initiation into the rough and tumble of racial politics and the importance of the ballot.[2]

A little more than fifty years ago the issue of who could, and who could not, participate in our cherished democracy came to a head in the voting rights campaign that took place in Selma, Alabama. On March 7, 1965, blacks and whites were brutally beaten on the Edmund Pettus Bridge as they sought to march from Selma to Montgomery for the right to vote. Two weeks later, more than 30,000 marchers arrived in Montgomery and listened to Dr. Martin Luther King's stirring oratory that signaled the march's triumphant conclusion. On August 6, 1945, Congress finally passed and President Lyndon B. Johnson signed the Voting Rights Act into law, removing once and for all those obstacles that had prevented African Americans from voting. But the ink had hardly dried before some began to come up with new schemes aimed at undermining the bill. Today, many in this nation continue to struggle to exercise freely the right to vote. This essay, which examines that ongoing struggle, is dedicated to Paul M. Gaston, my mentor and friend, who has devoted much of his career and life work to ensuring equal justice for all.

The passage of the Voting Rights Act had far-reaching implications regarding national politics as the electoral map changed almost overnight. The South had been solidly Democrat since the Civil War; but, while southern Democrats on the state and local level had remained largely conservative and still identified with white supremacy, the national Democratic Party had become more progressive over the years, as reflected in the increasing level of support for civil rights in the Truman, Kennedy, and Johnson Administrations. President Johnson expressed concern that the civil rights legislation passed in the 1960s would alienate large numbers of white southerners who had in the past supported national Democratic candidates, and that the Republican Party would soon become a more attractive alternative. Just two months after passage of the Civil Rights Act, life-long segregationist Strom Thurmond, first elected United States Senator from South Carolina in 1956 as a Democrat, switched to the Republican Party on September 16, 1964—a move repeated by many other southern Democrats over the next decade. Thurmond played a significant role in attracting white South Carolinians to the Republican presidential campaigns of Barry Goldwater in 1964 (who openly opposed the Civil Rights Act) and Richard Nixon in 1968 (whose campaign of "law and order" was clearly aimed at white conservative voters who had had enough of civil rights legislation and urban rebellions). Although Goldwater's extremist views did not resonate with most Americans in 1964, Nixon's more subtle appeals to race proved to be a successful strategy when he ran against Hubert Humphrey in 1968. Nixon and George Wallace (who ran as a third party independent) carried every southern state except Texas, Johnson's home state, which Humphrey won by less than two percentage points. By 1968, the handwriting was on the wall: the South, which had been solidly Democratic in past presidential contests, would soon become solidly Republican.[3]

No sooner had Republicans regained control of the presidency did the push begin to weaken enforcement of voting rights laws. Originally set to expire in 1970, the Voting Rights Act has been reauthorized periodically and for varying periods of time, with each extension being accompanied by debates over which changes should be made and which parts of the country should be covered under the enforcement provisions. When the act was up for renewal for the first time in 1970, President Nixon's attorney general John Mitchell attempted to weaken the bill—or perhaps eliminate it entirely—by calling for only a three-year renewal. Additionally, he wanted to eliminate the preclearance provision, which requires states or any areas covered under the Act to submit any voting changes to the Justice Department to be approved in advance—or "precleared"—before the changes could go into effect. Under Mitchell's proposal, the covered areas would not need Justice Department approval for any voting changes; rather, the states would be free to change their voting laws at their leisure, requiring the Justice Department to issue a challenge only *after* the changes had become law. In other words, the burden of proof would shift: the Justice Department would now have to prove that the states were still engaging in racially discriminatory voting practices rather than the states having to prove that they were not. Enraged by the attorney general's announcement, a group of civil rights activists staged a sit-in at Mitchell's office.

The Mitchell Bill, as it was called, set off a firestorm of debate and controversy within the Congress. While it appealed to southern supporters who felt that federal supervision of their elections was like a second Reconstruction, it angered those—including a number of pro-civil rights northern Republicans—who believed it was far too soon to remove federal oversight. One of the bill's more controversial provisions called for a *national* ban on literacy tests (fourteen states outside the South still used them). This provision not only pleased southerners who felt that they were being exclusively stigmatized, but it also put liberal politicians in a tough spot: while they knew that the real problems with voting discrimination were in the South, it would be difficult for them to oppose a provision that sounded fair on its face. But including more states meant that the Civil Rights Division's staff would be stretched to the limit, forcing them to divert attention away from the problem areas in the South, which of course was the original intent of Mitchell's proposal.

After contentious debate in both chambers, Senators Philip Hart, a Michigan Democrat, and Hugh Scott, Republican minority leader from

Pennsylvania, prepared a substitute bill. Their bill extended the Act for another five years (not the three that Mitchell had proposed) and it provided for a national ban on literacy tests. But a serious problem arose over the issue of the *triggering mechanism*, which, in a nutshell, brought federal scrutiny on those states where less than 50 percent of the jurisdiction's voting-age residents either were registered to vote or cast a ballot in the November 1964 presidential election. Under the terms of the Voting Rights Act, the 1964 presidential election returns were used as the benchmark. But in a few southern states voter participation had now reached 50 percent, as reflected in the 1968 presidential election returns. North Carolina Senator Sam Ervin proposed that the 1968 election returns be the new benchmark, which meant that those states that showed a satisfactory increase in voter participation might be released from coverage. The concern among liberals was that if the 1968 election returns became the new standard of measurement to define which states should be covered, those states with the worst record of voting discrimination—Alabama, Mississippi, Louisiana, Virginia, and North Carolina (Ervin's home state)—would be freed from coverage. While pleased with the progress these states had made in voter participation, many liberal and moderate lawmakers feared that exempting these states from coverage too soon would be an open invitation for them to revert to their past racially discriminatory practices; continued federal oversight was needed to ensure that they did not.

Kentucky Republican John Sherman Cooper broke the impasse by offering a compromise amendment that made the 1968 election returns the new standard, but none of the original southern states covered under the Act would be freed—or *bailed out*—on the basis of one election. Additionally, areas *outside* the South that failed to meet the 50 percent threshold would now also be covered. On March 13, 1970, the Senate voted sixty-four to twelve to substitute the Hart-Scott Bill for the Mitchell Bill. The House of Representatives approved the bill on June 17 by a vote of 272 to 132. The final version extended the Voting Rights Act for another five years, banned literacy tests nationally, and updated the triggering mechanism to reflect the 1968 election returns. As a consequence of this revision, three New York boroughs and jurisdictions in Arizona, California, and Wyoming were now covered (thus removing the scarlet letter that the South had worn exclusively). Section 5, which contained the preclearance provision, remained unchanged, and residency requirements to vote in presidential elections were now reduced from generally one year to thirty days, thereby making the ballot accessible to those who had moved only recently. President Nixon signed the Voting Rights Act extension into law on June 22, 1970. Unlike five years earlier, there was no public ceremony to mark the occasion.[4]

The Voting Rights Act had survived its first renewal test, but the experience provided civil rights activists with a glimpse of what lay ahead. Future presidents and congresses who owed their loyalties to other constituencies might be far less sympathetic to the idea of voting equality for African Americans, and because the Act was not permanent and subject to periodic renewal, it would always be vulnerable to conservative attacks. No psychic powers of clairvoyance were required to realize that such attacks were inevitable.

For the next few decades renewal of the Voting Rights Act was pretty much routine. Despite objections raised by the usual conservative suspects in Congress, one president after another, Democrat and Republican, signed the bill extending the Act, signaling that African American participation in the electoral process was now a permanent fact of life. Even most white southern lawmakers refrained from attacking the Act itself, choosing instead to aim their efforts at weakening the bailout provision that would have allowed their states to be removed from coverage. The affirmative decisions coming from the United States Supreme Court on the matter of voting rights played no small part in moving both the executive and legislative branches of government towards acceptance of fairness in the voting booth. Beginning in 1966, the Court ruled in *South Carolina v. Katzenbach* that the provisions of the Voting Rights Act were constitutional. In 1969, in *Allen v. State Board of Elections* (Virginia) the Court ruled that a state could not change electoral practices in a way that might affect minority voting without submitting those changes to either the Justice Department or the US District Court in Washington, D.C., thereby reaffirming the practice of preclearance. In 1973, in *White v. Regester*, the Court ruled against at-large (or multimember) voting districts in Texas, arguing that such districts discriminated against black and Latino voters. In that same year, in *Zimmer v. McKeithen*, the Court issued a similar ruling in a case originating in East Carroll Parish, Louisiana, holding that "multimember districts were unconstitutional, unless their use would afford a minority greater opportunity for political participation, or unless the use of single-member districts would infringe protected rights."⁵ Between 1973 and 1980 attorneys from the American Civil Liberties Union (ACLU), the National Association for the Advancement of Colored People (NAACP), and various other civil rights organizations filed at least forty lawsuits in an attempt to block at-large elections in local and city governments. When the Voting Rights Act was set to expire in 1975, Congress voted to reauthorize it for another seven years.

With consistent backing from the federal courts, African Americans continued to reach new milestones in electoral politics. On January 1, 1968, Carl Stokes became the first African American mayor of a major city (defined as having a population of more than 100,000) when he was sworn in as the chief executive of Cleveland, Ohio. Stokes had grown up in Cleveland's black ghetto, served in the armed forces, and earned a law degree. He served three terms in the Ohio House of Representatives, first elected in 1962, and then ran unsuccessfully to be Cleveland's mayor in 1965, receiving less than 5 percent of the white vote. Given the city's demographics, he would have to do better with white voters if he were to have any chance of ever being elected. He mounted a second attempt in 1967, reassuring white voters that his election "would not mean a Negro takeover." At the same time, he openly confronted the race issue, and challenged the city's white residents to put aside their prejudices. In one campaign speech he asked, "Are the people of Cleveland willing to vote for a candidate for mayor who has the best qualifications, but whose skin does happen to be black?"⁶ Not all Cleveland whites responded in the affirmative, but enough of them did to propel him to victory. On November 7, 1967, Stokes received 95 percent of the black vote and 20 percent of white vote, which allowed him to defeat his white Republican opponent Seth Taft by a slender margin of 50.3 to 49.7 percent. At the same time, Richard Hatcher was elected as the first black mayor of Gary, Indiana, eking out a slim 1,389 vote majority over his white opponent. Hatcher received 14 percent of the white vote and a whopping 96 percent of the black vote.⁷

Many other African American electoral victories soon followed in rapid succession. In 1973 Thomas "Tom" Bradley, the grandson of slaves, was elected mayor of Los Angeles, California, the first African American to be elected mayor of a major city that did not have a black electoral majority. Although blacks accounted for only 18 percent of the city's population, Bradley's message of hope and change—a message that an obscure U.S. senator from Illinois would capitalize on thirty-five years later—resonated with the city's voters who gave him a solid victory on election day. Racial issues had dogged Bradley's campaign in his first attempt at the mayor's office in 1969 when his white opponent, Sam Yorty, exploited racial fears by portraying Bradley as "anti-police" and asserting that a majority of the police force (predominantly white) would resign if Bradley were elected. Yorty also alleged that Bradley's campaign was being driven by "black militants, white radicals and Communists."[8] Bradley won the primary in 1969 but lost to Yorty in the runoff. Four years later, however, Bradley effectively downplayed race as an issue, arguing that it was only a cheap ploy to divide the city's residents. Building a solid multiracial coalition of liberal whites and minorities, Bradley would be elected to an unprecedented five terms as Los Angeles' mayor, holding that position for twenty years. In 1982 and in 1986 he ran unsuccessfully for governor of California. He won the Democratic primary but lost both times in the general election to Republican George Deukmejian. The racial dynamics that appeared to underlie his narrow and unexpected loss in 1982 (Bradley had maintained a solid lead in all the polls) gave rise to the political term "the Bradley effect," in which some white voters will tell pollsters that they intend to support the black candidate but then vote for the white candidate on election day.

History was also being made in the Deep South in 1973. Maynard Holbrook Jackson was elected mayor of Atlanta, Georgia, becoming the city's first black mayor and the first black mayor of a large southern city. He would eventually serve three terms (1974–82, 1990–94). Also in that year Coleman Young was elected first black mayor of Detroit, serving from 1974 to 1994. In 1978, Ernest Morial was elected as the first black mayor of New Orleans; in 1979, Richard Arrington became Birmingham's first black mayor; in 1983, Harold Washington and Harvey Gantt were elected as the first black mayors of Chicago and Charlotte, North Carolina, respectively; in 1984, Wilson Goode was elected the first black mayor of Philadelphia; in 1988, Kurt Schmoke was elected the first black mayor of Baltimore; and in 1989, David Dinkins was elected as the first black mayor of New York. In that same year, Lawrence Douglas Wilder was elected governor of Virginia, becoming the first African American ever to be elected governor of a state.

In addition to being elected as mayors of major cities, African Americans were also winning election as state legislators and as United States congressmen. In 1972, Andrew Young of Georgia and Barbara Jordan of Texas became the first African Americans elected to Congress from the South since Reconstruction. They joined a cohort of other blacks elected to Congress that officially organized as the Congressional Black Caucus. Membership in the CBC is exclusive to African Americans, and while the Caucus is officially non-partisan, the vast majority of its members have been and continue to be Democrats (some black Republicans have joined the Caucus, others have not). A predecessor to the caucus was founded in January 1969 as a "Democratic Select Committee" by a group of black members of the House of Representatives, including Shirley Chisholm of New York, Louis Stokes of Ohio and William Clay of Missouri. Black representatives had begun to enter the House in increasing numbers during the 1960s, and they wanted a formal organization. The first chairman, Charles Diggs of Michigan, served from 1969 to 1971. The organization was renamed the Congressional Black Caucus in February 1971 on the motion of Charles B. Rangel of New York. Founding members of the caucus were Shirley Chisholm, William L. Clay, Sr., George W. Collins, John Conyers, Ronald Dellums, Augustus F. Hawkins, Ralph Metcalfe, Parren Mitchell, Robert Nix, Charles Rangel, Louis Stokes, and Walter Fauntroy.

Black electoral gains notwithstanding, the idealism and optimism that had characterized much of the 1960s and the early 1970s gave way to white backlash and retrenchment in later years, and for the first time the significant gains made during the civil rights movement appeared to be in real jeopardy. Earl Warren's retirement as U.S. Supreme Court Chief Justice and Richard Nixon's election as president signaled a shift—gradual at first—in the Court's direction from liberal to conservative. For the next twenty-four years, from

1969–1993, luck would be on the side of the Republicans when it came to appointing judges to the federal bench (in addition to those appointed to the U.S. Supreme Court), and as a consequence, the political pendulum moved increasingly to the right. Richard Nixon appointed four justices to the Supreme Court, Gerald Ford appointed one, Ronald Reagan appointed three, and George H. W. Bush appointed two. Elected in 1976, Jimmy Carter was the only Democrat to serve as president during that period, but as fate would have it, he did not have an opportunity to appoint a single justice to the high court. Carter remains the only president in the nation's history to have served at least one full term in office without making a single appointment to the Supreme Court.

The Supreme Court's new conservative majority handed down a string of decisions that appeared to limit African Americans' electoral opportunities. In *Mobile v. Bolden* (1980) the Court ruled that because African Americans in Mobile, Alabama, could register and vote freely, the city's at-large election system did not discriminate against them, even if such a system made it more difficult for blacks to be elected to office. The Court held that discriminatory *effects* had to be accompanied by discriminatory *intent*. Justice Potter Stewart wrote that "disproportionate impact alone cannot be decisive, and courts must look to other evidence to support a finding of discriminatory purpose."[9] In several important decisions in the 1990s, the Court held that race could not be a factor in the creation of voting districts. In *Shaw v. Reno* (1993) the Court ruled that North Carolina's congressional redistricting plan (which had created two predominantly black congressional districts out of a total of twelve districts) constituted racial gerrymandering. The white plaintiffs who challenged the oddly-shaped district alleged that they were the victims of racial segregation by virtue of having been excluded from the district. Speaking for the 5–4 majority, Justice Sandra Day O'Connor agreed. She wrote that the configuration of North Carolina's twelfth district was so bizarre on its face that clear racial intent was the only possible explanation. Calling the district a version of "political apartheid" (a reference to South Africa's system of rigid racial separation), O'Connor condemned "racial classifications of any sort."[10] In a similar case in 1995, the Court ruled in *Miller v. Johnson* that Georgia's eleventh district, represented by Cynthia

McKinney, the first black woman elected to Congress from Georgia, was also flawed—not because of the shape of the district, but because race was the predominant factor in determining the configuration of the district. Writing for the majority, Justice Anthony Kennedy determined that race, "for its own sake," could not be tolerated as a criterion in drawing district boundaries.[11] Equal opportunity could never be achieved, Kennedy wrote, "by carving electorates into racial blocs." Dissenting from the majority opinion, Justice Ruth Bader Ginsburg, appointed to the Court by President Bill Clinton in 1993, argued that the Court's rulings in these cases handicapped the very minority group that the Voting Rights Act had been created to protect.[12]

When the Voting Rights Act was renewed for seven years in 1975, Congress expanded its scope to protect "language minorities," defined as "persons who are American Indian, Asian American, Alaskan Natives, or persons who are of Spanish heritage."[13] Congress also enacted a bilingual election requirement in Section 203, which requires election officials in certain jurisdictions with large numbers of English-illiterate language minorities to provide ballots and voting information in the language of the language minority group. The Voting Rights Act was renewed for twenty-five years in 1982 and in 2006, with new provisions being added both times. In 1982, Congress amended the Act to overturn the Supreme Court case *Mobile v. Bolden*, which had held that the general prohibition of voting discrimination prescribed in Section 2 prohibited only *purposeful* discrimination. Congress expanded Section 2 to explicitly ban any voting practice that had a discriminatory *effect*, regardless of intent. In 2006, Congress amended the Act to overturn two Supreme Court cases, *Reno v. Bossier Parish School Board, Louisiana* (2000) and *Georgia v. Ashcroft* (2003). At issue in both cases was whether state legislatures had an obligation to try to *maximize* minority electoral strength (by increasing the likelihood that blacks would be able to elect their preferred candidates) rather than just preserve their right to participate. In both cases, the Court's conservative majority ruled 5–4 that the Justice Department could not deny preclearance to local redistricting plans just because minority voters in some districts will have a reduced chance of electing a candidate of their choice.[14]

Despite occasional setbacks as a result of decisions handed down by an increasingly conservative Supreme Court, black participation in the electoral process had become a fact of American life by the 21st century. African Americans (as well as Latinos, who by now outnumbered blacks as the nation's largest non-white minority) were increasing their representation in local, state, and national elective offices. In 1965 there were only five blacks in Congress; in 2014, there were forty-three blacks represented in the 113th Congress. In 1965 there were roughly 1400 black officeholders nationwide; by December 2009 that number had grown to 10,000, including many who were elected in majority white districts, some of which were in the South. By 2007, African Americans had served as congressional representatives and senators, state governors, and state legislators. Only the nation's highest elective office, the presidency, appeared to be out of reach. And while a few African Americans had previously mounted presidential bids—New York congresswoman Shirley Chisholm in 1972, civil rights activist Jesse Jackson in 1984 and 1988, civil rights activist Al Sharpton and former Illinois U.S. Senator Carol Moseley-Braun in 2004—none had drawn enough white support to be considered viable candidates. But in 2007, a relatively obscure U.S. Senator from Illinois would shake up the political establishment and in one fell swoop would soon personify the penultimate achievement of the 1965 Voting Rights Act.

On February 10, 2007, Barack Obama announced his candidacy for President of the United States in front of the Old State Capitol building in Springfield, Illinois—the same place where Abraham Lincoln had delivered his famous "House Divided" speech in 1858. Born on August 4, 1961, to a white American mother and a black Kenyan father, and having grown up in multi-racial Hawaii where race is not defined in terms of black or white, Obama was in many ways the perfect symbol of ethnic and racial diversity. While he had obviously benefitted from the successes of the civil rights movement, he was not a product of that era, which in large part enabled him to approach issues in ways that transcended race, something that only increased his appeal among younger voters. Although the product of a biracial marriage, he clearly identified as African American, a fact that he emphasized when CBS correspondent Steve Kroft asked him on the news program *60 Minutes* when did he decide that he was black. Responding with his usual poise, Obama replied "Well I'm not sure I decided it. I think if you look African American in this society, you're treated as an African American. And when you're a child in particular that is how you begin to identify yourself. At least that's what I felt comfortable identifying myself as."[15] His marriage to an equally intelligent, politically savvy, and darker-skinned black woman, with whom he was raising two daughters, removed any doubts about his racial identity.

Obama's sudden appearance onto the political stage seemed to come out of nowhere. He had graduated from Columbia University and Harvard Law School, where he served as president of *Harvard Law Review*. He had been a community organizer in Chicago before earning his law degree, and later he taught constitutional law at the University of Chicago Law School from 1992 to 2004. From 1997 to 2004 he served three terms in the Illinois senate, and had run unsuccessfully for the U.S. House of Representatives in 2000. He first gained national attention in July 2004, when as a candidate for a U.S. Senate seat in Illinois he delivered the keynote address at the Democratic National Convention. In November of that year he would win the senate seat, becoming only the third African American to be elected to the U.S. Senate since Reconstruction. In the Senate, Obama voiced his opposition to the Iraq War which had begun under President George W. Bush, and championed government policies that created good-paying jobs and increased educational opportunities for all Americans. Agreeing with his University of Chicago colleague, acclaimed sociologist William Julius Wilson, Obama believed that class had replaced race as the most significant detriment to economic mobility. The fact that he himself had been raised by a single mother after his parents divorced certainly lent credibility to his argument.

While Barack Obama's presidential campaign generated unprecedented excitement and enthusiasm within the African American community, many wondered privately if the freshman senator from Illinois was experienced enough to be president, and whether the country was ready to send a black man to the White House. Further complicating Obama's path to the presidency was his main Democratic opponent, Hillary Clinton. Democrat Bill Clinton had won the presidency in 1992 and in 1996, both times drawing very strong support from black voters. Clinton appeared to have such a common bond with African Americans that Nobel laureate Toni Morrison once referred to him as the nation's "first black President."[16] As First Lady, Hillary Clinton had been just as popular with black voters. Polls taken in 2007 indicated that Hillary Clinton was running well ahead of Obama among registered black voters, 57 percent to 33 percent. Many in the black civil rights establishment felt a certain allegiance to Bill Clinton and subsequently transferred that to Hillary, some of which stemmed from the fact that many believed that Hillary's chances of being the first woman president were better than Obama's chances of becoming the first black president. Georgia congressman John Lewis and New York congressman Charles Rangel came out early for Clinton while Illinois congressman Jesse Jackson, Jr., campaigned for Obama. The other thirty-nine members of the Congressional Black Caucus were evenly divided between the two candidates.

Many who had doubted Obama's electability quickly reassessed their options after Obama's surprising win in the Iowa caucus in early January 2008. Capturing 37.6 percent of the caucus votes in a state where blacks constituted less than 5 percent of the population convinced many skeptics that Obama had crossover appeal. Hillary Clinton had come in third. Obama came in second to Clinton in New Hampshire, but solidified his Iowa win with a resounding victory in South Carolina's primary, where blacks made up 50 percent of the Democratic Party's electorate. Obama's impressive showing with black voters in South Carolina (he captured more than 80 percent of the black vote) brought racial tensions openly into the campaign for the first time. Campaigning for his wife, Bill Clinton tried to minimize the importance of Obama's South Carolina victory by implying, not so subtly, that Obama would need more than black votes to win the presidency. "Jesse Jackson won South Carolina in '84 and '88," the former president told reporters.[17] Clinton did not need to remind the reporters that Jackson had been unsuccessful in both presidential bids. Tensions between the Obama and Clinton camps would only escalate in the coming weeks.

On February 5, races were held in twenty-two states. Because of the number of delegates up for grabs, the day was referred to as "Super Tuesday." Although Clinton had been expected to take the lion's share of delegates and lock up the nomination, she and Obama ended up splitting the delegates, further convincing voters that Obama's candidacy was not a sideshow. Campaigning on a theme of change, his slogan of "Yes We Can" captured the imagination of minorities and younger voters who had grown weary of politics as usual. Following Obama's win in the Georgia primary on Super Tuesday, pressure began to mount on civil rights veteran John Lewis to support the first African American presidential contender who now seemed to have a real chance of winning. While acknowledging his allegiance to the Clintons, Lewis realized that his early endorsement of Hillary was at odds with most of Georgia's black voters (as well as most black voters in his own congressional district). Faced with the possibility of having to fend off a challenge to keep his seat in Congress, Lewis defected from the Clinton camp and endorsed Obama, an endorsement that carried considerable weight not only in Georgia but across the nation. And with that endorsement Lewis appeared to be passing the mantle of black leadership to a new generation. "Barack was born long before he could experience or understand the movement," Lewis said. "He had to move towards it in his own time, but it is so clear that he digested . . . the spirit and the language of the movement."[18] Obama went on to win eleven straight primaries and caucuses following Super Tuesday, and by the end of February he led Clinton in both the popular vote and the convention delegate count.[19]

As the primary season drew to a close, Clinton scored victories in Texas, West Virginia, and Kentucky while Obama won in North Carolina, Nevada, and Oregon. Obama had a narrow lead among pledged delegates while Clinton had accumulated more popular votes, but neither candidate had achieved the required 2,117 votes needed to secure the nomination. The decision was now in the hands of the "super-delegates"—the 824 Democratic members of Congress, governors, and other high-ranking party officials who vote at the convention, and who comprise roughly 20 percent of convention delegates. The fact that Obama had won more delegates in the primaries and caucuses tipped the scales in his favor, and in the end most of the super delegates threw their support to him which helped him secure the nomination. On August 28, 2008—the 45th anniversary of the historic March on Washington—Barack Obama stood before a crowd of

84,000 people gathered at the Democratic National Convention in Denver, Colorado, and accepted the nomination of his party. In so doing, he became the first African American to be nominated for president by a major political party. Ever mindful of the irony of accepting his party's nomination on this significant date, Obama reminded the crowd that "a young preacher from Georgia" had dared to dream that "in America, our destiny is inextricably linked, that together our dreams can be one."[20]

Obama chose Delaware senator Joseph Biden as his running mate. Biden had been a candidate for the presidency in 2008 and had also run unsuccessfully in 1988. On the Republican side, Arizona senator John McCain came out on top from a crowded field of contenders to secure his party's nomination. Having gained a reputation as being a maverick within his own party, McCain was a distinguished veteran of the Vietnam War. He had nearly been killed in a fire aboard the *USS Forrestal* in July 1967, and in October of that year was seriously injured when, while on a bombing mission over Hanoi, his plane was shot down. He was captured by the North Vietnamese and held as a prisoner of war until 1973. First elected to the U.S. House of Representatives in 1982, he served two terms and then won a U.S. Senate seat in 1986, which he continues to hold. He ran for the Republican Party's presidential nomination in 2000 but lost to George W. Bush. After winning his party's nomination in 2008, he surprised many by choosing Alaska governor Sarah Palin, virtually unknown, as his running mate.

At first, both sides tried to downplay the race issue. Obama went to great lengths to portray himself as an agent of change who happened to be African American, and his message of hope and change resonated with minorities, younger voters, white liberals, and white moderates who described themselves politically as independent. For his part, McCain also seemed to want to run a campaign devoid of racist innuendo, even if it meant having to call out some of his white supporters at his various campaign events. When a woman commented at a McCain rally that she could not vote for Obama because "he's an "Arab," McCain responded without hesitation, "No Ma'am. He's a decent family man . . . that I just happen to have disagreements with on fundamental issues." And when a man told McCain that he would be afraid to raise a child in this country if Obama were elected president, McCain responded that Obama was "a decent person and not a person you have to be scared of as president."[21]

But as the campaign heated up in late summer and when it appeared that Obama's lead in the national polls was holding steady, many of McCain's supporters began to resort to crude and vicious racism that quickly tainted McCain's campaign. Some of his events—which McCain himself certainly was not responsible for—resembled Ku Klux Klan rallies, as Obama was openly referred to as a "nigger;" cartoons were circulated lampooning him as an "ape," and bull's-eye targets were circulated with Obama's head in the crosshairs. The racist rhetoric on open display at some McCain events prompted congressman and civil rights veteran John Lewis to call on McCain to distance himself from some of his supporters. McCain's running mate Sarah Palin helped stoke the flames by repeatedly suggesting that Obama (who many Republicans incorrectly believed was a Muslim, and whose surname sounded like the first name of America's most-hated enemy, Osama bin Laden) was sympathetic to terrorists. Palin never missed an opportunity to fire up her crowds by insisting that Obama was "palling around with terrorists who would target their own country."[22] An Associated Press reporter wrote that while Palin carefully skirted overt racism in her comments, "there is a subtext for creating a false image of a black president" as "not like us."[23] Although he had taken the high road early in the campaign, McCain eventually gave in to desperation and joined his running mate in linking Obama to terrorists. But these last-minute acts of desperation were all in vain. With the country on the brink of financial collapse as a result of George W. Bush's failed economic policies, most Americans were ready for a change, even if it came in the form of a biracial man with a black Kenyan father and a Middle Eastern-sounding name.

On November 4, 2008, Barack Hussein Obama was elected the forty-fourth president of the United States. He defeated John McCain by a convincing margin of 53 percent to 46 percent in the popular vote, the first Democrat since Jimmy Carter in 1976 to win a majority of the popular vote, and his margin of victory was the largest for a Democrat since Lyndon Johnson's 1964 victory over another Arizonan, Barry Goldwater. Obama won twenty-eight states and the District of Columbia, and most significantly, won the key battleground states of Ohio, Pennsylvania, and Michigan. He also won three southern battleground states—Florida, Virginia and North Carolina—moving Virginia and North Carolina out of the Republican column for the first time since 1964 and 1976, respectively. His margin of victory in the Electoral College, 365–173, was decisive.

A variety of factors contributed to Barack Obama's historic win, not the least of which was an economy on the verge of collapse. The stock market had tumbled to near historic lows; the auto industry was in free fall; a crisis in the housing market meant that the dream of home ownership was becoming increasing elusive for many; the unregulated banking industry was teetering on the brink of insolvency; the income gap between those at the top and those at the bottom had never been wider; and the incomes of most Americans were stagnant as gas prices soared. And then there was widespread dissatisfaction with what appeared to be an endless war in Iraq amid growing American skepticism over President Bush's claim that the war had been necessary because of Iraq's weapons of mass destruction (which have yet to be found). In light of that economic and political climate, it is unlikely that *any* Republican ticket could have prevailed in the general election; but, John McCain certainly did himself no favor when he selected Sarah Palin as his running mate, someone whose lack of preparedness to occupy the nation's second highest office was almost embarrassing.

But without a doubt, the fact that an African American was at the top of the ticket excited and mobilized black voters like never before. Not only did black voters give Obama their overwhelming support (around 95 percent), but most important, they turned out in record numbers. Roughly two million more blacks voted in 2008 than in 2004, and the black electorate now comprised 13 percent of the total vote, up two percentage points from four years earlier. Obama also picked up support from most Democrats who had voted for Hillary Clinton in the primary. Comprising 53 percent of general election voters, women gave Obama 56 percent of their votes, with most of that support coming from unmarried women, who gave him 70 percent of their votes. Most of Obama's support from women came from black women and other women of color; white women cast only 41 percent of their ballots for him. Obama did well with other racial minorities, netting 67 percent of the Latino vote (now 9 percent of the total electorate) and 62 percent of the Asian-American vote. And across racial and ethnic lines, first time, mainly younger voters supported Obama over McCain by a lopsided margin of 71 to 27 percent.

While Obama's victory clearly represented a historic milestone in American politics, there remained unmistakable signs that race still mattered, something that was most evident in the states of the former Confederacy. Except for Virginia, North Carolina, and Florida, the rest of the South went heavily for McCain. In Alabama and Mississippi, Obama received 10 percent and 11 percent of the white vote, respectively. He got 14 percent of the white vote in Louisiana, 23 percent in Georgia, and 26 percent in South Carolina. Even in winning Virginia, North Carolina, and Florida, Obama lost the white vote in all three states. Nationally, Obama received 43 percent of the white vote. He won the votes of those describing themselves as independents by an eight-point margin, but won only 34 percent of white Protestants and 24 percent of white evangelicals. Catholics and Jews, however, supported Obama with 54 percent and 86 percent, respectively.[24]

The fact that the nation had elected its first African American president almost immediately prompted many political commentators to declare that America had arrived at the millennium, and that the Obama Presidency signaled the beginning of a post-racial society, one in which race no longer mattered. Not surprisingly, most of those assessments came from conservatives who had established their careers and reputations by opposing affirmative action programs and other governmental policies that they considered to be racial "quotas," minority "set-asides," "racial entitlements," or "racial preferences." Many of them had even distorted and misappropriated the language from King's "I Have a Dream" speech in their opposition to any program that favored minorities. For decades, they had argued that "color consciousness" should now give way to "color blindness," despite the persistence of segregation and racial discrimination in many facets of American life. To them, Obama's victory was proof that America had finally turned the corner on matters of race. Staunch conservative and right-wing intellectual Dinesh D'Souza (who would become one of the president's leading critics) applauded Obama's victory for affirming that "we are now living in a post-racist America."[25]

While they were busy promoting the fallacy of a post-racial America, many conservatives were beginning to take note of the nation's changing demographics. In 1976, whites made up 89 percent of the presidential electorate; in 2008, that had dropped to 74 percent. The percentage of older white male voters had dropped even more significantly. Further, Latinos now outnumbered blacks as the nation's largest minority group, and with nearly 50,000 Latinos turning eighteen every thirty days, they would soon be a political force to be reckoned with. In this world of changing demographics and increased minority voter participation, many white conservatives apparently caught a glimpse of the political future that was at once unsettling and alarming.

And then, just two years after Obama's election, the 2010 midterm elections resulted in a conservative backlash that led to Republicans taking control of the House of Representatives while increasing their numbers in the Senate. The GOP gained 63 seats in the House for a total of 242, the most Republican House seats since 1946. The Democrats retained control of the Senate, but lost six seats. On the state level, the results were even more disastrous for the president's party. Before the 2010 elections, Democrats held the majority of state governorships and state legislatures. But Republicans won 23 of 37 gubernatorial contests in 2010, gaining 11 new governorships for a total of 30 out of 50 states. Republicans also made gains in the state legislatures, now controlling *both* legislative bodies in twenty-six states, with twenty-three of those also having a Republican governor, the equivalent of a political trifecta. As one observer noted, "What happened next was so swift that it caught most observers off guard—and began surreptitiously to reverse the last half-century of voting rights reforms."[26]

In the aftermath of the 2010 midterm elections, Republican legislatures all across the country enacted a series of new laws and restrictions designed to make voting more difficult. While these laws did not specifically target any one group (and like earlier disfranchisement schemes, made no mention of race) it was obvious that the overwhelming majority of those affected were part of Obama's Democratic coalition—minorities, the poor, students, the elderly or handicapped. In 2008, the Supreme Court had upheld a new Indiana law requiring government-issued photo identification for voting. Soon thereafter, Republicans in other states drew up and hastily passed similar laws which they claimed were needed to combat widespread voter fraud. In reality, instances of voter fraud nationally were virtually non-existent. The real impetus behind such measures was to weaken Democratic Party fortunes at the polls. All of the studies have shown that the poor, minorities, and college-age students—those most likely to vote Democratic—were least likely to have government-issued identification. The nonpartisan Brennan Center for Justice at New York University Law School reported that approximately 25 percent of African Americans did not possess a photo ID card. Before 2010, only two states required voters to show government-issued photo ID at the polls. By August 2012, thirty-four state legislatures had considered photo ID laws and thirteen had passed them; five more states had such laws passed in the Republican-controlled legislatures only to be vetoed by Democratic governors. Some accepted state-issued student IDs while others (South Carolina, Tennessee, and Texas) accepted no student IDs whatsoever. In Texas, however, while a student ID is not considered a valid form of identification for the purpose of voting, a permit to carry a concealed handgun is accepted as valid ID. By the summer of 2012, many states already had the new restrictive voter ID laws in place: Pennsylvania (where it was estimated that 9.2 percent of registered voters had no photo ID), Alabama, Mississippi, Rhode Island, New Hampshire, Kansas, South Carolina, Tennessee, Texas, and Wisconsin.[27]

The Brennan Center for Justice also found that of the eleven states with the highest black voter turnout in 2008, seven passed laws making it harder to vote. Of the twelve states with the largest Hispanic population growth in the 2010 census, nine have new voting restrictions in place. And of the fifteen states that used to be monitored closely under the 1965 Voting Rights Act because of a history of racial discrimination in voting, nine have passed new voting restrictions. Instead of embracing efforts to encourage voter participation, Republicans have worked in concert to undermine the process.

These new laws requiring government-issued photo IDs were just the beginning. One after the other, Republican-controlled state legislatures adopted measures to reduce the number of days for early voting, which African Americans in particular had taken advantage of. Many black communities participate in something referred to as "Souls to the Polls," in which black voters head to the polls *en masse* following church service on the Sunday before Election Tuesday. Republican lawmakers in Ohio introduced a bill, H.B. 194, that would have cut the number of early voting days by more than half and that would also have prohibited voting on the last Sunday before Election Day, a ploy aimed squarely at black voters. The Brennan Center observed that the push to shut down Sunday early voting in states where it has been most successful "is a glaring example" of "especially egregious" targeting of minority voters.[28]

This sudden desire to trim early voting is yet another example of how new voting restrictions target minorities. For more than two decades, states had been *increasing* early voting opportunities. In fact, most states now offer early voting, and in the last two presidential elections, at least one-third of Americans voted early. But after the 2008 election, support for early voting eroded among Republican legislators in the South and Midwest, and a likely explanation for that was the dramatic surge in the numbers of African Americans who were voting early. In southern states, early voting by blacks nearly tripled between 2004 and 2008, overtaking early voting by whites by a significant margin. Since 2011, eight states that saw recent increases in minority early voting have sharply curtailed the number of days and hours allowed for early voting, among them Florida, Georgia, Nebraska, North Carolina, Ohio, Tennessee, West Virginia, and Wisconsin. Generally, the days and hours most likely to be cut were those most popular with minorities and hourly workers, like Sundays and evenings. According to a 2008 Ohio study, 56 percent of weekend workers in Cuyahoga County, the state's most populous, were black.[29]

Knowing full well that early voting expands the electorate, Republicans have publicly conceded that they oppose it because it hurts them at the polls. In a column for right-wing clearinghouse *WorldNetDaily*, longtime conservative activist Phyllis Schlafly admitted that reducing the days of early voting was aimed squarely at President Obama's constituency. As she put it, "The reduction in the number of days allowed for early voting is particularly important because early voting plays a major role in Obama's ground game. The Democrats carried most states that allow many days of early voting, and Obama's national field director admitted, shortly before last year's election, that 'early voting is giving us a solid lead in the battleground states that will decide this election.'" Schlafly went on to add that early voting "violates the spirit of the Constitution" and it allows for "illegal votes" that "cancel out the votes of honest Americans."[30] After the 2012 election, former Florida GOP chairman Jim Greer told *The Palm Beach Post* that the explicit goal of the state's voter ID law was Democratic suppression. "The Republican Party, the strategists, the consultants, they firmly believe that early voting is bad for Republican Party candidates," Greer told the *Post*. "It's done for one reason and one reason only . . . 'We've got to cut down on early voting because early voting is not good for us,'" he said.[31] Consequently, the Florida Republican Party imposed a host of new voting rules, from longer ballots to fewer precincts in minority areas, meant to discourage voting. And it worked. According to one study, as many as 49,000 people were discouraged from voting in November 2012 as a result of long lines and other obstacles.[32]

Not only has voting become more difficult, but Republican lawmakers have also made it much more cumbersome to register. Since 2010, ten states have passed laws making it harder for citizens to register to vote. These include laws eliminating the highly popular same-day registration (in Nebraska and North Carolina); a law making it harder for people who move to stay registered (in Wisconsin); laws curbing voter registration drives (in Florida, Illinois, Texas, and Virginia); rules requiring voters to provide documentary proof of citizenship, such as a birth certificate, when registering (in Alabama, Kansas, Tennessee, and previously in Arizona). Groups such as the League of Women Voters have been prohibited from conducting voter registration drives, which tend to enroll twice as many minorities as whites, and which over the years have helped close the racial registration gap. And for those who lack the proper documentation to register, a fee is usually required in order for them to obtain it, which is the modern day equivalent of a poll tax, which effectively disenfranchised African Americans for nearly a century.

Additionally, many states have made it all but impossible for those with prior criminal convictions to have their voting rights restored. In the states of Iowa and Florida, those citizens are essentially permanently disenfranchised. Florida Republican governor Rick Scott secretly reversed the policies of his Republican predecessors Jeb Bush and Charlie Crist that would have permitted 100,000 former felons, most of whom were black and Latino, to vote in the 2012 presidential election. Democrats were stunned, prompting former president Bill Clinton to comment that "There has never been in my lifetime, since we got rid of the poll tax and all the Jim Crow burdens on voting, the determined effort to limit the franchise that we see today."[33] Nationally, it is estimated that at least 5.85 million Americans who have done their time have lost their right to vote, 1.5 million of whom reside in Florida. Overall, 7.7 percent of blacks have lost their right to vote as a result of a felony conviction, compared to 1.8 percent of whites. The number and complexity of new voting restrictions across the country is staggering, prompting one observer to refer to these restrictions as "a death-by-a-thousand-cuts strategy."[34]

What do all of these new voting restrictions have in common? They are all championed by conservative groups and wealthy corporations, passed by Republican legislatures, and signed into law by Republican governors. In the forefront of these new disenfranchisement efforts is an ultraconservative organization known as the American Legislative Exchange Council (ALEC), founded by the late Paul Weyrich, a conservative writer who also founded the Heritage Foundation, a conservative think tank dedicated to limited government, less federal government regulation, and the sanctity of traditional marriage. With the financial backing of conservative corporations such as Coca-Cola, Philip Morris, AT&T, Exxon Mobil, and Walmart, among many others, and funded by right-wing billionaires Richard Mellon Scaife, the Coors brewing family, and David and Charles Koch (aka, the Koch Brothers), ALEC wrote and sponsored hundreds of bills aimed at suppressing the vote and then created the campaigns to get them passed. Its spokesmen boasted "that each year more than 1,000 bills based on its models are introduced in state legislatures, and that approximately 17 percent of those bills become law." The new voter ID laws were one of the group's top priorities. Speaking to a convention of evangelicals in 1980, Paul Weyrich said "Many of our Christians . . . want everybody to vote. I don't want everybody to vote. . . . As a matter of fact, our leverage in the elections quite candidly goes up as the voting populace goes down."³⁵

Surprisingly, many Republican politicians have been brutally honest about their real intentions in their support of voter suppression. New Jersey governor Chris Christie referred to same-day registration as a "trick," an underhanded, Democratic, get-out-the-vote tactic. Speaking to a U.S. Chamber of Commerce gathering in Washington, DC, Christie said that Republicans need to win gubernatorial races so that they are the ones controlling "voting mechanisms" going into the 2016 presidential election. Georgia state senator Fran Millar complained that some polling places were too convenient for black voters. Writing in the *Atlanta Journal-Constitution*, Millar expressed concerns about polling places located in South Dekalb Mall: "This location is dominated by African American shoppers and it is near several large African American mega churches . . . Is it possible [that] church buses will be used to transport people directly to the mall since the polls will open when the mall opens?"³⁶ When asked about his state's efforts to limit early voting, Doug Preis, adviser to Ohio governor John Kasich, said: "We shouldn't contort the voting process to accommodate the urban— read African American—voter-turnout machine."³⁷ (To be clear here, Preis actually said "read African American;" it was not inserted). In a letter to the Justice Department defending his state's newly-drawn voting districts, Texas attorney general Greg Abbott wrote that "It is perfectly constitutional for a Republican-controlled legislature to make partisan districting decisions, even if there are incidental effects on minority voters who support Democratic candidates."³⁸ While running for a Florida congressional seat in 2012, Ted Yoho admitted to having "some radical ideas about voting" and that he believed that only property owners should be allowed to vote. He also called early voting by absentee ballots "a travesty."³⁹ (Yoho won the election and is now a member of Congress). In an interview with *The Daily Show*, North Carolina precinct chair Don Yelton defended his state's new voter ID law, saying that "if it hurts a bunch of lazy blacks that want the government to give them everything, so be it." He went on to add that "The law is going to kick the Democrats in the butt."⁴⁰ And at a meeting of the

Pennsylvania Republican State Committee in June 2012, House majority leader Mike Turzai openly boasted that the state's new voter ID law boded well for Republican presidential nominee Mitt Romney in the fall. When listing the GOP's achievements, Turzai said, "Voter ID, which is gonna allow Governor Romney to win the state of Pennsylvania: Done."[41]

To ensure that their efforts at voter suppression were foolproof, and leaving nothing to chance, Republicans also engaged in a widespread campaign of voter intimidation, which includes but is not limited to the following: voters being threatened with arrest at the polling station if they had unpaid child support or unpaid parking tickets; misleading robocalls to black voters (in Maryland) saying that there was no need to vote because "our goals have been met;" fliers being circulated (in Ohio and Virginia) informing voters that Republicans vote on Election Day and that Democrats vote the day after; challenges to black voters (in Philadelphia) by men carrying clipboards who drove a fleet of cars with signs that looked like law enforcement insignia. Many states permit "voter challenges," which allows any person to challenge another's right to vote, often by suggesting that an individual is engaging in voter fraud. Depending upon the state law, these challengers may be appointed by political parties or other organizations. As one might expect, the challengers are white, and most of those challenged are minorities. An Ohio Republican Party plan in 2004, for example, would have involved challengers confronting 97 percent of new African American voters in one location while only challenging 14 percent of white voters in another. Organizations such as True The Vote, a Tea Party group, have attempted to purge thousands of voters from voting rolls across the country. The group vowed to send thousands of poll-watchers to the polls on Election Day in 2012 to "monitor" voters. Republicans have said the efforts are meant to protect against in-person voter fraud, which there is little evidence of, and to keep undocumented immigrants from voting.

Wealthy corporations and private donors have also supported GOP efforts at voter intimidation by erecting billboards in cities across the nation that either issue threats or contain misinformation. In October 2012, dozens of billboards appeared in predominantly black and Latino neighborhoods in Cleveland warning that "VOTER FRAUD IS A FELONY," punishable with prison time of "Up to 3 and ½ years and $10,000 fine." Stephen Einhorn, a Wisconsin venture capital fund manager and a major GOP donor, along with his wife Nancy, paid for dozens of anonymous billboards in and around Milwaukee and two Ohio cities warning residents of the penalties for voter fraud. The Einhorns have made substantial contributions to many Republican politicians, including Wisconsin governor Scott Walker, 2012 Republican presidential nominee Mitt Romney, Romney's running mate and Wisconsin congressman Paul Ryan, and other GOP House and Senate candidates. "All of these things taken together have such a detrimental impact on communities of color and low income communities," said Ohio state senator Nina Turner. "African Americans really feel insulted at the insinuation that black folks are involved in voter fraud. It makes no sense to me. What they are doing is reminiscent of what segregationist leaders did in the Jim Crow South with poll taxes and grandfather clauses." She added: "They are creating an environment whereby African American, Hispanic and poor people are being painted as offenders. They know exactly what they are doing. This is all about our president. Don't make any mistake about it. Those signs were not up four years ago or eight years ago." Senator Turner also noted the strategic placement of the billboards. "If you are a low-information voter, under all of this pressure . . . many voters will say 'to hell with it,'" and stay home on Election Day.[42]

Many of these new voting restrictions had been strategically timed to go into effect prior to the 2012 presidential election (with President Obama running for re-election), but various civil rights and civil liberties groups across the nation successfully challenged many of the laws in the federal courts. But just when it appeared as if the courts would step in to guarantee minority voting rights and uphold the integrity of the 1965 Voting Rights Act, the U.S. Supreme Court dealt voting rights activists a devastating blow. In 2013, in *Shelby County, Alabama v. Holder*, the Court ruled 5–4 that the act's coverage formula, Section 4, was no longer valid, and that affected jurisdictions no longer had to submit voting changes to the Justice Department before going into effect. The Court did not strike down Section 5 (preclearance), but without Section 4, no jurisdiction will be subject to Section 5 preclearance unless Congress enacts a new coverage formula, which as of this writing, Congress has not done. And since Republicans now control both houses of Congress (as a result of the 2014 midterm elections), it is highly unlikely that they will support any legislation that will hurt their chances at the polls.

Some background to this case might be useful. A predominantly white suburb of Birmingham, Shelby County had a lengthy history of racial bias in voting. Between 1975 and 2008, the county's elections laws had been found racially discriminatory twenty times. In 2008, the county redrew voting districts (over the Justice Department's objection) which resulted in the county's lone black incumbent being defeated. The election was declared invalid, but in 2010, lawyers for the county filed a suit challenging the two key provisions of the Voting Rights Act. The main issue to be decided was whether blacks in 2012 still faced discriminatory obstacles to voting. Writing for the 5–4 majority, Chief Justice John Roberts contended that the nation had made tremendous racial progress since 1965. He noted the election of the first black president, increased black voter turnout, and the election of black mayors in Selma, Alabama and Philadelphia, Mississippi, two cities with a rich civil rights history. If Congress wanted to extend federal oversight over state and local elections, Roberts suggested it should do so on the basis of current data. In its current form, however, Roberts wrote that the Voting Rights Act is "based on 40-year-old facts having no logical relationship to the present day." Responding for the minority of four, Justice Ruth Bader Ginsburg acknowledged the progress that African Americans had made, but also pointed out that there was a significant body of evidence suggesting that racial bias in voting continues, and that this Court "errs egregiously" in invalidating Section 4 of the Act. She wrote that battling racial discrimination in voting "resembled battling the Hydra. Whenever one form of voting discrimination was identified and prohibited, others sprang up in its place." And Justice Ginsburg was correct in her assessment. When Congress voted to renew the Voting Rights Act in 2006, it conducted twenty-one hearings over ten months, gathering 12,000 pages of testimony. Most of the voting rights challenges adjudicated in the federal courts as late as 2006 occurred in those jurisdictions covered under Section 4.[43]

One prominent voting rights scholar has noted that "In pronouncing a premature end to the ongoing struggle against racial disfranchisement, the chief justice's opinion appeared inspired by a long-standing political agenda."[44] In the 1980s, Roberts had worked in President Reagan's Justice Department and had argued for weakened enforcement of the Voting Rights Act, a position that he brought with him to the Supreme Court. One legal analyst wrote that Roberts' mission on the Court was "to declare victory in the nation's fight against racial discrimination and then to disable the weapons with which the struggle was won."[45] Joining Roberts in his opinion were Justices Anthony Kennedy, Samuel Alito, Antonin Scalia, and Clarence Thomas. Scalia commented that the Voting Rights Act was nothing more than the "perpetuation of racial entitlement," while his African American protégé Clarence Thomas, in typical fashion, took an ever more extreme view, insisting that the entire Voting Rights Act was unconstitutional.

Predictably, within hours of the Court's decision, Texas reinstated its photo ID law, which a federal court judge had previously rejected for imposing "strict, unforgiving burdens" on minority voters. Soon thereafter, North Carolina imposed tougher voter ID laws, reduced the number of days for early voting, eliminated same-day registration, ended pre-registration for 16- and 17-year-olds, and disqualified provisional ballots cast outside of voters' home precincts. Other than the stricter ID requirement, which will go into effect in 2016, all of the other laws are already in place. In 2008, more than 700,000 North Carolinians voted during the week that was cut from early voting—including nearly a quarter of all African Americans who voted that year. Even in the 2010 midterm elections, more than 200,000 voters cast ballots during that week. In 2012, nearly 100,000 voters used same-day registration in North Carolina, almost one-third of whom were black. Nationally, same-day registration is credited with boosting turnout by as much as 5 to 7 percent. In 2014, hundreds of citizens cast ballots that went uncounted because of the elimination of out-of-precinct voting. North Carolina now has the dubious distinction of having the nation's harshest and most sweeping voting requirements.

Georgia congressman John Lewis said of the Supreme Court's decision in *Shelby County v. Holder*, "When that decision came down I wanted to cry. Because too many people had suffered; too many people had died."[46]

U.S. Attorney General Eric Holder expressed similar disappointment with the Court's decision. At a press conference on the same day the decision has handed down, the attorney general said that he was "deeply disappointed with the Court's decision" and that "this decision represents a serious setback for voting rights—and has the potential to negatively affect millions of Americans across the country."[47] Speaking of the stated rationale behind the tougher photo ID laws, Holder said, "This whole notion of voter fraud . . . is really a solution in search of a problem."[48] Holder promptly filed suits against the new voting restrictions in Texas and North Carolina, seeking to have their laws overturned and to return both states to preclearance coverage. In an address to the National Action Network, an organization led by political commentator and civil rights activist Reverend Al Sharpton, President Obama called out Republicans for waging a war on voting rights:

> Now, it is wrong, President Johnson said, deadly wrong, to deny any of your fellow Americans the right to vote in this country. It's wrong to change our election rules just because of politics. It's wrong to make citizens wait five, six, seven hours just to vote. It's wrong to make a senior citizen who no longer has a driver's license jump through hoops and have to pay money just to exercise the rights she has cherished for a lifetime. . . . This has not been led by both parties. It's been led by the Republican Party. And in fairness, it's not just Democrats who are concerned. You had one Republican state legislator point out, and I'm quoting here, making it more difficult for people to vote is not a good sign for a party that wants to attract more people. . . . Out of 197 million votes cast for federal election between 2002 and 2005, only 40 voters out of 197 million were indicted for fraud. Now for those of you who are math majors, as a percentage that is 0.002 percent. That's not a lot. So, let's be clear. The real voter fraud is people who try to deny our rights by making bogus arguments for voter fraud.[49]

If there is a silver lining within this dark cloud of voter suppression, it is that African American voters are politically sophisticated enough to see these Republican efforts for what they are—blatant attempts to deny them participation in the electoral process. Since 2010, African Americans as well as other minorities have responded to these tactics by organizing suffrage campaigns to help voters obtain the necessary photo identification in states that require them and sign up new voters to defeat lawmakers who support voter suppression. In North Carolina for instance, the state NAACP organized something referred to as "Moral Monday," a weekly march to the capitol building in Raleigh to "dramatize the shameful condition of our state." Led by the Reverend William S. Barber II, Moral Monday has become a grassroots movement throughout North Carolina focusing on voter registration drives and political education campaigns. The trend nationally is equally promising. Election results from the 2012 presidential election show that in many African American communities, the percentage of black participation actually increased when compared to the number of blacks who voted in 2008.

But the recent upsurge in black voting and the election of the first black president do not tell the whole story, and the situation on the political front has not improved as much as it might appear at first glance. African Americans face greater obstacles to voting today than at any time since the passage of the 1965 Voting Rights Act. Twenty-five states have never sent an African American to Congress; since Reconstruction, only five states (California, Massachusetts, Illinois, South Carolina, and New Jersey) have elected an African American to the U.S. Senate; and, only two states (Virginia and Massachusetts) have elected a black governor. And despite being elected president in 2008 and re-elected in 2012 with huge majorities both times (popular vote as well as the Electoral College), President Barack Obama, as the nation's chief executive, has been the target of crude and racist insults, and a general level of contempt and disrespect unprecedented in American history.

It cannot be denied that much progress in the area of race relations has been made in the last fifty years, and that minorities in general, African Americans in particular, have become a part of the American electorate in ways that would have been unimaginable before the Selma voting rights campaign. But I am reminded of the words that author James Baldwin shared with his nephew in 1963 as the nation prepared to celebrate the centennial of the Emancipation Proclamation:

> They [white people] have had to believe for many years, and for innumerable reasons, that black men are inferior to white men. Many of them, indeed, know better, but, as you will discover, people find it very difficult to act on what they know. . . . you come from sturdy, peasant stock, men who picked cotton and dammed rivers and built railroads, and, in the teeth of the most terrifying odds, achieved an unassailable and monumental dignity. . . . [But] you know, and I know, that the country is celebrating one hundred years of freedom one hundred years too soon. We cannot be free until they are free.[50]

NOTES

1 *Hearings Before the Subcommittee on Civil and Constitutional Rights of the Committee on the Judiciary, House of Representatives, Ninety-Seventh Congress, First Session* on "Extension of the Voting Rights Act," Serial no. 24, Part 1 (H521–8.8), May 20, 1981, 365–401. For a detailed account of Richmond's 1970 annexation of portions of Chesterfield County, see John V. Moeser and Rutledge M. Dennis, *The Politics of Annexation: Oligarchic Power in a Southern City* (Cambridge: Schenkman Publishing Company, 1982).

2 See Robert A. Pratt, *The Color of Their Skin: Education and Race in Richmond, Virginia, 1954–89* (Charlottesville: University Press of Virginia, 1992), 48–9.

3 The only exceptions to the Republican Party's dominance in the South in presidential contests were in 1976, when Georgia governor Jimmy Carter won every southern state except Virginia, and in 1992 and 1996, when Arkansas governor Bill Clinton ran successfully for the presidency. In 1992, Clinton won Arkansas, Georgia, Kentucky, Louisiana, and Tennessee. In 1996, he won Arkansas, Florida, Kentucky, Louisiana, and Tennessee.

4 See Gary May, *Bending Toward Justice: The Voting Rights Act and the Transformation of American Democracy* (Durham: Duke University Press, 2015), 204–08.

5 *Zimmer v. McKeithen*, 467 F.2d 1381 (1972). See also Steven F. Lawson, *In Pursuit of Power: Southern Blacks and Electoral Politics, 1965–1982* (New York: Columbia University Press, 1985), 219–20.

6 See transcript from *Eyes on the Prize: America's Civil Rights Movement* ("Power! 1966–1968).

7 There is some confusion concerning whether Carl Stokes or Richard Hatcher was the first African American mayor of a major U.S. city. All sources report that Hatcher was actually elected days before Stokes, but that Stokes took office before Hatcher was inaugurated. Stokes was elected on November 7, 1967; I have been unable to confirm the date of Hatcher's election.

8 "Sam Yorty, 1909–1998," *LA Weekly*, June 10, 1998.

9   *Mobile v. Bolden*, 446 U.S. 55 (1980), at 62.
10 *Shaw v. Reno*, 509 U.S. 630 (1993), at 645, 647.
11 *Miller v. Johnson*, 515 U.S. 900 (1995), at 918.
12 *Miller v. Johnson*, 515 U.S. 900 (1995), at 947.
13 See James Thomas Tucker, Enfranchising Language Minority Citizens: The Bilingual Election Provisions of the Voting Rights Act," in *New York University Journal of Legislation and Public Policy*, 10:195.
14 The fundamental issue in both of these cases centered on the best way to maximize minority voting strength, and on this issue African Americans did not always agree on the best course of action. While some favor creating a few majority black districts, thereby making it easier to elect black candidates, others argue that when blacks are concentrated in a few districts, the other districts naturally became more heavily white and conservative. A better strategy, some believe, is to have a greater black electoral presence in many districts, thereby giving them more "influence" in those districts. Even if a black is not elected, white candidates would likely adopt a more moderate position owing to the increased number of black voters in their districts. Critics of majority-minority districts argue that carving out districts that favor black candidates often comes at the expense of moderate and liberal white Democrats, who are more likely than Republicans to support African Americans' interests.
15 Transcript excerpt of Steve Kroft's Interview with Senator Barack Obama, *60 Minutes*, accessed online February 11, 2007, http://www.cbsnews.com/news/transcript-excerpt-sen-barack-obama/5/.
16 When Barack Obama ran for president, Morrison was asked in an interview whether she regretted having referred to Bill Clinton as the first black president. She responded by saying: "People misunderstood that phrase. I was deploring the way in which President Clinton was being treated, vis-à-vis the sex scandal that was surrounding him. I said he was being treated like a black on the street, already guilty, already a perp." See Toni Morrison's interview in *The New Yorker*, October 5, 1998.
17 Bill Clinton, speaking to reporters in Columbia, South Carolina. Quoted in Eugene Robinson, "Cards from a Worn-Out Deck," *Washington Post*, January 29, 2008. http://www.washingtonpost.com/wp-dyn/content/article/2008/01/28/AR2008012802336.html.
18 David Remnick, "The President's Hero," *The New Yorker*, February 2, 2009.
19 See Steven F. Lawson, *Black Ballots: Voting Rights in the South, 1944–1969* (Lanham: Lexington Books, 1999), 345–49.
20 Steven F. Lawson, *Running for Freedom: Civil Rights and Black Politics in American since 1941* (Malden: Wiley Blackwell, 2015), 355.
21 Lawson, *Running for Freedom*, 356.
22 Lawson, *Running for Freedom*, 356.
23 Lawson, *Black Ballots*, 356–57.
24 Lawson, *Black Ballots*, 357–58.
25 Dinesh D'Souza, "Obama and Post-Racist America," *Townhall*, January 28, 2009.
26 May, *Bending Toward Justice*, 241.

27 Brennan Center for Justice, "Election 2012: Voting Laws Roundup," October 11, 2012.
28 Wendy R. Weiser, "Voter Suppression: How Bad? (Pretty Bad)," Brennan Center for Justice, October 1, 2014.
29 Tom Feran, "Analysis of Cuyahoga County voting finds cutback on in-person balloting hits minorities most," *Cleveland Plain Dealer*, October 6, 2012.
30 Jamelle Bouie, "Republicans Admit Voter-ID Laws are Aimed at Democratic Voters," *The Daily Beast*, August 28, 2013.
31 Bouie, "Republicans Admit Voter-ID Laws are Aimed at Democratic Voters," *The Daily Beast*, August 28, 2013.
32 Bouie, "Republicans Admit Voter-ID Laws are Aimed at Democratic Voters," *The Daily Beast*, August 28, 2013.
33 Darren Samuelsohn, "Clinton likens GOP effort to Jim Crow," *Politico*, July 6, 2011.
34 See Michelle Alexander, *The New Jim Crow: Mass incarceration in the Age of Colorblindness* (New York: The New Press, 2010).
35 May, *Bending Toward Justice*, 242.
36 Daniel Strauss, "Georgia GOPer Complains About Early Voting, Excessive Black Voting," *TPM Livewire*, September 9, 2014.
37 Karin Kamp, "Unbelievable GOP Statements on Voter Suppression," *Moyers & Company: Billmoyers.com*, October 24, 2014.
38 Kamp, "Unbelievable GOP Statements."
39 Kamp, "Unbelievable GOP Statements."
40 Kamp, "Unbelievable GOP Statements."
41 Kamp, "Unbelievable GOP Statements."
42 Trymaine Lee, "'Voter Fraud' Billboards in Ohio meant to Intimidate, Advocates Say," *The Huffington Post*, October 12, 2012.
43 *Shelby County, Alabama v. Holder*, 570 U.S. __ (2013).
44 Lawson, *Running for Freedom*, 385.
45 Jeffrey Toobin, "Holder v. Roberts: The Attorney General makes voting rights the test case of his tenure," *The New Yorker*, February 17, 2014.
46 Comments by Congressman John Lewis on National Public Radio, February 10, 2015.
47 Comments by Attorney General Eric Holder, June 25, 2013.
48 Comments by Attorney General Eric Holder in an interview on MSNBC, March 15, 2012.
49 Remarks by President Barack Obama at the National Action Network's 16th Annual Convention, April 11, 2014.
50 James Baldwin, *The Fire Next Time* (New York: Dell Publishing Company, 1962), 19–22.

8

What We Remember, What We Forget

Mythmaking and Civil Rights History in South Carolina

Stephen O'Neill

I first met Paul Gaston as his student in a graduate seminar on the civil rights movement in the fall of 1985. I had not come to Charlottesville to work with Paul or to study southern history as my main focus. This seminar and Paul's approach to history changed that. Our topic in the seminar was closer in time to the present than any history I had previously studied. The topic I chose to research for the course, the 1969 Hospital Workers' Strike in Charleston, brought history closer to me in space as well. I had grown up in Charleston, though I wasn't sure I could claim to be a Charlestonian, since I had arrived in the city as a young child, an Air force brat and the son of Yankees from Philly. Although all good history, of any time or place, connects the past to the present, at least implicitly, this seminar and my topic did that for me in very powerful and personal ways. That was even more true when, with Paul's encouragement, I expanded the topic of the hospital strike to a dissertation on the civil rights movement in Charleston. My efforts to explain the racial history of a place that I argued was very different than the rest of South Carolina or the wider South became an effort to understand not only what I had read and researched but also what I had experienced, in my young life, as a quasi-Charlestonian.

Paul's approach to history was well suited to my research topic. He helped me see clearly that the past influenced the present and future in at least two ways. First, material changes set the objective conditions that future generations faced; but, second, what people thought had happened in the past, whether accurate or not, also influenced the future, taking on a life of its own. This was especially true concerning decisions that ordinary folks and leaders made based on myths or faulty memories of the past. Paul's writing and teaching made clear to me that neither the hospital strike nor the larger history of race in Charleston could be understood without reference to historic myths of Charleston's past that still hung like a veil over the city in the civil rights years. Throughout his distinguished career, Paul saw his role as a teacher and a scholar to expose myths of southern history so that his students and the public that read his books or heard his talks might see more clearly ways to address problems of race and inequality in their midst.

Paul connected the past and the present in one other important way. In addition to understanding and explaining the South's history as a means to improve its present and future, Paul took action to create a better South, one that was more just and more equitable. Paul's work with the Southern Regional Council, his fight to create new programs and expand access at UVA, and his direct action efforts in the Charlottesville sit-ins set a standard of public engagement by an academic. Throughout his career, Paul has integrated who he was as a scholar and professor with what he did as an activist, with what he valued as a human being, and with what he was willing to fight for as a dissenter. Perhaps Paul's role in the movement was an inheritance or legacy from his grandfather, Ernest B. Gaston, the founder of Fairhope, the utopian community that nurtured Paul's intellect and his sense of social responsibility. For me and many others, Paul remains a model of combing the roles of scholar, teacher, and activist.

My essay here seeks to connect the past and the present by highlighting what I see as a danger in how ordinary folks understand South Carolina's civil rights past. The topic has come into focus for me over a long period of time, but was recently, in spring 2016, brought to sharper relief by protests and a sit-in at Clemson University over racial insensitivity and a claim that Clemson had refused to confront the racism in its history. The protests identified Benjamin Tillman and John C. Calhoun as targets, not the claim of "Integration with Dignity" that I analyze. As the protests mounted, however, I could not help but wonder if the claim of "Integration with Dignity" had helped to mask on-going racial issues at the center of the Clemson protests.

A paradox stands at the center of South Carolina history: no state in the union is more obsessed with its history, yet no state has had more difficulty learning from its past, finding in history a means to address present-day problems, especially racial ones. An inability to learn from the past, a trait evident in the wider South, seems hyper-concentrated in the Palmetto State. The parallel failures of the state's white leadership during the Civil War and Reconstruction, on one hand, and during massive resistance in the civil rights years, on the other, stand as the leading example of South Carolina ignoring the lessons of its history. Those parallels, so hidden to the state's leaders in the 1950s, so obvious to us today, are a reminder of the present generation's obligation to view its past with courage and clarity.

William Faulkner, someone Paul Gaston once described as the South's greatest historian, understood keenly the costs of his region's willful blindness to the lessons of the Civil War era. He warned of those costs in a talk to the Southern Historical Association (SHA) in 1955, a year after the *Brown* decision, at a time, in South Carolina and the wider South, when the scent of racial change was in the air, but no real change had yet occurred.

Faulkner issued this admonition even as he knew it would go unheeded:

> We speak now against the day when our Southern people who will resist to the last these inevitable changes in social relations, when they have been forced to accept what they at one time might have accepted with dignity and good will, say, "Why didn't someone tell us this before? Tell us this in time!"[1]

In his talk at the SHA conference, held in Memphis, Faulkner spoke to an integrated audience, of mostly academics. However, Faulkner's real audience, his more important audience, was the wider South, his generation of white southerners who, at that moment, were mobilizing all resources to defend segregation. (Indeed, that night, he could have been speaking directly to South Carolina's white political and business leaders as they rallied resistance to *Brown*.) Faulkner spoke as a sensitive and intelligent white southerner, but not one who particularly embraced the justice behind civil rights or racial change.[2] He spoke to the audience, the one inside hearing his voice and especially the one outside that might read his words, as a fellow white southerner of the mid-twentieth century, as one of them, and in a spirit of practical counsel. But he also spoke as someone who knew southern history. When he looked at that history, he saw in the Civil War and Reconstruction, in that past, a pattern of "resistance to the last" against the inevitable social changes that occurred eighty and one-hundred years before the night he spoke. Given that history, Faulkner believed, expediency if not justice demanded that the white South solve its own racial problems. Yet, as his words reveal, he believed in this case history's lessons would remain obscure.

Today we know more than Faulkner possibly could have about why the lessons of history proved so elusive to white southerners in the civil rights era. The path-breaking scholarship of Paul Gaston on the myth of the New South, C. Vann Woodward's sweeping revisionism, particularly in *The Strange Career of Jim Crow,* and a host of studies on the Lost Cause have helped explain how both the rise of legal segregation in the 1890s and the white South's resistance to black freedom in the 1950s were buttressed by false historical narratives.[3] Faulkner's lament "Why didn't someone tell us this before?" speaks to the limited historical vision of his audience, blinded as they were by Lost Cause myths, halcyon memories of happy slaves, reminders of the "Negroes who rode with Hampton,"[4] and host of other temporarily satisfying, but ultimately false—and costly—historical myths.

As a scholar and a teacher, Paul Gaston made it his work to expose myths about the southern past, myths that, typically speaking, the powerful used to shape the present and future in their own interest. His opus, *The New South Creed: A Study in Southern Mythmaking,* explained how, in the years after Reconstruction, spokesmen for the idea of a New South—journalists and other writers, politicians, industrialists, educators—invoked romantic images of the Old South and the Lost Cause to recruit support for a new order, a new industrial South that would "restore power and prestige" to their class, cement white supremacy against the reforms of Reconstruction, and, at least according to their promises, provide prosperity for the region.

Paul Gaston's scholarship on the myth of the New South and William Faulkner's warning to the massive resisters of the 1950s remind us that much is at stake, practically speaking, in how each generation ascribes meaning to its defining historical events. In *The New South Creed,* and especially its final chapter, "The Emperor's New Clothes," Gaston makes clear that the South's embrace of the myths of economic prosperity and racial justice in the face of all evidence to the contrary served, ironically, to perpetuate the region's poverty and racial injustice. "Unable to bequeath to the next generation of Southerners a legacy of solid achievement, the New South spokesmen gave them instead a solidly propounded and widely spread image of its success, a mythic view of their own times that was as removed from objective reality as the myth of the Old South."[5]

Today, in South Carolina, historical myth and something close to what Gaston called "objective reality" compete as underpinnings of South Carolina's civil rights history. And, just as in Gaston's New South era, much is at stake in the temptation to substitute the former for the latter. How non-historians—common folks, as well as leaders in business, civic affairs and politics—understand their civil rights past is vitally important for the collective decisions citizens and politicians make on the local, state, and national levels. Today, the general public's understanding of the civil rights movement in South Carolina springs from multiple sources. Scholarship resting on a careful examination of primary and secondary sources, validated by peer-review, represents only one source for the public, and certainly not the most important. Other sources such as commemorations, the inscriptions and symbolism of monuments, interviews given by participants in the events, oral histories, articles in popular periodicals or newspapers, speeches by politicians, and especially stories told around the kitchen table or at grandma's knee are more powerful in shaping the public's historical memory of defining episodes in the past. Whatever their source, historical myths and memories, rooted, as they often are, in strong emotions, sometimes overwhelm even the most well-documented and accurate scholarship.

For today's South Carolinians, confronting their civil rights history with accuracy and courage has proved as challenging as Civil War and Reconstruction history was for Faulkner's generation. In the 1950s, the Lost Cause, deeply ingrained in the minds of white southerners, touted the liberty of white southerners as the driving force behind secession, erasing slavery as a factor. Today, in a similar fashion, narratives of the civil rights movement in South Carolina audaciously omit central elements of that story. We hear memories of voluntary integration, even when court orders and federal legislation, in the record, contradict any notion of voluntarism. We read articles and interviews that recall integration with "grace and style" and that applaud blacks and whites "working together for integration," but these same articles and interviews leave out the essential fact that white South Carolinians, and especially the state's leaders, remained adamant in their opposition to racial change until federal coercion forced them to adjust.[6] In South Carolina, white co-operation in racial change almost always came when every mode of resistance short of violence had been exhausted. The myth of progressive white leadership during the state's civil rights crisis threatens to turn on its head more the more complete account of a bitter struggle between black activists and the white establishment that defined the civil rights years in South Carolina. Myths of whites embracing change with voluntarism and good will overlook the fact that litigation in federal courts and sweeping federal legislation in 1964 and 1965 won the gains that were achieved in the state—and did so over the objections of nearly all South Carolina's white leaders.

The power of historical memory, selective and often self-serving, to override evidence-based history was poignantly demonstrated at the Citadel Conference on the Civil Rights in South Carolina in 2003. The conference, held at the Citadel Military College in Charleston, convened the leading scholars of the civil rights movement in South Carolina, but it also invited surviving participants on both sides of the movement from thirty, forty, and fifty years before. Moreover, the co-directors of the conference, Vernon Burton, then of University of Illinois, and Winfred "Bo" Moore, of the Citadel, also invited to the conference journalists, present-day politicians, and the general public. As John Monk of Columbia's *State* newspaper wrote, "There was not just scholarship; there was witnessing."[7] It was a combustible combination, and for four days the topics in the sessions ranged from the lynching of Willie Earle, to the South Carolina roots of the *Brown* case, to the Klan in South Carolina, to the Orangeburg Massacre, and to dozens of other topics.

The defining clash between history and the memory came early in the conference, during the opening keynote address. The speaker was Anthony Badger, eminent historian from Cambridge University in England. Badger is a highly respected scholar of American history and the South, but was somewhat of an outsider on the specific topic of civil rights in South Carolina. The conference planners hoped Badger would bring fresh eyes to a topic very familiar to many of the attendees. It was a challenging task to address not only an audience peppered with experts in the field but also participants and eyewitnesses to the history itself. Badger proved able to the task.

His talk was entitled "From Defiance to Moderation: South Carolina Governors and Racial Change."[8] In his introduction, he stated his assignment for the address: "What I believe the organizers want me to do is to put the established narrative of White South Carolina's response to racial change into a regional context, to see what was distinctive about the state's reaction."[9] The title and the topic pulled the audience to the edge of its seats. No doubt, his focus on South Carolina governors in the age of segregation was a compelling topic. But there was more to the listeners' rapt anticipation. Listed in the conference program and on the stage, for the audience to see, sat former governor and then-sitting United States Senator Ernest F. "Fritz" Hollings. Hollings had been governor during the state's transition from segregation. Hollings, as most in the audience knew, had also been an ardent defender of segregation while governor.

Hollings had agreed to provide commentary or a rebuttal, as the case may be, on Professor Badger's remarks. The historian Badger would present a view of the past based on evidence and interpretation. Civil rights-era participant, in this case former-governor Hollings, a leader of white resistance to integration, would respond. It was symbolic of the special nature of the conference itself.

Badger's address focused on the way South Carolina's leaders from the 1950s and 1960s, especially its politicians, had remembered the civil rights movement in the state.[10] They had, he said, absolved themselves of responsibility for the state's defiance of the *Brown* decision. Badger explained, their "views constitute what I would call the self-exculpatory model of massive resistance in South Carolina, in which responsibility for massive resistance lies with everybody except the white political leaders in the state."[11] These leaders placed most of the blame on the shoulders of their constituents (although the Supreme Court, the NAACP, and northern liberals shared blame): "The argument [of these politicians] was that the forces of white mass racism were so powerful that no politician could challenge them and be reelected."[12]

Badger was not done. And Senator Hollings, the audience could see, sat expressionless behind him. If "self-exculpatory" was the response to the 1950s when the defense of segregation in South Carolina held strong, Badger argued that the memories of the civil rights years in the 1960s turned to "self-congratulations" to explain why segregation ended in the state when it did. He charged that politicians of that era—and some historians—had forgotten how racial change actually came about in South Carolina. Change was not a result of economic modernization. It did not come at the hands of progressive-minded business leaders. It was not an effort by urban and suburban state legislators persuading retrograde "county-seat elites" to accept integration.[13] All of these have been used as explanations. On this point, Badger was clear: "Racial change did not come to South Carolina through the efforts South Carolina's whites."[14]

To the contrary, he reminded listeners just how fierce and how successful the state's defiance of federal authority had been. For evidence, as his title promised, he surveyed the governors from James F. Byrnes in 1951 to John West who left office in 1975. Byrnes represented missed opportunity, returning to the state with enormous prestige from Washington where he had served as congressman, senator, Supreme Court justice, director of war mobilization, and secretary of state. "No one was better placed to lead South Carolina into realistic acceptance of racial change."[15] Instead, Byrnes led the state's resistance to racial change from his first day in office. Byrnes's successor George Bell Timmerman vowed "segregation would not end for a thousand years."[16] When Badger got to Governor Hollings's term in office, the crowd was tense with uncertainty. Would Badger pull his punches and how could Hollings respond if he did not? Hollings, for his part, sat without a hint of worry on his face. Badger, aware of the sensitive dynamics of the situation, made appropriate effort to be courteous in his assessment. He was helped in that effort by the fact that Hollings's term in office from

1959 to 1963 did indeed represent the transition in Badger's title "From Defiance to Moderation." That permitted the professor to highlight the realism Hollings showed in accepting the inevitability of the changes forced on the state toward the end of Hollings's term. Nonetheless, Tony Badger had traversed the Atlantic and arrived in Charleston with the intention of puncturing some myths about civil rights history in South Carolina, and he proceeded to do that.

As the senator sat without apparent emotion, Badger called Hollings "part of the inner circle masterminding South Carolina's strategy of defiance."[17] He cited Hollings's self-serving claim that most blacks in South Carolina favored segregation. He recalled Hollings's threat to outlaw the NAACP as a subversive organization. On the other hand, Badger did credit Hollings with refusing to abolish public education and with using black deputies and state agents to police demonstrations in an effort to avoid violence. And, Badger reminded the audience that when the inevitable tide of federal court orders had swept through Virginia, Georgia, Alabama, and Mississippi, when that tide reached South Carolina, Hollings began to tell South Carolinians to prepare for change. That was the "moderation" in Badger's title. As Hollings told the people of the state when Harvey Gantt was ordered admitted to Clemson College in 1963, "South Carolina was running out of courts."[18] Yet, while acknowledging Hollings's willingness to bow to the inevitable, in concluding Badger left no doubt about where he saw the state's leaders on the defining question of the day: "Far from dousing the fire of popular racist sentiment, the leaders of South Carolina sought to fan the flame."[19] He did concede that South Carolina avoided the worse consequences that stained Alabama and Mississippi in the early 1960s—hardly worthy of celebration, but worth noting, nonetheless.

So there it was: a few compliments for the senator but mostly a matter-of-fact assertion that South Carolina's leaders had fought against racial change to the end and had since refused to acknowledge what they had done. Everyone in the audience waited tensely. What could Senator Hollings say in his own defense? He did not disappoint. He stepped to the podium with calm and confidence and in his Geechee accent said, "I feel very much like Elizabeth Taylor's seventh husband, who on the wedding night said, 'I know what I am supposed to do, but it is going to be difficult to make it interesting.'"[20] The crowd roared, as much to relieve tension as in response to the joke, which was in fact very funny and timely.

What came next, however, nobody could have expected, especially given the indictment that Badger had leveled. Hollings took the audience back to his days in the state legislature in the early 1950s. He did so to take credit for pushing "Jimmy's Tax" through the legislature: "I put in the [three percent] sales tax. . . . That's the most progressive thing I have ever done."[21] The tax was named after then-governor James F. Byrnes. Nearly every person in the auditorium knew, what Hollings failed to acknowledge, that the three-percent sales tax of 1951 was designed for one purpose: to maintain segregation. Yes, it was true, as Hollings made sure to tell the crowd, the money would be used to improve black schools, but what he left unsaid was that the school improvements were conceived to give South Carolina's lawyers a case to make before the Supreme Court, namely that the state's racially separate schools were indeed equal for blacks and whites. Hollings, in spite of himself, had made Badger's case for self-congratulations, and indeed self-exculpation, more strongly than a mountain of evidence might have. The audience was left to wonder whether Hollings *knew* that the audience *knew* the real purpose of Byrnes's tax. Regardless, Hollings's memory fueled by self-interest and, no doubt, some measure of defensiveness flew in the face of what the audience knew to be the accurate history—and the whole story—of South Carolina's 1951 school equalization tax.

The exchange between Badger and Hollings, coming as it did before that particular audience, brought into sharp relief the myth of white racial progressivism in South Carolina during the civil rights movement; however, perhaps the boldest assertion of the myth, in the face of evidence to the contrary, came during Clemson University's commemoration of its desegregation. In 2003, the university marked the fortieth anniversary of the court-ordered enrollment of its first black student, Harvey Gantt. Under the title, "Integration with Dignity: A Celebration of Forty Years," Clemson sponsored a symposium, erected a permanent historical marker on campus, hosted a ceremony upon the marker's unveiling, built a website, and commissioned a short written history of events leading to Gantt's enrollment.

The "dignity" in Clemson's commemoration referred not to Gantt, not to his persistence in the face of endless obstacles created by Clemson officials, nor to his courage in the face of injustice; rather Clemson employed the term to describe actions by the school leaders, state officials, and a small group of powerful businessmen who worked to prevent violence on the day of Gantt's arrival in January 1963, even as they refused to concede the right of Gantt, or any African American, to attend Clemson.[22]

Clemson borrowed the title and theme of its "celebration" from an article by George McMillan, "Integration with Dignity—The Inside Story of How South Carolina Kept the Peace," which was published in the *Saturday Evening Post* six weeks after Gantt's enrollment. McMillan credited a "small group of responsible citizens" for engaging a "conspiracy for peace" to counteract the state's "passionate defense of its southern customs."[23] According to McMillan, this group, which included Governor Hollings, construction magnate Charles Daniel, textile executive John Cauthen, state senator Edgar Brown, and Clemson President Robert Edwards, had the dignity to prevent an explosion of violence like that which had greeted James Meredith four months previously in Oxford, Mississippi. McMillan contrasts these progressive-minded peace-keepers (who, nonetheless, continued to support segregation) with the rank-and-file whites of South Carolina and especially with three potential troublemakers among the state's leaders, James F. Byrnes, state senator and chair of the state's "Segregation Committee" Marion Gressette, and state legislator A. W. "Red" Bethea. Thus the central struggle, in McMillan's estimation, was between progressive white leaders and retrograde racists; and not between the federal courts and defenders of South Carolina's right to discriminate, nor between civil rights activists, such as Gantt and his lawyers, and state and college officials who defended segregation.

McMillan leads his readers to focus on what he paints as a dramatic battle over tactics among like-minded segregationists, while overlooking the central struggles of both the larger civil rights movement in South Carolina and the specific events at Clemson. For McMillan, "When South Carolina's turn came to face the inevitable fact of racial change, its responsible people, its leadership group, its 'power structure' took the initiative and handled the crisis with dignity, dignity for the Negro as well as the white man. This is why the South Carolina story is one of the most significant—and reassuring—stories in the recent history of race relations in this country."[24] In this scenario, any dignity associated with Gantt and other black activists was dignity bestowed upon them by South Carolina's "power structure." Moreover, the article as a whole seems to suggest, although it never states explicitly, that this "power structure" had undergone a change of heart on the matter of segregation at Clemson. They had not. None of the leaders in McMillan's cabal, the "conspirators for peace," spoke in favor of desegregation or Gantt's enrollment during the crisis. Their position was carefully enunciated by Senator Edgar Brown, "If the ultimate decision of the Federal courts directs that Harvey Gantt should be admitted, my response is that the administration at Clemson College will not tolerate violence on the Clemson campus."

Of course, it is important to realize that McMillan did not breathe life into the myth of "integration with dignity" by himself. We can imagine McMillan, a free-lance writer, one born in west Tennessee, steeped in the culture of Jim Crow, with a deadline for his article looming, trying to find an angle for his story and seizing upon one that might appeal to his audience. On the other hand, in 2003, Clemson University officials, with forty more years of hindsight, chose to resurrect McMillan's "integration with dignity" as a unifying theme for its commemoration. Clemson, like McMillan, connected the concept of dignity to the same white leaders who executed the "conspiracy for peace." And as part of the commemoration, Clemson permanently enshrined "Integration with Dignity" by unveiling a monument, in the shadow of Ben Tillman Hall, with that phrase as its title, on January 28, 2003, forty years to the day after Gantt's enrollment. The text on the monument echoes the interpretation in McMillan's article. It reads:

> Clemson University became the first white college or university in the state to integrate on January 28, 1963. Harvey B. Gantt, a Charleston native wanting to study architecture, had applied for admission in 1961. When Clemson delayed admitting him, he sued in federal court in the summer of 1962. President Robert C. Edwards, meanwhile, worked behind

the scenes to make plans for Gantt's eventual enrollment. Edwards and several leading businessmen, politicians, and others drew up an elaborate plan, described as "a conspiracy of peace," designed to ensure that Gantt would enter Clemson without the protests and violence that marked the integration of other Southern universities. After a federal court ruled that Clemson should admit him, Gantt enrolled without incident. He graduated with honors in 1965. Erected by Clemson University, 2003[25]

In choosing to remember "a conspiracy of peace" and "integration with dignity," Clemson has simultaneously chosen to forget the indignities the school imposed on Harvey Gantt for exercising his right as an American. It was a right Gantt asserted in a letter to the registrar at Clemson: "I am a citizen of South Carolina. Clemson is a state-supported institution . . . and I have a right to attend."[26] Clemson's self-proclaimed dignity was contradicted by its far-reaching, and somewhat deceitful, efforts to bar Gantt's enrollment. The written history of events surrounding Gantt's enrollment, published by Clemson as part of the commemoration, highlights (in a way that seems unwitting) the incongruity between what the commemoration emphasized and the actions of school officials in years and months leading to Gantt's matriculation, in other words between myth and reality. Historian Henry L. Suggs, in his introduction, follows the track established by McMillan, "The desegregation of Clemson on January 28, 1963 was characterized by 'Integration with Dignity' and . . . was a well-planned and coordinated effort to prevent violence, to enhance the image of the university and the state, and to elevate the character of the civil rights movement." And, like McMillan, Suggs heaps praise on Clemson President Robert C. Edwards, calling him a "strategist, innovator, and risk-taker" and "a man clearly in charge."[27] However, in the body of his essay, Suggs describes actions by Clemson officials, including Edwards, that seem to stretch any notion of dignity to the breaking point. Suggs's evidence makes clear that Clemson rejected Gantt's application solely because he was black, despite the fact that the admissions office knew he was an honors student and highly qualified to be admitted. Yet when the case went to court, Clemson's lawyers denied point blank that race was an issue in refusing to admit Gantt. Rather, Clemson's lawyers claimed Gantt's application was denied because it was incomplete. That legal defense was made possible, according to Suggs, only by the fact that Clemson developed a changing policy on admissions, a moving target of sorts, in order to foil Gantt's application efforts. President Edwards, Senator Edgar Brown, and Senator Marion Gressette were at the center of this conspiracy on the new admissions policy. Suggs reports that fifty-one other applicants were denied admission so that Clemson could have a rationale, other than race, to reject Gantt's application.[28] Dignity demands better.

Clemson's characterization of its desegregation as "integration with dignity" bears some special costs for posterity. The importance of this specific episode in the overall span of the civil rights movement in South Carolina gives added significance to Clemson's interpretation of events. Gantt's victory in federal court and his enrollment at Clemson in January 1963 represent the single most important turning point in South Carolina's civil rights history. The desegregation of Clemson ended massive resistance in the state. It fulfilled the promise of the *Brown* decision, which had been issued nearly a decade before. It forced a concession, of sorts, from some state leaders, most notably outgoing Governor Fritz Hollings, on the practical need to accept desegregation, although not on the justice behind it. Gantt was the first black to enroll in an all-white school at any level in twentieth-century South Carolina. And if race is a central theme in the state's history, as it certainly seems to be, then Gantt's admission to Clemson stands as a watershed moment in the twentieth century, beside the introduction of rice in the seventeenth, the invention of the cotton gin in the eighteenth, and the end of slavery in the nineteenth. Two hundred years from now, when books are written on the history of South Carolina, Gantt's enrollment will be the defining episode of the civil rights movement, the symbol, the microcosm. Given the importance of this episode, and its inherent connection to events before and after, any general or simple characterization, even of the narrow episode, is bound to extend in the public's mind to the larger movement in ways that do harm to the complexity and the accuracy of our understanding of the past.

The false memory of "integration with dignity" not only threatens to erase, in the thinking of the general public, the injustices that Clemson imposed upon Harvey Gantt; but, indeed, to erase from the minds of white South Carolinians the indignities that segregation imposed on all African Americans in the age of Jim Crow. Furthermore, the unwarranted praise of the states' white leaders during the civil rights era threatens to absolve leaders and ordinary citizens, alike, in the present, of any sense of responsibility for addressing on-going injustices in their midst. For many, the "conspirators for peace" have paid any debt owed for the injustices of segregation. This sentiment was clearly at work in 2003, at the celebration on the fortieth anniversary commemoration, a member of the Clemson Board of Trustees, an African American, reflected on the meaning of desegregation at his school, saying that today's students at Clemson "don't have to think about race because that generation before them made it happen." Another trustee at the celebration, who had been student-body president when Gantt enrolled in 1963, stated, "I always felt we were going through the motions. There were no acts of defiance,"[29] thereby overlooking massive resistance and the fact that the entire state's white establishment had been engaged in defiance of the spirit of the federal courts' interpretation of the Constitution since the *Brown* decision, for nine years before Clemson was forced to desegregate.

South Carolina's past as a wellspring of American slavery, as the birthplace of the Confederacy, as the instigator of the Civil War, and epicenter of Redemption has long provided the state an incentive, if not an obligation, to view its past with all the courage and clarity it could muster. The state has struggled to do so. The history of the civil rights movement in the state provides one more chance to see clearly into our present by looking more accurately at our past. Without a sound understanding of our civil rights history, the state is certain to flail blindly in search of racial and economic justice in the future. A state that prefers the reassuring memories to hard truths, that remembers the civil rights struggles as internal battles among white leaders, and that recalls freedom as something given by whites to blacks is a state that will remain mired in the mistakes of the past. We cannot escape our history. We can face it with courage and honesty and thereby hope to wrest some insight and advantage from it. Or we can evade it or mythologize it into satisfying but false narratives. But if we take this second course, the evasion is always temporary. The past will always come out, will always come back. If we are not prepared for it, it will come back at the most inopportune times and force painful change on us, under duress and at the cost of good will and dignity.

Let us speak now against that day.

Notes

1. William Faulkner, "American Segregation and the World Crisis" in Bell Wiley, William Faulkner, Benjamin Mays, and Cecil Sims, *The Segregation Decisions: Papers Read at a Session of the Twenty-First Annual Meeting of the Southern Historical Association, November 10, 1955* (Atlanta: The Southern Regional Council, 1956), 9.
2. See Joel Williamson, *William Faulkner and Southern History* (New York: Oxford Press, 1993), 299-312.
3. Paul Gaston, *The New South Creed: A Study in Southern Mythmaking* (New York: Alfred A. Knopf, 1970); C. Vann Woodward, *The Strange Career of Jim Crow* Woodward, (New York: Oxford University Press. 3rd rev. ed. 1974); David Blight, *Race and Reunion: The Civil War in American Memory*, (Cambridge, Mass.: Belknap Press, 2002): Bruce Baker, *What Reconstruction Meant: Historical Memory in the American South*, (Charlottesville: University of Virginia Press, 2009).)
4. Quote is from an editorial by Thomas R. Waring editor of *Charleston News and Courier*, September 14, 1956, who tried to convince whites that blacks did not really want to end segregation in the 1950s. It refers to the historical claim that South Carolina blacks supported the end of Reconstruction in the 1876 South Carolina gubernatorial race by riding with the para-military group called the Redshirts, who swung the election for the Democrat General Wade Hampton.
5. Gaston, *New South Creed*, 196.
6. The phrase "grace and style" was first used by Dr. Ernest F. Harrill, a leader of the effort in February 1970 to make a smooth transition of Greenville's schools from a dual system to a unitary one. Since that time multiple historical accounts have employed that or similar terms to describe civil rights in Greenville or the state as a whole. For accounts that use that term or that stress voluntarism and co-operation between whites and blacks to integrate see Keith Morris, "Desegregation and Dignity: Those Who Made It Work—In Their Own Words," *Upcountry Review* (Fall 1999): 28-51; Betty Stall, "With Grace and Style: The Desegregation of the Greenville County Schools in 1970," *Proceedings and Papers of the Greenville County Historical Society* 9 (1990–1991): 80-92; Alfred Burgess, "Working together for Integration," *Carologue: Bulletin of the South Carolina Historical Society* 8 (Winter 1992): 7, 14.
7. Winfred B. Moore and Orville Vernon Burton, *Toward the Meeting of the Waters: Currents in the Civil Rights Movement of South Carolina during the Twentieth Century*, (Columbia: University of South Carolina Press, 2008), ix.
8. Badger's remarks that night have been published in *Toward the Meeting of the Waters*. All the quotes from that night included in this essay are drawn from that book. Other descriptions of that evening are my own, based on what I witnessed and on notes of the conference sessions I took while in attendance.

9   Moore and Burton, *Toward the Meeting of the Waters*, 3.
10 Badger spoke primarily of the memory and memoirs of participants in the movement but links the self-exculpatory view to interpretations by historians as well. See p. 5 in Moore and Burton.
11 Moore and Burton, *Toward the Meeting of the Waters*, 4.
12 Moore and Burton, *Toward the Meeting of the Waters*, 4.
13 Moore and Burton, *Toward the Meeting of the Waters*, 5, 15–18.
14 Moore and Burton, *Toward the Meeting of the Waters*, 17.
15 Moore and Burton, *Toward the Meeting of the Waters*, 3.
16 Moore and Burton, *Toward the Meeting of the Waters*, 9.
17 Moore and Burton, *Toward the Meeting of the Waters*, 11.
18 Moore and Burton, *Toward the Meeting of the Waters*, 15
19 Moore and Burton, *Toward the Meeting of the Waters*, 18
20 Moore and Burton, *Toward the Meeting of the Waters*, 23.
21 Moore and Burton, *Toward the Meeting of the Waters*, 23.
22 Integration of Clemson University, 1963, in S.C. Historical Marker Program, box 19, S.C. Department of History and Archives; Skip Eisiminger, editor, *Integration with Dignity: A Celebration of Harvey Gantt's Admission to Clemson* (Clemson, S.C.: Clemson University Press, 2003), http://cup.sites.clemson.edu/pubs/gantt.
23 George McMillan, "Integration with Dignity: The Inside Story of How South Carolina Kept the Peace," *Saturday Evening Post*, March 16, 1963, 16.
24 McMillan, "Integration with Dignity," 19.
25 Photograph in author's possession.
26 Henry L. Suggs, "Harvey Gantt and the Integration of Clemson University," in Skip Eisiminger, editor, *Integration with Dignity: A Celebration of Harvey Gantt's Admission to Clemson* (Clemson, S.C.: Clemson University Press, 2003), http://cup.sites.clemson.edu/pubs/gantt, 23.
27 Suggs, "Harvey Gantt," 16, 24.
28 Suggs, "Harvey Gantt," 23–26.
29 Anna Simon, "Clemson Integrates Past into Strategy for Future, *Greenville News*, January 26, 2003, B.1.

9

Racial Buffer Zone

How Geography and Residential Housing Patterns around Fort Jackson Fostered Armed Forces Integration and Limited Its Effect on the Civil Rights Movement in South Carolina

ANDREW H. MYERS

Though separated by forty years, Paul Gaston and I shared the common bond of having been infantrymen in the United States Army. Both of us completed peacetime tours of active duty in South Korea—he during the late 1940s and I during the late 1980s. I remained in the Army Reserves throughout my time as his student, so the topic had frequent opportunity to arise. He always spoke favorably of his service.

Paul seemed to relish our disparity in rank. I held a commission as a Regular Army first lieutenant when I first met him during 1991 as a graduate school applicant and reached lieutenant colonel in the Reserves before retiring in 2008. He would sometimes greet me with a jaunty salute and a twinkle in his eyes. "Corporal Gaston reporting," he would say in a soft drawl. Having a mentor who understood military culture helped me acclimatize to the University of Virginia and Charlottesville, where veterans were few and where an atmosphere of affluence and gentility prevailed. Paul's ability to chuckle at the transience of titles and class distinctions had added benefit for someone like me, who had grown up on army posts only a generation removed from a textile mill village.

Paul understood that duty as well as friendship transcended politics. Although he made clear his opposition to the toppling of Saddam Hussein, he never allowed his position to overshadow his concern for my wellbeing during 2006–2007 when I advised an Iraqi battalion in Nineveh Province. He in fact spread word of my situation to others, many of whom joined him and Mary in bolstering my morale with kind messages. "You will learn a lot and help me to learn more," he said.

As historians, both of us valued our time in uniform because of the ways in which it had shaped our views about race relations. Paul describes in Coming of Age in Utopia his *"first experience of interracial socializing"* while undergoing basic training at Fort Eustis, Virginia.[1] Like him, I had positive encounters on military bases that made me think outside the boundaries of civilian possibilities. Deciding upon a dissertation topic thus became an easy matter. When I told Paul that I wanted to study the effects of armed forces integration upon the civil rights movement, he grasped immediately that I had found a subject that would resonate with my background and abilities.

Paul continued supervising my dissertation for more than a year after he retired. He helped me revise the work into a manuscript that was published in 2006 as the book Black, White, and Olive Drab. *His dedication was all the more notable given that I had moved to South Carolina at the end of 1994 to immerse myself in sources. We communicated between Columbia and Charlottesville via the then-cutting-edge technology of electronic mail. Paul embraced the Internet, especially social media. I had set up my first email account because of him. He seemed to enjoy the novelty of receiving messages this way. I used a landline modem, telnet protocol, and keyboard commands to reach the university server. The days of reading scanned documents over the World Wide Web and manipulating images still lay in the future.*

The following essay updates Black, White, and Olive Drab *by leveraging computer resources that have only recently become available or practical for historians: scanned, searchable telephone directories; digitized historical maps; search engine maps; and software capable of combining the data to generate usable information. It was originally presented in San Francisco as a paper at the 2013 meeting of the Organization of American Historians. This work, I hope, is in keeping with Paul's optimism about the potential of both new technology and the armed forces.*

Few places in the United States contain as rich a mixture of Americans as armed forces installations. These bases bring together people of diverse race, class, ethnicity, and regional background. They foster new bonds forged through teamwork, shared hardship, and common ideology. They provide avenues for social mobility and settings for seminal life moments. Their presence ripples outward to shape the populations, economies, and infrastructure of nearby communities. They accomplish these things—ironically—within the context of an organization that brings death and ruin to other parts of the world, where being killed or maimed is an occupational hazard, and where the bureaucracy routinely crushes individuals.

Black, White, and Olive Drab examines only a facet of this kaleidoscopic institution: racial integration. The book addresses two major questions. First, how did a post located next to the capital of South Carolina become in 1950 the first in the U.S. Army to desegregate soldiers on a large scale? Second, how did this change at Fort Jackson influence Jim Crow practices in Columbia over the next two decades?[2]

The answer to the latter is the most intriguing. Fort Jackson had virtually no effect upon the desegregation of buses, schools, public facilities, or housing in the surrounding area. Post authorities hesitated to use the moral and economic power they wielded to improve conditions for soldiers under their command. In fact, they went to considerable lengths to appease local whites. Soldiers stationed at Fort Jackson—even those with prior histories of activism—almost never participated in civil rights demonstrations. Those few who did were motivated more by the Vietnam War than the racial situation in South Carolina.

The scope of *Black, White, and Olive Drab* is limited to the 1950s and 1960s because this was the time when the American armed forces stood in advance of civilian society. The book focuses primarily on political and institutional causes. This essay will reassess the case of Fort Jackson and Columbia during the same decades by taking into consideration two additional factors—residential housing patterns and local geography.

The idea was inspired by the works of Carol McKibben and Tracy K'Meyer. Published in 2012, McKibben's history of Seaside shows the role played by the California town's proximity to Fort Ord. Other municipalities in Monterey County were wealthier and more developed, but none was physically closer, and none was more closely associated with the post. Similarly, K'Meyer's 2009 analysis of the civil rights struggle in Louisville emphasizes the significance of the Kentucky city's position on the border between North and South.[3]

Digitalization of city directories and computer-generated maps make a spatial analysis of Fort Jackson much more feasible than when the original research for *Black, White, and Olive Drab* was completed at the turn of the century. The results suggest that the physical arrangement of black and white neighborhoods in Columbia both facilitated the desegregation of the post in 1950 and limited its subsequent effects on the civil rights movement. Before these findings are discussed, some background information will perhaps be helpful for readers unfamiliar with the book or the region.

Columbia is the capital of South Carolina. It was founded for that purpose in 1786. It is situated near the center of the state in Richland County. It serves as host to various offices of the state government, the main campus of the University of South Carolina, and several industries.

African Americans have comprised a significant part of the population since the 1800s. They outnumbered whites in the county from 1800 until 1920 and in the city from 1870 until 1900. As of the 2010 census, blacks make up 46 percent of the county's 389,000 residents and 42 percent of the 130,000 who live within Columbia's municipal limits.[4]

Fort Jackson is located approximately six miles to the east of the Statehouse. The post was established in 1917 as part of the mobilization for World War I and used as a National Guard training facility during the 1920s and 1930s. The War Department reopened it in 1939 and designated it as a "fort." It remains on active status at this writing.

The main purpose for Fort Jackson has been to conduct initial entry training, which is commonly called "basic." Under the close supervision of drill sergeants, recruits make the transition from civilian to soldier. The period of this instruction has varied over the decades from eight to eleven weeks in duration. At present, more than fifty percent of all new soldiers and sixty percent of all incoming women in the army go through Fort Jackson.[5]

That the post became the first in the United States to be racially integrated on a large scale is surprising given the reputation it gained for racism during World War II. In 1941, a mob of white National Guardsmen marched to the "Colored Area" and shot holes in the barracks.[6] Black civilians suffered beatings at the hands of military policemen, who conducted patrols on the streets of Columbia.[7] According to some accounts, German prisoners of war held at Fort Jackson enjoyed better treatment.[8]

When the army tried in 1947 to send all of the nation's African American soldiers to the South Carolina post for basic training, a firestorm of criticism arose among civil rights activists.[9] The reasoning of military planners made sense on paper. The preponderance of black recruits and conscripts came from the South. Concentrating them at Fort Jackson saved money. Although Pentagon leaders had already begun assembling a cadre to conduct basic training on a segregated basis, they backed down. African Americans would go elsewhere.[10]

Not being able to assign black trainees to the post significantly decreased its utility. In 1949, when budget cuts prompted base closures, Fort Jackson was among those chosen. Other factors played a part in the decision, too, most notably the lack of permanent brick buildings at the installation.[11] Regardless, the white legislators, municipal authorities, and Chamber of Commerce officials who lobbied mightily to keep the post open never considered the possibility that treating African Americans better might have prevented the crisis.[12] Many of them concluded incorrectly that Harry Truman ordered the shutdown to punish South Carolina because Governor J. Strom Thurmond had run against him in the 1948 presidential election.[13]

The Korean War saved the post. Responding to Kim Il Sung's surprise attack during June 1950 required a rapid mobilization of troops. Within weeks, the skeleton crew that had remained to shut down Fort Jackson expanded into a division headquarters. By the end of September, more than twenty thousand new soldiers had arrived at the post for basic training.[14]

Ironically, Fort Jackson's legacy of racism contributed to its desegregation. Because of the previous decision to assign only whites, the post did not have separate barracks or an established cadre of trainers to handle black soldiers on a segregated basis. The lifting of race-based quotas on enlistment during April 1950 compounded the challenge of maintaining Jim Crow. Nobody could predict the race of anyone arriving on any given day. Desegregation became the most practical course of action.

Brigadier General Frank McConnell decided that "if we didn't ask for permission, they couldn't stop us." He based his authority upon a new regulation titled *Utilization of Negro Manpower* that had been published in January 1950 and that made post commanders responsible for implementing equality of opportunity in the ranks in accordance with Truman's Executive Order 9981. McConnell also relied upon the precedent set during 1949 when desegregation took place at Fort Ord. In that case, the commander had decided against the wastefulness of using a cadre of seven officers and 165 enlisted men to administer basic training to groups of African Americans that sometimes numbered as low as twenty.[15]

This kind of policy change obviously had a greater potential to cause controversy in South Carolina than it did in California, but several factors worked to keep the situation peaceful. The recent memory of Fort Jackson's near-closure and the urgency of the war in Korea made local whites hesitant to protest anything military authorities did. In addition, nearby civil rights activists were too preoccupied with other issues to celebrate or protest. Furthermore, the dominance of the Democratic Party in Palmetto State meant that the 1950 elections had already been settled during the primaries and that state politicians had little to gain by race baiting. Brigadier General McConnell still took no chances. He informed local civilian leaders of his plans, and he persuaded the editors of Columbia's two major dailies to keep the story out of the papers.[16]

In September 1950, Fort Jackson became the first army post within the United States to desegregate on a large scale. The experiment worked with surprising smoothness. Social scientists studying race relations as part of the military's Project Clear visited during 1951.[17] Although their praise would remain classified for another decade and a half, favorable word began to leak. Positive reports appeared in the *Pittsburgh Courier*, which had long criticized conditions at Fort Jackson.[18] Lee Nichols—a white reporter from United Press International—made two trips there. His account became a central part of his 1954 classic *Breakthrough on the Color Front*.[19]

Despite the model of racial harmony that Fort Jackson provided and despite the power that the commanding general could wield, the post had little or no effect on the civil rights movement in Columbia during the 1950s and 1960s when the installation stood at the forefront of change.

Army leaders tried to distance themselves from civilian conflicts over race. This sense of restraint revealed itself in 1953 when fifty-two black soldiers from Fort Jackson were arrested after one of the men sat down next to a white woman while riding a Columbia city bus. The incident, which drew national attention and came at a time of heightened tensions in South Carolina, had the potential to spark a local movement against segregated transportation. From Fort Jackson to the Pentagon to the White House, people at all levels worked to prevent the armed forces from becoming embroiled in the controversy. Ultimately, municipal leaders in Columbia agreed in the future not to prosecute soldiers for disobeying Jim Crow laws and to instead turn any violators over to the post commander for unspecified punishment.[20]

Reluctance at the Department of Defense to use the military as an agent of social change did not prevent other parts of the federal government from trying to do so. During the early 1960s, the Department of Health, Education, and Welfare attempted to leverage school desegregation with funds earmarked for the children of parents stationed at Fort Jackson. The initiative did not accomplish its goal, and it actually made segregation profitable in the short run for local civilians. Post authorities tried to steer clear of the fray. They opened an elementary school that served 245 students on an integrated basis, but the preponderance of military dependents continued to attend segregated civilian facilities.[21]

The ability of the Fort Jackson commander to bring about change beyond installation boundaries by using the off-limits sanction or other means of desegregating public facilities was limited by the complexities of military-social relations. Commanding generals normally served for two-year tours of duty. They relied heavily upon municipal leaders for institutional knowledge. They needed the support of local congressional representatives to obtain funding for new programs and buildings. As presidential appointees, they could fail to win confirmation for another star if they offended a senator. The factors converged with especial intensity in the Palmetto State because all of its politicians during this period belonged to the Democratic Party and many of the most powerful were reelected until they died. Furthermore, the members of the congressional delegation gravitated towards committees that handled the armed services and veterans affairs.[22]

White leaders in South Carolina thus had no fear that their resistance to desegregation would bring about any sort of retaliation from the military. In 1955, the governor said that "so long as our basic training installations are used as sociological camps for compulsory race mixing . . . it is reasonable to expect a continued lack of voluntary enlistments and a continued lessening of morale and esprit de corps in our armed forces."[23] In 1956, the General Assembly called for the president "to restore segregation of the races in the Armed Forces."[24] In 1957, when Fort Jackson again faced the possibility of closure, a delegation from Columbia was visiting Washington to lobby against the cut at the same time that Senator Thurmond was making his famous filibuster against the civil rights bill of that same year.[25] "The thought that the post in Columbia might suffer never entered into my mind," Thurmond wrote in a 1997 letter.[26]

When the sit-in movement began in 1960, commanders at Fort Jackson had little need to worry about their soldiers getting involved. Basic trainees had limited opportunities to venture into town, and they rarely stayed at the post long enough to establish relationships with local protesters. Even those who had the motivation and connections declined to join. James Felder, for example, was a South Carolina native who participated in the Atlanta student demonstrations and the founding of the Student Nonviolent Coordinating Committee (SNCC). He was drafted in 1962 and sent to Fort Jackson for basic training. Although he visited friends and family in the Columbia area, he put his activism on hold. He was such an impressive soldier, in fact, that he was selected to become a member of the army's ceremonial unit in Washington. The most notable moment of his time in uniform occurred when he served as the sergeant in charge of the casket team for President Kennedy's funeral. Felder returned to South Carolina after completing his enlistment and went to work with a voter registration project. He eventually attended law school, won election to the legislature, and served as president of the state NAACP.[27]

Not until later in the 1960s would protests by soldiers become a concern for authorities at Fort Jackson. The best-known case involved Captain Howard Levy, a white dermatologist from New York who had been drafted and assigned to South Carolina. Levy made friends with local civil rights leaders and began helping to register black voters during off-duty hours. These activities brought him under the scrutiny of post security investigators, who learned that Levy had been counseling black recruits to refuse deployment to Vietnam. The doctor subsequently disobeyed orders to train medics who were preparing for combat in Southeast Asia. He was court martialed in 1967 and sentenced to three years imprisonment.[28]

Nearly all of the unrest at Fort Jackson during the 1960s arose out of opposition to the Vietnam War rather than over local conditions for blacks. These incidents are relevant to because they reveal the close relationship that existed between post officials and Columbia's white elite. The two joined forces, for example, to undermine an antiwar coffeehouse that had opened in town. A former Fort Jackson chief of staff remembered that "we just called the police department, the chief, and he closed the coffeehouses. And the way they did it . . . the fire department went in, and said, 'Ah! Fire hazard here, fire hazard there, you know, gotta be closed.' Whether it was true or not, you know, you could go to court and sue them to reopen it."[29] Eventually, the owners were prosecuted for operating a public nuisance and driven out of the state.[30]

Segregated housing was the issue in which Fort Jackson authorities arguably had the greatest opportunity to fight Jim Crow practices in the Columbia area. On July 17, 1967, Secretary of Defense Robert McNamara instructed commanders to place off-limits any civilian landlord or realtor who discriminated on the basis of race. They were required to survey conditions within the surrounding community and to send periodic status reports to the Pentagon. Issued in advance of the Fair Housing Act, McNamara's directive marked the first overt use of the American armed forces to influence domestic social practices by means of economic suasion.[31]

The policy had especial potential to help at Fort Jackson because the post had little housing available for the officers and soldiers who handled the day-to-day operations and provided administrative and logistical support.

Most of these men and their families went into the civilian community to purchase or rent quarters. Columbia had a shortage of dwellings that met military standards for acceptability. Real estate advertisements often listed properties as being designated for "colored" or "white." A white officer who commanded a basic training battalion in 1967 remembered that "black NCOs who came here had a terrible time finding anything decent."[32]

Humiliation and basic unfairness aside, the physical arrangement of segregated housing in the Columbia area imposed a disproportionate burden upon African Americans stationed at Fort Jackson. Black neighborhoods were clustered close to the city center. To the east, Allen University and Benedict College provided twin anchors for this community. The most prestigious district—called Waverly—was located to the south of these institutions. Residents included I. S. Leevy, who operated a nearby funeral home and who helped organize the only bank in South Carolina to be controlled by African Americans. Also in this area was the office of John H. McCray, who edited the *Lighthouse and Informer* newspaper and who organized the South Carolina Progressive Democratic Party of the 1940s.

Other prosperous African Americans settled to the north and northeast

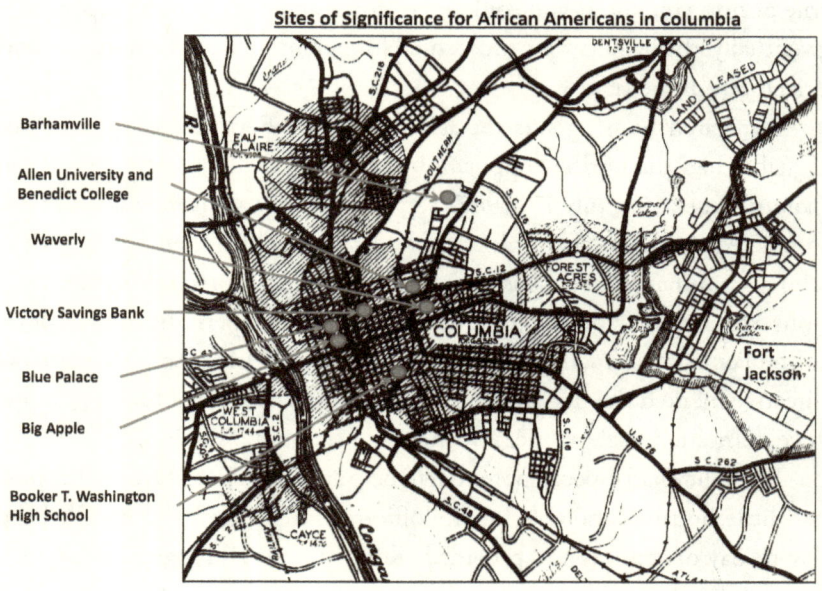

of Allen and Benedict in what came to be known as Edgewood, Barhamville, and Colonial Heights. Among the inhabitants were Ethel Bolden, who became one of the first black librarians to desegregate Columbia schools and whose son Charles attained two-star rank in the Marine Corps, piloted space shuttles, and directed the National Aeronautics and Space Administration (NASA).[33]

Many less-affluent African Americans lived to the west of Assembly Street. This area enjoyed a brief moment of glory during the 1930s when its "Big Apple" nightclub gave rise to a popular dance fad. The area was home to several black-owned businesses and an important center of civil rights protest—Zion Baptist Church. This part of town also had a reputation for prostitution and bootlegged alcohol stretching back to the Civil War. Almost all of the conflicts that took place during World War II between civilians and military policemen from Fort Jackson occurred here. White soldiers called the district "Congo Square."[34]

Another concentration of African Americans was located south of the campus of the University of South Carolina. It was home to Booker T. Washington High School, the second such institution ever to be opened in South Carolina and the only one available for blacks in Columbia until after the Second World War.[35]

These housing patterns shifted during the middle of the twentieth century as municipal leaders obtained federal funds for urban renewal. Black families were frequently removed from dwellings that had been designated as slums and moved to public housing projects. Almost all of these were built in or near predominantly black neighborhoods. In 1965, African Americans comprised thirty percent of the city population while occupying fifty-five percent of the available public housing units.[36]

Whites meanwhile moved to the outskirts of town. Many found places to live in Lexington County, which lay west of the Congaree and Broad Rivers. The wealthier ones went eastward in the direction of Millwood, which had been the plantation of Confederate General Wade Hampton III. The oldest of these neighborhoods was Shandon, which Robert Shand developed during the early 1900s. Others included Heathwood, Melrose Heights, and Rosewood.

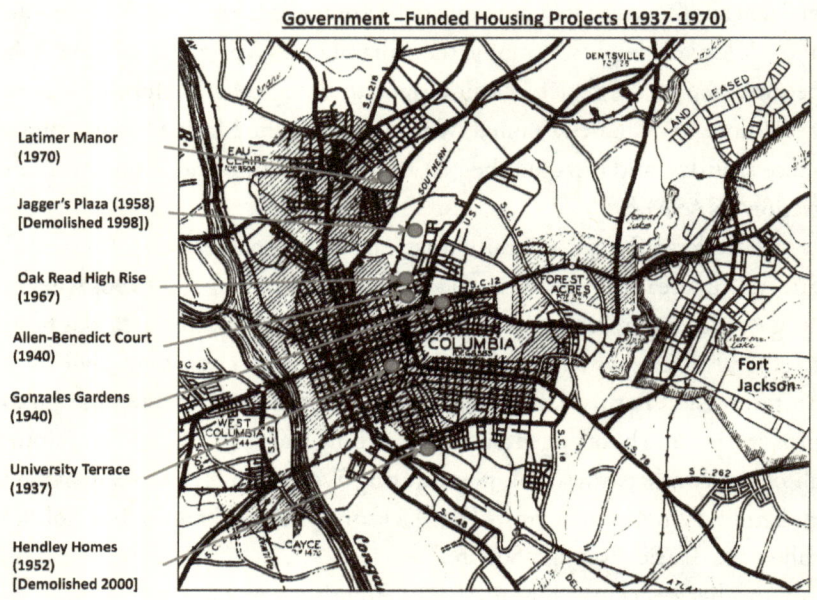

Government –Funded Housing Projects (1937-1970)

Latimer Manor (1970)

Jagger's Plaza (1958) [Demolished 1998])

Oak Read High Rise (1967)

Allen-Benedict Court (1940)

Gonzales Gardens (1940)

University Terrace (1937)

Hendley Homes (1952) [Demolished 2000]

Builders moved farther eastward during the 1930s into the watershed of Gill's Creek, which flows along the edge of Fort Jackson's cantonment area. They drained swamps and constructed dams to create a series of lakes surrounded by expensive homes. Several communities in this area underwent incorporation to take advantage of federal programs or avoid annexation by Columbia. The towns of Arcadia Lakes and Forest Acres were the most significant and enduring.

Black people were not welcomed in these enclaves. In fact, the deed for the Forest Lake Country Club explicitly prohibited African Americans from becoming members. The extensive acreage of the club's golf course—combined with the predominantly-white neighborhoods and municipalities—created a racial buffer zone between Columbia and Fort Jackson.

This situation caused especial hardships for African Americans sergeants and junior officers. None of them could purchase homes nearby even if they could afford to buy one. They faced a long waiting list to find quarters on post, and these were of dubious quality. They included the Jackson Homes—which the Work Projects Administration had built during the 1940s and turned over to the army—and the pinewood buildings of an old

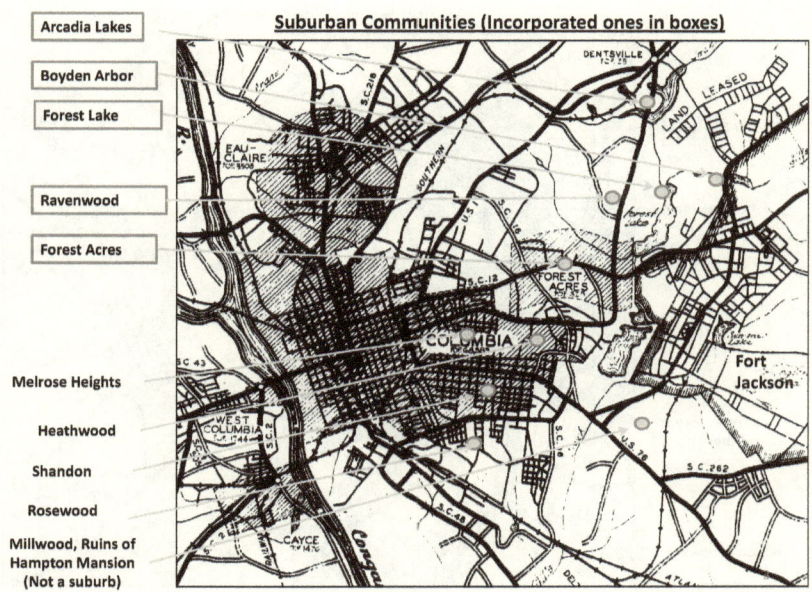

World War II hospital—which had been partitioned for family occupancy. A few privately-owned apartment complexes near the main gate on Jackson Boulevard and some trailer parks on Percival Road and Decker Boulevard provided the last of the nearby alternatives. Most of the other available rental properties in the Columbia area required a much longer commute.

The story of Captain Ernest Porter makes these challenges apparent. An ophthalmologist from Ohio, he moved to Columbia with his wife to work at the post hospital. He testified under oath on May 26, 1967, that "prior to my moving on post . . . we found it very difficult to find living accommodations. . . . I was, to say the least, very despondent. . . At the time, I felt that, as I drove home, seeing signs 'white only' on laundromats . . . and having to drive so far each evening to get back and forth to post, I felt that my first venture into the Southland was rather a negative one."[37]

Dr. Porter made this statement during the same month and year that Fort Jackson officials began conducting telephone surveys and preparing to comply with the housing directive that Secretary of Defense McNamara would issue fifty-two days later. Here was an issue in which the post commander had the full authority of the Pentagon behind him. Here was an

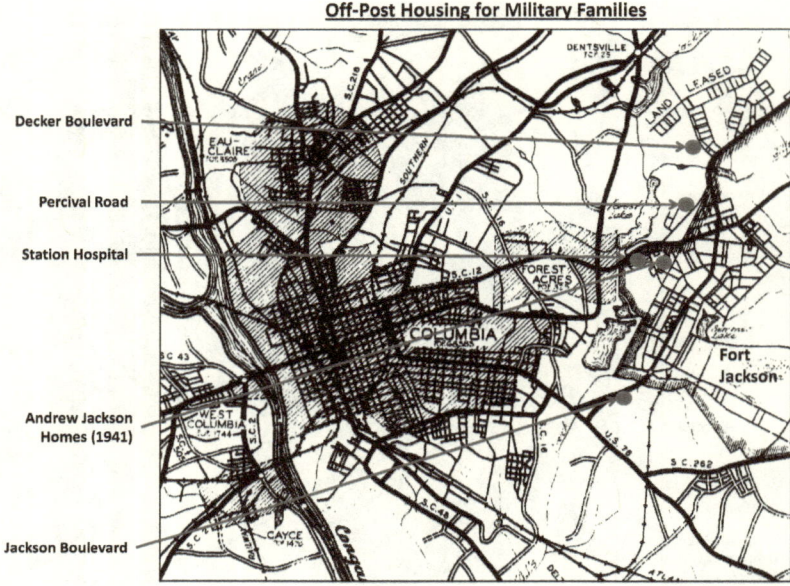

issue that directly affected the morale and welfare of his subordinates. That he would use the off-limits sanction would seem to be a foregone conclusion.

According to the evidence, he did not. Although installations were not required to preserve such papers, a copy of a 1967 study at the post level by happenstance found its way into a filing cabinet at the Fort Jackson Museum. These documents show that the commanding general misled his superiors into thinking that the housing situation for African Americans in Columbia was better than it actually was. His staff accomplished this deception by fudging statistics and shading the words of reports.[38]

Nothing in the record suggests that anyone from Fort Jackson consulted with local black leaders. A 1969 letter to the Deputy Assistant Secretary of Defense for Manpower said that

> an analysis of the narrative and statistical housing reports filed by Fort Jackson . . . has revealed that the base's statistics do not illustrate what we believe to be the true housing situation for Negro servicemen. . . . These statistics infer that there has been little integration of housing facilities since our staff visit, at which time we found that the only facilities housing

Negroes were trailer courts and slum-type dwellings. Our report also recommended that a dialogue be established between the base command, their Negro personnel, and the local Negro community, but the narrative reports from these bases make no mention of any minority group contact.[39]

Rather than sanction discriminatory landlords and realtors, post authorities worked with white elites from Columbia to increase the number of quarters on post. A former member of the general's staff said later that "the feeling was, we were not going to force integration downtown, period. So the downtown real estate community said, well, if you all want to build housing out there for the black NCOs, you know, essentially fine."[40] In 1960, African Americans comprised eleven percent of the military population and eighteen percent of the ones who lived on Fort Jackson. By 1970, these numbers had risen to eighteen and twenty nine.[41]

The closeness that existed between military authorities and white city officials was confirmed in 1968 when Columbia annexed Fort Jackson into the city limits. Taking this step allowed the absorption and taxation of suburban developments that bordered on federal land.[42]

As discussed in *Black, White, and Olive Drab*, the general based his priorities on politics and bureaucratic idiosyncrasies. The maps suggest that the physical positioning of black and white neighborhoods played a part as well. According to the May 1967 survey, the apartment complexes closest to Fort Jackson were already integrated. Forcing the issue with the others brought limited returns given their distance away and given the attendant problems that would arise with laundromats and other public facilities not covered by Secretary McNamara's order. From the general's perspective, constructing on-post housing and drawing black soldiers closer to post perhaps did make better sense.

Mapping the racial geography of Columbia and Fort Jackson supports broader conclusions as well. The location of the post could very well have contributed to the ease with which it was desegregated in 1950. Black and white soldiers living and training together posed no threat to the white neighborhoods and municipalities that surrounded Fort Jackson, and they remained out-of-sight to local African Americans.

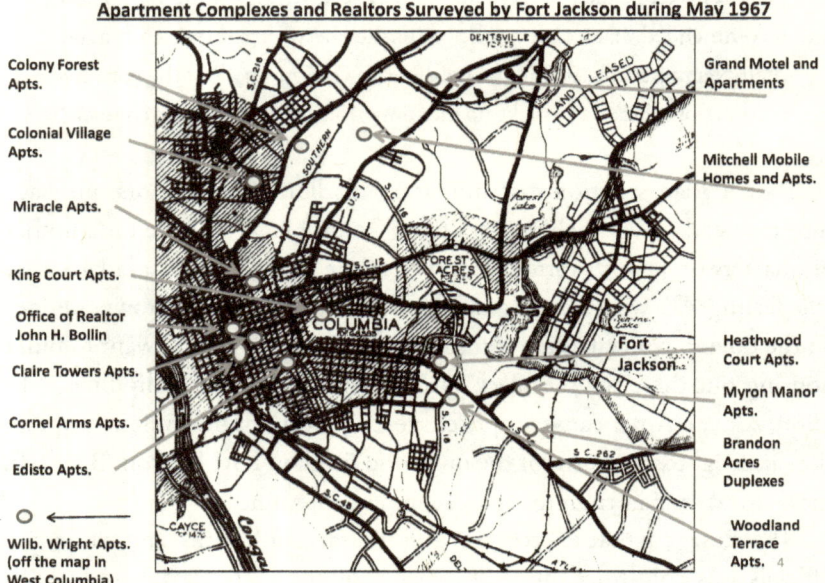

Apartment Complexes and Realtors Surveyed by Fort Jackson during May 1967

Basic trainees rarely left the post, and when they did, they gravitated toward the USO for blacks in Waverly or the one for whites at the corner of Assembly and Laurel Streets. They also frequented a block of nightclubs on Main Street nicknamed the "Combat Zone."[43]

The same racial geography that fostered integration also helps to explain why Fort Jackson had such a limited effect on the civil rights movement. The 1953 bus incident involving the fifty-two soldiers occurred in the Waverly district. The lunch counter sit-ins of the 1960s took place during the day in the downtown and affected virtually no one in uniform. Unlike the black civilians of Seaside, California, the ones who lived in Columbia were physically removed from each other and had no opportunities to interact socially with high ranking military officers.

Fort Jackson did not have much of an impact on the racial practices of its civilian neighbors until the start of the 1970s, when African Americans in South Carolina began voting in sufficient numbers to influence the state's congressional delegation. This development coincided with the aftermath of the Orangeburg Massacre, a federal court decision regarding schools, and a bitter gubernatorial election. It also coincided with efforts at the Department

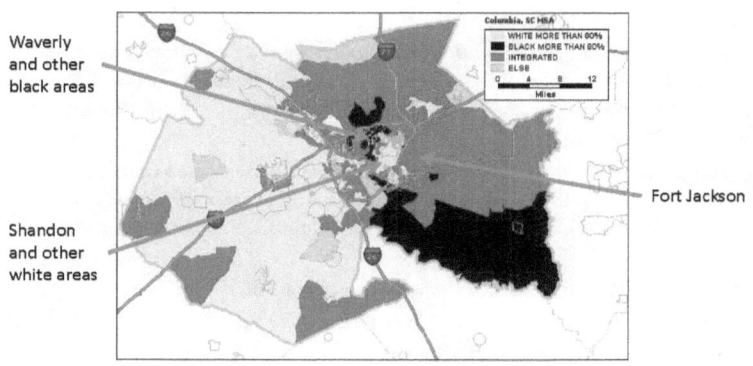

Racial Segregation in the Columbia Metropolitan Area as of 2000

"Maps of the African American and White Populations in the Columbia, SC MSA," http://www4.uwm.edu/etl/Integration/columbia.htm [Accessed 27 March 2013].

of Defense level to combat racism. In other words, Fort Jackson did not make a difference until other factors made local civilians ready to end Jim Crow. The post did provide a model of racial harmony—and for that it deserves credit—but the evidence demonstrates clearly that it had little effect when it stood at the forefront of the civil rights movement. Analyzing the racial geography of the Columbia-Fort Jackson area reinforces this conclusion.

Although two new interstate highways and sprawl have expanded Columbia deeper into Richland County, these earlier neighborhood patterns have persisted.[44] A year 2000 map of racial demographics in the Greater Columbia Metropolitan Area shows that the buffer zone of white people remains between the post and the city center. The Forest Lake Country Club still did not have any black members as of 2014.[45] Nobody noticed until the early twenty-first century that Forest Drive, one of the major thoroughfares connecting Columbia to Fort Jackson, gained an additional letter "r" to recognize Confederate General Nathaniel Bedford Forrest when the road crossed onto federal property. Keeping with the South Carolina tradition of quiet change, the signs honoring the founder of the Ku Klux Klan disappeared without fanfare during the early 2000s.[46]

Notes

1. Paul M. Gaston, *Coming of Age in Utopia: The Odyssey of an Idea* (Montgomery: New South Books, 2010), 103.
2. Andrew H. Myers, *Black, White, and Olive Drab: Racial Integration at Fort Jackson, South Carolina, and the Civil Rights Movement* (Charlottesville: University of Virginia Press, 2006).
3. Carol Lynn McKibben, *Racial Beachhead: Diversity and Democracy in a Military Town, Seaside, California* (Stanford: Stanford University Press, 2012); Tracy K'Meyer, *Civil Rights in the Gateway to the South: Louisville, Kentucky, 1945–1980* (Lexington: University Press of Kentucky, 2009).
4. John Hammond Moore, *Columbia and Richland County: A South Carolina Community, 1740–1990* (Columbia: University of South Carolina Press, 1993), 481; U.S. Census Bureau, "State and County Quick Facts" for Columbia, S.C., http://quickfacts.census.gov/qfd/states/45/4516000.html.
5. "About Fort Jackson," http://www.jackson.army.mil/sites/info/.
6. "Report of Investigation, Civilian Conservation Corps," April 23, 1941, and "Report of Proceedings of Board of Officers at Fort Jackson, S.C.," April 28, 1941, National Archives and Records Administration (NARA), Record Group (RG) 407 (declassified) decimal (dec.) file 291.2. Duplicate copy in RG 159, dec. file 333.1; *Columbia Record*, April 21, 1941; *Columbia State*, April 21, 1941; *Pittsburgh Courier*, May 3, 1941; June 14, 1941.
7. Colonel Andrew Krieger, Inspector General's Department, First Army, "Report of Investigation of Alleged Unwarranted Assaults on and Mistreatment of Colored Civilians in Columbia, South Carolina by Military Police," May 16–24, 1941, NARA, RG 407, dec. file 291.21; Colonel Charles Richtel, "Investigation of Alleged Mistreatment of Negroes by Military Police at Columbia, South Carolina," February 1942, NARA, RG 159, Fort Jackson file.
8. Anonymous letter from soldier in the 1700th Engineer Battalion to *Pittsburgh Courier*, September 1, 1944, NARA, RG 107, entry 91, box 208.
9. 1947 Survey of Negro Conditions at Fort Jackson and Columbia, S.C., February 14, 1947, NARA, RG 159, IG General Correspondence, 1939–1947, box 241, Fort Jackson file; *Pittsburgh Courier*, January 25, 1947.
10. Outgoing Clear Message, February 18, 1947, NARA, RG 107, entry 91, box 208.
11. Memorandum for Record, August 29, 1949, Subject: Inactivation of Fort Jackson, South Carolina, NARA, RG 319, entry 26, dec. file 323.3, box 653.
12. "To the Honorable Louis A. Johnson, Secretary of Defense, and the Honorable Gordon Gray, Secretary of the Army, In support of its Petition that Fort Jackson be preserved as a training and tactical base for the use of the Army," September 1949, NARA, RG 319, dec. file 333.1, box 653.
13. *Columbia Record*, August 31, 1949; Letter from Esther Bonnet to President Truman, October 7, 1949, NARA, Truman Papers, Official File 300B, box 982; Letter from E. C. Townsend to Senator Olin Johnson, September 21, 1949, Johnston Papers, Modern Political Collections, University of South Carolina, box 15; John Riley to Strom Thurmond, June 29, 1955, Thurmond Papers, Clemson University, Subject

Correspondence, MS100, box 17.

14 *Columbia Record*, September 16, 1950; October 2, 1950; Report of Command Inspection, November 30, 1950, NARA, RG 319, entry 26, dec. file 333.1, box 1167.

15 Lee Nichols, *Breakthrough on the Color Front* (New York: Random House, 1954), 97–99; Incoming Clear Message to the Adjutant General dated January 29, 1949, NARA, RG 319, MacGregor Papers, box 7.

16 Nichols, *Breakthrough*, 99.

17 Leo Boart, *Social Research and the Desegregation of the U.S. Army* (Chicago: Markham Publication Company, 1969).

18 *Pittsburgh Courier*, April 21, 1951.

19 Lee Nichols, personal interview by Andrew Myers, tape recording, June 21, 1995; Lee Nichols, "The Army's Secret War Against Racism," *The Freeman*, July 1, 1990, http://www.fee.org/the_freeman/detail/the-militarys-secret-war-against-racism#axzz2ON6jwHnX [Accessed March 23, 2013].

20 "Mass Jailing and Fining of Negro Soldiers in SC," NARA, G1 Staff Files, RG 319, dec. file 291.2; NARA, RG 335, dec. file 291.2; NARA, Eisenhower Library, Central File, Official File 124-A, box 910; Complaints re Incident, Columbia, S.C.—Military Personnel in Custody of Civil Authorities, NARA, RG 407, dec. file 291.2.

21 *Southern School News*, April 1962, March 1963, April 1964; *Columbia State*, February 6, 1963; February 22, 1963; February 27, 1963; April 3, 1963; April 20, 1963; August 31, 1963; September 3, 1963; September 6, 1963.

22 The district to which Fort Jackson belongs has been represented by John Riley (1945–49 and 1951–1962), Hugo Sims (1949–1951), Corinne Riley (1962–1963), Albert Watson (1963–1971), Floyd Spence (1971–2001), and Joe Wilson (2001–present). Another strong supporter of Fort Jackson was L. Mendel Rivers of Charleston, who served in Congress from 1941 until 1970 and was the Chairman of the House Armed Services Committee during the late 1960s.

23 *Columbia Record*, December 1, 1955; *Southern School News*, January 1956.

24 Copy of resolution located at Eisenhower Library, Central File, General File 123, box 903, S.C. Senate Resolutions file.

25 Hyman Rubin, personal interview by Andrew Myers, tape recording, Columbia, S.C., January 27, 1997. Rubin was a member of the delegation that went to Washington during 1957 to lobby against the closing of Fort Jackson. His grandson and namesake is a historian of the South.

26 J. Strom Thurmond, letter to Andrew Myers, April 21, 1997.

27 James Felder, interview by Andrew Myers, Columbia, S.C., no tape recording, April 26, 1995; James Felder, *I Buried John F. Kennedy* (Columbia: Lee Books, 1994).

28 The Office of the Clerk of Court, United States Army Judiciary, maintains control of the transcript of the Howard Levy court martial. In 1995, it was located at the National Records Center in Suitland, Maryland.

29 Angelo Perri, personal interview by Andrew Myers, Columbia, S.C., tape recording, January 30, 1997.

30 *New York Times*, August 12, 1968.

31 MacGregor, *Integration*, 603–604; Nalty, *Strength for the Fight*, 299.
32 Perri interview.
33 The papers of Ethel Bolden (1918–2002) are housed at the University of South Carolina.
34 Moore, *Columbia and Richland County*, 415, 416.
35 Ashley Nichole Bouknight, "'Casualty of Progress:' The Ward One Community and Urban Renewal, Columbia, South Carolina, 1964–1975," Master's Thesis, Public History, University of South Carolina, 2010.
36 "Citizens Design for Progress," Greater Columbia Chamber of Commerce, 1965, 98. Copies located at the Greater Columbia Chamber of Commerce and at the Richland County Public Library.
37 Testimony of Captain Earnest Porter, May 26, 1967, Howard Levy Court-Martial transcript, pp. 2068–2087.
38 The file folder at the Fort Jackson Museum contained the following seven items:
    - Single page from the instruction memorandum received from the Department of Defense
    - Memorandum from First Lieutenant Carr to Major McCracken, Subject: Equal Opportunity for Military Personnel in Rental or Off-Post Housing, May 12, 1967.
    - Sheet titled "Party Line" containing a text for survey takers to read.
    - Memorandum for Record, Subject: Equal Opportunity for Military Personnel in Rental of Off-Post Housing. (This document contains the results of the survey.)
    - Memorandum to Commanding General, Third United States Army, May 17, 1967, Subject: Equal Opportunity for Military Personnel in Rental Off-Post Housing.
    - Text of speech given by the deputy commanding general at the military/civilian liaison council meeting, May 19, 1967.
    - Memorandum for the Commanding General, May 24, 1967, SUBJECT: Resume of Oral Presentation Given at 1000 hours Meeting, subject: Rental of Off-Post Housing.

    The papers collected by Morris MacGregor for an uncompleted sequel to *Integration of the Armed Forces* contain the two items below that include data collected from Fort Jackson. In 1995, the papers were housed at the U.S. Army Center for Military History in Washington, D.C.:
    - DCSPER-DAHC, Fact Sheet, SUBJECT: Equal Opportunity in Off-Post Housing, December 20, 1967.
    - DCSPER-DAHC, Fact Sheet, SUBJECT: Equal Opportunity in Off-Post Housing, October 28, 1968.

    The *Fort Jackson Leader* contains articles about housing in its issues for July 7, 1967, and July 12, 1968.

    Attempts were made to interview Fred Stuck, who was the civilian housing officer, and Colonel Johnnie Duffie, who was the staff officer for the project who answered directly to the commanding general. Mr. Stuck agreed to an interview at his home on February 12, 1997, but was either gone or refused to answer his door at the appointed time. He refused to answer subsequent telephone calls and died in 1999. Colonel Duffie responded to an October 1996 request for an interview by citing illness in the family and abruptly hanging up the phone. He died in 2001.

39   *In the United States District Court for the Middle District Court for the Middle District of Pennsylvania. Howard B. Levy, Petitioner, v. Jacob J. Parker, as Warden of the United States Penitentiary, Lewisburg, Pennsylvania, and Stanley R. Resor, as Secretary of the Army*, p. 137. This source is heavily biased against Fort Jackson authorities. The lawyers who quoted this source appeared to have been looking for information to discredit their opponents. Regardless, it is likely accurate for two reasons. First, if untrue, the claim could easily have been disproved. Second, the claim is extremely tangential to the matter discussed in the appeal. If a lawyer is going to make up something, one would think he would create something more germane. The emphasis was in the original.

40   Perri interview.

41   Census tracts 1960 and 1970.

42   *Columbia Record*, September 9, 1968.

43   Moore, *Columbia and Richland County*, 405.

44   The neighborhoods of the buffer zone made national headlines during the fall of 2015 after a weather system dumped sixteen inches of rain onto the Gill's Creek watershed within a period of twenty-four hours. The resulting runoff washed away multiple dams, killed several people, and ruined hundreds of houses.

45   *Columbia State*, September 4, 2014. The Forest Lake Country Club tradition of inviting the commander of Fort Jackson to become a member came to an end during the 1980s after a Jewish general was assigned to the post.

46   Nothing ever appeared in the news about the renaming of Forrest Road. Knowledge of the change comes from firsthand observation.

10

The Open Schools Revolt

The Southern Regional Council and the Construction of the Moderate South

Matthew D. Lassiter

I really began grappling with the white southern response to the civil rights movement during the fall of 1992, my first semester in graduate school at the University of Virginia, in a seminar on twentieth-century southern history that met in the living room of Paul and Mary Gaston's house on Rugby Road in Charlottesville. About a year later, after Paul had become my Ph.D. advisor, I visited his office on campus in search of ideas for a research paper on some aspect of the civil rights era. Paul pulled four or five folders stuffed full of documents from a cabinet and said that he had been waiting for the right time to give these to a graduate student. The folders contained the confidential reports, referenced in this essay, that Virginia journalist Benjamin Muse submitted to the Southern Regional Council during the late 1950s and early 1960s as part of the Southern Leadership Project, designed to convince moderate white leaders to speak out against massive resistance and endorse compliance with the Brown *decision. Paul explained that he had made copies of these documents during his tenure as president of the Southern Regional Council, between 1984 and 1988, for a potential book on white liberal southerners and the civil rights movement that he had ultimately decided not to write. Instead, as I later came to realize, he was entrusting responsibility for chronicling this history to more than a dozen graduate students who worked with him at the University of Virginia and whose dissertations and books would collectively reorient the scholarship on twentieth-century southern history and the American civil rights movement.*

My research seminar paper on Benjamin Muse and the Southern Leadership

Project became the first chapter in the anthology The Moderates' Dilemma: Massive Resistance to School Desegregation in Virginia *(University Press of Virginia, 1998), which I coedited with Andrew B. Lewis and which features six essays written by UVA graduate students under Paul's mentorship. The first three chapters of the book based on my dissertation,* The Silent Majority: Suburban Politics in the Sunbelt South *(Princeton University Press, 2006), also covered this episode and the broader history of the open-schools movement in the South during the massive resistance era. I wrote this previously unpublished essay, "The Open-Schools Revolt: The Southern Regional Council and the Construction of the Moderate South," for a 2003 conference on the Southern Regional Council and the civil rights movement sponsored by the University of Florida. Although the planned anthology based on that conference did not transpire, a large group of scholars and activists had a productive and at times contentious debate that weekend in Gainesville, with Paul Gaston sitting on the front row throughout. I have not updated the historiographical framing of this essay but instead present it as written in 2003, when I was seeking to produce a synthetic, regionwide account of an open-schools movement that several scholars had written about in specific states and localities. The essay also excavates the Southern Regional Council's covert intervention in the massive resistance debate by orchestrating the emergence of a grassroots moderate South and critically assesses its support for open-schools groups that promoted a position of gradual and minimal compliance with* Brown *that the SRC's white liberal leaders soon came to view as insufficient and obstructionist. This is a messy and complex history, a reflection of the Faulknerian ways that Paul Gaston taught me and several generations of undergraduate and graduate students to think about race, politics, and power in the South, and ultimately in the nation as well. Paul Gaston's fusion of scholarship and political activism has long inspired so many of us, and this essay is a small tribute to that legacy.*

∼

I. Massive Resistance and the Divided South

During the decade following the *Brown* decision, a grassroots open-schools movement led by white middle-class parents from the metropolitan

South defeated the massive resistance program of the region's political leadership and marginalized the egalitarian agenda of the civil rights movement. Many white southerners, including an eventual majority outside the Black Belt, did not support the political strategy of massive resistance, which sought to unite the region behind an uncompromising defense of the caste system through the sacrifice of public education if necessary. In 1958, a year after three cities in North Carolina pioneered the moderate formula of minimal compliance through tokenism and gradualism, the governors of Virginia and Arkansas responded to court-ordered racial desegregation by closing public schools in four communities. As massive resistance to the *Brown* decision became the dominant political stance across the South, white liberals and white moderates joined forces in a compliance movement designed to save the institution of public education. By shifting public discourse away from the choice between segregation and integration, and emphasizing instead the educational and economic costs of defiance, the open-schools movement depicted massive resistance as a showdown between the Black Belt version of the past and the Sunbelt vision of the future. The desegregation dramas of the late 1950s and early 1960s played out in the public sphere not primarily as a racial conflict between black and white southerners but instead as a political battle between civic-minded middle-class families and backward-looking rural demagogues. Instead of a moral confrontation between segregationists and integrationists, the open-schools movement recast massive resistance as an internal power struggle within the white South, matching upwardly mobile urban and suburban families against reactionary state politicians.

The Southern Regional Council (SRC) played a vigorous although largely clandestine role in the emergence and expansion of the open-schools movement during the massive resistance era. As the South's leading interracial public policy organization, the Atlanta-based SRC watched with alarm as the majority of southern states enacted legislative safeguards designed to close all desegregated public schools and subsidize an ersatz system of private segregated alternatives. The arrival of grassroots protests against the implementation of massive resistance in Virginia and Arkansas reinforced the SRC's long-standing faith in the existence of a moderate South that historically had been submerged beneath the politics of white supremacy, which empowered the region's conservative rural leadership through pervasive voting discrimination, systematic electoral malapportionment, and severe intimidation of black activism and white dissent. The liberals in the SRC drew two key lessons from the parallel showdowns in Virginia and Arkansas: that the refusal of open-schools groups to debate the moral issue of segregation versus integration represented the strategic breakthrough in moving the entire region from defiance to compliance, and that pragmatic appeals to the self-interest of business leaders could convince the so-called "power structure" of local communities to take a public stand for public education before court orders triggered massive resistance. Despite lacking a mass membership, the SRC embarked upon an ambitious mission to guide the region into compliance with the *Brown* decision through the political construction of a moderate South.[1]

Between 1959 and 1964, the SRC pursued a two-pronged "research and action" plan designed to defeat the state-level program of massive resistance through the community-based mobilization of open-schools sentiment. The Southern Leadership Project, led by a liberal white journalist from Virginia named Benjamin Muse, represented a comprehensive outreach to influential civic leaders throughout the region, reinforced by a steady stream of research reports sent to businessmen, newspaper editors, municipal politicians, and others identified as "submerged moderates" and "cautious liberals." For five years, Benjamin Muse and other SRC consultants traveled to trouble spots across the South, holding confidential meetings with more than five hundred contacts identified as part of the local "power structure," and keeping faith that pragmatic businessmen would lead their communities into the future through preemptive opposition to the dangers of segregationist defiance. Instead of appeals to "conscience and moral principle," the Southern Leadership Project emphasized economic arguments based on "common sense and self interest," portraying massive resistance as a futile last stand that would destroy the educational prospects of white children and devastate the industrialization agenda of the New South. Since desegregation was inevitable, the SRC argued, pragmatic southern leaders should manage the process of racial transition instead of allowing segregationist ideologues to create the conditions for civic chaos and mob violence. SRC leaders believed that the population would follow moderate leaders in embracing a policy of "good-faith gradualism," and peaceful desegregation in the metropolitan centers and the Upper South could create a ripple effect that would spread throughout the region.[2]

The Southern Leadership Project largely failed in its principal mission to convince the southern business community to speak out openly against massive resistance and initiate a good-faith process of legal compliance before the arrival of court orders and civic disorder. At the same time, the liberal strategy of changing the rhetorical terms of debate proved to be remarkably successful in rallying white moderates behind an ostensibly race-neutral defense of public schooling and economic progress. As demagogic politicians promised defiance and prominent businessmen remained silent, the middle-class parents who organized the open-schools movement stepped into the vacuum created by the profound default of moderate leadership in most corners of the South. To shift legislative policy from massive resistance to local option, the dynamics of the open-schools movement required one major grassroots breakthrough in each state that had chosen the path of defiance. The SRC quickly moved to capitalize on the effectiveness of the grassroots compliance movements in Virginia and Arkansas, first through the covert provision of financial support and strategic advice to burgeoning open-schools groups in the moderate metropolitan regions of Atlanta and New Orleans, and later by secretly creating save-the-schools organizations in segregationist strongholds such as Mobile and Jackson. The broader open-schools movement represented a grassroots phenomenon of middle-class political consciousness and suburban/metropolitan economic priorities that emerged independently of the desegregation initiatives of the Southern Regional Council. But then white liberals made a tactical decision to embrace the moderate open-schools revolt as the political vehicle for their civil rights agenda, a practical response to the extreme and immediate threat of massive resistance that would have significant consequences for the long-term prospects of school integration and racial equality in the South.[3]

II. "Fighting Moderates"

During the 1950s, white middle-class residents of the cities and suburbs of Virginia exercised almost no formal political influence in a state government dominated by the rural conservatives in the Byrd Organization. The political culture of Virginia depended upon the disfranchisement of black and poor citizens along with a system of malapportionment that prevented metropolitan regions from enjoying the electoral influence that should have flowed from the demographic shifts of recent decades. In 1956, faced with clear evidence that suburban communities in northern Virginia planned to comply with court-ordered desegregation, the Byrd Organization abandoned a local option formula approved by voter referendum and designed a program of massive resistance to be implemented at the state level. Two years later, when a clash between the federal judiciary and the state government appeared imminent, the organized opposition to massive resistance first emerged in one of the most affluent suburbs of northern Virginia. The Arlington Committee to Preserve Public Schools included members of religious, educational, and civic groups along with ordinary white parents who supported legal compliance and contended that state-subsidized private schools could never provide an adequate replacement for public education. In its mission statement, the Arlington Committee demanded local control of educational policy and insisted that the activists in the open-schools movement "are here concerned neither with perpetuating segregation nor in hastening integration."[4]

The open-schools movement in Virginia rapidly expanded into a formidable statewide revolt in the fall of 1958, after Governor Lindsay Almond closed public schools in three communities that faced immediate desegregation mandates. The enactment of the massive resistance program deprived thirteen thousand white students of public schooling in Norfolk, Charlottesville, and Front Royal. The save-the-schools movement rapidly mobilized in the port city of Norfolk, where white parents filed an equal-protection lawsuit to force the state government to reopen their children's schools. In Charlottesville, upper-middle-class white mothers opened temporary facilities to prevent local segregationists from converting to a permanent system of private education. Demands for open schools also came from a broad spectrum of PTA groups, religious organizations, and League of Women Voters chapters—a statewide surge of opposition to massive resistance from a coalition labeled Virginia's "fighting moderates" by the SRC activist Benjamin Muse. Not until December, four months after the closing of schools, did corporate leaders express collective opposition to the program of massive resistance, but only in an off-the-record meeting between the governor and the Virginia Industrialization Group. By the time that business leaders in Virginia took a formal stand, the open-schools movement had already established a framework for compliance in the public sphere, and the tide of public opinion in the state had shifted decisively. In Norfolk, for example, one hundred businessmen signed a petition explaining that "while we would strongly prefer to have segregated schools, . . . the abandonment of our public school system is . . . unthinkable." The manifesto appeared in late January, after months of pleading by the parents in the open-schools movement and also days after the successful resolution of the litigation against massive resistance.[5]

In December, the local open-schools movements joined forces in the Virginia Committee for Public Schools (VCPS), which ultimately included twenty-five thousand members in fifteen chapters based in the state's largest cities and suburbs. The organization decided to restrict membership to whites because of the "present climate of public opinion." The VCPS statement of principles declined to take a position on the issue of integration but warned that the sacrifice of public education would trigger corporate flight from the state, create a populace unqualified for representative government, and cause demoralization and delinquency among young people. VCPS literature observed that the organization "probably includes a majority who would prefer continued segregation of the schools," but all members were "brought together in the united belief that free public education must continue to be available to all who want it." The unprecedented political revolt by white Virginians based in the metropolitan regions exposed the fragility of popular support for massive resistance and threatened the Byrd Organization's domination of the state government. The VCPS made endorsement of legal compliance a safe and respectable position through a highly effective public relations campaign that defended public education as an essential institution in a democratic society and emphasized the costs of defiance to the futures of white children. In the early months of 1959, federal and state courts invalidated the school-closing legislation, and black students peacefully broke the caste barrier in Virginia's secondary school system. That spring, with considerable assistance from a lobbying operation coordinated by the VCPS, moderate forces in the state legislature passed a local option plan over the fierce opposition of diehard massive resisters who sought to repeal the constitutional guarantee of free public education.[6]

The Southern Regional Council trumpeted the successful efforts of the VCPS in its publications and presented the organization as a model for other communities caught in the showdown between segregationist defiance and federal supremacy. The November 1958 edition of *New South*, the monthly newsletter published by the SRC, highlighted the emergence of Virginia's grassroots opponents of massive resistance and explained that every state in the region faced a similar and simple choice between "desegregation or no public education." A few months later, in the dispassionate 'just the facts' style that typified SRC literature, *New South* offered a bleak forecast of the economic consequences that would follow the abandonment of public education in Virginia, including the departure of the state's industrial base and the absence of a skilled workforce adequate to the requirements of a modern society. By the spring of 1959, the Virginia experience had become the cautionary tale that the SRC projected for consumption by the still resistant states of the Deep South, a warning of the need for white moderates elsewhere to organize before rather than after the implementation of massive resistance. But the liberal celebration of the triumph of moderation in Virginia also revealed the extent to which the extreme program of massive resistance had rearranged the political discourse within the South. The decentralized policy of "freedom of choice" and local option that replaced massive resistance included tuition grants for segregated private education and allowed rural Prince Edward County to close its public schools for five years. White moderates and liberals in Virginia had opposed both of these proposals in the 1956 statewide referendum, but three years later the VCPS lobbied for the passage of the local option plan despite privately considering several of its components to be part of a transparent effort to circumvent federal law and a dangerous attack on the institution of public education.[7]

The SRC also immediately began to establish a communications network between the Virginia Committee for Public Schools and its nascent counterparts in other southern states. SRC leaders recruited William Lightsey, the executive secretary of the VCPS, to serve as an external consultant through an informal arrangement that anticipated the subsequent outreach initiatives of the Southern Leadership Project. In early 1959, the SRC paid for Lightsey to travel to Little Rock, where he met with the leaders of the Women's Emergency Committee to Open Our Schools as well as local business executives and moderate members of the school board. Harold Fleming, the executive director of the SRC, insisted that his organization's role in orchestrating the consultations remain confidential, in order to prevent massive resisters from slandering the open-schools movement for its affiliation with supporters of integration. A few months later, under the same undercover arrangement, the SRC brought Lightsey to Atlanta to meet with the founders of HOPE, the grassroots parents organization leading the assault on Georgia's massive resistance laws. The SRC also funded a report written by Lightsey that described the organizing techniques and rhetorical strategies adopted by the VCPS. This handbook for other open-schools movements, excerpted in *New South* and distributed by the SRC, emphasized the importance of appealing to the broadest possible range of white moderates by choosing leaders unaffiliated with liberal institutions and circumventing the debate between integrationists and segregationists through a single-minded focus on the preservation of public education.[8]

The dynamics of desegregation in Arkansas paralleled the events in Virginia, with the Women's Emergency Committee to Open Our Schools (WEC) playing the grassroots role of the VCPS, and the circumspection of business leaders mirroring the public silence of their counterparts in the Old Dominion. In the fall of 1958, Governor Orval Faubus closed all four of the high schools in Little Rock, one year after his efforts to obstruct desegregation had provoked mob violence and resulted in the military enforcement of federal court orders. Immediately following the enactment of massive resistance legislation, upper-middle-class white women from some of Little Rock's most exclusive neighborhoods organized the WEC as an organization "dedicated to the principle of free public school education and to law and order. We stand neither for integration nor for segregation, but for education." The WEC ultimately boasted 1,600 active members engaged in a multifaceted grassroots campaign to reopen the schools through radio and television advertisements, informational mailings to parents, neighborhood meetings, and reports sent to businessmen that emphasized the economic consequences of massive resistance. The organization led the resistance to Faubus's attempt to convert the city's white public schools into a "private" taxpayer-funded system, a scheme approved by 72 percent of the voters in Little Rock but promptly invalidated by the Supreme Court. The open-schools movement also established temporary facilities to withstand the efforts by local segregationist forces to begin a permanent private school system. The turning point came in December, when voters elected three white moderates to the Little Rock school board in a campaign organized by the WEC and supported by an open-schools coalition that included local ministers, lawyers, physicians, and education officials.[9]

The Southern Regional Council quickly established a working relationship with the WEC through its local affiliates in the Arkansas Council on Human Relations, including Harry Ashmore of the *Arkansas Gazette* (whose wife served on the WEC's advisory board). "We are indeed interested in the fine work of the Women's Emergency Committee," Harold Fleming wrote to the group's chairwoman in January 1959, "and will be happy to do anything we can to further it." In February, the WEC invited the leaders of the Little Rock Chamber of Commerce and the moderate members of the school board to a meeting with William Lightsey, where the SRC-funded consultant touted the strategies of Virginia's open-schools movement. A few days later, the three school board members released a statement arguing that events in Virginia meant that massive resistance had failed, and presenting Little Rock with a choice between "open[ing] the schools with controlled integration, or . . . uncontrolled integration with all of its adverse effects, economic and social." The Chamber of Commerce immediately followed with a public endorsement of a "controlled minimum" integration plan that would operate along the North Carolina model (a pupil placement scheme to transfer a small number of black students to identifiably white schools after they passed a battery of aptitude screening tests). The WEC and business leaders also joined forces in a successful recall campaign against the massive resistance faction on the school board, and the judicial invalidation of the school-closing laws allowed moderates to implement a limited desegregation plan in the fall of 1959. Businessmen received most of the credit when public schools in Little Rock reopened without incident, but the president of the Chamber of Commerce acknowledged privately that they would not have succeeded without the actions of the Women's Emergency Committee.[10]

The SRC, in a centralized effort to create a chain reaction of grassroots mobilization, quickly began advertising the WEC as the model for preemptive open-schools movements in New Orleans and Atlanta, the next cities to confront massive resistance. In June, *New South* published a feature on Arkansas that highlighted the political activities of the WEC and republished the Little Rock Chamber of Commerce statement for open schools and "controlled integration." The WEC also released an extensive report that convincingly documented the damage to industrial recruitment and white-collar corporations caused by two years of massive resistance in Little Rock, where "the business and cultural climate was clear and bright until a storm broke over its public school system." The SRC distributed the report to thousands of business executives and other civic leaders around the South, and the resource became a central component of the strategic outreach by open-schools forces in Louisiana and Georgia. Paul Rilling, the director of field activities for the SRC, traveled to New Orleans during the fall of 1959 to assist local activists in the effort to establish an ad-hoc organization that would defend public education in Louisiana. In the spring of 1960, open-schools supporters in New Orleans announced the formation of SOS (Save Our Schools) under the leadership of middle-class white women, religious leaders, and college professors. Drawing on the strategic platform of other open-schools movements, SOS refused to "argue the relative merits of segregation or desegregation" and expressed support for "any reasonable plan . . . which will keep the public schools open."[11]

SOS launched an advertising campaign, before the arrival of the full-blown massive resistance crisis, warning of the economic devastation that would accompany the closing of public schools and the outbreak of mob violence. A more conservative open-schools group, the Committee for Public Education, also began a public relations initiative that emphasized the inadequacy of "makeshift private schools" and informed New Orleans that "we no longer have a choice between integration and segregation." In the fall of 1960, Governor Jimmie Davis seized control of the New Orleans public school system to prevent compliance with court orders, and thirty white parents filed litigation to keep their children's schools open. District Judge J. Skelly Wright responded by invalidating the massive resistance program passed by the state legislature, which produced a new round of demagoguery from state politicians. Despite a constant stream of public and private appeals by the open-schools movement and the SRC, the business leadership of New Orleans refused to take a public stand throughout the fall as the city descended into disorder and violence. In November, when four first-grade girls finally desegregated two facilities, New Orleans became the site of the worst scenes of mob resistance since Little Rock, and the vast majority of white families abandoned the desegregated schools and sought private school tuition grants provided by the state legislature. Not until December, after four months of chaos, did a group of leading businessmen publish a statement of support for public education. The next fall, additional desegregation in New Orleans proceeded far more smoothly, although the metropolitan brand of moderation that replaced the state program of massive resistance remained committed to policies of minimal desegregation rather than the SRC's vision of good-faith integration flowing from gradualism and local control.[12]

III. HOPE in the New South

On January 7, 1959, as public schools remained locked in Virginia and Little Rock, the NBC affiliate in Atlanta televised a community meeting conducted by a new organization called HOPE (Help Our Public Education). Frances Breeden, introduced as HOPE's president, led a cadre of upper-middle-class white mothers who represented the core leadership of the group, which drew heavily from the affluent annexed suburbs of northside Atlanta. The telecast outlined HOPE's mission to defeat the massive resistance program of Georgia's political leadership by disseminating the basic facts about public education and transforming public opinion across the state. HOPE's statement of philosophy refused on principle "to argue the pros and cons of segregation versus desegregation, or states' rights versus federal rights." After an opening prayer and a message of encouragement from the Women's Emergency Committee in Little Rock, four fathers in HOPE (all mid-level white-collar professionals) offered pragmatic critiques of massive resistance from the perspectives of medicine, education, business, and the law. The overall program presented a compelling case for what HOPE called its single-minded agenda: "To champion children's rights to an education within the State of Georgia, an education they can be proud of, and a public school system that the balance of the United States can look to as an example."[13]

From its inception in December 1958, HOPE promoted an image of itself as nothing more and nothing less than a collection of concerned parents who cared only about their children's future and their city's reputation. The official version of the group's origins emphasized the spontaneous activities of a small group of middle-class housewives, "in response to the demands of thousands of parents in Atlanta for leadership in the present education crisis." An early press release explained that HOPE originated when two Buckhead mothers, Muriel Lokey and Maxine Friedman, began conducting a series of meetings in their homes, and then the open-schools message spread across northside Atlanta like wildfire. The Atlanta news media—print, radio, and television—immediately began featuring in-depth interviews with HOPE's founders, and the national media followed closely behind. The storyline that emerged emphasized the telephone trees and morning coffee gatherings organized by the four women at the center of HOPE's public leadership: "a petite mother of five," a "tall, attractive, dark-haired" mother of three, "a chic society matron" with four children, and "Atlanta's best looking mother of six children." This powerful iconography framed HOPE's appearance onto the Georgia landscape: an organization that was public-spirited and respectable, explicitly apolitical and implicitly maternal. "We read *Better Homes and Gardens* and got recipes out of *Good Housekeeping* magazine and read Dr. Spock and had these babies," Muriel Lokey later explained. None of them "had ever started a movement."[14]

This account of HOPE's origins was not false but incomplete. Beyond the impromptu mobilization of suburban mothers and fathers lay the submerged narrative of an organization grounded in the city's legacy of female political activism and facilitated by a broad spectrum of powerful local interests. Three weeks before HOPE received its charter, the Atlanta League of Women Voters decided to establish an ad-hoc citizens' committee to address the massive resistance crisis. All four women credited with founding HOPE were active members of the League, an interracial organization that endorsed the *Brown* decision and considered itself to be too controversial to lead the open-schools revolt. During the next two years, as HOPE became the leading voice of white moderation in Georgia, an informal steering committee chaired by the League of Women Voters operated as a shadow organization, with secret monthly meetings attended by representatives of HOPE, the NAACP, the Southern Regional Council, and a dozen other civil rights and religious organizations. Helen Bullard, a close confidant of Mayor William Hartsfield and the second most powerful figure in Atlanta politics, joined the HOPE executive committee and served as an unofficial liaison to City Hall. Ralph McGill, the editor of the *Atlanta Constitution* and a longtime member of the Southern Regional Council, became HOPE's most enthusiastic booster in the press. The local media provided constant and extremely favorable coverage of HOPE's efforts, celebrating the democratic and forward-looking agenda of selfless white parents while denouncing the undemocratic and backward-looking extremism of Georgia's rural political establishment. And although the business community's refusal to provide leadership in the open-schools movement would become a source of constant frustration for the parents in HOPE, several Atlanta corporations anonymously donated money, office space, supplies, and even undercover security at open-schools rallies.[15]

The Southern Regional Council played a quiet but crucial role throughout HOPE's three-year battle to defeat massive resistance in Georgia. With an emphasis on secrecy, the SRC supplied strategic advice and informational literature, coordinated communications with open-schools movements in other states, and provided desperately needed financial support. In a letter to the chairman of HOPE, Harold Fleming of the SRC observed that "the arrangement about expenses is understood on all sides." Much of HOPE's budget was "laundered through the Southern Regional Council," one of the founders of the group believed, because "someone was looking after us or watching us or knew we were important for the city." When HOPE adopted the SRC's business outreach but failed to convince any prominent corporate leaders to serve on its State Advisory Board, the organization obtained commitments from Rabbi Jacob Rothschild of the Atlanta Temple and Reverent Norman Shands of West End Baptist Church, both of whom were active in the SRC through the affiliated Georgia Council on Human Relations. Soon after HOPE's emergence, the SRC installed several of its own members as paid staffers, apparently without the knowledge of most of the ordinary parents who made up the nucleus of the executive committee and volunteer personnel. Paul Rilling, the head of field activities for the SRC, designed the lobbying strategies followed by HOPE in its interaction with the state legislature. The SRC also orchestrated the decision to name another of its members, a retired white liberal named Harry Boyte, as the chairman of HOPE in a maneuver that eventually created a serious internal dispute regarding the tactics of the open-schools movement.[16]

HOPE's inner circle consisted of white liberals who believed that racial segregation was immoral and white moderates who described themselves as "liberal-minded segregationists." The open-schools group ultimately subsumed internal uncertainty about its official stance on racial equality beneath a pragmatic decision to highlight the ways that massive resistance threatened the self-interests of white Georgians. "We just knew it was a total loss to make any impression on changing anybody's minds publicly by coming out with statements that segregation was wrong," Muriel Lokey later explained. By the same rationale, HOPE decided to restrict membership to whites only, a policy made easier when an NAACP attorney privately assured several HOPE leaders that an integrated group would be less effective. "Everyone knew that black people wanted the schools kept open," observed Nan Pendergrast, a liberal activist in HOPE who also belonged to the NAACP and the Greater Atlanta Council on Human Relations. "What was important was that white people wanted them open." The open-schools movement mapped out an ambitious grassroots campaign to emphasize the inevitability of legal compliance, the inadequacy of private schools, and the disastrous economic consequences of abandoning public education. After some debate, HOPE decided to highlight but not specifically endorse desegregation options that could serve as a compromise between massive resistance and "massive integration." To fend off anticipated attacks, HOPE also resolved to deny any charges that its leaders were racial integrationists, northern liberals, or allied with the NAACP and the Southern Regional Council—four political liabilities that were all at least partially true. Each founding member even took a loyalty oath swearing that she or he was not a communist.[17]

Soon after HOPE's emergence, Governor Ernest Vandiver delivered an inaugural address that denounced "advocates of surrender" and "fomenters of division and discord." The governor promised that almost all Georgians were united behind resistance of the Supreme Court, "whatever the cost," and warned "that the few raindrops of 'token integration' would become a downpour, a deluge and then a flood which would engulf our people." Six weeks later, HOPE held its first major demonstration at Atlanta's Tower Theater. The fliers for the event urged concerned citizens to "Stand up and be counted!" and "Fill the Tower with HOPE!" Two thousand supporters of the open-schools movement attended the rally, which included speeches by Mayor William Hartsfield and Ralph McGill of the *Atlanta Constitution*. The SRC also secretly funded an appearance by a Little Rock leader from the Women's Emergency Committee, who warned white moderates to organize before the politicians closed down their schools or face the disruption of their children's education and the destruction of their city's reputation. The coverage by the city's leading newspaper underscored "an overwhelming majority" of Atlanta residents who supported public education, whatever their feelings about the *Brown* decision. *Time* magazine praised the white parents in HOPE for speaking with "a fervor and eloquence" too often absent among the ranks of intimidated southern moderates. The favorable publicity highlighted HOPE's strategy of framing massive resistance as a clash between the past and the future, and offering itself as indisputable evidence of the vitality of the New South. HOPE quickly turned the momentum of the Tower rally into a comprehensive grassroots political campaign that convincingly demonstrated the popular opposition to massive resistance in Atlanta and also led to the establishment of affiliated chapters in six other metropolitan regions.[18]

During the first year of Atlanta's open-schools movement, the parents in HOPE attempted to prove the SRC theory that involvement by the "power structure" would be the turning point in the massive resistance crisis. In the spring of 1959, HOPE systematically informed hundreds of civic and business leaders that the time had come to take a stand for law and order, and warned that continued silence amounted to a tacit endorsement of massive resistance. The complete failure of this strategy led HOPE to inform the Atlanta Chamber of Commerce that "this community wants and expects the business community to speak out on behalf of public education." Pointing to the "lack of foresight" exercised by corporate executives in Virginia and Arkansas, HOPE insisted that the mobilization of thousands of ordinary citizens in Georgia had already created a safe climate for the involvement of business leaders. Under the auspices of HOPE, the SRC also arranged for two leaders of the Little Rock Chamber of Commerce to travel to Atlanta in the fall of 1959 to warn their corporate counterparts against waiting too late before speaking out against massive resistance. But it would take two additional years, a descent into mob violence, and an overwhelming shift in public opinion before the Atlanta Chamber of Commerce abandoned its default position of neutrality. A revealing moment came when Nan Pendergrast of HOPE paid a personal visit to the chairman of the board of the Coca-Cola Company to ask for a public endorsement of the open-schools movement. Business leaders knew that those "out front" would be attacked, Harrison Jones informed the HOPE emissary, so they would "let someone else lead, and then we will follow at a respectful distance."[19]

HOPE's strategic decision to embrace a discourse of pragmatic segregation broadened its political influence but created a simmering internal controversy. In the summer of 1959, when the federal district court ordered the Atlanta school board to submit a desegregation plan, HOPE issued a press release explaining that Georgia faced two choices: closing down every public school in the state, or allowing "a few Negro children" to attend white schools in Atlanta. James Dorsey, the head of HOPE's legal committee, insisted that desegregation did not require "all-out race-mixing" and observed that HOPE was being "called 'integrationists' because we recognize the Supreme Court decision as the law of the land." HOPE promoted the pupil placement scheme used by North Carolina as a compromise that would prevent "massive integration" while securing statewide support, and the *Atlanta Constitution* assured readers that the plan would "maintain for years what would amount only to token desegregation." In the fall, a deepening rift over HOPE's all-white membership policy and pragmatic willingness to endorse token desegregation culminated in the resignations of chairman Harry Boyte and League of Women Voters leader Eliza Paschall, both of whom promptly became officers in the Greater Atlanta Council on Human Relations (a local SRC affiliate). Paschall explained her break with the open-schools movement in a passionate essay in the *Atlantic Monthly*, where she rebuked white liberals who believed that the evils of racial segregation could be dismantled through a cautious strategy that avoided questions of justice and morality. The "realistic liberals" of the white South were in danger of losing their souls, Paschall concluded, but "I can no longer live with my own silence."[20]

HOPE's lobbying campaign during 1960 revolved around the theme of "controlled desegregation," a phrase that the leaders of Atlanta's open-schools movement borrowed from their counterparts in Little Rock. Attorney James Dorsey defined HOPE's agenda as saving public education "from destruction by segregationists and integrationists." With thirty thousand official members and many more sympathizers, HOPE mobilized for the annual session of the state legislature with an open-schools platform that enjoyed popular support in the metropolitan regions but exercised almost no formal political strength in Georgia's severely malapportioned and rural-dominated electoral system. Governor Vandiver opened the new decade with a no-compromise speech that denounced token desegregation as a betrayal of Georgia's heritage and pledged "to resist again and again and again." HOPE responded by labeling the governor a liar for promising that public schools could remain open and segregated, warning that political leaders would be responsible if Atlanta became the scene of mob violence and federal troops. The organization also delivered an open-schools petition to the legislature containing ten thousand names from eighty-seven different localities, along with a pointed reminder that "we are all first Americans, then Georgians." This growing moderate revolt, combined with the judicial invalidation of massive resistance in other southern states, convinced the Vandiver administration of the wisdom of seeking an exit strategy. In February, with the tacit approval of key members of Atlanta's business establishment, the governor convinced the General Assembly to establish a task force called the Sibley Commission in order to plot a tactical retreat.[21]

During March 1960, the Sibley Commission held public hearings throughout the state and asked Georgians to choose between two alternatives: very limited desegregation in a few big cities, or wholesale conversion to a system of private segregated schools subsidized by state tuition grants. Like the discursive strategy of the open-schools movement, this formula rejected the segregationist argument that integration was an all-or-nothing proposition and excluded the civil rights position of good-faith compliance with the spirit of the *Brown* decision. Open-schools supporters dominated the hearings in the metropolitan regions and in the predominantly white sections of rural North Georgia, while massive resisters overwhelmed moderates in the Black Belt areas of South Georgia. At the Atlanta hearing, HOPE and its allies organized a tour de force for the open-schools movement. In a continued reflection of the tensions between its progressivism and its pragmatism, HOPE reluctantly endorsed the local option formula as a compromise solution, while expressing the belief that private schools would be too expensive or too inadequate to function as a replacement system in any part of the state. Harry Boyte, the former chairman of HOPE, delivered the ethically driven position of the Greater Atlanta Council on Human Relations: "The proposed pupil placement plan of the Atlanta school board is designed deliberately to evade insofar as possible the mandate of the federal court. We would like all compulsory racial segregation and resulting discrimination abolished." The Sibley Report, released in April of 1960, urged the state legislature to repeal the massive resistance laws and adopt a "freedom of choice" program that included pupil placement plans to minimize desegregation, tuition grants for private schools, and local option to close public schools by voter referendum.[22]

HOPE immediately issued an endorsement of the "freedom of choice" plan, despite almost unanimous internal opposition to the tuition grant and local option policies. Led by the Atlanta media, the other key groups in the open-schools coalition also closed ranks behind the Sibley Commission. The federal judge overseeing the Atlanta litigation postponed the desegregation deadline until after the next meeting of the General Assembly, after pointing out from the bench that state leaders should realize that the city's patterns of residential segregation would prevent "massive integration." In the fall of 1960, HOPE launched "Operation Last Chance" to prepare its formidable statewide network for the narrow task of convincing the legislature to ratify the Sibley Report. When New Orleans descended into disorder in November, HOPE blamed the violence on the deception of the public by state leaders and launched an advertising campaign with the refrain "Don't Let It Happen Here!" The showdown came in a place that no one expected, after a federal judge ordered the desegregation of the University of Georgia in January 1961. Governor Vandiver temporarily closed the university but made it clear that the state could not suffer the loss of its flagship institution, and the General Assembly quickly passed a version of the Sibley Report called the "Child Protection Plan." Almost two weeks after mob violence broke out at the University of Georgia, and four days after the governor asked the legislature to repeal the massive resistance program, one thousand businessmen affiliated with the Georgia and Atlanta Chambers of Commerce signed a manifesto endorsing "freedom of choice" and declaring that the "disruption of our public school system would have a calamitous effect on the economic climate of Georgia." It is hard to imagine who was left for the silent moderates from the "power structure" to influence.[23]

IV. "A Negative Peace"

Georgia's new policy of local option meant that the city of Atlanta, the self-proclaimed epicenter of enlightenment in the New South, bore full responsibility for the pace and degree of compliance with the *Brown* mandate. HOPE and its allies in the open-schools movement launched a comprehensive public relations campaign to prepare for the court-ordered desegregation of the Atlanta public school system in the fall of 1961. The leadership for the initiative came from OASIS (Organization Assisting Schools in September), a new umbrella organization that included HOPE, the Southern Regional Council, the League of Women Voters, the NAACP, and more than fifty other civic and religious groups that mobilized behind the agenda of "peaceful and orderly desegregation." Under the pupil placement plan, the Atlanta school board only approved 10 out of 123 transfer applications filed by African American students. The members of HOPE's inner circle privately expressed disappointment at the limited degree of school integration, although the policies of the school board accurately reflected the open-schools movement's assurances that desegregation would be minimal if controlled by white moderates at the local level. Segregationist opponents denounced "Ralph McGill's Southern Regional Council" for pushing a "communist program for Atlanta's children" disguised as token desegregation. The religious leaders who belonged to both HOPE and the SRC initially called for a statement "supporting the principle of desegregation and calling for more complete desegregation in the near future," but ultimately decided to honor the OASIS mission of single-minded focus on peaceful compliance. The Greater Atlanta Council on Human Relations remained a member of the umbrella organization but also formally registered its disapproval that "any discussion of the acceptance of desegregation as a desirable measure . . . is outside the scope of OASIS."[24]

OASIS acknowledged and then deflected civil rights opposition toward token desegregation in a handbook prepared for the national media representatives who descended on the capital of the New South: "Whatever the views that divide them, Atlantans are united in a single hope that the story that unfolds on August 30 will be much different from the one you might have expected." When nine black students entered formerly all-white schools in Atlanta, the city orchestrated the events so elaborately that it is hard to see how anything could have gone wrong. "All that remains is this final question," OASIS asked its network. "Have we done all that we can to insure that Atlanta makes good her illustrious image?" The Chamber of Commerce launched a public relations campaign with the theme "How Great is Atlanta?" and boasted that "the business leaders of this city have never faltered in our solid support" for the rule of law. Mayor Hartsfield instructed the media on its obligation to portray the city as a progressive example for the rest of the South and a shining example to the world beyond. HOPE observed that massive resistance had been defeated by "a bunch of starry-eyed amateurs—a strictly grassroots-type operation . . . [of] ordinary housewives and mothers who left beds unmade and meals uncooked to insure their children's educational future." Soon after the desegregation of Atlanta's public school system, HOPE and OASIS each disbanded. "I think all of us were disappointed at the way in which segregation had been killed, if it had been," SRC member Nan Pendergrast later remarked. "We were willing to settle for less than we probably should have settled for. . . . Had we been able to look down the road through the decades to see where we would be now, it would have broken our hearts."[25]

In the early 1960s, the widespread celebration of token desegregation in Atlanta reflected the broad national approval of the politics of racial moderation that defined the metropolitan landscapes of the Sunbelt South. President Kennedy applauded the peaceful desegregation of Atlanta public schools and saluted the "vigorous efforts for months . . . by groups of citizens throughout the community." The *New York Times* portrayed Atlanta as "an island of moderation" in the Deep South and praised the city for demonstrating "what can be accomplished if the people of goodwill and intelligence, white and Negro, will cooperate to obey the law." The United States Information Agency even filmed the events in Atlanta in order to combat Soviet propaganda about the violence of Little Rock and New Orleans. One year later, an SRC activist who served as a "volunteer" in HOPE's open-schools revolt assessed the three-year experience in a reflective essay published by *Harper's Magazine*. HOPE successfully mobilized "the uncommitted center," Florence Robin observed, but only through reliance on a pragmatic strategy that circumvented the moral imperative at the heart of the *Brown* decree. "We have kept the schools open by forcing token integration," she concluded. "Will we now allow the politicians to use token integration as a new weapon to defy the 'deliberate speed' of the Supreme Court decision?"[26]

During their grassroots campaign to defeat massive resistance, the activists in HOPE became prominent exceptions to Martin Luther King, Jr.'s devastating indictment of the "appalling silence of the good people" in the white South. But the region's open-schools movement, like the nation at large, remained vulnerable to the trenchant critique that white moderation favored "a negative peace which is the absence of tension to a positive peace which is the presence of justice." HOPE's public authority revolved around its claim to speak the truth: about the inevitability of compliance with the law, the self-defeating futility of defiance, the inadequacy of private education, and the economic consequences of massive resistance. But HOPE's strategic refusal to discuss either segregation or integration ultimately reflected the short-term effectiveness and long-term liabilities of the open-schools movement. White liberals and moderates did not tell the truth about the policies of pragmatic segregation that replaced massive resistance—pupil placement plans restricting desegregation to "a few" black students, "freedom of choice" that only existed in affluent white neighborhoods—which represented bad-faith tactics that merely postponed an eventual reckoning.

Three distinct strains of gradualism temporarily converged around the agenda of open schools during the late 1950s and early 1960s: the pragmatic efforts by white liberal activists who hoped that good-faith compliance would be the first step toward genuine integration; the self-interested actions of a white moderate majority that embraced token desegregation as necessary to keep schools open; and the belated recognition by diehard segregationists that tokenism represented the best legal method to maintain the ethos if not the policy of massive resistance. Although "token desegregation" eventually became identified with the forces of racial conservatism and white supremacy, historical verdicts of the southern response to the *Brown* decision must recognize that dedicated white liberals and organized white moderates initially championed and ultimately legitimated the path of gradualism and the policy of tokenism. The new desegregation formula that permitted individual exceptions to the dual school system represented a metropolitan blueprint designed to accommodate the class privileges and residential patterns of the white-collar neighborhoods of the urban and suburban South.[27]

In the aftermath of the triumph of moderation in Atlanta, the Southern Regional Council continued to promote the strategic model of the open-schools movement in the most resistant states of the Deep South. During 1963–64, the SRC diverted the bulk of the resources of the Southern Leadership Project away from business leaders in favor of establishing local open-schools groups through a covert process branching off of its local Councils on Human Relations. HOPE veteran Florence Robin prepared a community handbook, "Transition Without Tragedy," using the Atlanta experience as a grassroots organizing model for parents and religious leaders who opposed massive resistance. The SRC secretly distributed the report to open-schools supporters in Mobile, Alabama, where violence loomed as a distinct possibility, and Jackson, Mississippi, where segregationist forces threatened to abandon public education under the local option formula. In Mobile, the SRC used its local human relations council to orchestrate the creation of a group called ABLE (Alabamians Behind Public Education), led by four white mothers who warned that massive resistance would bring economic chaos and insisted that "public schools are the bulwark of democracy—we must keep them open." Publicity of the SRC's involvement compromised the effectiveness of ABLE, however, and segregationist groups attacked the mothers for participation in an allegedly communist plot devised by liberal integrationists from Atlanta. The SRC's field organizers also played central roles in starting an ad-hoc organization called Mississippians for Public Education, staffed by affluent white women who refused to "debate the pros and cons of desegregation" and demanded that public schools remain open. When Jackson implemented court-ordered desegregation without violence in the fall of 1964, the SRC claimed a major victory in its efforts to achieve compliance "peacefully and with good will."[28]

In 1965, in the annual report of the activities of the Southern Regional Council, executive director Leslie Dunbar observed that "a seemingly invariable" lesson had emerged during the transition from massive resistance to desegregation in community after community across the region: "No progress until the right of public discussion and dissent has been established." Since the most important battles of the massive resistance era took place in the public sphere, creating a consensus for legal compliance "has been the task and great achievement of save-our-schools groups." Six years after the SRC launched a comprehensive outreach to moderate business leaders in the South, Dunbar acknowledged that "seldom has the 'power structure' led in gaining this right. Its weighty role comes later, after the windows have been opened." While acknowledging the role played by the grassroots open-schools movement, Dunbar also declared that "our society has been systematically oppressive, and the change from a discriminating to a nondiscriminating social order cannot be a merely superficial alteration." Then the SRC executive director argued that the structural rather than superficial nature of the civil rights movement had been most clearly understood by the extreme segregationists who opposed any desegregation compromise and the young black activists who gave new meaning to the promises of equality. In a series of essays published a year later, Dunbar went even further in crediting black southerners with showing white southerners—including white liberals—that segregation was simply a policy that could be changed by government intervention, instead of a deeply ingrained way of life that could only be dismantled with caution and through gradualism.[29]

Leslie Dunbar's observations reflected the substantial intellectual odyssey of white southern liberals during the decade following the *Brown* decision, and symbolized a new departure in the relationship between the Southern Regional Council, the black freedom struggle, and the federal government. In his 1965 report, Dunbar endorsed the internal catalyst of the civil rights movement and the external catalyst of federal intervention in the South, and he informed SRC members that "this nation is only still beginning the necessary work of making ours a republic of equal citizenship." The political defeat of massive resistance had brought secondary school desegregation to every southern state, but the structural legacies of the dual school system and the inherent limitations of the moderate approach to race relations meant that almost 98 percent of black students remained in segregated institutions. The lessons of the previous decade seemed to contradict the SRC's constant refrain that "each community in the South must find its own answers to social issues within the framework of law and conscience, . . . white and Negro, coming together in equal dignity to find the best ways to move ahead." But even as the Southern Regional Council praised protest from below and demanded intervention from outside, the resilient liberal faith in the necessity of transformation from within recognized an essential truth about the civil rights era. "The really key decisions will not be made by Presidents, Congress, or civil rights leaders," Leslie Dunbar told the SRC's annual convention in 1965. "They will be made individually by millions of church-goers, parents of school children. . . . They will choose whether they want an . . . integrated society or one built on the principles of social exclusion and isolation."[30]

NOTES

1 David Chappell, *Inside Agitators: White Southerners in the Civil Rights Movement* (Baltimore: The Johns Hopkins University Press, 1994); Morton Sosna, *In Search of the Silent South: Southern Liberals and the Race Issue* (New York: Columbia University Press, 1977); John T. Kneebone, *Southern Liberal Journalists and the Issue of Race, 1920–1944* (Chapel Hill: University of North Carolina Press, 1985); John Egerton, *Speak Now Against the Day: The Generation before the Civil Rights Movement in the South* (New York: Alfred A. Knopf, 1994); Julia Anne McDonough, "Men and Women of Good Will: A History of the Commission on Interracial Cooperation and the Southern Regional Council, 1919–1954," (Ph.D. Dissertation, University of Virginia, 1993).

2 Matthew D. Lassiter, "A 'Fighting Moderate': Benjamin Muse's Search for the Submerged South," *The Moderates' Dilemma: Massive Resistance to School Desegregation in Virginia*, eds. Matthew D. Lassiter and Andrew B. Lewis (Charlottesville: University Press of Virginia, 1998), 168–201; Benjamin Muse, "The Southern Leadership Project—After Five Months," Sept. 1, 1959, reel 56: frames 1489–93, Southern Regional Council Papers (microfilm). [Note: hereinafter cited as 56: 1489–93, SRC Papers].

3 The five-year history of the Southern Leadership Project and the parallel story of the open-schools movement challenges the historiographical emphasis on the centrality of public leadership by businessmen in the resolution of the crisis of massive resistance. See, for example, Elizabeth Jacoway and David Colburn, eds., *Southern Businessmen and Desegregation* (Baton Rouge, Louisiana State University Press, 1982); David R. Goldfield, *Black, White, and Southern: Race Relations and Southern Culture, 1940 to the Present* (Baton Rouge, Louisiana State University Press, 1990), 118–48; James C. Cobb, *Industrialization and Southern Society, 1877–1984* (Lexington, Ky.: University Press of Kentucky, 1984); Numan Bartley, *The Rise of Massive Resistance: Race and Politics in the South during the 1950's* (Baton Rouge: Louisiana State University Press, 1969), 118–48.

4 William M. Lightsey, "Organizing to Save Public Schools," 71: 1899–1932, SRC Papers; Benjamin Muse, *Virginia's Massive Resistance* (Bloomington: University of Indiana Press, 1961); Ronald Heinemann, *Harry Byrd of Virginia* (Charlottesville: University Press of Virginia, 1996), J. Harvie Wilkinson III, *Harry Byrd and the Changing Face of Virginia Politics, 1945–1966* (Charlottesville: University Press of Virginia, 1968).

5 "Special Report: Background Summary on Charlottesville, Arlington, Norfolk, and Newport News," Aug. 11, 1958, 220: 0947–70, William M. Lightsey, "Organizing to Save Public Schools," 71: 1899–1932, "A Public Petition to the Norfolk City Council," n.d., 71: 1869, William M. Lightsey to Harold C. Fleming, March 10, 1959, 71:

1820–1826, SRC Papers; Benjamin Muse speech to Charlottesville Council on Human Relations, July 20, 1957, box 3, Papers of Benjamin Muse, University of Virginia; John C. Jeffries, Jr., *Justice Lewis F. Powell, Jr.* (New York: Charles Scribner's Sons, 1994), 145–52; Lassiter and Lewis, eds., *Moderates' Dilemma*.

6   VCPS, "Report on the School Situation," Jan. 9, 1959, 71: 1797–1801, VCPS, "Questions and Answers Concerning the Committee for Public Schools," March 20, 1959, 71: 1864–65, VCPS, "Summary of Legislative Activity," April 30, 1959, 71: 1856–60, William M. Lightsey, "Organizing to Save Public Schools," 71: 1899–1932, SRC Papers. Also see James H. Hershman, Jr., "A Rumbling in the Museum: The Opponents of Virginia's Massive Resistance" (Ph.D. Dissertation, University of Virginia, 1978).

7   "Resistance Growing to School Closings," *New South* (Nov. 1958), 3–7; Lorin A. Thompson, "Virginia Education Crisis and Its Economic Aspects," *New South* (Feb. 1959), 3–8; "Desegregation—Or No Public Schools," *New South* (March 1959), 3–6; VCPS to Members, April 30, 1959, 71: 1854–55, SRC Papers.

8   Harold Fleming to Mrs. Joe R. Brewer, Feb. 12, 1959, 74: 1735–36, Brewer to Fleming, March 2, 1959, 74: 1740, William M. Lightsey to Fleming, March 10, 1959, 71: 1820–26, Fleming to Harry Boyte, Feb. 13, 1959, 212: 0011, Lightsey to Fleming, June 22, 1959, 71: 1887, Fleming to Lightsey, July 21, 1959, 71: 1888, Paul M. Rilling to Lightsey, Aug. 17, 1959, 71: 1933.

9   WEC, "Policy and Purpose," Sept. 1959, 74: 1728, WEC, "What is the Women's Emergency Committee?", n.d., 74: 1727, SRC Papers; *Southern School News*, Oct. 1958, Nov. 1958, Feb. 1959; Nat Griswold, "Arkansans Organize for Public Schools," *New South* (June 1959), 3–7; Sara Alderman Murphy, *Breaking the Silence: Little Rock's Women's Emergency Committee to Open Our Schools, 1958–1963*, ed. Patrick C. Murphy II, (Fayetteville, Ark.: University of Arkansas Press, 1997).

10 *Arkansas Gazette*, March 1, 3, 1959; Nat Griswold, "Arkansans Organize for Public Schools," *New South* (June 1959), 3–7; "Chamber of Commerce Seeks Open Schools," *New South*, (June 1959), 8–10; Benjamin Muse Memo, July 6, 1959, 56: 1181–82, SRC Papers.

11 WEC, "Little Rock Report: The City, Its People, Its Business, 1957–59," Aug. 1959, 74: 1651–1727, Brewer to Fleming, Jan. 16, 1959, 74: 1734, Fleming to Brewer, Jan. 23, 1959, 74: 1732–33, Brewer to Fleming, March 17, 1960, 74: 1743, Fleming to Brewer, March 22, 1960, 74: 1742; Mrs. Moise S. Cahn to Paul Rilling, Nov. 10, 1959, Rilling to Cahn, Nov. 16, 1959, "Save Our Schools, Inc.," n.d. (1960), SRC Papers; Nat Griswold, "Arkansans Organize for Public Schools," *New South* (June 1959), 3–7, "Chamber of Commerce Seeks Open Schools," *New South*, (June 1959), 8–10.

12 SOS, "Our Stake in New Orleans Schools: A Study of Education and Economics," Aug. 1, 1960, 137: 1675–94, SOS, "Close Our Schools?" 137: 1876–85, SOS, "Constitutional Aspects of School Closing," Aug. 1960, 137: 1697–1710, Committee for Public Education advertisements, 137: 1635–38, Benjamin Muse New Orleans Memos, 56: 1205–16, 1737–38, SRC Papers. Also see Adam Fairclough, *Race and Democracy: The Civil Rights Struggle in Louisiana, 1915–1972* (Athens: University of Georgia Press, 1995), 234–64; Juliette Landphair, *"For the Good of the Community": Reform Activism and Public Schools in New Orleans, 1920–1960* (Ph.D., University of Virginia, 1999).

13 HOPE Minutes, Jan. 7, 1959, 212: 1457, HOPE Policy Statement, Jan. 1959, 212:

1399, SRC Papers.

14 HOPE Press Release, Jan. 19, 1959, 212: 1747–48, HOPE Minutes, Dec. 17, 1958, 212: 1453, SRC Papers; *Atlanta Constitution*, Dec. 15, 1958; *Time*, (March 16, 1959), 71–72; "Around Town," n.d., folder 6, box 1, Nan Pendergrast Papers, Special Collections Department, Robert W. Woodruff Library, Emory University; Gerald Walker, "How Women Won the Quiet Battle of Atlanta," *Good Housekeeping*, (May 1962), 76–77, 194–96, 202; Florence B. Robin, "Honeychile at the Barricades," *Harper's Magazine*, (Oct. 1962), 175; Hamilton and Muriel Lokey interview, Jan. 26, 1989, "Public Figures" Series, box 5, Georgia Government Documentation Project, Special Collections, Georgia State University, pp. 55–63 [hereinafter GGDP].

15 Atlanta League of Women Voters Minutes, Nov. 25, 1958, box 21, Eliza Paschall Papers, Special Collections Department, Robert W. Woodruff Library, Emory University; HOPE Minutes, Dec. 9, 1958, 212: 1455–56, Grace Hamilton, "The Beginning of HOPE: The Story of the Struggle for Open Schools in Georgia," April 1960, 137: 1783–87, Hamilton, "A Record of Process—Community Preparation for Desegregation of Public Schools in Atlanta, Georgia," July 28, 1961, 213: 0267, SRC Papers; Nan Pendergrast Interview, June 24, 1992, box 14, GGDP, 77–78; Lokey interview, GGDP, pp. 64–78.

16 Harold C. Fleming to Harry Boyte, Feb. 13, 1959, 212: 0011, HOPE Minutes, April 30, 1959, 212: 1463, HOPE Minutes, Oct. 29, 1959, 212: 1500, HOPE Press Release, Jan. 19, 1959, 212: 1747–48, Feb. 6, 1959, 212: 1750–51, SRC Papers; Lokey interview, GGDP, 76–78.

17 HOPE Minutes, Dec. 14, 1958, 212: 1454, Dec. 17, 1958, 212: 1453, Dec. 29, 1958, 212: 1452, Policy Committee Plan, Dec. 18, 1958, 212: 1391–92, Publicity Committee Plan, Dec. 22, 1958, 212: 1433–36, SRC Papers; *Atlanta Constitution*, Feb. 17, 1960; Nan Pendergrast, "Integration or Ignorance," *Vassar Quarterly* (1960), folder 9, box 1, Pendergrast Papers; Lokey interview, GGDP, 58, 65–69; Pendergrast interview, GGDP, 73–75; Frances Pauley interview, April 11, 1988, "Public Figures" Series, GGDP, 24.

18 *Atlanta Constitution*, Jan. 14, March 5–6, 1959; Tower Rally Program, March 4, 1959, 212: 1762–64, Speech by Mrs. Gordon Wilson, March 4, 1959, 212: 1765–69, HOPE Leaflet, 212: 1772, HOPE Press Release, n.d., 212: 1745, Here's How You Can Help Spread HOPE!," n.d., 212: 1763, HOPE, "Progress Report," 1959, 212: 1443, HOPE Minutes, April 19, 1959, 212: 1461–62, Aug. 6, 1959, 212: 1481, SRC Papers; *Time*, (March 16, 1959), 71–72; "Georgians Resist Closed Schools," *New South* (April 1959), 3–8.

19 Harry Boyte to Jack Adair, March 18, 1959, 212: 0076, HOPE-businessmen correspondence, 212: 0019–0075, 1827–96, Benjamin Muse to Boyd Ridgeway, Aug. 31, 1959, 56: 1695, Ridgeway to Muse, Nov. 9, 1959, 56: 0886, HOPE Press Release, Oct. 28, 1959, 212: 1649, HOPE Minutes, Oct. 1, 1959, 212: 1495, SRC Papers; *Atlanta Constitution*, Nov. 5, 1959; Pendergrast interview, GGDP, 78–79.

20 James W. Dorsey, "There is 'HOPE' for the Public Schools," *The Emory Alumnus* (December 1959), 10–11, 37, folder 5, box 8, Frances Freeborn Pauley Papers, Special Collections Department, Robert W. Woodruff Library, Emory University; *Atlanta Constitution*, Oct. 13, 27, Nov. 7, 25, 28, Dec. 1–2, 1959; HOPE Press Release, June 8, 1959, 212: 1627–28, HOPE Minutes, June 11, 1959, 212: 1471–72, Sept. 10,

1959, 212: 1488–89, Sept. 17, 1959, 212: 1493–94, Oct. 9, 1959, 212: 1497–98, HOPE Pamphlet, Fall 1959, 212: 1417–18, Harry Boyte to Fran Breeden, June 15, 1960, 212: 1516, SRC Papers; Eliza Paschall, "A Southern Point of View," *The Atlantic Monthly* (May 1960), 66–67.

21 HOPE Press Release, Jan. 12, 1960, 212: 1678–79, Jan. 26, 1960, 212: 1688–92, Feb. 14, 1960, 212: 1694, n.d., 212: 1698–1701, SRC Papers; *Atlanta Constitution*, Jan. 5, 11–12, 26, Feb. 5, 17, 1960; Griffin Bell interview, Sept. 12, 1990, "Public Figures" Series, box 3, GGDP, 31–37.

22 "HOPE Statement for the Georgia Study Commission," March 23, 1960, 212: 1704, HOPE Memo, March 1960, 212: 1741, SRC Papers; GACHR, "Notes and News," July 1961, box 1, series I, Paschall Papers; *Atlanta Constitution*, Feb. 18, March 4–25, April 28–29, 1960. Also see Jeff Roche, *Restructured Resistance: The Sibley Commission and the Politics of Desegregation in Georgia* (Athens: University of Georgia Press, 1998); Paul E. Mertz, "'Mind Changing Time All Over Georgia': HOPE, Inc. and School Desegregation, 1958–1961," *Georgia Historical Quarterly*, (Spring 1993): 41–61.

23 HOPE Press Release, April 28, 1960, 212: 1707, HOPE Minutes, April 28, 1960, 212: 1509, May 25, 1960, 212: 1511, "HOPE Asks Some Unanswered Questions," Feb. 15, 1960, 212: 1695, "Operation Last Chance' documents, 212: 1546–51, 1589–1616, 1716–31, 1934–46, HOPE Flier, n.d., 212: 1570, HOPE Mass Mailing, Nov. 28, 1960, 212: 1569, SRC Papers; *Atlanta Constitution*, May 10, 27, 1960, Jan. 7–14, 17–21, 23, 28, Feb. 1, 1961.

24 OASIS Press Release, May 17, 1961, 213: 0873–75, "The Purpose of OASIS," 213: 0006, "History of OASIS," June 12, 1961, 213: 0163–64, OASIS Membership, 212: 1425, Memo to OASIS supporters, June 1961, 213: 0064; Beverly Harris to Anne Sawyer, June 12, 1961, 213: 0160, OASIS Religious Committee Minutes, Aug. 14, 1961, 213: 0517–18, SRC Papers; Separate Schools, Inc., "Newsletter," April 1961, box 3, William Berry Hartsfield Papers, Special Collections Department, Robert W. Woodruff Library, Emory University; GACHR Memo, June 1961, GACHR Minutes, July 11, 1961, GACHR Memo, Aug. 17, 1961, Box 1, Paschall Papers.

25 OASIS, "Background: A Handbook for Reporters Covering the Desegregation of Atlanta's Public Schools," box 22, Paschall Papers; OASIS mailing, July 13, 1961, 213: 0104–05, SRC Papers; *Atlanta Constitution*, Aug. 30–31, Sept. 1–2, 1961; Pendergrast interview, GGDP, 92–93.

26 OASIS mailing, July 13, 1961, 213: 0104–05, SRC Papers; *New York Times*, Aug. 27–28, 31, 1961; Florence B. Robin, "Honeychile at the Barricades," *Harper's Magazine*, (Oct. 1962), 173–77.

27 Martin Luther King, Jr., "Letter from Birmingham Jail," in *A History of Our Time: Readings on Postwar America*, 4th ed., eds. William H. Chafe and Harvard Sitkoff, (New York: Oxford University Press, 1995), 182–95. Also see Tony Badger, "Fatalism, Not Gradualism: Race and the Crisis of Southern Liberalism, 1945–1965," *The Making of Martin Luther King and the Civil Rights Movement*, eds. Brian Ward and Tony Badger (New York: New York University Press, 1996), 67–96, and Walter A. Jackson, "White Liberal Intellectuals, Civil Rights and Gradualism," *The Making of Martin Luther King and the Civil Rights Movement*, 98–102.

28 Florence Robin, "Transition Without Tragedy: A Community Preparation Handbook,"

Dec. 1963, 219: 0306–0437, Paul Anthony, "Memorandum," Jan. 7, 1964, 138: 1681, Frances Pauley to Anthony, March 31, 1964, 138: 1686–87. On Alabama, see Anthony to Leslie Dunbar, May 20, 1963, 59: 0431–32, Oct. 17, 1963, 59: 0437–38, March 6, 1964, 59: 0446–48, ABLE, "Join and Support ABLE," n.d. (1963), 137: 1886, ABLE, "Keep Mobile Schools Open," n.d. (1963), 137: 1887–92, Mobile County White Citizens Council Flier, n.d. (1963), 59: 0439. On Mississippi, see Anthony to Dunbar, May 26, 1964, 59: 0463–64, Feb. 6, 1963, 59: 1878–79, J. Kenneth Morland to Anthony, Aug. 15, 1964, 144: 1563–72, Mississippians for Public Education, Press Release, July 30, 1964, 144: 1561–62, MPE letter to supporters, n.d., 144–1587, Leslie Dunbar, "Annual Report of the Executive Director of the Southern Regional Council, April 1965, 219: 0743–68, SRC Papers.

29   Leslie Dunbar, "Report of Program Activities, 1964," April 1965, 6: 2020–43, SRC Papers; Leslie W. Dunbar, *A Republic of Equals* (Ann Arbor: University of Michigan Press, 1966).

30   "The Southern Regional Council—Its Origins and Aims," 221: 0876–77, Dunbar, "Report of Program Activities, 1964," 6: 2028, SRC Papers; *Statistical Summary of School Segregation-Desegregation in the Southern and Border States, 1964–65* (Nashville: Southern Education Reporting Service, 1964), 2–3.

11

White Southern Students and University Reform in the 1960s

Gregg L. Michel

One day in early 1993, I stopped in Paul Gaston's office to discuss a research topic I was considering for an upcoming seminar paper. I recently had come across a brief mention of the activist student group the Southern Student Organizing Committee (SSOC) in Clayborne Carson's seminal work on the Student Nonviolent Coordinating Committee (SNCC).[1] Carson noted that SSOC was the creation of native white southerners who dissented from the white supremacist attitudes and policies that prevailed across the region and instead promoted racial reform and social justice. I was intrigued, because the only southern whites to appear in the scholarship on the civil rights movement typically were those whose words and deeds helped form the bulwark against racial change in the region.

I explained my interest in the group to Paul and asked if he knew anything about it. He leaned back in his chair and with a wry smile, whose meaning I could not yet understand, commented that he knew a thing or two about SSOC. The group, Paul explained to me that afternoon, had been part of the activist community that helped bring sweeping changes to the state's most prominent university in the 1960s. More than that, it had been composed of a group of dedicated, humane, and reformist young men and women, students whom he had grown close to as they worked for social justice on their campuses and in their communities. Yes, he told me, there might be a story I could tell about these white students and SSOC.

Paul was right about that. But as I delved into the research for what would become my dissertation, I came to realize how closely Paul's own story intersected with that of the students I studied. In both his personal and professional life,

Paul displayed an unwavering commitment to civil rights, devotion to the free exploration of ideas, and faith that an honest reckoning with the past could be liberating in the present. I, of course, had known of the important supporting role he had played in the Charlottesville civil rights movement; the assault he suffered at Buddy's Restaurant in 1963 was a key moment in local movement history. What I discovered, though, was that Paul was just as committed to reforming his academic home, the University of Virginia. From the moment of his arrival in 1957, he struggled alongside a growing number of white and, in time, black students to transform a university that basted in elitist traditions and clung to exclusionary policies into a more open and diverse school that lived up to its founder's highest ideals.

In the 1960s, white students at Virginia, like their peers across the region, worked in support of civil rights. They also pleaded, argued, demanded, and protested to make their universities treat them as the adults they were rather than the adolescents they had been. They insisted that their schools abandon policies that tightly regulated student life and circumscribed academic freedoms. Paul Gaston encouraged students in these efforts. More than that, he taught them that southern history was populated with dissenters and non-conformists, people who, in different contexts and in different ways, rebelled against the status quo and the stifling grip of tradition. That many of these earlier dissenters were white was not lost on his students. They understood that they were not alone or even unique in their activism, that they were part of a long tradition of white southerners who battled for social justice and racial equality. With this understanding of history and with Paul's own activism as a model and inspiration, the students challenged how their universities were run, and, like activists across the region, won more freedom for students, forced an adoption of a more diverse curriculum, and made their school more democratic and modern.

~

In early 1966, University of Florida undergraduates Lucien Cross and Alan Levin found themselves in the school administration's crosshairs for setting up literature tables on the Gainesville campus without first obtaining the requisite approvals. Cross and Levin were veterans of the student activist movement that had blossomed at the university earlier in the decade to support civil rights and advocate for more freedoms for undergraduate students, and both were active in the Freedom Party, a progressive student political organization. Free speech was a central issue for the student activists because rules restricting the types of permissible activities on campus were embedded in the student code and were enforced by the administration. By setting up their tables in front of the library to display and sell copies of the antiwar *Viet Nam Report* and the locally produced humor magazine *The Charlatan*, Cross and Levin sought to challenge university policies and provoke an administrative response that would highlight the absurdity and unfairness of free speech regulations. The administration did not disappoint them.[2]

At first, though, the literature tables did not attract officials' attention. But others had noticed, and soon tables with literature promoting the legalization of marijuana, support for the Congress of Racial Equality, and, curiously, one set up by two women to sell fruit, appeared in front of the library. After two weeks, the administration acted, banning the tables and charging Cross and Levin with violating university policy for not obtaining permission to set up their tables or to sell literature. The subsequent disciplinary hearing displayed the administration's contempt for the students. Marshall Jones, a sympathetic professor who was active in progressive causes on campus and who was an observer at the hearing, described it as a "savage, stupid grilling," as the university inquisitors asked such questions as "are you an anarchist?"; "How can you know what your constitutional rights are? Are you a lawyer?" and "How many children do you have that you know of?" Unsurprisingly, both Cross and Levin were found in violation of university policy and sentenced to probation for the remainder of their days as Florida students.[3]

But the administration had blundered. Its handling of the disciplinary hearing appalled students and faculty members who did not believe that Cross and Levin's actions warranted such condescending treatment. Moreover, by allowing themselves to be goaded into responding to the students' actions, school officials inadvertently stoked student unease regarding free speech on campus. The issue was not just the activists' right to promote their causes, but the right to free speech for all students. As Lucien Cross remarked shortly after his hearing, students simply wanted a place on campus where "all forms of free speech protected under the first amendment [sic] of the Constitution" were permitted. To put an end to the controversy, the administration issued a new policy in April 1966 that guaranteed students' right to free speech—including the right to picket, pass petitions, and distribute free literature—so long as they did not disrupt the normal workings of the university. With the new policy in place, literature tables soon proliferated at the University of Florida.[4]

The Florida episode, though unique in its particular circumstances, exemplified efforts undertaken by students to win progressive reforms on predominantly white southern campuses in the 1960s. In the language of the day, the goal was "university reform," a broad and flexible term that defied precise definition but encompassed everything from calls for greater free speech protections for students to campaigns to force a relaxation in the rules governing student life—the hated *in loco parentis* policies. Although the student activists who promoted and led university reform efforts on their campuses typically came from the political left, they shrewdly focused on issues that would appeal to students across the political spectrum. Moreover, university administrators unwittingly helped to popularize the cause of university reform and unite disparate groups of students by typically opposing reforms of any type. And their commonly harsh and vindictive responses to student activists' initial provocation—from sit-ins and rallies to petitions and silent vigils—only stirred resentment among the student body, deepening activists' commitment to their cause and prompting students who never before had engaged in activism of any sort to get involved. Thus, rather than defusing the crisis at hand, school officials' actions created a backlash among students and ensured the popularity of university reform in the campus community, thereby enabling the advocates of reform to achieve many of their goals. Administrators may have feared their campuses becoming a "Berkeley of the South," in Marshall Jones's words, but their swift condemnation of reform campaigns undercut their opposition and assured Berkeley-like protests—and victories—on their campuses.[5]

University reform efforts in the South had their roots in the burgeoning movement against Jim Crow that drew support from increasing numbers of white college students in 1963 and 1964. Many of these students were outraged by the violence directed at civil rights activists, such as the use of police dogs and fire hoses on demonstrators in Birmingham and the murder of James Chaney, Andrew Goodman, and Michael Schwerner at the outset of Freedom Summer in Mississippi. Likewise, the March on Washington, with its rhetoric of love and goodwill to all and its vision of a racially harmonious future, gave the goal of black rights national legitimacy and inspired many young white southerners previously indifferent to the cause of black equality to assume an active role in the movement.

As a result of this surge in interest in civil rights, white students joined together to form civil rights groups on numerous southern campuses during the 1963–64 school year. These groups frequently made civil rights struggles close to home the focus of their work. For some, like the Virginia Council on Human Relations at the University of Virginia, the opening of their school to black students was the top priority.[6] For others, the desegregation of public facilities near their campuses was the priority. At the University of Florida, the Student Group for Equal Rights organized a picketing campaign against a whites-only eatery near the school, and in Nashville, the Joint University Council on Human Relations, composed of students from Vanderbilt University and Scarritt and Peabody Colleges, organized demonstrations at the Morrison's Cafeteria near the three campuses.[7] White students at the University of Louisville, Tulane University, Florida State University, and the University of Georgia were among others who also formed campus-based groups to promote civil rights. As Sam Shirah, the white student organizer in the Student Nonviolent Coordinating Committee remarked in late 1963, "no longer is it one or two white students active; often there are hundreds."[8]

In 1964, many of these students came together to form the Southern Student Organizing Committee (SSOC), a nearly all-white group devoted to bringing social change to the South. Since the black struggle had inspired the activism of most of the group's founders, civil rights was initially SSOC's primary concern, though as time passed it took on other issues, including the Vietnam War and university reform. Over the course of its five-year existence, white students established SSOC chapters on campuses across the region, and the group came to play a significant role in university reform efforts.[9]

The Free Speech Movement that roiled the University of California in 1964 served to introduce campus reform issues to many white activists in the South. The images from Berkeley flashing across these students' television screens piqued their interest in university reform and legitimized activism that focused on campus issues. Further stoking their interest was a tour of southern campuses in early 1965 undertaken by Steve Weismann, a veteran of the Berkeley movement. Weismann visited more than two dozen schools in ten southern states to discuss the Free Speech Movement and encourage students to pursue university reform on their campuses.[10] Many student activists were receptive to his message because their previous work on civil rights and, increasingly, Vietnam had sensitized them to the interconnectedness of societal problems. University reform was another concern to be added to the mix, and, in fact, gained particular salience when seen in the context of the struggle for self-determination that underlay many students' interest in civil rights and antiwar movements. As University of Virginia activist David Nolan argued in the SSOC pamphlet "The University of the Status Quo," the lack of freedoms on college campuses was "merely a reflection of the closed minded society that in other spheres perpetuates racism and wages a war of genocide upon the people of Vietnam." Similarly, Emory's Jody Palmour, in the wake of a Florida-like episode in which he was charged with setting up literature tables on campus without permission, placed university reform alongside the Black Power movement and revolutionary struggles in the Third World in the effort to displace the "colonial" power structures that governed people's lives. Florida's Alan Levin highlighted these connections more directly: "Individuals [should] be permitted to play a part in the making decisions that affect their lives. We hold this for the people of Vietnam, Greece, Harlem, Selma, and the University of Florida."[11]

Establishing the link between university reform and other progressive issues helped galvanize student activists to take a hard look at the situation on their campuses. They were not happy with what they saw: boards of trustees which happily accepted federal money for research to support the military's efforts in Vietnam, administrators who ruled student life with an iron fist, faculty who meekly supported their administration's positions, and students who seemed oblivious to the repressive state of affairs at their school. At the University of Arkansas, one activist bluntly compared the campus to an antebellum plantation, with the administration and board of trustees as "masters," the faculty as "slave drivers," and the students as "niggers." Writing in the *Daily Tar Heel*, one University of North Carolina student used the all-too-familiar racial epithet to argue that students were treated as second-class citizens. "Can't you see," he addressed his fellow white students, "you are the biggest nigger of all" since the university controlled everything from where they live to what classes they take to where they eat? "Anything the 'mastahs' say, de slaves obey. And you think you're not niggers!"[12]

The use of such raw, offensive language suggested a lack of racial sensitivity among certain activists and a tendency to conflate the grievances of a relatively privileged group of students with the state-sponsored oppression African Americans long had endured. But it also reflected these students' growing alienation from their campuses and an awareness of the limitations on their own freedoms. Just as white society had deprived black Americans of their rights, university administrators had crafted a system which did not treat students fairly and which prevented them from contributing to the decisions that shaped their lives. To alter this situation, students needed to follow the lead of black activists and engage in direct action.

Starting in 1965, student activists in the South began to push back. Over the next several years they formed reformist political parties that competed for control of student governments, challenged the legitimacy of compulsory participation in the Reserve Officer Training Corps (ROTC), worked for curricular reform, launched alternative newspapers, protested the dismissal of politically active faculty, and engaged in a variety of other campaigns designed, in the words of one SSOC publication, "to organize students to acquire the power to make important decisions on their campuses."[13] Their efforts resulted in greater freedoms for students and liberalizing policy revisions that diminished administrators' previously unchallenged and near-total control of campuses.

One area that drew student attention focused explicitly on their formal education—what they were being taught and the environment in which they were supposed to learn. At Knoxville College in Tennessee, for example, students organized protests demanding longer library hours. In Atlanta, students from Emory and Georgia State organized a petition drive opposing state education budget cuts and the lack of intellectual freedom on their campuses. In 1967, forty of the students held a "study-in" in the Appropriation Committee's chambers in the Capitol to press their demands.[14] Activists frequently expressed dissatisfaction with the curricula at their schools. They complained that administrators were unwilling to make curricular revisions to take into account subjects of burgeoning student interest and contemporary importance. The "study-in" students in Georgia had made this one of their demands, insisting that "students and faculty . . . have increased power to add to curricula." Students organized teach-ins as a mechanism for giving students opportunities to learn about subjects that formal curriculums bypassed or ignored. Whether informal, haphazardly comprised "open mic" sessions or highly-structured, scholarly debates and presentations, teach-ins stood as thinly-veiled rebukes of the existing curricula.[15]

White students also organized in support of creating academic courses, departments, and programming focused on black history and culture. The growing number of African American students on these campuses typically took the lead in agitating for these changes. White students, though, offered critical support that ensured the biracial character of the campaigns, thereby immunizing them to charges that they were the work of radical black activists. Nonetheless, school officials did not typically accede to student demands without first trying to suppress or ignore their efforts, steps that usually backfired by drawing even more support for the students' goals. At Duke, the call for black studies programming was one of the demands of black students who took over the administration building in early 1969 that culminated in President Douglas Knight's resignation. After police stormed the campus, shooting tear gas and clashing with students, an outraged study body staged a three-day strike to protest the violence and support the black students' demands. Forced to soften its stance, the administration negotiated a settlement with the Afro-American Society that included a pledge to establish a black studies program on campus.[16]

At the University of Virginia, biracial curricular reform efforts reflected white activists' long-standing commitment to civil rights. A small but hardy group of white students had agitated for opening the school to black undergraduates since earlier in the decade. They also had connected the enduring racial segregation of the campus with the cause of university reform, such as when they attacked the university's hallowed honor code. The activists charged that it was absurd for the institution to maintain an honor code that penalized students for academic infractions while the administration engaged in the decidedly dishonorable practice of denying admission to an entire class of people.[17] Starting in late 1968, white students at Virginia joined their African American peers to insist that school officials develop a black studies curriculum. With white activists, student government, and Black Students for Freedom, the black student group, all behind the demands, administrators relented. Subsequently, in the spring of 1970, history professor Paul Gaston, long active in the civil rights movement and a mentor to many student activists at Virginia, designed and taught the introductory course. And beginning with the 1970–71 academic year, the university formally established an Afro-American and African Studies program.[18]

The rules and regulations that governed student life were an even more frequent target of attack by southern activists. Crafted by administrators who considered it their solemn duty to rule in place of absentee parents, *in loco parentis* policies reached deeply into student academic and social life. They determined where students could live, how—and with whom—they could spend their free time, whether they were permitted to drive on campus, and how they were expected to act in the classroom (e.g. no talking back to professors). In short, they shaped students' entire collegiate existence. Such policies were not unique to the South. Indeed, anti-*in loco parentis* sentiment fueled the Berkeley Free Speech Movement and inspired student protest at colleges and universities nationally. Like their peers elsewhere, southern students increasingly chafed under policies which many believed were designed to infantilize students. As University of Virginia activists asked in a letter they surreptitiously distributed to new students' dorm rooms in the fall of 1965, "Do we really have a university here, or just an advanced high school?"[19]

At several schools, white activists worked to undo *in loco parentis* policies through officially sanctioned avenues for student participation in campus affairs, most notably student government. At Greensboro College, for example, activists presented student government with a "student bill of rights and responsibilities" in an effort to win the student leaders' support for reformist measures. More commonly, student activists tried to take control of student government itself, reasoning that only by displacing the mainstream leaders who they assumed would take the administration's side in policy disputes would they be able to build student support for their position in opposition to *in loco parentis* policies. With the backing of a significant number of students, they believed, administrators would be forced to scrap restrictive student policies. To pursue this goal, activists organized political parties and sought to win the highest elective offices in student government. At Marshall University in West Virginia, a party advocating the liberalization of student regulations emerged in the spring of 1965, and several months later student activists at the University of Arkansas ran candidates for student government on a platform calling for greater protection of free speech and the abolition of student regulations.[20]

A particularly well-organized activist political party emerged in 1965 at the University of Florida, where activists accused the existing student government of being "an echo of the administration and the deans." With strong support from the activist community on campus, the Freedom Party fielded candidates for a wide array of elective offices in 1965 and 1966 and played a major role in shaping the debate during the election campaigns. University reform was at the heart of the Freedom Party's platform each year. The party called for the abolition of compulsory ROTC, the recognition of students' free speech rights, the end to racial and religious discrimination in university organizations, and the revamping of the student dress code. By reducing university control over students, the party, in the words of its 1965 vice-presidential candidate, sought to achieve "a radical re-orientation of the basic campus relationships between students, faculty, and administration."[21] The Freedom Party did not capture student government, as most of its candidates lost. But it injected university reform into the electoral process on campus and paved the way for the 1967 student government victory by an anti-establishment, pro-university reform political party. Despite this important legacy, the Freedom Party's lack of electoral success revealed the difficulty student activists had in garnering support for all-encompassing attacks on *in loco parentis* policies. The Florida activists, like those on other campuses, discovered that their appeal for student support resonated most strongly when they defined their goals narrowly or organized single-issue campaigns. By seizing on one specific issue, white southern activists found it easier to unite broad cross sections of students, thus giving their efforts a level of support which put administrators on the defensive and made students' demands difficult to ignore.

The many special regulations that shaped the daily lives of female students were frequent targets of student discontent. Opposition to rules that set curfew hours for women, banned them from men's dorms, and prohibited immodest dress united students, transcending ideological or political differences that otherwise divided them. In a perspective shared by many students, the editors of the University of Georgia student newspaper complained in 1964 that "university coeds are governed by unfair, unrealistic rules befitting sixth-graders but not college women."[22] When challenged, school administrators typically ignored student complaints, refused to consider modifying the offending policies, or disciplined students who protested. Such actions only strengthened students' resolve and inspired to action students who never before had participated in protests.

Schools across the region experienced unrest over women's rules in the late 1960s. At the University of Arkansas in Fayetteville, women students led mass meetings in 1969 to build opposition to women's rules, while at Vanderbilt more than 1,500 students—both men and women—took part in a protest calling for their repeal. Clemson University, a formerly all-male military academy, saw the emergence of a women's organization devoted to challenging women's policies on campus, a campaign that dovetailed with a drive by SSOC chapters in South Carolina to eliminate curfew policies for women in the state.[23] At the University of North Carolina in Chapel Hill, a broad movement of male and female students developed in 1968 to challenge rules that placed a curfew on women who lived on campus and barred students from opposite sexes from visiting each other's rooms in residence halls, fraternities, and sororities. The SSOC chapter on campus helped coordinate the effort. The group led a petition drive that ultimately collected nearly 4,000 signatures calling for revamping the policy. And it organized a rally around the theme "Are you ready to run your own social life?"[24] Curfews and social life, on one level, can seem trivial concerns. But for reform-minded students they were an affront that symbolized their powerlessness on campus. To push for a revocation of the rules was to assert student rights. Sam Austel, the SSOC leader on campus, declared that "students have the right to decide if and when they want visitation in their rooms." The student newspaper, the *Daily Tar Heel*, concurred, editorializing that the petition drive demonstrated that "students want the opportunity to run their own lives."[25]

The Chapel Hill administration moved quickly to address the students' concerns. First, as the petition drive swelled and the rally drew more than 1,000 students, school officials announced a student-faculty committee would study the issue. Then, later in the fall, it announced two significant policy changes: junior and senior women would be permitted to set their own dorm hours, and students who lived on campus would be allowed to receive visitors of the opposite sex in their rooms.[26] Whether out of agreement with the students' position or a desire to defuse the issue mattered less to students than the fact that the administration had taken concrete steps in response to their demands.

Few other universities' administrations were willing to make similar concessions when faced with student calls for abolition of gender-specific restrictions. To these officials, North Carolina's revamping of its policies was disconcerting because it signaled that, with enough pressure, students could blur the traditional lines of authority on campuses. Administrators elsewhere would have disagreed strongly with Dean of Student Affairs C.O. Cathey when, after receiving the petition from the Chapel Hill students, he declared: "We believe in participatory democracy, and that's the procedure we're following now." In their view, universities were not democracies, and to suggest that they were would sow problems for the future. What they failed to comprehend, though, was that the Chapel Hill administration had removed women's hours as a source of tension on campus. School officials who rebuffed students' calls to revise women's rules served only to inspire more opposition, as students interpreted their resistance as an effort to keep control over students' lives.[27]

At the University of Georgia, administrative intransigence on the issue helped propel the student effort to overturn existing women's rules in 1968. The issue had simmered on the Athens campus for several years, where especially restrictive policies were in place, such as requiring faculty chaperones at all official campus social events and mandating that women wear non-transparent raincoats while attired in gym uniforms. In 1964, the Women's Student Government Association won administrative support for permitting senior women to take "day trips" away from campus and extending from 8:30 p.m. until 11:15 p.m. the time at which women who had been out on trips needed to check-in to their dorms. These were modest changes and did little to dampen student discontent. Early in 1968, male and female students created the Movement for Co-Ed Equality explicitly to challenge the rules. In April, the organization led a march of 500 students to the main administration building to protest the rules. Three hundred of the students then occupied the building for two days. Caught off-guard by the occupation and unmoved by the students' voluntary withdrawal from the building in an effort to spur negotiations, administrators took a hard-line approach: they refused to negotiate about women's rules, obtained a restraining order against 400 of the students that sharply limited their ability to protest, and began disciplinary proceedings against the march's leaders, one of whom received a one-year suspension from the university. Neither the officials' actions nor the summer break disrupted student efforts and, in fact, helped to increase student support for the cause. To the students, the administration's staunch opposition was confirmation that the ideas of shared governance or participatory democracy were foreign concepts to the adult leaders of the campus. The protests restarted with the advent of the fall 1968 semester and continued through the term. Finally, in early 1969, the administration bowed to student demands and began dismantling women's rules on campus.[28]

Like their counterparts in Georgia, University of Tennessee administrators discovered that efforts to quell student protest over women's rules actually helped popularize the issue on campus. Initially, school officials summarily dismissed a 1968 request from a student organization, Associated Women

Students (AWS), to abolish curfew hours for women students over twenty-one who lived on campus on the grounds that it would be too disruptive and impractical to implement. The refusal to consider this modest policy change stoked unrest across campus. The AWS was predictably outraged, but so too was student government and the *Daily Beacon* newspaper, hardly bastions of radical activism on campus. The newspaper, for example, editorialized in favor of revision and compared Tennessee's policy unfavorably with those at Vanderbilt and Georgia, pointedly noting that civil disobedience had led to change on the latter campus. And three student government members, in an effort to stir opposition to the official policy, distributed leaflets that said, in part, "Freedom for the Blacks, but you're just a woman—so forget it."[29] Additionally, students who may not have considered women's dorm hours to be a personally relevant issue, such as commuters and some men, rallied to the cause because the administrative position made student rights the core concern of the dispute. Student opposition crested in early 1969 with a late-night dorm walkout by several dozen women students followed the next evening by a midnight march by 1,000 women dorm residents who were cheered on by an estimated 2,000 men. Concerned that the situation was spinning out of control, the administration quickly announced that a new no-hours policy for all women over twenty-one (with parental approval) would begin. Supporters celebrated the change. As a joint student government-AWS statement declared: "we have met the issue of equality for women—and we have won."[30]

Free speech joined *in loco parentis* as a focal point of university reform efforts on southern campuses in the latter half of the 1960s. Major state universities and smaller, private colleges alike were convulsed by protests over efforts by school officials to implement speech codes, speaker bans, and other policies designed to silence voices and views they judged to be immoral, obscene, or simply disagreeable. Students from across the political spectrum readily understood that such policies posed a threat to the free flow of ideas on campus. They also saw free speech restrictions as yet another assault on their rights as well as evidence that school administrators did not consider them adults with the ability to make informed judgments about contemporary issues. Thus, rather than preserving peace and quiet on campus and protecting students from distasteful ideas, as administrators had hoped, policies regarding free speech served to unite students in common cause and frequently forced school officials to abandon efforts to control discourse on campus. If, as Emory student and first SSOC Chairman Gene Guerrero asked, "the question is whether or not the university will guarantee the free expression of its students," students were increasingly finding that universities answered the question in the negative.[31]

It was not uncommon for free speech to be fused to other student concerns on southern campuses as a result of administrative actions. The heavy-handed response of school officials to the threat of student protest could amplify student demands and frustrate efforts to quell dissent on campus. At Duke, the University of South Carolina, and the University of Alabama, for instance, prohibitions on anti-Vietnam War demonstrations on campus compelled students to rally in support of the right to protest as much as in opposition to the war itself.[32] In a particularly notable incident, SSOC activists who were visiting southern campuses in 1967 on a "Peace Tour" to educate and rally students about the war were barred from the campus of Miami Dade Junior College and subsequently arrested when they tried to defy the ban and address students. The arrests, which included police physically dragging away one of the activists, generated media coverage and student interest. Indeed, the free speech issue appeared to galvanize students who previously had paid little mind to the activists. After the arrests, they formed a "Students Rights Committee" and successfully pushed the administration to allow the activists to return. Had the administration allowed the Peace Tour to proceed as planned, the activists would have reached perhaps fifty students with their antiwar message. Instead, they triumphantly appeared before an overflowing crowd of 250 students in a campus auditorium.[33]

In similar fashion, *in loco parentis* regulations could be recast as free speech restrictions, a coupling that advanced the cause of university reform. Such was the case at the University of Florida in early 1967, when activists baited school officials into severely disciplining a university coed for appearing nude in the *Charlatan*, the same local humor magazine Alan Levin and Lucien Cross had distributed on campus when the university stepped in to dismantle their literature tables. The magazine's editor, Bill Killeen, precipitated the controversy as a means of challenging the student code's threat of disciplinary action for any conduct, on- or off-campus, deemed inappropriate or immoral by administrators. "Sexual promiscuity, vulgarity, obscenity, sex perversion, participation in bawdy affairs, " the code warned, "are illustrations of offences that may well be grounds for disciplinary action." Killeen intended to break the code—or rather, since he was not a student, encourage someone who was to break it—in hope that the administration would overreact and thus turn students against the regulations. Officials responded to Killeen as expected: they charged the student, Pamme Brewer, with "indiscreet and inappropriate conduct" for undressing for the camera, and, then, after winning a guilty verdict from the disciplinary committee, placed her on probation. The administration's actions created an outcry among students, not the least because Brewer had posed off-campus in an off-campus publication. Within hours, students rallied in opposition to her punishment in the Plaza of the Americas, the open space situated near several important campus buildings that was a central gathering spot for students. The protest then moved to the administration building, Tigert Hall, where 150 students spent the night in an impromptu sit-in and followed-up the next day with calls to restrict administrative oversight to on-campus student behavior only.[34]

While the Florida activists' deliberate defiance of university policies galvanized student protests over freedom of speech issues, activists elsewhere in the South typically did not have to manufacture a crisis in order to raise free speech concerns among students. Administrative restrictions on free speech at many southern schools were usually so blatant that students often could not help but bump up against them. These restrictions typically took the form of speaker bans, policies that prohibited individuals who administrators deemed undesirable or inappropriate for speaking on campus. The nation's most notorious speaker ban, in fact, had developed in North Carolina in 1963, where state law barred from state-supported schools speakers who were Communist Party members or who previously had invoked the Fifth Amendment in sworn testimony. The law's primary target was the university in Chapel Hill, which, with its reputation for liberalism, stood in sharp contrast to the rural conservatism of the rest of the state.[35]

Unlike in North Carolina, speaker bans typically originated with school administrations, not state legislatures. School officials had established such policies in their role as stand-in parents, protecting students from dangerous and inflammatory rhetoric and ideas. In practical terms, that meant advocates of politically unorthodox ideas—black nationalists, communists, socialists—and anyone who could be construed as supporting violent change would run afoul of university rules. Unsurprisingly, speaker bans deeply angered a wide cross-section of students resentful that administrators reserved for themselves the power to determine who could, and who could not, be invited to campus to speak.

Students protested speaker bans at numerous schools. At the University of Georgia in 1963, school leaders refused to allow the Phi Kappa Literary Society to stage a debate between a faculty member and a representative of the Communist Party. In editorials and letters in the *Red and Black* student newspaper, students expressed their disagreement with the policy, believing it was a blow to their free speech rights. But the president of the university, O. C. Aderhold, defended the ruling, saying, "We cannot be a party to inviting to our campus a communist whose avowed purpose is to destroy the idea and fruits of freedom."[36] At Memphis State University in 1967, students organized in opposition to new university restrictions on outside speakers. The policy served to unite long-time activists on the Memphis campus with student government leaders and the editors of the school newspaper, the *Tiger Rag*, segments of the student body that usually identified with the administration.[37]

Across the state in Knoxville, students involved in civil rights and antiwar activity joined with Young Republicans, the Interfraternity Council, and members of student government to assail a speaker ban policy in 1968 that had canceled speaking invitations to Congressman Adam Clayton Powell, comedian and black activist Dick Gregory, and LSD-advocate Timothy Leary. Dr. Charles H. Weaver, the university's chancellor, rebuffed calls for revising the policy on the grounds that doing so would undermine his authority on campus. Students were unimpressed and suggested that, far from seeking to challenge his authority, they simply wanted input into who could address them. As Chris Whittle, the student government president explained, "we're not asking to run the University; we simply want sincere consideration of our position within it."³⁸ The chancellor was unmoved by the request. In response, as the fall semester of 1968 progressed, students became more vociferous in their opposition to existing policy. The *Daily Beacon* editorialized in support of a revised policy, student government passed resolutions supporting change, and, most notably, students rallied in demonstrations, including one that drew over 1,000 students despite a driving rain, to pressure the administration to adopt a more open speaker policy.

For students, the dispute over the speaker policy, like the simultaneously occurring conflict over women's rules, represented not just bureaucratic overreach, but attempts to stifle students. Infuriating as this was, student activists were also shrewd enough to recognize the benefits of such administrative opposition. "It has been to the advantage of UT-SSOC," the group's leader commented, "that the administration has acted in such an indecisive manner in regard to an open speaker policy by playing bureaucratic games with inalienable rights guaranteed by the Constitution." After continued protest and an adverse federal court ruling, the administration finally reversed course and in late 1969 authorized a new policy that gave student organizations the freedom to invite speakers of their choosing to campus without fear of an administrative veto.³⁹

Opposition to speaker ban policies at a flagship public institution like the University of Tennessee may seem overdetermined since this was the type of campus—large, increasingly diverse—where student activism flourished in the 1960s. But restrictive speaker policies proved repugnant to students wherever they emerged, and protests bubbled up on numerous campuses, regardless of their size or location. For instance, at Furman University, a small, Baptist school in Greenville, South Carolina, the implementation of a policy designed to protect students from "inappropriate" speakers stirred significant unrest. School officials had created the speaker policy in the wake of a fiery 1968 speech by Black Power advocate George Ware. Determined to keep people like Ware off campus in the future, administrators crafted a policy prohibiting anyone from speaking who had a reputation for promoting violence or illegal activities. As a result, the speaker policy was invoked in fall of 1968 to keep Chicago Seven defendant Rennie Davis from addressing students.

The ruling outraged students, regardless of whether they shared Davis's political views. Through student government and the school newspaper, the *Paladin*, students complained that the policy limited the free exchange of ideas and tarnished the university's reputation as a place where freedom of inquiry was putatively a cherished ideal. It also united them. The College Republicans, Young Democrats, Baptist Student Union, and Pershing Rifles joined together to support a candidate for student government president in spring 1969 who distinguished himself from his peers by making revision to the speaker policy the central plank of his campaign. When this candidate, Ronald McKinney, scored an upset victory, he proposed a liberalized speaker policy for the campus. And when administrators quickly rejected it, students organized a petition drive to revise the policy and held a free speech rally on campus.

The continued opposition to the speaker ban policy dismayed school officials. Student respect for their rulings and policies seemed to have suddenly disappeared. No longer could they simply insist that students accept their interpretation of the issue as a matter of public and campus safety. Instead, students viewed the matter through the lens of academic freedom and believed their fundamental rights of citizenship were at stake. As one of the students, Steve Compton, remembers, "It was a very clear case of the administration violating what seemed to be, to a lot of people . . . a very basic right." In January 1970, hoping to quiet student protests, school officials adopted a new policy which ceded greater control of the speaker process to the students.[40]

In the fall semester of 1968, Tom Gardner, a student activist at the University of Virginia and a former SSOC chairman, submitted a paper on the history of SSOC for Paul Gaston's class on southern history. In his paper, the first historical study of SSOC, Gardner downplayed the significance of university reforms achieved by activists in the region over the previous several years. "The powers-that-be," he wrote, "were less concerned about altering dormitory hours, having a few more seminars or pass-fail courses, and turning over some disciplinary problems to student lackeys, especially if such concessions would help buy the students off and avoid the necessity of dealing with more basic issues such as admitting blacks or women or allowing controversial speakers on campus."[41]

In one respect, Gardner was right; administrators could trumpet the changes they ultimately had agreed to as a sign of their support for student rights and thereby avoid discussion of more difficult issues involving race and equal rights. Gordon Blackwell, the president of Furman, for example, touted reforms on that campus as proof that the university "is moving, kicking and struggling to be sure, into the last third of the twentieth century."[42] But Gardner underestimated the significance of these changes. Rarely achieved without a struggle, they brought important reforms, often for the first time, to many campuses. It was no small matter or achievement to win the abolition of gender rules, institute curricula reforms, or safeguard academic freedom. And the opposition they garnered from school officials united students who otherwise were unlikely to have cooperated on campus issues.

Moreover, their achievements extended well beyond forcing administrators to revamp student codes or to scrap policies which infringed on students' free speech rights. The work of student activists played a key role in prompting university officials to take a number of progressive steps, including ending compulsory ROTC and, where it existed, mandatory chapel; prohibiting military recruiters from visiting their campus; opening the undergraduate college to women; and reforming the curriculum by reducing the number of course requirements and, for the first time, offering classes in African American history and the history of women. On the predominantly white campuses of the South, student activists were able to effect broad-based, long-lasting progressive reforms that helped to make southern colleges and universities more open, democratic, and modern institutions.

NOTES

1. Clayborne Carson, *In Struggle: SNCC and the Black Awakening of the 1960s* (Cambridge: Harvard University Press, 1981).
2. Marshall B. Jones, *Berkeley of the South: A History of the Student Movement at the University of Florida, 1963–1968* (unpublished manuscript in the possession of the author), 61–63; interview, Alan Levin, December 26, 1994.
3. Jones, 63–67 (quote p. 66); interview, Alan Levin, December 26, 1994.
4. *Florida Alligator*, February 16, 1966; *New South Student*, 3:3 (March 1966); interview, Alan Levin, December 26, 1994; Jones, *Berkeley of the South*, 67–70.

5   Jones, *Berkeley of the South*.
6   Bryan Kay, "The History of Desegregation at the University of Virginia, 1950–1969" (Undergraduate Honors Essay: University of Virginia, 1979); Archie Allen, untitled essay, ca. November 1964 (draft of "Report of Field Secretary," *Newsletter: Southern Student Organizing Committee*, 1:3 [November 1964]), folder 2, Southern Student Organizing Committee Papers, Alderman Library, University of Virginia; interview, Bill Leary, April 2, 1995; interview, David Nolan, March 13–14, 1995; interview, Tom Gardner, September 2, 1994.
7   On the University of Florida, see *Florida Alligator*, January 6, 13, 15, and 30, 1964; and January 19, 1965; Judy Benninger to Carl Braden, December 17, 1963, folder 1, box 42, Carl Braden and Anne Braden Papers, 1928–1972, State Historical Society of Wisconsin, Madison, Wisconsin; Jones, *Berkeley of the South*; interview, Marilyn Sokaloff, September 30, 1996; Stuart Howard Landers, "The Gainesville Women for Equal Rights, 1963–1978" (Master's Thesis: University of Florida, 1995), 41–45, 87–89. On the Nashville efforts, see *Southern Patriot*, May 1964; The *New Rebel*, 1:1 (May 27, 1964), in the Southern Student Organizing Committee Papers, Archives and Library, The Martin Luther King, Jr., Center for Nonviolent Social Change, Atlanta, Georgia; *Newsletter: Southern Student Organizing Committee*, 1:3 (December 1964); *Student Voice*, 5:10 (May 5, 1964) and 5:11 (May 19, 1964); *Nashville Tennessean*, May 4, 1964; interview, David Kotelchuck, August 31, 1994.
8   Shirah quoted in "Minutes of the Meeting of the SNCC Executive Committee," December 27–31, 1963, *Student Nonviolent Coordinating Committee Papers, 1959–1972* (Sanford, North Carolina: Microfilm Corporation of America, 1982), A:II:4, reel 3; *Southern Patriot*, May 1964; *The New Rebel*, 1:1 (May 27, 1964), 3–4; Bryant Simon, "Southern Student Organizing Committee: A New Rebel Yell in Dixie" (Honors Essay: University of North Carolina, 1983), 5; Irwin Klibaner, *Conscience of a Troubled South: The Southern Conference Educational Fund, 1946–1966* (Brooklyn, N.Y.: Carlson Publishing, 1989 [originally published 1971]), 209–210; Sam Shirah, "A Proposal For Expanded Work Among Southern White Students and an Appalachian Project, folder 5, Sam Shirah Papers, State Historical Society of Wisconsin, Madison, Wisconsin.
9   For a history of SSOC, see Gregg L. Michel, *Struggle for a Better South: The Southern Student Organizing Committee, 1964–1969* (New York: Palgrave Macmillan, 2004).
10 *Newsletter: The Southern Student Organizing Committee* 2:4 (May 1965), in the author's possession.
11 David Nolan, "The University of the Status Quo," 1966, Steve Wise Papers (Southern Student Organizing Committee Additional Papers, 1963–1979 *and* Southern Student Organizing Committee Papers, 1959–1977), Alderman Library, University of Virginia, Charlottesville, Virginia; *Emory Wheel*, November 2, 1967; Levin quoted in *New Left Notes* 1:31 (August 19, 1966).
12 Joe Neal quoted in *New South Student* 6:1 (January 1969); *Daily Tar Heel*, March 14, 1969. The use of the explosive racial epithet in reference to students was first made by Jerry Farber in his essay "The Student as Nigger," originally published in 1967 in the *Los Angeles Free Press*. Jerry Farber, *The Student as Nigger: Essays and Stories* (North Hollywood, Calif.: Contact Books, 1969), 7.
13 Southern Student Organizing Committee: On the Move," ca. 1967, in the author's

14 "Letter to Supporters," ca. January 1965, box 17, Boyte Family Papers, Special Collections Library, Duke University, Durham, North Carolina; "SSOC Protests Maddox Educational Budget," January 1967, in the author's possession; "Changes," SSOC Membership Mailing Number Five, February 14, 1967, in the author's possession. The author thanks Harlon Joye for providing him access to these and other materials related to student activism in Georgia and other locales around the South.

15 Quote from "Changes," February 14, 1967. Teach-ins were a regular occurrence on southern campuses in the second-half of the decade, particularly on the Vietnam War and the draft (Emory, Arkansas, Florida, and Kentucky) and labor rights (Virginia). *New South Student*, 2:5 (October 1965), 2:6 (November 1965) and 2:7 (December 1965); *Emory Wheel*, October 1, 15, 29, 1965; and November 4, 1965; interview, Jody Palmour, April 2 and 18, 1995; *New Left Notes* 1:3 (February 4, 1966); Jan G. Owen, "Shannon's University: A History of the University of Virginia, 1959- 1974" (Ph.D. Dissertation: Columbia University, 1993), 133.

16 *Southern Patriot*, April 1969; *Phoenix*, 1:6 (March 1969), and North Carolina SSOC, "Worklist Mailing #1," February 17, 1969, "NC-SSOC Worklist #2," ca. April 1969, Wise Papers; Knight, *Street of Dreams*, 134–150. On the development of black studies programs, see Martha Biondi, *The Black Revolution on Campus* (Berkeley, Calif.: University of California Press, 2012); Jeffrey A. Turner, *Sitting in and Speaking Out: Student Movements in the American South, 1960–1970* (Athens, Ga.: University of Georgia Press, 2010); Stefan M. Bradley, *Harlem vs. Columbia University: Black Student Power in the Late 1960s* (Urbana, Ill.: University of Illinois Press, 2009), 110–132; Ibram Rogers, *The Black Campus Movement: Black Students and the Racial Reconstruction of Higher Education, 1965–1972* (New York: Palgrave Macmillan, 2012). The seminal work on the development of black studies programs is Armstead L. Robinson, Craig C. Foster, and Donald H. Ogilvie, *Black Studies in the University: A Symposium* (New Haven, Conn.: Yale University Press, 1969).

17 For another trenchant critique of the honor code, see Paul M. Gaston, *Coming of Age in Utopia: The Odyssey of An Idea* (Montgomery, Ala.: NewSouth Books, 2010), 174–175.

18 Ibid., 274–287, 311–314; Kay, "The History of Desegregation at the University of Virginia, 1950–1969," 141–154; Lisa Anne Severson, "A Genteel Revolution: The Birth of Black Studies at the University of Virginia" (unpublished seminar paper: University of Virginia, 1995), in the author's possession; interview, Bill Leary, April 2, 1995.

19 *The New South Student*, ca. September 1966; Gaston, *Coming of Age in Utopia*, 261.

20 "N.C. -SSOC Worklist no. 1," ca. 1967, in the author's possession; *Newsletter: Southern Student Organizing Committee*, 2:3 (April 1965); *Southern Patriot*, March 1966.

21 Quotes from *Florida* Alligator January 26, 1965; and February 8, 1965. On the Freedom Party, see Newsletter: *Southern Student Organizing Committee*, 2:1 (January 1965) and 2:2 (February 1965); *New South Student*, 3:3 (March 1966); "The History of the Freedom Party," folder 4, box 61, Braden Papers; "Freedom Party Proposal for Action, 1966," folder 37, box 2, Southern Student Organizing Committee Papers, Archives and Library, Martin Luther King, Jr., Center for Nonviolent Social Change; Jones, *Berkeley of the South*, 42–44; and *Florida Alligator*, January 22 and 29, 1965; February 3, 5, 12, and 15, 1965; January 24, 1966; and February 4, 1966.

22 *Red and Black*, May 26, 1964.
23 *The Phoenix*, 1:6 (March 1969), Wise Papers; Wells, "A Movement for Us," *Great Speckled Bird*, February 28, 1969; David Littlejohn to all SSOC chapters [in South Carolina], February 6, 1969, box 17, Boyte Family Papers.
24 Quote from *Daily Tar Heel*, September 28, 1968. Also see *Daily Tar Heel*, October 4, 1968; and October 18, 1968.
25 Quotes from *Daily Tar Heel*, October 4, 1968; October, 18, 1968. Also see *Daily Tar Heel*, October 1, 1968; November 19, 1968; and December 12, 1968.
26 *Daily Tar Heel*, October 4, 1968; November 19, 1968; and December 12, 1968.
27 *Daily Tar Heel*, October 18, 1968.
28 "Press Release," April 14, 1968, and "A Report on the Demonstrations at the Administration Building," April 15, 1968, 3:28, reel 22, *Students for a Democratic Society Papers, 1958–1970* (Glen Rock, N.J.: Microfilming Corporation of America, 1977); "Worklist Mailing" (publication of the Southern Student Organizing Committee), April 20, 1968; *Phoenix* (1:1), August 1968, Wise Papers; *Southern Patriot*, June 1968; University of Tennessee *Daily Beacon*, January 22, 1969; interview, David Simpson, March 15, 1995; Thomas G. Dyer, *The University of Georgia: A Bicentennial History, 1785–1985* (Athens, Ga.: University of Georgia Press, 1985), 345–349.
29 Quote from *Daily Beacon*, November 23, 1968. Also see *Daily Beacon*, November 27, 1968; and December 3, 1968.
30 Quote from *Daily* Beacon, February 8, 1969. Also see *Daily Beacon*, January 22 and 23, 1969; and February 4, 1969; *Great Speckled Bird*, February 28, 1969; and *Phoenix* (publication of the Southern Student Organizing Committee), 1:6 (March 1969), Wise Papers.
31 *New South Student* 2:5 (October 1965).
32 "Worklist Mailing," 1:5 (February 14, 1968); *Phoenix*, 1:5 (January 1969); "Notes from the Field," December 15, 1968, file "Southern Student Organizing Committee," box 2S427, Field Foundation Archives, 1940–1990, Briscoe Center for American History, University of Texas at Austin, Austin, Texas.
33 *Southern Patriot*, April 1967; *Miami Herald*, March 30, 1967; Tom Gardner, Nancy Hodes, and David Nolan, "Florida Peace Tour, February 23–April 7, 1967," in the author's possession; "Peace Talkers Arrested at Dade Junior College," March 30, 1967, folder 8, box 6, Southern Student Organizing Committee and Thomas N. Gardner Papers, Alderman Library, University of Virginia, Charlottesville, Virginia.
34 *Florida Alligator*, February 15 (quote) and 16, 1967, and March 10, 1967; Jon Nordheimer, "Activists: Big Men on Campus—or Big Menace?", *Miami Herald (Tropics Magazine)*, May 19, 1968; Jones, "Berkeley of the South", 72–77; interview, Alan Levin, December 26, 1994; interview, Bo Lozoff, March 10, 1995; interview, Nancy Lewis, September 30, 1996.
35 William J. Billingsley, *Communists on Campus: Race, Politics and the Public University in Sixties North Carolina* (Athens, Ga.: University of Georgia Press, 1999).
36 Quote from *Red and Black*, October 8, 1965. Also see *Red and Black*, October 10, 1965.
37 *New South Student* 4:3 (April 1967).

38 Quote from *Daily Beacon*, September 26, 1968. Also see *Daily Beacon*, April 17 and 18, 1968; September 19 and 28, 1968.
39 Quote from *Daily Beacon*, January 29, 1969. Also see *Daily Beacon*, October 1, 15, and 19, 1968; January 28, 1969; February, 4, 5, 7, 11, 12, 13, 21, and 28, 1969; March 7, 1969; April 19, 1969; and June 20, 1969.
40 Interview, Steve Compton, March 12, 1995; interview, Jack Sullivan, August 31, 1994; interview, John Duggan, March 16, 1995; "Worklist Mailing," April 5, 1968, and *Phoenix* 1:5 (January 1969), Wise Papers; Gregg L. Michel, "It Even Happened Here: Student Activism at Furman University, 1967–1970," *The South Carolina Historical Magazine* 109:1 (January 2008), 38–57; Alfred Sandlin Reid, *Furman University: Toward a New Identity, 1925–1975* (Durham, N.C.: Duke University Press, 1976), 229–231, 247–248.
41 Tom Gardner, "The Southern Student Organizing Committee, 1964–1970" (October 1970), in the author's possession.
42 Gordon Blackwell, "Changes at Furman in Last Four Years," ca. March 1969, "SSOC (Southern Student Organizing Committee)" folder, Gordon Blackwell Presidential Papers, Furman University Archive, James Buchanan Duke Library, Furman University, Greenville, South Carolina.

12

Hugo Black and a Lost Alabama Political Tradition

Southern Economic Liberalism, Populism, and Fairhope's Mission

STEVE SUITTS

I met Paul Gaston when I went to Atlanta to interview for the post of executive director of the Southern Regional Council (SRC) in the spring of 1977. He was serving on SRC's search committee, and I was director of the Alabama Civil Liberties Union. We both were from an "other" Alabama. He grew up in the single-tax colony of Fairhope, which socialists and utopians, including his grandparents, had settled in the 1890s on Mobile Bay. I grew up in north Alabama in Winston County, known to some as the "Free State of Winston," where citizens announced their secession from Alabama after the state seceded from the Union at the outbreak of the Civil War.

After I arrived at SRC, Paul was on the executive committee and later served as SRC's vice-president and president. Bless his heart, Paul did not know much about fundraising and cared little for organizational matters, but he knew the South, its history, the importance of work on issues of race and poverty, and many of the region's liberals. Also, with almost everyone, Paul could be charming—although never quite as charming or captivating as Mary, his wife. During some summers, Paul and Mary would retreat from Charlottesville to Fairhope and invite my wife, Ginny Looney, and me to spend time with them. Those summers proved to be graduate seminars on the single-tax colony and its economic principles.

Wherever we were together, Paul and I also talked about Alabama—its people, its politics, its history, its failures, and its uneven struggles with racism. Amid these discussions, we usually included Hugo Black of Alabama. I had been researching a book on Black for years, and Paul served as one of those friends all writers need—one willing to appear as interested in your book's subject as you are. Because his grandfather and father knew Black and shared much of Black's outlook on economic issues, Paul often broached topics about liberalism, radicalism, and economics that would refer to Black.

Paul and I were also mutual friends of another Alabamian, Virginia Durr—Black's sister-in-law—who was an SRC member and later an SRC Life Fellow. Virginia was a delightful raconteur of southern history who remembered events and people that the young could only know through books and the teaching of people like Paul. Whenever we three were together, the conversation often included Black, Fairhope (Black and his family often vacationed near there until he was appointed to the U.S. Supreme Court), the old days of the New Deal, and Alabama demagogues, past and present.

Throughout those years, while never believing that white southerners should be allowed to escape coming to terms with the racism that their ancestors and they sustained, Paul was no less genuinely concerned about the ravages of the South's colonial capitalism built on biracial poverty. It was not a "New South" Paul wanted.

Little wonder, therefore, when preparing an essay to honor my old friend, I have written about Hugo Black's southern economic liberalism and its echoes of the early Fairhope values. The exercise was no substitute for those lazy, meandering conversations that took place on Fairhope's public beach or in a sailboat skimming the Mobile Bay, or even sitting in a bar after an SRC meeting. But this essay did remind me of those past moments and, in important respects, is a product of those shared good times with a friend who has been a friend indeed.

～

Introduction

Paul Gaston's grandfather, E. B. Gaston, an ardent Populist, led settlers in 1894 into the Deep South to establish on Mobile Bay the town of Fairhope, Alabama, one of the South's most radical economic experiments of the nineteenth and twentieth centuries. It was an attempt to create and sustain an intentional community, a single-tax colony embodying the spirit of Populism and the economic principles of Henry George, who had proclaimed that poverty existed amid progress and prosperity because a community's common wealth, especially its land, was hoarded by "monopolistic capitalism."[1]

At the time of Fairhope's founding, Populist ideals were spreading across Alabama, and there was a "fair hope" that both this new utopian community and the political movement it represented could fashion—almost thirty years after the Civil War—a different economic order that served primarily the state's common folk. History records that the vision did not succeed. Fairhope struggled valiantly into the twentieth century to be a model community, but hostile economic, social, and political forces were eventually more powerful than the ideals and resources of the town's founders. In Alabama generally, Populism fizzled even more quickly, with only a limited impact on the established order.

Yet Populist ideals and ideas were born again in Alabama politics three decades later with the election of Hugo Black to the U.S. Senate. Black is most often remembered as the U.S. Supreme Court justice from Alabama who as a lawyer joined the Ku Klux Klan and as a judge later joined the Court in declaring racial segregation unconstitutional in America's public schools. But he was also the political leader in Alabama history who most embodied what Fairhope represented. Black became the South's foremost economic liberal spokesman who strived before and during the New Deal to put into national practice many of the principles and sentiments that Fairhopers and Populists espoused.

Southern historians have generally acknowledged Black's credentials as one of the South's few true-blue Roosevelt Democrats. But Black served for less than two terms, held no top position of Senate leadership, and was sponsor of only one piece of legislation that was a part of the Roosevelt administration's agenda, so his senatorial years have commanded relatively little ink.[2] Politically, Black was admired by many surviving Populists, including the leaders of Fairhope, but in the Senate's southern delegation, he was overshadowed on the left by Huey Long's three years of senatorial grandstanding and on the right by the near-life tenure of senators who were skeptical of the New Deal at its beginning and by its end considered President Roosevelt a communistic carpetbagger.

Yet Black played a singular role in the early twentieth century as political spokesman for a southern liberalism anchored primarily on economics, not race. Black's senatorial career represents a long-lost southern liberal political creed that elevated economic self-interest above all other agents of change. The creed was based on the belief that common economic concerns among the South's poor—often in conflict with corporate interests—offered the most powerful means of solving the South's problems, including its racial problems. As a senator from the dirt-poor, segregated Heart of Dixie during the Great Depression and the heydays of the New Deal, Hugo Black stood out, in the words of *Montgomery Advertiser* editor Grover Hall, as "the first genuine philosophical radical that the Deep South" had sent to Washington.[3] And, in most respects, Black alone carried forward in Alabama and the South the aspirations and hopes that had motivated the Fairhopers' mission to keep alive Populist economic values.

Coming of Age in the Era of Populism

When Fairhope was founded in 1894, eight-year-old Hugo Black was 250 miles north, attending Populist rallies at the Clay County courthouse, a few blocks from his home in Ashland in east central Alabama. After a close election in 1892, Populists held most of Clay's county offices. Black heard Populist speeches, including those by local leaders like Joe Manning who often derided "the bluster of Bourbons in their feigned warnings of 'Negro domination' . . ." and advocated the "principles of Thomas Jefferson and Andrew Jackson." Manning interpreted those principles as endorsing government support for public schools, a graduated income tax, government ownership of railroads and telegraphs, and the issuance of more money into the economy. Black's closest childhood friend was the son of Clay's Populist probate judge, whose office was a hangout for both boys. The two young friends also did odd jobs for the editor of the local Populist newspaper as they came of age.

However, by the time Black had earned a law degree at the University of

Alabama and returned to Ashland to practice, the Populist movement had withered almost completely in Clay and across Alabama, and the foundations of the Jim Crow South had been cemented with the state constitutional disfranchisement of African Americans and many poor whites. A few years afterwards, Black moved to Birmingham, where he became an active labor lawyer representing union members, often in bitter, violent strikes, and a successful plaintiff's lawyer usually suing the state's major corporations. When he left Clay County, Black had fifty dollars, two worn suitcases holding all his worldly possessions, and a set of homegrown political and economic ideas that would help him build an anti-corporate law practice and, twenty years later, win statewide office.[4]

A SOUTHERN VOICE AGAINST CORPORATE INTERESTS: 1926–1932

When elected to the U.S. Senate in 1926 with, at that time, the largest turnout of white voters in Alabama history, Black relied on what he called a "Dry-Protestant-Progressive" coalition of partisan interests.[5] But within two years, Al Smith's Democratic presidential campaign had fractured the solid South over the issues of liquor and Catholicism and obliterated Black's coalition. Within two more years, confronted with widespread deprivation from the Great Depression, Black was heckled by both old corporate opponents and former Dry-Protestant supporters, who believed he had abandoned them on the social issues of the day.[6]

These political eruptions broke apart Black's initial base of political support, but he kept faith throughout his first Senate term with the "progressive"[7] core of his original coalition and with "his first public profession of political faith," which he had delivered in Ashland in March 1926 at the launch of his senatorial campaign.

"Wealth is piling up in the hands of a few with ever increasing power," Black had proclaimed from the balcony of the Clay County Courthouse, as he described a need for public servants who had not lost touch with "the common people" in times of economic peril. "Great railroad systems are rolling under one control . . . Power systems spring up in one state and spread their wires over many states in a gigantic web that entangles the destiny of our children."

"I am not opposed to wealth honestly acquired and honestly used . . ." Black continued. "We must turn a deaf ear alike to the selfish appeals of those who attack property rights or human rights . . . I am not now, and have never been a railroad, power company, or corporation lawyer," Black solemnly intoned. "They have never shaped my ideals, fashioned my political creed, nor helped me in my aspirations for public office," he assured voters. "I could not compete with the millionaire opponents on an advertising or moneyspending campaign. I would not, if I could."[8]

In this political statement, used throughout 1926 as his primary campaign literature, Black specifically named only one corporation when discussing the problems of vast wealth and power. In referring to the Muscle Shoals dam, built in north Alabama on the Tennessee River shortly before World War I, Black reminded voters: "It was originally built to give the farmer cheap fertilizer in time of peace. Selfish interests have succeeded in thwarting the people's will . . . If you want your great property at Muscle Shoals given away to the Alabama Power Company, or any other privately owned power company, do not vote for me," Black declared.[9]

Black's economic views and especially his opposition to "monopolistic capitalism" won him strong support among the Gastons and other Fairhopers. He carried the town's votes with a large plurality in the 1926 Democratic primary. In his role as editor of the *Fairhope Courier*, E. B. Gaston often praised Black's opposition to corporate interests, including the Alabama Power Company. Long before his senatorial campaign, Black had taken an interest in the single-tax colony and visited there whenever he was nearby. He valued the "friendship of the Gaston family" who knew that Black, in his own words, "can work in behalf of the whole people without having any strings tied to me by any selfish corporate interests."[10]

"Corporate interests" were, in fact, the animating concerns of Black's first term in the Senate, although as a southern Democrat in a national government where northern Republicans controlled the White House and both houses of Congress, Black had few opportunities in his first six years to do more than express his anxieties and objections for the record.

In 1928, one of the first bills Black introduced in the Senate was to forbid the Federal Radio Commission granting a license for any radio station to a company owned wholly or in part by a public utility corporation.[11] Black's first major speech in the Senate, which his wife attended in the public gallery, concerned the Muscle Shoals dam, which he feared would be transferred by the Hoover administration to the Alabama Power Company for its private profit instead of producing cheap fertilizer for farmers. Black declared, "Here is the whole gist of this controversy: Should the power from Muscle Shoals be turned over to prosperous industry or should it be turned over to the impoverished farmer?"[12]

The following year, Senator Black reintroduced his bill to ban public utility corporations from operating radio stations and proposed the public registration of lobbyists in Washington. "The people of this nation have suffered enough already from secret propaganda and fraudulent lobbies," Black told his colleagues in 1929.[13] When the Senate Judiciary Committee, led by independent Republican Senator George Norris, established a special lobby inquiry committee, Black asked the special committee to investigate the influences responsible for the delay in Muscle Shoals. Black insisted that "the great power of money behind the Power Trust and the Fertilizer Trust has been able to confuse the public and keep the plants at Muscle Shoals idle." Black, however, was unable to block the Hoover administration from renewing a lease of the Muscle Shoals plant to the Alabama Power Company.[14]

When the lobbying committee held hearings on the Muscle Shoals dam in early 1930, Black participated as a guest member, cross-examining witnesses to expose how power companies and other large corporations were financing the "Tennessee Valley Improvement Association," whose officers and agents, including the current chairman of the National Republican Committee, had prepared speeches and letters for members of Congress. The group had even written a first draft of the report of the House Military Affairs Committee in support of corporate control of the dam.[15]

National coverage of the Committee's work gave Black an opportunity to speak for the first time on national radio. "Monopoly stalks abroad in our land," Black began his address. "Competition has all but passed away . . . In this era of monopoly . . . plunder of the many seems to have become the privilege of the few." Condemning the "most gigantic, well-organized, and well-financed effort of the power companies to control public opinion known in our history," Black accused the power trust of obscuring their lobbying activities so that they could continue to "unjustly enrich a few from the pockets of the many." The best example of this national "spirit of greed," he said, was Muscle Shoals.[16]

According to Black, President Herbert Hoover also was attempting to place the federal government under the control of large corporations by appointing corporate lawyers and corporate officials to run the government. "I want to know why that each time the President has sent a name to the Senate . . ." for confirmation, "it has been the name of a man who represents or has represented the railroads," Black asked from the Senate floor. "It is a strange coincidence that the President, out of all the available men, could have selected only . . . a man who is a corporation lawyer," Black observed in another speech opposing Hoover's nominee to the Interstate Commerce Commission.[17]

By early 1932, unemployment and hunger were at unprecedented levels in Alabama and across the nation. With a sense of helplessness and despair, Black informed a former law partner: "Jobs seekers are multitudinous."[18] Ten months later, after his reelection, Black had his first opportunity to go beyond obstructing and complaining about the misuse of the federal government by corporate interests and start advancing a "progressive" agenda.

A Southern Agent for Big Economic Changes: 1933–1937

The election of Franklin Roosevelt and Democratic majorities in both houses of Congress in November 1932 offered the chance to put into practice the agenda Black believed would address the nation's poverty and the source of its economic problems.

Even before Roosevelt took office, Senator Black introduced a three-paragraph bill to "prevent the interstate commerce of any commodity or article produced by American industry where persons were employed more than five days in any week or six hours per day." Any person who engaged in such interstate commerce would be punishable with a fine of $200 and three months imprisonment. When Black's simple proposal became fully known, the *New York Times* editors called it the "most socially revolutionary bill offered in this Congress, or probably in any other American Congress."[19]

In a national radio address, Black explained his bill: "My own belief is that the major contributing cause to our present dilemma is that labor has been underpaid and capital has been overpaid ... When greed and privilege grasp unearned wealth and condemn millions to undeserved poverty and misery, government is useless if it does not curb greed and destroy privilege." In a second radio talk, Black stated that millions "cannot buy shoes, cannot buy food, and cannot buy shelter because they have no way to work." By limiting work, Black proposed to spread jobs to millions and to force industries to increase the wages for all workers—without creating a federal bureaucracy.[20]

The passage of Black's bill in the Senate in early April 1933 spurred the White House to move furiously with its own proposals for economic recovery. When Black's bill stalled in the House because of opposition from business groups (and delaying tactics by those who wanted to require the same standards for imported goods), the Roosevelt administration used the slowdown of Black's bill to collect support for its own National Recovery Administration (NRA). Black declined to sponsor the NRA as a substitute for his bill, but Senator Robert Wagner of New York introduced the administration's legislation providing more than $3 billion in public works, voluntary self-government of industry by business committees, and a general guarantee that the business committees would set fair wage and hour standards. The proposed law prohibited monopolistic practices, but at the same time it suspended antitrust laws. Citing Adam Smith and Thomas Jefferson in a single breath, Black bitterly opposed the NRA and voted against it in all forms until the final vote.[21]

Black continued to push his thirty-hour work week bill in each session of Congress, but his economic reform agenda also included ending extravagant federal subsidies of private companies. His first target was the shipping industry, in which, as chairman of a special investigative committee, Black exposed a widespread system of graft and corruption. In one case, the federal government under prior Republican administrations had sold ships for $1 million to one company while the government spent $44 million to build and repair the same ships for sale. The same company also received federal subsides of more than $45 million to carry U.S. mail across the ocean—at a calculated cost of $66,000 per pound. In another case, a corporation began with assets of only $500 and after three years, entirely due to federal contracts and subsidies, showed a profit of more than $1 million. America needed a strong merchant marine, Black declared, but it did not need a system of federal subsidies that paid a few men "thousands upon thousands of percent profit" on meager investments.[22]

In the emerging airline industry, Black's investigative committee found similar patterns of ill-gotten gains from federal contracts to support mail delivery. Black demonstrated that more than 90 percent of government contracts were let to the four largest airline carriers, while smaller airlines like Delta and Braniff were barred from bidding. Black charged that the Big Four had become big primarily through exorbitant, no-bid government contracts. He pointed out that the founder of United Aircraft—while receiving $40 million in federal contracts—had seen his company stock grow from a value of $253 to more than $10 million.[23]

As a result of his investigations, Black guided passage of the Air Mail Act of 1934 that required competitive government contracts; prohibited holding companies and interlocking directorates with manufacturers of airline equipment; limited government payments and corporate salaries; and authorized the U.S. Secretary of Commerce to set maximum hours and minimum wages for pilots and mechanics. The latter provision enabled the first federally mandated minimum wage.[24]

Black's investigations into federal mail contracts only sharpened his interest in curbing corporate influence and control of government. In 1934, Black introduced a bill requiring the public registration of lobbyists, and in 1935 he created another special committee to investigate lobbying activities. This committee exposed a variety of lobbying organizations that were secretly funded by large corporations and their wealthy stockholders in an unsuccessful attempt to defeat the New Deal's Public Utilities Holding Company Act.[25]

Black spent a huge amount of his time and energy in the Senate from late 1932 through 1936 addressing excessive corporate influence and federal government corruption, but not to the exclusion of his agenda for other economic reforms that involved the development of an American system of social welfare. By mid-1934, Black announced in Alabama newspapers that his study of America's problems had led him to believe that the country must have "some form of old age pension and unemployment insurance." Black also added that he was convinced that "the health of the nation" warranted consideration of "a system of national hospitalization" or a system of "state or national health and accident insurance."

By the start of 1935, Black had drafted legislation for a national health insurance system that would be financed by contributions from wage-earners but available to all in need. Black also prepared bills to increase payments to workers under the Workmen's Compensation Act for on-the-job injuries or deaths and to require corporations to report to stockholders on corporate officers' salaries or bonuses of $25,000 or more. At the same time, Black opposed the Roosevelt administration's proposal to finance old-age pensions—what became Social Security—by payroll deductions. Black advocated for a tax on wealth. Invoking the principles of Thomas Jefferson, Black declared his support of social security programs "is not intended to destroy wealth but to use it."[26]

In a strategic maneuver, Alabama's senior senator gave up his third-ranking seat on the Judiciary Committee to get a position as the junior member of the Senate Finance Committee, chaired by Mississippi's Pat Harrison. Black decided that the switch was necessary so that he could influence essential social legislation and push for a redistribution of wealth through tax policies. "Taxes that reduce the buying power of the masses are harmful," Black declared. For the country to get out of the Depression, he stated, it would have to shift taxes "from the little man who consumes onto the rich man who saves."[27]

In 1936, Black and Senator Robert La Follette, Jr., led a rearguard action in the Senate Finance Committee and on the Senate floor to tax large amounts of undistributed corporate profits as a way to stop tax avoidance by the wealth. Black claimed the proposal would stop America's wealthiest individuals from avoiding as much as $600 million in annual taxes.[28]

In 1937, as chairman of the Senate Committee on Education and Labor and while continuing to push his thirty-hour work week, Black developed a wide range of federal legislation to address the nation's economic problems. In March, he reported to the full Senate the Black-Harrison-Fletcher Bill to provide "federal aid to the states for the support of public schools." Senator Black proposed a permanent change in the federal role in education—the first serious effort to establish a permanent federal role in public education (K–12) since the Blair Bill of the 1880s—and began by proposing to allocate $1 billion to the states over five years. The funds were to be distributed to all states that maintain "a system of schools uniformly throughout its territory open for no less than 160 days in each school year."

"For a great many years, "Black told *Anniston Star* publisher Harry Ayers, "I have looked forward to the time when the equality of educational opportunities would be given throughout our entire nation."[29] In a nationwide radio address, Black invoked the wisdom of President George Washington, "In a country like this—if there cannot be money found of education, there is something amiss with the ruling power." Black argued: "There is no longer reason for us to depend upon the old theory that the poor shall educate the poor. It produces grossly unfair educational opportunities. This great nation of ours needs an educated citizenship. . . . American children are entitled to this chance. Education is the hope of our nation. Federal assistance alone can meet the widespread educational needs of our American youth."[30]

As Education and Labor chairman, Black pushed efforts in the Senate in the summer of 1937 to provide permanent federal support for safe and sanitary housing across the United States; to create a permanent Civilian Conservation Corps; to sustain Robert La Follette's subcommittee investigations into corporate abuse and terrorism against union organizers (including organizers in Alabama); and to establish the nation's first minimum wage and fair labor standards act.[31]

When he accepted President Roosevelt's appointment to the U.S. Supreme Court in August 1937, Black left all of these initiatives pending. Most died on the Congressional vine; some took decades to enact into law. Only the Fair Labor Standards Act—which Black co-sponsored at Roosevelt's request as an alternative to his own bill for a thirty-hour work week—had passed the Congress by the end of the decade.

BLACK AS A SOUTHERN ECONOMIC LIBERAL

A little more than ten years after leaving the Senate, Black's credentials as a New Deal Democrat were confirmed by V. O. Key's tally of roll call votes. The compilation showed that whenever Democrats split their support for the New Deal, Senator Black broke ranks with southern Democrats to join national Democrats more than any other southern senator—almost 80 percent of the time. Senator Huey Long ranked second—joining the national Democrats in two-thirds of his votes.[32]

Senator Long may have voted against the New Deal economic proposals (when he bothered to show up for a roll call) because he considered them too tepid.[33] If so, he was not alone. Black usually considered the New Deal proposals too weak and timid, although he was more willing than Long to go along when no better could be had. For instance, in 1934–35, Senator Black heard loud carping from Alabamians who believed that the New Deal had gone too far in disturbing the nation's economic system. An old friend, Horace Turner of Mobile, asked him: "Is it not about time to stop experiments and let business, not bureaucracy, adjust business?" Many of Black's Alabama critics labeled him a socialist or communist. Yet, Black's response was unequivocal: "The only complaint I would have about this 'New Deal' is not the direction in which it is going, but that it has failed to go far enough" in redistributing wealth and economic opportunity in America.[34]

In promoting his agenda for economic justice, Senator Black often ignored, evaded, or opposed direct attempts to advance racial justice. To some extent, as he admitted two and half years after leaving the Senate, Black's posture on racial issues was a political necessity: "Any candidate . . . would jeopardize his chances for election by being too liberal on the race question." But, for the most part, Black simply considered many public efforts for racial justice to be secondary in effect and importance to economic justice.

Black stated to Ralph Bunche in February 1940,

> The real core of the problem is economic, and that must be worked out before anything significant along other lines can be hoped for. Give the poverty-stricken South economic opportunity and opportunity for education, and the race issue will work itself out. Many people unfortunately ignore the economic nature of the problem, and in raising extraneous issues, unconsciously play into the hands of corporate interests that are

eager to keep people from understanding the real nature of the problem.³⁵

As events unfolded into World War II, Senator Black had no true political heir who could survive southern politics, and his own militant economic vision for a New Deal America withered in the Congress. As a Supreme Court justice for more than three decades, Black was hog-tied in publicly expressing his own radical economic views,³⁶ although he privately condemned the "economic royalists." Closeted in the chambers of the Supreme Court, Black remembered his Senate days and his attempts to advance economic issues. He also read a wide range of southern history, examining how books about past political and economic movements squared with his own understanding of the issues and periods through which he lived. Among those works was Paul Gaston's *The New South Creed, A Study in Southern Mythmaking*, which sat on Black's book shelf until he died in 1971.³⁷

Occasionally, an action by one of the emerging New South politicians of the late 1960s encouraged Black to believe that the politics of his economic creed would be reborn. But he did not live long enough to see and hear any southern political leader—or for that matter, any American political leader—revive a version of the Alabama-born economic manifesto that he proclaimed in 1926: "Equality under the law to millionaire and pauper, factory owner and worker, is the test of a successful democracy . . . The vision I see shines from justice for all and special privilege to none . . . Such is the spirit of America."³⁸

Notes

1. Paul M. Gaston, *Man and Mission: E. B. Gaston and the Origins of the Fairhope Single Tax Colony* (Montgomery: NewSouth, 1993), 3–5, 22–34, 48–61. Also, see Paul M. Gaston, *Coming of Age in Utopia: the Odyssey of an Idea* (Montgomery: NewSouth, 2010), 32–49.
2. See George B. Tindall, *The Emergence of the New South, 1913–1945* (Baton Rouge: Louisiana State University Press, 1967), 354–390, 607–649; William E. Leuchtenburg, *Franklin D. Roosevelt and the New Deal: 1932–1940* (New York: Harper and Row, 1963); Alan Brinkley, "The New Deal and Southern Politics," in *The New Deal and the South* (Jackson: University Press of Mississippi, 1984), 97–115.
3. See Morton Sosna, *In Search of the Silent South: Southern Liberals and the Race Issue* (New York: Columbia University Press, 1977), 60–101, 198–205, and E. David Cronon, "A Southern Progressive Looks at the New Deal," *Journal of Southern History* 24 (May 1958): 151–74; *Baltimore Evening Sun*, Aug. 13, 1937.

4. Steve Suitts, *Hugo Black of Alabama: How His Roots and Early Career Shaped the Great Champion of the Constitution* (Montgomery: NewSouth, 2005), 57–71, 82–92, 101–105.
5. Suitts, *Hugo Black of Alabama*, 482–525.
6. Virginia Van Der Veer Hamilton, *Hugo Black: The Alabama Years* (Baton Rouge: Louisiana State University Press, 1972), 200–203; Interview with Herbert Baughn, 1972, in possession of author. Ed Pettus to Hugo Black, May 13, 1932, Hugo L. Black Papers, Library of Congress, Washington, DC.
7. While there were ideological differences in the political movements that shaped and spanned most of his years before appointment to the U.S. Supreme Court, Black and others, including E.B. Gaston and many Fairhopers, used the terms "populist," "progressive," and "liberal" as virtually synonymous terms when referring over time to economic views that were based on a suspicion of or opposition to large corporate control in the economy as well as large concentrations of wealth.
8. Suitts, *Hugo Black of Alabama*, 495–496.
9. Suitts, *Hugo Black of Alabama*, 496.
10. Black to C.L. Gaston, Sept. 18, 1926, Black to E.B. Gaston, June 28, 1927, W. M. Olive to Black, Sept. 23, 1926, E. B. Gaston to Black, Nov. 20, 1934, E. B. Gaston to Black, March 4, 1937, Black to E. B. Gaston, March 10, 1937, C. A. Gaston to Black, May 17, 1938, Black to C. A. Gaston, May 20, 1938, Black to D. C. Arthur, June 18, 1926, Black Papers.
11. *New York Times*, Feb. 24, 1928.
12. *Congressional Record*, 40874093, March 5, 1928; *Birmingham News*, April 24, 1941.
13. *New York Times*, Sept. 26, 1929.
14. *New York Times*, Oct. 5, 1929; Black to M. M. Striplin, Dec. 30, 1929, Black Papers.
15. *New York Times,* Feb. 21, 1930, Feb. 27, 1930; *Mobile Register*, Feb. 22, 1930; Feb. 26, 1930.
16. *Congressional Record*, 71st 2d, 44684470.
17. *Congressional Record*, 71st 2nd, 846938.
18. Black to Crampton Harris, Jan. 28, 1932, Black Papers.
19. *Congressional Record*, 72nd, 2nd, 819–820; Black to Elizabeth Brandeis, July 22, 1955, Black Papers.
20. *Washington Daily News*, Aug. 21, 1937; *Congressional Record*, 72nd, 2nd, 14431444; Black to Kingman, Dec. 29, 1932, Black Papers.
21. Leuchtenburg, 55–58; Frantz interview with Hugo Black, Black Papers.
22. Hearings of the Special Committee on Investigation of Air Mail and Ocean Mail Contracts, 73rd, 2nd, 1933, Part 1–3; *New York Times,* Sept. 27, 1933–Dec. 8, 1933.
23. Hearings of Air Mail and Ocean Mail Contracts, 73rd, 2nd, 1933, Part 1–3.
24. Hamilton, *Hugo Black*, 233–234. After the air mail contracts were exposed, E.B. Gaston wrote Black that he had "certainly done great service for the people in the investigation and the action that followed . . ." E.B. Gaston to Black, May 28, 1934, Black Papers.
25. William A. Gregory and Rennard Strickland, "Hugo Black's Congressional Investigation of Lobbying and the Public Utilities Holding Company Act: A Historical View

of the Power Trust, New Deal Politics, and Regulatory Propaganda," *Oklahoma Law Review*, vol. 29, 543–576.

26. *Montgomery Advertiser*, June 28, 1934, Dec. 28, 1934; *Birmingham News*, Dec. 4, 1934, Dec. 28, 1934; *New York Times*, Dec. 16, 1934, Jan. 6, 1935, Jan. 26, 1935, Feb. 24, 1935; Hugo Black, "Social Security," *Vital Speeches of the Day,* January 14, 1935.

27. *Birmingham Herald,* Jan. 29, 1935. Black's father as a rural Alabama merchant, usually quite adroit when sober, once advertised to customers the approach that Black suggested was now needed for the country: "Buy Yourself Rich." See Suitts, 92.

28. *Minority Views* of Report on Revenue Bill of 1936, Report 2156, Part 2, 74th, 2nd .

29. Black to Harry M. Ayres, May 10, 1937, Black Papers.

30. Federal Aid to the States for the Support of Public Schools, Report 217, 75th 1st, March 19, 1937; Black to Harry M. Ayers, May 10, 1937, Black Papers; "Radio Address, Black-Harrison-Fletcher Bill," undated, Black Papers.

31. Creating a United States Housing Authority, Report 933, 75th, 1st, July 22, 1937; Making the Civilian Conservation Corps a Permanent Agency, Report 538, 75th, 1st, May 12, 1937; Joint Hearings Before the Committee on Education and Labor, United States Senate, and the Committee on Labor, House of Representatives, on S. 2475 and H.R. 7200, 75th, 1st, Part 1, June 2 to June 5, 937.

32. V. O. Key, Jr., *Southern Politics* (New York: A. A. Knopf, 1949), 366.

33. William Ivy Hair, *The Kingfish and His Realm: The Life and Times of Huey P. Long* (Baton Rouge: Louisiana State University Press, 1991), 265–271; Tindall, 613–15.

34. *New York Times*, Dec. 15, 1935; Horace Turner to Black, Oct. 8, 1934, and Black to Horace Turner, Oct. 11, 1934, Black Papers; John Temple Graves to Black, July 1, 1937, Black Papers.

35. Greg Robinson and Peter Eisenstadt, "Two Dilemmas: Ralph Bunche and Hugo Black in 1940," *Prospects*, Vol. 22, 453–478, 467; Black to John Temple Graves, June 28, 1937, Black Papers. This view of the role of economic justice was shared by the Fairhopers. See Gaston, *Man and Mission*, 83.

36. Justice Black rendered an early dissent that attempted to make a profound change in the role of corporations in American law and society. His opinion objected to the notion that the Fourteenth Amendment recognized corporations as "persons" who are afforded the guarantees of due process and equal protection of the laws—a constitutional amendment that, as Black said, was passed to protect the rights of former slaves. See *Connecticut General Life Insurance Company v. Johnson*, 303 US 77 (1938).

37. See Daniel J. Meador, *Mr. Justice Black and His Books* (Charlottesville: University Press of Virginia, 1974). Black learned as a boy the speech by Henry Grady that coined the "New South." See Hugo L. Black, "There Is a South of Union and Freedom," *Georgia Law Review* 2 (1967): 10, 15.

38. Suitts, *Hugo Black of Alabama*, 496–497. Lyndon Johnson and his "Great Society" programs probably came closest to fulfilling Black's vision for a New Deal America. Had he lived until 2016, Black perhaps would not have been surprised to hear his creed echoing in the words of a self-proclaimed Democratic Socialist senator from Vermont; Black might have been tempted to call him a Populist.

13

Southern Family Trees, Wrong and Right

EDWARD L. AYERS

Paul Gaston and I shared teaching the history of the American South for more than twenty years even though neither of us bore the proper pedigree. Paul spoke with the sonorous voice of his Deep South and I with the high lonesome sound of my native mountains, but we were both frauds. Our genealogies were wrong.

Paul, as he himself has amply documented, came from radical Midwestern roots. He grew up in Alabama because his family had migrated there to change Alabama. The Single Taxers had in mind something like the opposite of what the Alabama of Paul's youth was, something egalitarian, transparent, and fair. When Paul arrived in Virginia in the 1950s, he worked for decades to make that place, too, something better than it was. And he did. Paul knew exactly who he was and what he was supposed to do and he did it with courage, grace, and success.

My family genealogy was wrong in a different way. As far as I knew, it barely existed. I do have a copy of a photograph from what appears to be the 1890s, of some ancestors, perhaps great-great-great-grandparents. The man, John Edwards, has a beard, recognizable from hillbilly cartoons, streaming down his chest. The woman, Martha Edwards, has her hair done up tightly in the back and—sadly, I have always thought—her ears bearing drawn-in jewelry. A great uncle gave me the copy and, on the back, wrote in the outlines of the genealogy of that side of our family. A note on the back says that a photo of my great-great-grandfather was available from my great uncle for five dollars, but I never took him up on the offer. As far as I know, everyone on both sides of my family lived in the mountains of North Carolina from the 1830s on until my *parents moved us to the mountains of Tennessee an hour away. No Civil War stories, no stories of Mammies or loyal retainers, no lost plantation or burned manor house. Just hard-working mountain folk who seemed to live outside of what we knew as southern history.*

It is possible that Paul and I became historians of the South precisely because we were poor fits in the South. In some ways, we both wrote larger genealogies of the South we knew, Paul tracing the myths in which his generation grew up, me tracing the paths that led to the new and awkward South in which I came of age. We both brought a lot of energy to our teaching, a kind of urgency. Perhaps displaced family history in some form fed that spirit.

Paul worked hard to create a broader genealogy for the South, a genealogy that included black southerners, radical southerners. I did the same in a different way, including, in line with my generation of scholars, women and poorer southerners, religious people and rambunctious people.

Today, a new kind of possibility for southern genealogy presents itself—an actual genealogy, of family trees and documented connections. This is not the genealogy within which neither Paul nor I fit, the genealogy of the First Families of Virginia and the Sons of the Confederacy, but a new and more inclusive genealogy. Paul Gaston worked for years to broaden our sense of what history could be. Following his example, I accepted an opportunity to give a talk to the Afro-American Historical and Genealogical Society about opportunities before us if we connected history and genealogy. Here is some of what I said.

~

Like the twin strands of DNA, the strands of history and genealogy have twisted together throughout American history, sometimes more tightly than at others. Genealogy is flourishing as the second most popular hobby in the United States, after gardening, both of which are about growing things, about organic connections to where we live. Genealogy helps sustain our public archives and libraries and is finding new audiences and new purposes in the latest and most sophisticated technologies, as well as in television and in books.

History is flourishing, too, though we often take its presence for granted.

History is the most-taught subject across all grades and all students. It accounts for large sections in every bookstore and offers some of the top bestsellers every year. The study of history has never been more capacious, embracing groups and individuals that previous generations have neglected. Millions of students in college take history every year even when they don't have to. History attracts millions of people to national parks, to museums, to TV audiences. The books historians write have never been more inclusive or more sophisticated.

We might say that genealogy gets more love and history gets more respect. As we will see, they are part of the same family tree, a recognition that we all live in time and place, that we are all shaped, every day and all the time, by patterns larger than ourselves. But the studies of family history also demonstrate that, in every generation, the decisions people make can shape themselves and the generations that follow.

I don't have much genealogical knowledge or many genealogical memories, to tell you the truth, but I do remember receiving, when I was 11 or 12, an embossed Bible from my grandmother—from Sears, I think—and the motto written on the box: "As the twig is bent, so grows the tree." Family history is the history of many twigs being bent on many trees.

My job as a historian is to understand those many trees, that forest. My job is show how it is that every tree can be different and yet still take its shape from the soil and climate in which it grows. Genealogy teaches that we have power over our lives, but it also teaches us how things over which we have no control shape our lives as well. That power is not always visible when its shaping us—when we are deciding how many children to have, for example, or what kind of work we might do, or what kind of religious commitment we make, or whether we move or stay put—but it is profoundly apparent in retrospect.

Thus, genealogists and historians should be closer than we are. We are like relatives who have lost track of each other. It's time to get in touch.

Now, as we all know, getting to know each other better must begin with a little family history, so let me sketch for you the history of genealogy. Fortunately, an excellent book appeared a couple of years ago by Francois Weil, a historian of the U.S. who also happens to head the most prestigious university in France. His book is called *Family Trees* and it offers the unusual and fascinating history of American genealogy.

The first generations of European Americans basically copied a culture of genealogy that had been in Europe for a couple of centuries, especially that of England. By the late eighteenth and early nineteenth centuries, though, Americans felt they needed to develop their own kind of genealogy, one that would be democratic and open.

American genealogy, from the beginning, was marked by two basic traits that distinguished it from its counterparts elsewhere. It was oriented toward marketing, tapping the interest in family history to grow rapidly and to make profits and create institutions. Second, American genealogy has always been fascinated with documentation and method and replicability. Genealogists have adopted every new technology as it came along, from microfilm in the 1930s to computers in the 1960s to the Internet in the 1990s to DNA in the 2010s.

From the beginning, too, genealogy has served lots of different purposes in a nation based on movement and self-invention. Every different ethnicity has created and sustained its own form of family history.

Frederick Douglass said that "genealogical trees do not flourish among slaves."[1] But Africans and then African Americans carefully fostered their understanding of their families' history. That memory became a way for them to fight the cultural as well as physical violence of slavery. That tradition would be one of the most important in American genealogy throughout our history.

American genealogy was distinguished, too, by the role of women among all ethnicities. Girls were raised to think about their families' histories and needlework samplers often displayed symbols such as vines, touching hearts, and links. Many single women specialized in this work, drawing, painting, and stitching family trees, which became popular throughout the country.

The movement west deepened interest and activity in genealogy. As people uprooted themselves—or in the case of enslaved people, were uprooted against their wills—they worked even harder to remember where they had come from. That may be one reason that Americans have been especially interested in family history; the most rootless of people have the most interest in their roots.

As early as 1829, the first genealogical information was published beyond a specific family—John Farmer published the *Genealogical Register of New England*. "The preparation, publication, and subsequent revision of Farmer's [book] transformed the practice of genealogy in the US," Francois Weil tells us. "Antiquarians defined genealogy as scholarship and agreed on a series of guidelines, practices, rules, and goals that defined the contours of their shared investigations." People now demanded "evidence," primary sources. They talked of "genealogical data."[2] In the 1840s and 1850s, genealogical societies were founded across the nation, North and South.

Genealogy pivoted after the Civil War. White families in the United States after that war tried to heal their wounds by imagining a shared racial heritage as Anglo-Saxons or Aryans. People of rapidly growing wealth also sought to distance themselves from the democratic genealogy that had spread before the war. They returned to the obsession of tracing their ancestry back into English history even as they stocked their new mansions with armor, tapestries, and paintings exported from the Old World. They paid people to invent coats of arms and to find ancient lineages.

Wealthy white Americans in the Gilded Age decided that their lineage passed on unique abilities and talents for rule, for morality, for democracy. Good "blood" came to count for much more than it had before the Civil War.

Earlier, most women had practiced genealogy privately, in the home. But around the turn of the twentieth century, women became much more visible. Some influential women emphasized, along with their male relatives and counterparts, white supremacy and Anglo-Saxonism with a new energy and public attention. Some African-Americans developed their own version of this exclusive genealogy, creating hereditary societies based on lineage. They did not put their work in print very often, but genealogy became an important part of a culture of pride and respectability.

But far more common was the older tradition in African American genealogy, in which the emphasis was not on *exclusivity* but *inclusivity*, not on keeping people out of the family tree but inviting them in. That tradition stretched far back into slavery but became newly visible with emancipation. As soon as they could, as all of you well know, African Americans began working to reconstitute families that had been separated by the slave trade, by movement, and by war.

African Americans emphasized kinship rather than blood, connection rather than separation. They wrote to the Freedmen's Bureau for help, hoping that somehow they might connect with mothers, father, sons, daughters, brothers, and sisters lost decades, years, or months earlier. Others set out on personal journeys, looking for loved ones farm by farm, town by town, following only hints of where they had been sold or taken. Many more ran advertisements in black newspapers, including the *Christian Recorder*, asking that pastors read the notices to their congregations. Their searches went on for decades and, as you know, they go on still.

In the meantime, another distinctive branch of the tree of American genealogy grew with the Mormon church. Joseph Smith's 1840 vision was that Mormons would baptize the dead, ensuring the salvation of family members who had died before the Church of Jesus Christ of Latter-Day Saints had emerged. In the 1880s, the church greatly accelerated its efforts on this front, sending missionaries back east from Utah to do genealogical work. Women played a large role—by the early twentieth century, about thirty thousand women pursued genealogy through church programs. On the other hand, all the resources were concentrated in Salt Lake City, and as recently as 1955 nearly all visitors to the Family History Library in Salt Lake were church members.

You may have noticed that to this point I have not mentioned the other strand of the DNA I mentioned at the outset: history. Genealogy had gone through all these changes before what we think of as professional history began. To this point, history was the preserve of a relatively few men—Francis Parkman and George Bancroft, for example—who worked on their own, largely with private wealth. American history was not taught in colleges and universities.

In the 1890s and the first decade of the twentieth century, though, graduate schools started granting Ph.D.'s on the German model. For history, that meant that scholarship would be based on rigorous research in original sources, building on the work of those who came before.

That sounds a lot like genealogy by this time, but these first professional historians did their best to distance themselves from genealogy. In historians' austere vision, they were doing science and genealogists were involved in antiquarianism and romance. The marker of professional success was not the market but peer review.

These new professional historians, in fact, created their discipline in part by distinguishing themselves from as many people as they could—not only genealogists but also journalists, amateur historians, high school teachers, and others. They thought they could serve the public best by upholding a rigorous standard of scholarship that required years of post-graduate training, often abroad. They participated in a new kind of writing—the monograph, in which a specialist studied, with great and documented, care, a single, focused, topic—thus, the "mono" in "monograph" (not, as one of my students wondered, whether the root was "monotonous.") The American Historical Association was founded in 1884, and it had no place for genealogy or what they considered antiquarianism—an interest in history for its own sake, without a larger contribution to make.

Genealogists, though they were equally devoted to documentation and verifiability by this time, did not professionalize. They did not have a place in universities, and few could make full-time careers from their passion and skill.

The branches of our shared tree began to grow apart, though both continued to flourish in their own ways. Genealogy began to boom after World War II across the nation as people looked for connection in what felt like an ever more disconnected country. Public librarians and archivists became more welcoming. The National Archives became more active for genealogists in the 1960s, and it appointed a full-time genealogist to help visitors. Professional genealogists, for their part, improved the quality of their research and created the Board of Certification of Genealogists in 1964.

The Mormons strengthened their efforts a great deal, too. They had introduced a massive microfilming initiative in 1938, and by 1945 they had about 2,000 reels. Those numbers grew with remarkable speed, with 50,000 reels in 1950, 270,000 in 1960, 660,000 in 1970, and 880,000 in 1975. By the early 1960s the church began to develop computers to aid their genealogical work. The Mormons also decided in 1964 to open branch libraries, with seventy-five branches by 1968, and develop genealogical seminars, conferences, and various outreach programs, open to non-church members. These branch libraries received sets of copies of the original microfilm rolls and so made genealogical research possible for many people who could not travel to Salt Lake City.

So the stew of genealogy was beginning to grow richer in the 1960s and '70s. Several books about Sicilian, Armenian, and eastern European Jews became bestsellers in the early 1970s, and then, of course, *Roots* overshadowed them all. Alex Haley had been working on his project throughout the 1960s and had spoken to five hundred campuses. As word of his book grew, it became a phenomenon before it was even published, with Haley signing a major television deal. The book sold one and a half million copies, and the twelve-hour series on ABC, on eight consecutive nights, attracted the largest television audience in history to that time. African American genealogy flourished after this moment, of course, and that flourishing benefited all genealogy. People felt the presence of the past in their lives as they never had before. Every family in this country now felt that it had, and deserved, a family history. This very organization was founded in 1977, and you only need to look around you to see how it has grown.

In fact, since the 1970s interest in American genealogy has increased exponentially. In 1977, 29 percent of Americans professed themselves to be "very interested" in their family history; in 1995, 45 percent; in 2000, 60 percent; in 2005, 73 percent. I have no doubt that today it is higher yet, in part because of all this momentum from the preceding half century and in part because of technology.

In the late 1990s a small genealogy firm, Ancestry, Inc., merged with Infobases, an electronic publishing company formed in 1990 by two young Mormons. The company went through a number of reorganizations and mergers, changing names several times. It has been Ancestry.com since 2009. It has raised millions of dollars from venture capitalists, and its founders have been replaced. The company now provides access to more than fifteen billion records and provides the leading genealogical software, Family Tree Maker. In 2013 it collected $561 million in revenue and had more than two million subscribers. Those numbers continue to mount, in the US, in the UK, and in Germany.

Its most recent innovation has been DNA research, and AncestryDNA now has seven hundred thousand samples in its database. Television shows on ancestry, especially African American ancestry, have greatly accelerated the adoption of a technology that would have seemed impossible and imposing not long ago.

We are just beginning to feel the effects of the transformation brought by democratized DNA research. On the one hand, everyone can see what some scientists and historians have been saying for decades: we are all multiracial, we are all descended from the same foremothers and forefathers, we share so much more than separates us.

On the other hand, DNA can only point us in the right direction. Or, rather, right directions. It may be just as useful in closing some doors, some imagined pasts and lineages, as opening others that people never suspected. One British genealogist argued that "what DNA represents is a shift in the nature of authority—a shift away from the authority of the book to the authority of the test, away from the library to the lab."

Americans, generally, trust labs more than libraries. Many people would rather a sample of their saliva tell them who they are than to go to all the work of genealogy. But the DNA results are actually far more vague than old-fashioned genealogical work, only probabilistic calculations rather than documented proof of descent. We will still need to do the hard digging of genealogical research to understand what the DNA means for our families.

So, as we can see, genealogy has a history, one that changes with almost every decade and it is changing now. Certain tendencies are clear, though. First, genealogists have always seized on the latest technology, whether a register, an archive, a reel of microfilm, a database, the Internet, or DNA. Second, American genealogy has been enabled to a remarkable extent by the Church of Jesus Christ of Latter-Day Saints. Without the pioneering and tireless work of the Mormons, who for generations were persecuted, our vast and distended nation would not have anything like the genealogical infrastructure that we do.

Third, African Americans have led the way, for generations, toward a more generous and inclusive understanding of what genealogy could be.

While European Americans were putting forward a fictional idea of "race," and guarding its boundaries ferociously (as here in Virginia, with the Racial Purity Act of 1924 and the eugenicist office it sustained until after World War II), African Americans recognized and honored the fact that people of all sorts have intermingled. While other Americans were defining ancestry ever more narrowly, African Americans were defining heritage more broadly and generously. While other Americans were turning to what they imagined to be "scientific" notions of racial purity, African Americans were using oral, family, neighborhood, and other sources in ingenious and effective ways.

In the meantime, professional history was working on parallel paths. History, too, became much more inclusive. Starting with African American history, the study of the American past opened to women's history, working-class history, immigrant history, the history of gay and lesbian people, the history of the disabled.

Here, too, African Americans led the way. Even as Virginia's government was sponsoring the inhumane work of the racial purity machinery, another Virginian—Carter G. Woodson—was helping to develop a place within professional academic history for African Americans. He had allies, of course, in W. E. B. DuBois, John Hope Franklin, and other bold pioneers, but Woodson understood the importance of journals, of monographs, of meetings, of professional identity. Because of him, African American history developed deep roots in the profession, in colleges and universities. We all owe him a debt. Just as all American genealogists, in other words, are indebted to African American genealogists, so are all American historians indebted to African American historians.

Those of us who were excited by these developments back during the first wave of a newly democratic social history in the 1970s found ourselves sharing microfilm readers with genealogists in libraries and archives. We were interested in people we called awkward names back then—the inarticulate, the common people, everyday people. In some ways, the more neglected the more interested we were in them.

Not only did academic historians piggyback on the public investments in records, machines, spaces, and archivists that simply would not have been there without genealogists creating the demand, but academic historians found themselves using the same techniques that genealogists had long used, exploring church records, court records, cemetery records, and the back pages of newspapers, poring through family histories and local histories that previous generations of historians would have considered merely antiquarian.

I certainly followed that path: I decided to look into the history of crime and punishment in the American South, tracing people convicted of crimes in obscure county courts, following them into penitentiaries, into convict labor camps, and, too often, into lynchings. I found that while the genealogists I met were uniformly friendly, they could not really understand why I would be interested in people's families other than my own, why I would do so much digging into hard records for scholarly generalizations rather than for the satisfying particulars of real people who belonged to real families—including my own. As one new genealogist friend asked me: "Why don't you study somebody worth studying?"

Over the last several decades, genealogy and academic history have developed along a lot of the same trajectories, but those trajectories intersected only irregularly. When they have intersected, the results have been important. I think of the case of Thomas Jefferson and Sally Hemings. Annette Gordon-Reed, back in the 1990s, used genealogical and legal methods to show how great the likelihood was that Jefferson had fathered several of Hemings' children. But when early DNA tests confirmed that, people grappled with it in ways they had not before. And then when Gordon-Reed's remarkable book on the Hemings family came out in 2009 it won every prize there is—and justifiably so. She carefully used all kinds of evidence to weave together a compelling account of one of the most complicated genealogical and historical mysteries in American history.[3]

Despite that important case, the possibilities of collaboration between genealogy and history have barely begun to be explored. When I had the kind invitation to speak with you, I jumped at the chance because I believe our two guilds would benefit so much from working together far more closely than we have.

The possibilities are growing rapidly. The biological turn in genealogy created by DNA makes clear the need for a newly enriched sense of context. Now that we no longer think of racial "purity" as a reality, much less a goal, we realize we need the shared context of many families. DNA can point in interesting directions, but only history can take us where we want and need to go.

Genealogy has never been as enabled as it is now. An ever-broader array of people are exploring their past themselves with powerful new tools, growing more powerful by the day. At the same time, professional academic history has never been more democratic in its subjects. We take it for granted now that every group has a history worth telling, worth knowing. We take it for granted that all Americans make the history of all other Americans. We take it for granted now that all people in the past deserve to be chronicled with dignity and respect and care.

So here's my plea: Let's work together. We can't see the forest unless we see all the trees, and we can't see the trees without the forest that gives them life and shape. The purpose of genealogy in America has changed from a search for purity to a search for connection. The purpose of history has changed from telling the stories of famous men to seeing the big processes, structures, and patterns that give shape to lives of all families. We have remarkable new tools, not only DNA and vast databases and blogs but ways to see and share patterns we've never been able to see before.

We are all kin, and it's about time that we came to know each other better, that we teach each other things we cannot learn alone.

Notes

1. Frederick Douglass, *My Bondage and My Freedom* (New York: Miller, Orton, and Mulligan, 1855), 34.
2. Francois Weil, *Family Trees: A History of Genealogy in America* (Cambridge: Harvard University Press, 2013), 62.
3. Annette Gordon-Reed, *The Hemingses of Monticello: An American Family* (New York: W. W. Norton, 2008).

Contributors

EDWARD L. AYERS is Tucker-Boatwright Professor of the Humanities and President Emeritus at the University of Richmond. His major publications include *The Promise of the New South: Life after Reconstruction* (1992); *In the Presence of Mine Enemies: Civil War in the Heart of America* (2003); and *The Thin Light of Freedom: Civil War and Emancipation in the Heart of America* (2017). He and Paul Gaston were colleagues on the history faculty at the University of Virginia from 1980 until the latter's retirement in 1997.

RAYMOND GAVINS (1970)[1] was Professor of History at Duke University until his death on May 22, 2016. He was the first African American to receive a doctorate from the Graduate School of Arts and Sciences at the University of Virginia, and he was the first African American on the history faculty at Duke, where he served as Director of Graduate Studies. He oversaw the collection of more than 1,250 oral histories as Co-Director of "Behind the Veil: Documenting African American Life in the Jim Crow South." His publications included *The Perils and Prospects of Southern Black Leadership: Gordon Blaine Hancock, 1884–1970* (1977); *Remembering Jim Crow: African Americans Tell about Life in the Segregated South* (2001), which he co-edited with William Chafe; and *The Cambridge Guide to African American History* (2016).

JAMES H. HERSHMAN, Jr., (1978) served on the Senior Faculty of Governmental Affairs at the U.S. Office of Personnel Management; on the Senior Staff at the Brookings Institute; and as a Senior Fellow for the

---

1 Indicates year of completing Ph.D. dissertation under the supervision of Paul Gaston.

Government Affairs Institute at Georgetown University, where he is presently a Lecturer for the Graduate Liberal Studies Program. He has published articles in the *Virginia Quarterly Review* and the *Journal of Negro Education*; an essay in *The Moderates' Dilemma: Massive Resistance to School Desegregation in Virginia* (1998) entries in the *Dictionary of Virginia Biography* and the online *Encyclopedia Virginia*; and the afterword for *Scalawag: A White Southerner's Journey through Segregation to Human Rights Activism* (2014).

JOHN T. KNEEBONE (1981) is Associate Professor and Chairman of the Department of History at Virginia Commonwealth University, where he has taught since 2003. He was an editor and then director of Publications and Educational Services at the Library of Virginia from 1986 to 2002 and prior to that taught history at Princeton and Harvard Universities and at the University of Alabama. He is author of *Southern Liberal Journalists and the Issue of Race, 1920–1944* (1985). At the Library of Virginia he was co-editor and contributor to the first four volumes of the *Dictionary of Virginia Biography* and other publications. More recently, in 2015, he was a collaborator in a digital history project, *Mapping the Second Ku Klux Klan, 1915–1940* (https://labs.library.vcu.edu/klan/).

MATTHEW D. LASSITER (1999) is Associate Professor of History, Associate Professor of Urban and Regional Planning, and Arthur F. Thurnau Professor at the University of Michigan. He is author of *The Silent Majority: Suburban Politics in the Sunbelt South* (2006), which won the 2007 Lillian Smith Award presented by the Southern Regional Council. His article for the *Journal of Urban History*, "The Suburban Origins of 'Color-Blind' Conservatism: Middle-Class Consciousness in the Charlotte Busing Crisis," was republished in *The Best American History Essays 2006* (Palgrave). He is also coeditor of *The Myth of Southern Exceptionalism* (2009) and *The Moderates' Dilemma: Massive Resistance to School Desegregation in Virginia* (1998). Lassiter formerly served on the Board of Directors of the Urban History Association (2007–2010) and currently serves on the editorial boards of *Urban History*, the *Journal of Policy History,* and the Justice, Power, and Politics series published by the University of North Carolina Press. His current book project is *The Suburban Crisis: Crime, Drugs, and the White Middle-Class America*. Essays drawn from this book have appeared in the special *Journal of American History* issue "Historians and the Carceral State" (2015) and the special *Journal of Urban History* issue "Urban America and the Carceral State" (2015).

GREGG L. MICHEL (1999) is Associate Professor and Chairman of the Department of History at the University of Texas at San Antonio. He is author of *Struggle for a Better South: The Southern Student Organizing Committee, 1964–1969* (2004). He has contributed chapters to *The Edge of the South: Life in Nineteenth-Century Virginia* (1991), *The New Left Revisited* (2003), and *Rebellion in Black and White: Southern Student Activism in the 1960s* (2013). He also has published articles in *Labor History* and the *South Carolina Historical Magazine*.

LYNDA J. MORGAN (1986) is Professor of History and Africana Studies at Mount Holyoke College. She is author of *Emancipation in Virginia's Tobacco Belt* (1992) and *Known for My Work: African American Ethics from Slavery to Freedom* (2016). Her other publications include an article in the *Journal of African-American History* and entries for the *Encyclopedia of Colonial and Revolutionary America* (1988) and the *Dictionary of Virginia Biography* (1990).

ANDREW H. MYERS (1998) is Professor of American Studies at the University of South Carolina Upstate. He is author of *Black, White & Olive Drab: Racial Integration at Fort Jackson, South Carolina, and the Civil Rights Movement* (2006). He has contributed essays to *Military Culture and Education* (2011); *Recovering the Piedmont Past: The South Carolina Upcountry during the Nineteenth Century* (2013); and *Citizen Scholar: Essays in Honor of Walter Edgar* (2016). He also has written a chapter for the forthcoming *Recovering the Piedmont Past II: Bridging the Centuries in the South Carolina Upcountry, 1877–1941*, which he is co-editing with Timothy P. Grady.

ROBERT J. NORRELL (1984) holds the Bernadotte Schmitt Chair of Excellence and is Professor of History at the University of Tennessee. He was formerly Professor of History and Director of the Center for Southern History and Culture at the University of Alabama. He received a Mellon Research Fellowship in American History at the University of Cambridge during 1984–85 and held the Fulbright Distinguished Chair in American Studies at the University of Tuebingen during 2010–2011. His publications include *Reaping the Whirlwind: The Civil Rights Movement in Tuskegee* (1985); *The House I Live In: Race in the American Century* (2005); *Up from History: The Life of Booker T. Washington* (2009), *Eden Rise* (2012), and *Alex Haley and the Books That Changed a Nation* (2015).

STEPHEN O'NEILL (1994) is Professor of History at Furman University. He has served as a consultant in fields of museum and exhibit design, organized conferences designed for the general public, and is interested in how ordinary southerners make sense of their past. He is author of articles in *The Proceedings of the South Carolina Historical Association* and "Memory, History, and the Desegregation of Greenville, South Carolina" in *Toward 'The Meeting of the Waters': Currents in the History of the Civil Rights Movement during the Twentieth Century* (2009). In 2016, he was awarded Furman University's inaugural Meritorious Diversity and Inclusion Award for work promoting diversity and justice on Furman's campus and in the Greenville community.

ROBERT A. PRATT (1987) is Professor of History at the University of Georgia. His essays have appeared in the *Virginia Magazine of History and Biography*, *Rutgers Law Journal*, *Georgia Journal of Southern Legal History*, and other journals and magazines. He is author of *The Color of Their Skin: Education and Race in Richmond, Virginia, 1954–89* (1992); *We Shall Not Be Moved: The Desegregation of the University of Georgia* (2002), and *Selma's Bloody Sunday: Protest, Voting Rights, and the Struggle for Racial Equality* (2016).

STEVE SUITTS spent nearly eighteen years as executive director of the Southern Regional Council where in this capacity he first met Paul Gaston during 1977. Prior to joining SRC, he worked for the Selma Inter-religious Project and the Alabama Civil Liberties Union. He has worked for the past twenty years as program coordinator, vice president, and senior fellow at the Southern Education Foundation. He also teaches as an adjunct lecturer at the Graduate Institute of Liberal Arts at Emory University. He is author of *Hugo Black of Alabama* (2005).

RANDOLPH D. WERNER (1977) was a Managing General Partner of Dominion Ventures, L.L.C., an institutional venture capital fund. He has published articles in the *Journal of Southern History* and elsewhere. He is currently completing a history of nineteenth-century Augusta, Georgia.

www.ingramcontent.com/pod-product-compliance
Lightning Source LLC
Chambersburg PA
CBHW032017230426
43671CB00005B/112